THE CEASE OF MAJESTY

THE CEASE OF MAJESTY

A Study of Shakespeare's History Plays

by

M. M. REESE

The single and peculiar life is bound
With all the strength and armour of the mind
To keep itself from noyance; but much more
That spirit upon whose weal depend and rest
The lives of many. The cease of majesty
Dies not alone, but like a gulf doth draw
What's near it with it; it is a massy wheel,
Fix'd on the summit of the highest mount,
To whose huge spokes ten thousand lesser things
Are mortis'd and adjoin'd; which, when it falls,
Each small annexment, petty consequence,
Attends the boisterous ruin. Never alone
Did the king sigh, but with a general groan.
                              Hamlet III iii 11.

NEW YORK
ST MARTIN'S PRESS

© M. M. REESE 1961

First published 1961
LIBRARY OF CONGRESS CATALOG CARD NO. 61–16926

Printed in Great Britain by
Butler & Tanner Ltd., Frome and London

Contents

Preface

IT has been customary for quite a long time not to take Shakespeare's politics very seriously. In *The Political Characters of Shakespeare* the late John Palmer declared him to be in the final analysis indifferent to society's demands. At the crisis of the action it was only the fate of the individual that interested him, and his view of professional politicians was always detached and cynical. Then the recent emphasis on the importance of order and degree in Elizabethan society has had the effect of seeming to reduce his political thinking to a mere formula. His apparently automatic responses whenever authority is called in question have given him a reputation as an all-weathers champion of the Establishment, always cautious and conservative. As a man of property he just wanted to be left in peace, and so he was a defender of rank and privilege. But as an artist he was much too pessimistic about mankind to believe that any man was virtuous enough to resist the temptations of power; and so his examination of political virtue in the histories had no moral depth, and his famous celebration of a royal hero in *Henry V* was just a catchpenny piece for the playhouse. His inner conviction accepted Commodity as the bias of the world.

To such opinions this book tries to offer a modest corrective. An important difference between Elizabethan society and our own is that, whereas we are accustomed to chaos and expect it to continue, the sixteenth century regarded it as an unnatural departure from a norm that must and would be restored. Order was the supreme political virtue because it was a condition of all other virtue, and when Shakespeare wrote of 'majesty' he had in mind a common attribute of man, not an attribute of kings alone. A society threatened with chaos cannot be saved just by its institutions; nor, although they obviously bear the heaviest responsibility, just by its rulers. Thus Shakespeare's quest in the histories was not only the ideal king, since even the most dedicated ruler must fail when his subjects are corrupt; he was seeking also the ideal social relationship in which king and people were united in a conception of their mutual duty.

That is what Shakespeare meant by majesty: a recognition of mutual duty. Nearly a hundred years later the Marquess of Halifax, whose mind had in many ways a strong affinity with Shakespeare's, wrote that king and kingdom 'ought to be one creature . . . and when either of them

vii

undertakes to act apart, it is like the crawling of worms after they are cut in pieces, which cannot be a lasting motion, the whole creature not stirring at a time'. That was exactly Shakespeare's view, the traditional view of mediaeval society. Majesty is that instinct in mankind that unites them not just for their own preservation but for the attainment of virtue. To quote Halifax again: 'There is a natural reason of state, an undefinable thing, grounded upon the common good of mankind, which is immortal, and in all changes and revolutions, still preserveth its original right of saving a nation.'

Shakespeare's political plays belong to social history as well as to literature, and the first three chapters of this book indicate the circumstances in which they were written. I must apologise here for summarising some rather elementary Tudor history, and also for taking the reader briefly over ground much better covered by Dr. E. M. W. Tillyard in his *Shakespeare's History Plays*, but we shall be much less likely to accuse Shakespeare of cynicism or indifference if we realise the immense contemporary significance of the histories. The Tudor historian had an important didactic duty to perform, and it would be absurd to suppose that Shakespeare was not aware of it. The 1590s being a period of sustained anxiety and unrest, that duty was especially urgent, and I believe that Shakespeare conceived the histories not, as Dr. Tillyard has suggested, because he wanted to write a fashionable epic, but because he had something vital to say to contemporary England. It was additionally fortunate that in the prevailing mode of historical writing, in which the humanist faith in man's capacity for self-determining action was tempered by mediaeval notions of providence, he found the sort of contradictory view of human behaviour that always liberated his genius. If, finally, his conclusions seem over-sympathetic to authority, we have to remember that, contrary to the usual assumptions about the sixteenth-century state, Elizabethan government was divided and weak. Tudor 'absolutism' was a bid from weakness, not an assertion of overpowering strength.

Shakespeare was a poet, not a writer of political tracts, and no interpretation of his work can ignore the many-sidedness of his vision, that two-eyed scrutiny in which ideas of good and bad are called to no single account. He never supposed that politics made up the whole of life, or that the dedicated statesman was in that respect alone a complete man. In political success there was always a sense of personal sacrifice and loss, and a short closing chapter shows Shakespeare to have been aware of the flaws in the idea of the successful king. What matters, however, is that he never repudiated this idea as something that was valid on its own terms, and he continued to uphold it as the condition of a happy and well-ordered society. His recognition of its defects strengthens his assertion of its value; since the affirmations of an artist carry more conviction than the arguments of a propagandist.

I gratefully acknowledge my debt to the work of Dr. Tillyard, although I question some of the inferences that have been made from it. Professor Irving Ribner's *English History Play in the Age of Shakespeare* is an exhaustive and valuable study, particularly illuminating on the didactic role of contemporary historical drama, and the relevant chapters in Professor Arthur Sewell's *Character and Society in Shakespeare* have, I hope, enabled me to keep the characters in Shakespeare's history plays in their right perspective. Although he would not agree with my conclusions, I have also found some stimulating suggestions in Mr. D. A. Traversi's minute analysis of the second tetralogy, *Shakespeare from 'Richard II' to 'Henry V'*. Lastly, I have to acknowledge the inspiration I have received from Professor L. C. Knights's *Shakespeare's Politics* (the British Academy Shakespeare Lecture, 1957). I had already started to work on this book when I read this lecture, and it gave me great encouragement to find that Professor Knights was challenging the dangerous incompleteness of what I may call the 'Elizabethan world picture' analysis of Shakespeare's political thought. He suggests that the Elizabethan orthodoxy about degree and order did not by itself furnish Shakespeare with an adequate explanation of man's behaviour in society. Shakespeare's political ideas expanded with his imaginative experience of life as a whole; and so far from being cynical about the state, he found it to be a natural development of the organic relationship between man and man. In short, the true foundation of society is what Halifax called a 'principle of love'.

Shakespearean references are to the Oxford Shakespeare, edited by W. J. Craig. The reference *SWW* in the footnotes is to Reese, *Shakespeare: his World and his Work* (Arnold, 1953).

CHAPTER ONE

The Uses of History

Our history shall with full mouth
Speak freely of our acts.
Hen. V I ii 230.

WHEN Shakespeare (or someone) wrote *Henry VI*, the prestige and importance of history in England had never been higher. As a storehouse of moral and political examples, as a warning against the capricious ways of fortune, or simply as a means to praise great nations and famous men, it spoke with the authority of poetry itself.

The change in its status began when the historical writers of the Renaissance recovered something of the spirit and purpose of the classical historians of Greece and Rome, and partially discredited the mediaeval belief that the record of man's actions was of trifling significance, since all that man did was but in fulfilment of the will of God. History in its modern sense was born with the fifth-century Greeks: perhaps, we do not know, in the lost books of Hecateus of Ionia, a historian much esteemed in his own time, who travelled widely in the Near East to discover his materials and applied his learning in an unsuccessful attempt to convince his countrymen of the unwisdom of rising against the Persians; more certainly in his great successors, Herodotus and Thucydides. Writing midway between the Old Testament books of Kings and Samuel, dated about 700 B.C., and Chronicles some three hundred years later, the Greek historians broke away from the mere compilation of genealogies, military expeditions and payments of tribute, and approached the past in a true spirit of enquiry. Whereas the patient annalists of China, Assyria and Egypt asked no questions about the meaning of their records, the Greeks gave some pattern to their narrative, however tentative and inexact, by analysing the causes, effects and implications of the events of which they wrote. For Herodotus the great war with Persia was not just a haphazard struggle between two peoples. He saw it in abstract terms as a conflict between a clumsy, over-centralised autocracy and the self-governing city states of Greece, and hinted that victory would always be to the free. Thucydides, writing of the war between Athens and Sparta, disclosed in the speeches he invented for his historical characters his own

I

conception of the motives which govern human action. From facts
he attempted to deduce psychological laws.

This method of writing, like those parts of the Old Testament
which rise above the noting of facts to an organised vision of the Jewish destiny, is recognisably modern. In the Greek war against Persia,
as Herodotus interpreted it, the Elizabethans could identify their own
struggle with Spain; and in Thucydides the more thoughtful of them
might find revealed the subtle perversities of human behaviour which
in their own day made civil war a frightening possibility.[1]

Classical historiography could appeal to the Elizabethans because,
like their own, it was quite unscientific, although for different reasons.
Renaissance humanism was never absolute, and the sixteenth-century
mind had not outgrown the idea of a providence which has a controlling influence in man's affairs. The Greeks were not seriously disturbed
by this idea. Although the ordaining power was ferocious and ill-
disposed towards man—'bloody-minded' is the word our modern
idiom would instinctively select for its operations—foresight and
common prudence were often proof against its thunderbolts. It tended,
moreover, to act repetitively, and so predictably. Fate was destructive
only when humans were blind to their own dangers, and the victim
the gods loved to strike down was the man who stuck his neck out
($ὕβρις$). But the general laws which the Greeks inferred from their
study of the past were not of a kind to be classified as scientific knowledge. The inevitability of change was the one thing of which they
were certain; but instead of comprehending change as a gradual force
linking the passing generations into a coherent pattern, their historians,
like their great dramatists, saw life as a series of violent reversals
($περιπέτειαι$), of catastrophic precipitations from wretchedness to
glory, from prosperity to ruin. Life's rhythm moved restlessly from
one excess to its opposite.[2]

It was the same spectacle of great ones toppled from their high
estate that furnished mediaeval moralists with the most fruitful of all
their texts, but they found a ready explanation of it in the will of God.
The Greeks were equally conscious of change, but they could not explain
it. They did not know why it happened, nor did they think of it as
leading to any ultimate goal. Thus their historical writing produced no
true philosophy of history, no theory of origins and ends. The only

---

[1] An English translation of Thucydides, based on a French version, was produced in 1550 by Thomas Nicolls, a London goldsmith, who dedicated it, with
elaborate expository prefaces, to Sir John Cheke, a tutor of Edward VI.
[2] See R. G. Collingwood, *The Idea of History*, 21-8.

conclusion they offered was that events moved in recurrent cycles; and since in their thinking there could be no such thing as a science of the changeable, the highest claim they made for history was that it offered an approximate understanding (δόξα) of the transitory and perceptible.

But if the nature of the historical process was not scientifically knowable, it could be perceived, and so could contribute to the formation of right opinion, which was just as necessary to the conduct of life as scientific knowledge. The Greeks found in history the same rich didactic content as the Elizabethans. It might have no value as theory, but it had immense practical value in arming mankind against the blows of fate. Because change is repetitive, events may be forecast with some probability and preparations made to meet them, Man was seen as a rational being, capable of choosing his own ends and by strength of his unfettered will achieving them. Because he was a free agent, he was even able—if he profited by the lessons of history—to challenge the displeasure of the gods, who had no general plan for human affairs but merely decreed success or failure to certain individuals. By discipline and character their doom could be met and overcome.

• 'Untruss your slaveries'. In the Induction to Marston's *Antonio and Mellida* the actor playing Piero was so directed:

> Thus frame your exterior shape
> To haughty form of elate majesty,
> As if you held the palsy-shaking head
> Of reeling chance under your fortune's belt
> In strictest vassalage.
>
> Ind. 7.

The intention here was satirical, but freed of the essential Greek moderation there is a recognisable connection between the classical conception of the sovereignty of man and certain high-souled heroes of Elizabethan drama—Guise, Mortimer, Biron and the whole ambitious crew who played their several variations on the theme of 'I am myself alone': men of 'commanding soul', each one 'to himself a law rational'. The Greek view of life was over-optimistic in attributing the control of events to deliberate human agency: an error from which Elizabethan orthodoxy was protected by its sense of a pervasive providence. This optimism led to a dangerous over-simplification in Greek historiography, for human motives are seldom clear and untrammelled and action is mostly tentative. The actor is acted upon, by environment, tradition, contemporary culture and a dozen other modifying forces, so that what eventually happens may not be what anyone has deliberately wished to happen, and the seeming agents are

no more than instruments of the historical process. No one understood
this better than Shakespeare, whose conception of character, revealed
in all his drama, was of man's will and passions endlessly disturbed
and moulded by conflicting visions of what constitutes right action.

The Greek glory, in any case, did not last, and we find a different
interpretation of history in Polybius (c. 204–122), the Arcadian who
witnessed the Roman victories over Macedonia and Carthage and
wrote a generalising account of the stages by which Rome became
mistress of the world within, as it seemed to him, a couple of generations.[1] Although his narrative only covered the years 220–146, he
made large claims for his medium and has some right to be regarded as
the first writer to sketch a conscious philosophy of history. Using
ίστορία, which originally meant any kind of enquiry, as the particular enquiry of history, he held that it was possible to develop practical
lessons from human experience, and that the best education for real
life was the knowledge of affairs which could be gained from a study
of the past. He asserted a universal and scientific value for his analysis
of the Roman conquest of the world, tracing the subjugation of Greece
and Carthage to the operation of general and inevitable laws whose
influence he was also able to detect in the agrarian and social disturb-
ances (it was the time of the Gracchi) that broke out during the last
years of his life. Polybius too often holds up the story while he points
his moral and underlines, too emphatically, the lessons to be inferred
by future generations; but, being a logical and level-headed man, he
would have admitted that there was no reason why Rome herself
should not one day perish by the same ineluctable laws that had destroyed Carthage and Greece.

The significant change in his work is, however, the admission of
chance (τύχη), the element which the historians of classical Greece had
always denied. The reason for this lay partly in the enlarged scope of
his history. Small as it was, he used a broader canvas than the classical
historians, whose principles confined them to a narrative of events that
could be verified by people still alive. The wider the canvas, the less
the historian is likely to attribute to the deliberate action of human
wills. An element of determinism must creep in, and Polybius taught

---

[1] Like several Tudor historians, Polybius had a personal part in some of the
events he described. As a leading statesman of the Achaean League, he was one
of the thousand hostages taken to Italy in 167 for refusing to fight against
Perseus. He grew to understand and admire his conquerors, and was allowed to
accompany Scipio in the final campaign against Carthage. He later returned to
Greece to try to dissuade his countrymen from the rising which led to the final
extinction of Greek independence.

that the effort to see the past as an organic whole necessarily revealed the frequent operation of fortune. In this conclusion he was only uttering the new wisdom of the Hellenistic world. The collapse of Greek civilisation had humbled man's assurance that he was master of his destiny, and with the loss of that splendid but vain self-confidence he had come to acknowledge the existence of an alien, inscrutable force that would often frustrate his purposes. He could only call it chance, and hate it, and withdraw into an inner citadel where it could not reach him. The lessons to be learned from history were no longer those which instruct the successful life of action. Its study would not provide a training ground for statesmanship, nor enable men to avoid the mistakes and tragedies of their predecessors.

> Are these things then necessities?
> Then let us meet them like necessities.
> 2 *Hen. IV* III i 92.

Men were no longer able to control events, and the virtue Polybius would have them learn from history was the courage and self-mastery to endure bravely what they could not prevent.[1]

For this stoicism, or for a more specifically Christian resignation, men would presently have much need. In 410 Alaric and his Visigoths sacked Rome, and nineteen years later the Vandals, the most savage of the barbarian invaders, crossed from Spain into Africa and attacked the coastal fortress of Hippo. Before it fell its bishop had died, leaving a book that was to have a tremendous influence on the nature and purposes of historical writing.

St. Augustine was not a historian. He was a passionate, fallible man (*Da mihi castitatem et continentiam, sed noli modo*: give me chastity and continence, but do not give them yet) who was brought to his salvation by God's overwhelming and irresistible grace. His days were the last of the Roman Empire, when the ancient imperial order, buttressed by immense wealth, a mature administrative system and a culture deeply rooted in the centuries, suddenly collapsed before the tribal pressure on its frontiers. *The City of God* gave a vision of the kingdom that would not perish. It was not that Augustine despised the earthly city. He recognised that the Christian idealist would always have need of the magistrate, who would enforce society's necessary laws, punish the transgressor, maintain order and protect property. Civil government was desirable if only to avoid worse things, and its very imperfections corresponded to the nature of fallen man. Augustine even

[1] Collingwood, *Idea of History*, 35–6.

allowed it justice, 'of a kind', and warned men against losing themselves so deeply in contemplation of the eternal and divine that they neglected their common duty to their neighbours. But earthly kingdoms were at best 'fair thievish purchases', their glittering empty prizes mere deceits of the flesh. Man's only true reward was in the service of God.

If man is merely the agent of the divine purpose, it follows that the only worthwhile function of history is to record the will of God as constantly manifested in human affairs. This had already been asserted, a hundred years before the fall of Rome, by Eusebius (c. 264–340), Bishop of Caesarea, who led the moderate Arian party at the Council of Nicaea. In his hands history found a new pattern, centred upon the birth of Christ, and he searched the past for anything that might be regarded as an anticipation of this event. In history that was truly universal, since it collated the records of diverse peoples and civilisations as testimony to a single end, Eusebius held that Jewish religion, Greek philosophy and Roman Law had all combined to create the unique soil in which the Christian revelation could take root and flourish.[1]

A change in the purposes of historical writing followed inevitably from the Christian conception of man as a being impotent in himself but, with God's grace, heir to the everlasting kingdom. It received crushing authority from the fall of Rome, the human empire that had seemed eternal, and it dominated the writing of history for a thousand years. The *Historia adversus Paganos*, written in 416 by the Spanish theologian Orosius, the disciple and companion of Augustine, defended Christianity against the attacks of pagan writers and came to be regarded for centuries as the classic statement of the Christian case.[2] It was the standard manual of profane history in the mediaeval schools, and under its influence history became a record of events conditioned by divine intervention and revelation. The historical writing of Greece disappeared along with the rest of its secular literature, and Roman history survived only through its law; broadly speaking, nothing was recorded of the ancient civilisations of the Near East, the Aegean and the Mediterranean except the events that had been considered significant by Orosius and Augustine. Mediaeval historians looked back through the Jewish prophet-priests and kings to the Creation, valuing the history of Egypt, Tyre and Babylon only for what it revealed about Israel and the implacable judgments of Jahveh.

This unprofessional eclecticism gave a new unity to history, since all

---

[1] Collingwood, *Idea of History*, 50–1.
[2] It was translated into Anglo-Saxon by King Alfred.

significant events were thought to have proceeded from a single cause, the will of God, and progress was marshalled towards a single and desirable goal: for which the trumpets have not sounded yet. National and particularist history gave way to the simple narration of *gesta Dei*. It was impious, and also bad history, to fail to detect the hand of God everywhere, and mediaeval writers were less anxious to illustrate from the past the operation of general and permanent laws than to demonstrate that such laws were liable to continual interference and suspension. Human history being merely the working-out of God's purpose for mankind, man himself was reduced to the insignificance of a secondary agent, important only for the part[1] assigned to him in the divine purpose. Gone altogether was the brave self-confidence which claimed for him the power to control events. Human action was now thought to be essentially blind, the outward working of passion, and its success or failure was an incidental result depending not upon the quality of the act but upon a particular wish of God. Thus events had a necessity of their own, and the subjective purposes of the individual had no effect upon them. The old Greek conception of ἁμαρτία, by which they meant missing the mark, a momentary and almost accidental failure to achieve one's ends, came to be roughly equated with sin, for it was not in the nature of fallen man to be able to realise his self-proposed objects. Mediaeval historiography was fundamentally anti-humanist. With the insignificance of man, and the imminence of a Second Coming which would establish the eternal kingdom, it could not be anything else.

In such circumstances little was demanded of the writer. So far from the historian choosing his subject, the subject chose him; and as history was the progressive manifestation of the will of God, it was capable of ordering itself without the historian's help. One may not generalise about a thousand years, and there was, as always, a difference between the theory and the practice. Some writers rebelled against the limitations that bound their art and did work that was proper to a historian. They gave their subject the authority of men speaking to men, approaching it in a more scientific spirit and indulging in literary adornment and philosophical speculation that were held to be outside their province.[2] But the great mass of mediaeval historical writing was

[1] If indeed he had a part. Some mediaeval writers held that God worked transcendentally, outside and above man, not through him.
[2] Froissart, for instance, heightened his narrative with a natural instinct for the dramatic, and he allowed himself to speculate about purely human motives. Nor was all mediaeval history portentous. It was a legitimate exercise to record the past simply in order to satisfy man's natural curiosity and his pleasure in a good

servile in spirit, unscrupulous in invention and hopelessly uncritical in
its attitude to evidence. Forgery was endemic in the Middle Ages, and
having before them the fraudulent example of the trading and municipal
corporations, and even of the Church itself, it would have been surprising if the historians too had not fabricated their facts. Not that they
saw it in quite that way, for their concern was not with historical
truth as we understand it, but with examples and demonstrations of an
overriding truth that was beyond question. Determined to reveal the
unfolding of the divine plan, they were relatively indifferent to the
acts of men and took little trouble to discover what had really happened
in the past. For the same reason they accepted without much critical
examination the heroic legends in which most races have veiled their
origins, and one of the primary tasks of the more critical historians of
the Renaissance would be to separate the facts from the cumulative
accretions of falsehood, folk lore and sheer romantic nonsense.

None the less the mediaeval view of man has had a lasting influence
on the writing of history. Scorning the pseudo-history compiled as
national or political propaganda, it has taught that the true scope of
history is universal in time and space. The only reason for its specialisation into periods and the record of particular nations is the fallibility
of the human instrument. Secondly, it has taught that providence has
some part to play in men's affairs. This is an old, inscrutable question,
belonging as much to theology and ethics as to history.

> We are merely the stars' tennis-balls, struck and bandied
> Which way please them.
> > Webster, *Duchess of Malfi* V iv 52.

The human mind likes to reject this as too positive, and too pessimistic.
It is probably most men's experience—it was certainly Shakespeare's—
that we can at the same moment make our own decisions and yet be in
the hands of the gods. This is man's peculiar dilemma, which makes
him alone a proper subject for tragedy. We may call it chance if we
like, and exclude the emotional assumptions that underlie the word
providence. But the historian cannot exclude from his study of man's
past the sudden advent of the unexpected, the unforeseeable and the
unmerited. Even when at the Renaissance the religious and philosophical systems of the Middle Ages went out of fashion and man was
restored to the centre of the universal stage, puny no longer but self-
determining and free, he was still not the undisputed master of events.

story. Writers with a gift for narrative were much more interested in their story
than in the moral which they rather perfunctorily attached to it, see E. M. W.
Tillyard, *Shakespeare's History Plays*, 24–9.

Although often crude in its superficial manifestations, the humanism of the Renaissance lacked, deep down, the invincible confidence of classical times. In Shakespeare, whose thought was always remarkably central in matters of this kind, it was the bad men—Cassius, Iago, Edmund; and indeed it was this presumption in them that made them bad—who challenged 'the divine thrusting on'.[1] How like an angel, and also how like a beast: man still knew himself to be, as the theologians had for centuries depicted him, a creature of passion, incapable of achieving his chosen ends by unaided reason. Even when he no longer called it the hand of God, accident was always at his heels. The sixteenth century's view of human action oscillated between an exaggerated faith in man's supreme potentiality and the conviction that he would be brought down by forces he could neither anticipate nor control. In the territory separating these extreme conceptions Shakespeare found opportunities for speculation supremely suited to his genius; and the quality he was to demand of his ideal ruler was a self-discipline which first subdued all distracting passions and then so limited its ends as to reduce to insignificance the possible intervention of the unforeseen. In historiography, the recognition of providence made for a better understanding of the past than the classical belief that events happen because man has so willed them. It is more in harmony with human experience.

Some Renaissance historians, and many critical writers who were not primarily historians, did a great service by insisting upon an accurate testing of evidence and paring away the legends and deliberate falsifications that obscured the truth. The exposure of the Donation of Constantine, the Isidorian Decretals and the writings falsely attributed to Dionysius the Areopagite was chiefly anti-clerical in its immediate effects, but the textual and historical method applied to the task revolutionised the lethargic attitude to written evidence. Everywhere there was a hunt for original manuscripts and incontrovertible data, and it was typical of the new scholarship that in England Polydore Vergil should risk the displeasure of his royal masters by rejecting the cherished legend that Brut, the grandson of Aeneas, in his wanderings after his banishment from Italy came eventually to Britain and established there the New Troy. William Camden, Jonson's beloved mentor at Westminster, had discreet doubts on the same point, and in his reconstructions of the past from topographical and written data he employed the same exact methods as the physical scientists in another field. John Leland, appointed King's Antiquary by Henry VIII, with

[1] *SWW*, 436 n.2, 544–7.

authority to search all the cathedrals, colleges and religious houses of England for manuscript records, left it to others to ransack the rich storehouse of jottings made for the *magnum opus* he never wrote. John Stow, the peripatetic tailor who paupered himself by his love of books and was licensed by James I to seek 'gratuities', edited mediaeval chronicles and devoted his great learning and homely style to producing the most accurate historical works written in England during the sixteenth century. This widespread zeal for an honest discovery of the past taught the English more of their history than they had ever accurately known before. Its incidental products were Archbishop Parker's Society of Antiquaries, the foundation of the Bodleian, and Sir Robert Cotton's manuscript collection; and later, when the debates of scholars were brought into the political arena, the furnishing of deadly academic ammunition against the Crown's pretensions in the seventeenth century.

This dispassionate concern for the truth, was not, however, characteristic of the general run of Renaissance historians; or, rather, most of them pursued truth of a somewhat different kind. If, for instance, someone had told Sir Thomas More that his *History of Richard III* was untrue, meaning that it was founded on evidence and assumptions that had not been verified, he would have been not so much shocked as uninterested. He would have claimed that his portrait of Richard was essentially true; and if imagination had touched up some of the details, was not the proper exercise of the imagination a form of truth? Historical truth, that is to say, was to be tested by the historian's fidelity to the object he had set himself; which in More's case was to justify the Tudor usurpation by showing what a bad king Richard had been. The only truth the historian needed to profess, in this view (and it was certainly the only form of truth that Shakespeare needed or recognised in his history plays) was a conviction[1] of the justice and rightness of the cause he was defending. His aim was to persuade by power of eloquence rather than by the overwhelming accumulation of fact; and if he used material that he knew or suspected to be false, the duty of persuasion, in a cause he believed to be right, outweighed any faint obligation he might feel towards historical accuracy. George Buchanan, the Scots tutor of James VI, illustrates this attitude in its extremer forms. His *Rerum Scoticarum Historia* purported to be a general history of his country, but of its twenty books eight were devoted to events of the sixteenth century, and its real purpose was to

---

[1] Conviction might, of course, be procured by intimidation, material inducement and similar pressures. There are hacks and renegades in every age.

justify, in terms both theoretical and practical, the deposition of Mary, Queen of Scots. Buchanan was a genuine scholar, and one of the few British humanists of the sixteenth century to enjoy a European reputation. But he did not hesitate to suppress or invent facts to suit his purpose, and his work is not so much a history as a partisan manifesto.[1] His duty, as he saw it, was to demonstrate that what had been done was rightly done.

Except, therefore, for the antiquaries and memorialists, always a small minority, who really cared what had happened, the humanist historians of the Renaissance esteemed various moral and political objectives more highly than they esteemed the bare truth. This they regarded as a fruitful development, and not a betrayal of their art, for what was the use of a mere bundle of records, existing *in vacuo* without a beginning or an end, or of a collection of potentially informative anecdotes unrelated to any scheme of history? At the Renaissance classical didacticism, never wholly extinguished in the Middle Ages and newly invigorated as the control of the Church weakened, joined hands with the mediaeval belief in providence to produce a highly specialised and tendentious form of historical writing that has no exact parallels in any other century.

The Renaissance historians insisted, first, upon the dignity of their subject. History was worth writing for its own sake and therefore demanded to be written in the grand manner; in Italy, where style was an obsession, it called for their highest literary endeavours. Cicero, who spoke of history as '*lux veritatis . . . magistra vitae*', Quintilian and other ancient writers were cited as authority for holding it to be the legitimate exercise of a creative mind. Delightedly getting it both ways, its apologists ensured that the subject should be popular with those who shared Plato's mistrust of poetry as dangerous 'imitation', and at the same time proudly quoted Aristotle's observation that if a poet should come to take a theme from actual history, 'he is none the less a poet for that'. History, they felt, was worthy to be the prose sister of epic, no less.

But it did not derive its importance merely from the sense of technical difficulties triumphantly overcome. Its supreme value was that it enabled men to teach moral and political lessons and to glorify their native cities. Patriotism is the eloquent and often moving undertone to all sixteenth-century history, and to serve it the Renaissance writers abandoned universal history for a more concentrated study of their own peoples, rejecting Lucian's advice that the historian should be

[1] See *The Tyrannous Reign of Mary Stewart: George Buchanan's Account*, ed. by W. A. Gatherer, Introduction, 11–43.

'the citizen of no city'; and so strong was their feeling that the past was
a guide to the present that they tended to choose for particular study
periods whose problems seemed to resemble their own, so that the
lessons of history might be instantly applied where they were most
needed and would do most good. This explains the almost pathological
interest of the Elizabethans in the period from 1399 to 1485. The
identifying mark of sixteenth-century historiography was to limit
itself—sometimes after a perfunctory summary reaching back to
remoter times—to the records of particular nations studied over a
comparatively short period. Shakespeare's two main groups of histories fall into two tetralogies, and they may well have been conceived
in that way.

It was Isaac Casaubon, the Swiss scholar who ended his days in
England, who, anticipating Bolingbroke, described history as 'nothing
else but a kind of philosophy using examples'. Because man was
thought to have recovered some control over his destiny and to be no
longer helplessly at the mercy of divine intervention, the humanists
taught that his past experiences could furnish a warning and an inspiration to the future. Bodin's *Methodus ad facilem historiarum cogni-
tionem* (1566) argued that from an objective study of history men could
discover the universal laws which guide the development of political
institutions, and learn from them the unvarying principles of good
government. If this was something too absolute for the less exalted
thinking of humbler theorists, it was at any rate fairly generally assumed that the challenges and crises of history tended to recur: 'like
time brings like examples', as Thucydides had said, and we may learn
what to pursue and what to avoid. History links the scattered generations by making the blunders of one the corrective medicine of another.
It gives to youth the wisdom of age and by preserving the memory of
noble deeds may stir the emulation of less heroic times. In a famous
passage in *Piers Penniless* Nashe praises

> our English chronicles, wherein our forefathers' valiant acts (that have
> lain long buried in rusty brass and worm-eaten books) are revived, and
> they themselves raised from the grave of oblivion, and brought to plead
> their aged honours in open presence: than which, what can be a sharper
> reproof to these degenerate effeminate days of ours?

Chief of all history's lessons was the admonition, example and
inspiration it gave to rulers, and even the humblest writer felt himself
to be an exigent dominie to the throne. Regretting that ill-health had
prevented his giving due attention to the education of the young
James, Buchanan proffered as 'the next best thing . . . that kind of

writing most calculated to improve your mind': by which he meant his lying *History*; and he hoped to make good his neglect 'by sending you faithful advisers from history, whose counsel would help you in your affairs, and whose virtues you might emulate in the business of your life'. Wanting similarly to advise a prince, Bacon turned to Tudor history because it was so valiant in example, and held up for emulation Henry VII, who even by Shakespeare's time had become a copy-book king. The anonymous translator of Tito Livio's life of Henry V dedicated it to Henry VIII, then (1513) at war with the French, with the hope that 'the knowledge and sight of this pamphlet' would inspire Henry to the noble and chivalrous acts of his predecessor. An identical claim was made by Shakespeare in the Chorus before the last Act of *Henry V*, when he anticipated the return of Essex from Ireland 'bringing rebellion broached on his sword' and moved to high deeds by history's evocation of this mirror of all Christian princes.[1] North justified his translation of Plutarch by urging that kings would find history a better guide than flattering counsellors; Stow had no doubt that it imparted 'some colours of wisdom, invitements to virtue, and loathing of naughty facts'; and Thomas Norton, introducing Grafton's *Chronicle at Large* (1569), said that it would give every man 'a glass to see things past, whereby to judge justly of things present and wisely of things to come'.[2] Lord Berners declared that his aim in translating Froissart was to ensure that 'the chivalrous feats and martial prowesses' of former times should not pass out of remembrance. Chronicles were to be studied because they 'show, open, manifest and declare to the reader by example of old antiquity what we should enquire, desire, and follow, and also what we should eschew, avoid and utterly flee'.

The more consistent humanists, in no fear that their deductions might be overturned by the eruptions of providence, did not hesitate to advance the didactic functions of history into a new area. Rejecting altogether the mediaeval view that society, like the individual, was hopeless of perfection, they believed that it was possible to generalise the lessons of history into valuable speculations about the nature of government. Granted the premise, that historical patterns recur and men are always seeking remedies for the same mistakes, the inference is logical. There is no reason why the test of experience should not show which courses of action are most likely to succeed. If there are

---

[1] Scholars who believe in a closer association between Shakespeare and Essex will find this explanation too simple.

[2] Tillyard, *Shakespeare's History Plays*, 57–8.

discoverable laws of permanent and universal validity, as Bodin held
that there were, it should, in theory, be possible to construct in any
given conditions the right form of society and government. Much history came to be written, therefore, to document an abstract political
theory, and it was in a mood of apocalyptic triumph that Buchanan
produced his history of Scotland to prove the rightness of the theory
of government that he had already proclaimed in his more philosophical *De Iure Regni*. More often, however, the nature of controver-
sialists being what it is, the theory preceded the history. Machiavelli's
History of Florence is an example of this. From an analysis of the conditions of his own time he came to certain conclusions about the
nature of man and society and proceeded to read them back into the
past. Many Tudor dramatists and historians did the same, attributing
the troubles of former times to those very things that were causing
the writers anxiety in the present. If a man feels that his own age is in
peril from revolution, then revolution is the dissolvent he is most
likely to find in his study of the past.

In general, however, this close identification of history with the
science of politics—an important extension of its scope and a further
tribute to its authority—had to come to terms with an actively surviving belief in providence. Not everyone had the mental toughness
(cynicism, clear-sightedness, consistency, realism, or whatever one
chooses to call it) of Machiavelli, Guicciardini and other writers of the
Italian school. The existence of some higher power, either specifically
Christian or corresponding to the old Greek nemesis, was still generally acknowledged,[1] and providence can wreck the neatest of theories.
The two interpretations of history, seemingly irreconcilable but in
fact capable of being held simultaneously by the majority of intelligent men, are contrasted in Henry IV and Warwick. Sleepless and
worn out with care, the King sighs how different things might be if we
could foretell the future:

> O God! that one might read the book of fate,
> And see the revolution of the times
> Make mountains level. . . .
>
>   *2 Hen. IV* III i 45.

In his own case he would never have started on the way that has
brought him to his present greatness and unease, had he known then

> how chances mock,
> And changes fill the cup of alteration
> With divers liquors.

---

[1] See above, p. 8.

But his conclusion is wholly pessimistic, for he suggests that if the future, with all the relentless turns of fate, were revealed to us, the knowledge would be more disturbing than our present blindness:

> O! if this were seen,
> The happiest youth, viewing his progress through,
> What perils past, what crosses to ensue,
> Would shut the book, and sit him down and die.

Warwick answers him with an orthodox statement of history's power to teach practical lessons. There was nothing mysterious, he says, in Richard II's successful prophecy that the Percies would one day turn against Bolingbroke: he merely had to deduce it from the many precedents.

> There is a history in all men's lives,
> Figuring the nature of the times deceas'd;
> The which observ'd, a man may prophesy,
> With a near aim, of the main chance of things
> As yet not come to life, which in their seeds
> And weak beginnings lie intreasured.
> Such things become the hatch and brood of time:
> And by the necessary form of this
> King Richard might create a perfect guess. . . .
> *2 Hen. IV* III i 80.

The sixteenth century blended these two conceptions of history by teaching that while God ordains human affairs after a pattern that is rational and inevitably good, secondary causes may be found in the behaviour of men. As moralists, historians had a duty to reveal the logic and benevolence of God's plan and to explain and justify His interventions. 'All men in seeing the course of God's doings may learn to dread his judgments and love his providence,' Norton wrote in his introduction to Grafton's chronicles; and Edmund Bolton, whose *Hypercritica* was written at about the time that Shakespeare died, spoke of the historian as 'a Christian cosmopolite to discover God's assistances, disappointments, and overrulings in human affairs'. Most of the characters in Shakespeare's histories recognise in this way God's association with their destiny, and feel that their own lives are part of a larger pattern in which they may be already foredoomed to success or failure. But the humanist belief in the dignity and self-determination of man would not permit him to be merely the plaything of fate, even if it were God who directed it. There was a sense in which man's independent choice might fulfil the will of God. This is not as intellectually absurd as it sounds. In finite terms God's omniscience and God's omnipotence are self-cancelling, but finite terms are not appropriate in matters of this kind. Man's own acts were felt to have a positive value.[1] Although enclosed within a foreordained scheme, sixteenth-century history was not determinist. There is a significant difference between Lydgate's *Falls of Princes* and the Tudor *Mirror for Magistrates*, in which the reversals in men's fortunes, although acknowledged as part of a larger plan, are always traced to some particular fault in the individual or his inheritance, and the moral is pointed so that later generations may avoid the same mistakes.

The divergent ideas about history current in the sixteenth century were magnificently reconciled at its close in Raleigh's *History of the World*. In Raleigh's life there was a baffling admixture of intransigence and grace, the same co-existence that we find in Bacon of a noble mind and ignoble, predatory action. On the surface his *History* is just as contradictory. He confidently asserts the educative discipline of his subject, which was axiomatic at the Renaissance, claiming that 'it hath triumphed over time, which besides it, nothing but eternity hath triumphed over: for it hath carried our knowledge over the vast and devouring space of many thousands of years, and given so fair and piercing eyes to our mind'. It tells us

> how kings and kingdoms have flourished and fallen; and for what virtue and piety God made prosperous. . . . And it is not the least debt which we owe unto history, that it hath made us acquainted with our dead ancestors, delivered us their memory and fame. In a word, we may gather out of history a policy no less wise than eternal; by the comparison and application of other men's fore-past miseries, with our own like errors and ill deservings.

Why, he asks, do historians exhibit 'the fall and fortunes of the dead: seeing the world is the same that it hath been'? His answer is that the same pattern repeats itself in the history of every people and every recorded century, and there are certain general propositions—as, for instance, that nations without liberty are also without courage[2]—which may, if men will only heed them, prevent the recurrence of disaster.

---

[1] In extreme cases men of outstanding virtue could even persuade God to suspend His overriding plan, as, for instance, He stayed for the brief reign of Henry V the wrath incurred by England for the deposition of Richard II. But the inevitable consequences were immediately felt again in the following reign.

[2] 'The sum whereof is this. Wheresoever the prince doth hold all his subjects under the condition of slaves; there is the conquest easy, and soon assured: Where ancient nobility is had in due regard, there it is hard to win all, and harder to keep that which is won.'

All this is quite orthodox. Here are the conventional ideas about learning from experience, the repetitive sequence of events, the preservation of worthy deeds from oblivion, the spur of emulation. We should be grateful to history, Raleigh says, for 'the reverend respect that is held of great men, and the honour done unto them by all sorts of people'; for of such will be 'the greatening of our posterity, and the contemplation of their glory whom we leave behind us'. Yet these practical advantages of history are apparently diminished by Raleigh's uncompromising acceptance of the whole of the human past as an awe-inspiring panorama of the judgments of God.[1] The reported atheist and leader of 'the School of Night' finds in history the endless operation of a superior will. God's judgments may not be related in particular, for 'the sea of examples hath no bottom'; it is sufficient for men to know that He is not to be mocked and His principles are unchangeable: 'neither is He wearied by the long process of time, and won to give His blessing in one age, to that which He hath cursed in another'. 'Think not,' Sir Thomas Browne was to say, 'that morality is ambulatory.'

In this mood Raleigh scorns moralists and historians 'that ground their opinions on second causes'. The only true explanation of the vicissitudes of life is that God has appointed them.

If we truly examine the difference of both conditions; to wit of the rich and mighty, whom we call fortunate; and of the poor and oppressed, whom we account wretched: we shall find the happiness of the one, and the miserable estate of the other, so tied by God to the very instant, and both so subject to interchange (witness the sudden downfall of the greatest princes, and the speedy uprising of the meanest persons) as the one hath nothing so certain, whereof to boast; nor the other so uncertain, whereof to bewail itself. For there is no man so assured of his honour, of his riches, health, or life; but that he may be deprived of either or all, the very next hour or day to come. . . .

God, who is the author of all our tragedies, hath written out for us, and appointed us all the parts we are to play: and hath not, in their distribution, been partial to the most mighty princes of the world; That gave unto Darius the part of the greatest emperor, and the part of the most miserable beggar, a beggar begging water of an enemy, to quench the great drought of death; that appointed Bajazet to play the Grand Signior of the Turks in the morning, and in the same day the footstool of Tamerlane; . . . that made Belisarius play the most victorious captain, and lastly the part of a blind beggar; of which examples many thousands may be produced: why should other men, who are but the least of worms, complain of wrongs?

[1] Cf. Richard Knolles, a provincial schoolmaster, produced in 1603 a *General History of the Turks*, in which he argued that God used the might of Islam to punish the sins of the Christian nations.

Certainly there is no other account to be made of this ridiculous world, than to resolve, That the change of fortune on the great theatre, is but as the change of garments on the less.

Here is the full mediaeval doctrine '*de casibus virorum illustrium*', and Raleigh carries it to a thoroughly pessimistic conclusion. The dismal record of the same misfortunes occurring over and over again suggests to him that they always will. 'Boundless ambition' continues in mortal men, despite the catastrophe that always attends it, and although in the constant flux of men and nations it may be tonic to recall the example of the true heroes, death is the inevitable end of all. From the welter of human misery *contemptus mundi* is the only refuge.

It is not easy for us to recognise that the contradictions in this state of mind are only apparent, but we shall never understand Shakespeare and his generation unless we do. Shakespeare was never so obtrusively dogmatic as Raleigh; for one thing, he was a dramatist, and the medium afforded him other means of saying what he needed to say; but his attitude to the fundamental questions of human responsibility was not essentially different. Raleigh himself did not conduct the whole of his history in the rather windy moralising vein of his preface. Within the scheme of God's providence he surveyed secular history with the sharp perceptions of a man of the world, regarding the political cut-and-thrust with the detached irony of one well versed in courtly shifts and discussing naval and military tactics with the insight of an experienced commander. In literature, as in life, he was not indifferent to material concerns. But in his general approach to his subject, which was characteristic of his time, he was less classical than religious, poetical and romantic. So was Shakespeare. They remind us to what a very large extent Tudor England was dominated by traditional and mediaeval ways of thought. Even in 1600 Renaissance humanism was still contesting a foothold with the older conceptions of Mutability and *memento mori*. With the struggle as yet unresolved, there was a limit to the trust man dared to place in his own capacities. It was not only that the hold of traditional ideas was too strong for him; each passing day, with its lot of disillusion, justified his caution. In the rapid and devastating changes of the sixteenth century only an ideological imbecile could suppose that individual man was in conscious control of events. It was more natural to suppose, as many did, that Change itself was the only directing force, and all coherence gone. Indeed, it says much for the robustness of the age and the strength of its faith that it managed to salvage from the turmoil some assurance of human responsibility. If the Elizabethan half of the century had not been consciously conservative, this could never have been done; and in a conservative generation historiography found itself with a special function to seek to preserve what had been gained and to persuade each man that his own individual contribution (expressed through an uncritical obedience) was of value. But it could not be done without help. There must be no importunity towards the higher powers, and the historian's attitude to providence was accordingly placatory. He needed to feel that God was on his side; and thus the visitations that he could not regard as immediately benevolent, like plague, civil war or defeat by a foreigner, he ascribed to God's punishment for wrongdoing or to an unusually devious unfolding of the divine plan. The ultimate goodness and reasonableness of the plan were not in question, for God was the stay of the universe against Mutability and it was only the obduracy of human sin and error that frustrated Him. The power to make a free and rational choice was the specific attribute of man, even though he often exercised it wrongly. In this reading of life, the two conceptions of history, as following God's inexorable pattern and as offering a storehouse of practical lessons to guide man's independent choice, were complementary and not mutually exclusive.

In 1590, then, the uses of history were various but generally agreed and understood. Many influences had combined to evolve the Elizabethan attitude to its study.[1] One of the main purposes of history was to demonstrate the logic and reason of God's control of human affairs, an inheritance from the Middle Ages; but this was blended also with classical and humanist traditions that exalted one nation at the expense of others and allowed man a positive role in life. Shakespeare thus used history to glorify England, to teach moral and political lessons and to assert the intrusive sway of providence. A further element in history, less important to Shakespeare than to Jonson and Chapman, was the belief that by recalling the calamities that men had had to suffer in the past, it taught them to bear misfortune in the present. This survival from Stoicism became fashionable with the popularity of Senecan drama after the middle of the century.

The next chapter will consider in more detail the energy and interplay of these various influences in determining the contemporary tradition at the time when Shakespeare wrote his histories.

[1] See the introductory chapter in Irving Ribner, *The English History Play in the Age of Shakespeare*. Ribner usefully defines the true historical play as one in which the moral choices of the characters are determined by national and political concerns which the dramatist accepts and does not try to alter. He may vary the details and draw his own conclusions, but the 'plot' is essentially predetermined.

CHAPTER TWO

The Tudor Image

Take but degree away, untune that string,
And, hark! what discord follows; each thing meets
In mere oppugnancy.
Troilus and Cressida I iii 109.

TUDOR England offers no exception to the general rule that every age writes history in the light of its own necessities and beliefs. The particular need of the century was strong government, its corresponding fear any factor that might lead to weakness and disunity: dynastic rebellion, for instance, a divided succession, a bad king, religious individualism, agrarian discontent. Both need and fear have been known at some time to every nation, and no age, however secure, can be wholly indifferent to them. The Tudors experienced them with an intensity bordering at times on hysteria.

Tudor theorists and historians therefore extolled the strong and reviled the weak. 'A king that is soft as silk and effeminate,' Tyndale said, '. . . shall be more grievous unto the realm than a right tyrant.' In this reckoning they had a poor opinion of Stephen, during whose reign, according to the chronicler, Christ and His saints slept. The fact that his mother later married a Tudor partly, and perhaps irrelevantly, rescued Henry VI from a similar disesteem, but his reign had a morbid fascination for the sixteenth-century mind. It was engraved there as a period, perilously close to their own, that had suffered all the ills which their own age, thanks to God's providence and the character of their rulers, had miraculously escaped. The three generations from Richard II to Richard III, treated by many writers besides Shakespeare, were seen as a dreadful example of what happened when God's kindly watchfulness was turned to wrath by the crimes, ambition and misgovernment of men. The writer's duty was to discover what particular sin or weakness caused this kind of suffering, and by seasonable admonition to prevent its recurrence.

The sixteenth century was seldom far from civil war. In the early years men had no reason to suppose that Bosworth would be the last battle of the Wars of the Roses. Margaret of Burgundy certainly did not accept it as a final decision, and it was some while before Henry

20

VII, by shrewdly exploiting the exhaustion of his enemies and the country's need of peace, made himself secure from immediate challenge. Then the sudden death of Arthur, Prince of Wales, raised the bogey of an uncertain or disputed succession that was to plague the country for a hundred years. As it turned out, Mary was the only Tudor whose accession was challenged, even momentarily, by armed resistance; on the other hand, Henry VIII was the only one to whom there was not some formidable alternative. Throughout the century men always lived in fear of an uprising when the ruling monarch died. Although vast energies of statesmanship and intrigue went into the continual efforts to ensure a smooth succession, the future was never really certain. The sixteenth-century Englishman lived on his nerves.

When Arthur died, the survival of the new dynasty depended solely upon the ten-year-old boy who later became Henry VIII.[1] True, he had two sisters, but only one queen had sat on the English throne since the Conquest, and that was Matilda. As an omen she was not encouraging. It is impossible to say what would have happened if Henry had died before 1509, and in those days even the healthiest boys did die, and with great suddenness. Once he was on the throne, his lack of an heir made him suspicious of men with royal blood in them, and every crisis of the reign was marked by an execution: Suffolk in 1513, Buckingham in 1521, and later Montague, Exeter and the old Countess of Salisbury. These killings were a dreadful example to pretenders; and also a sign that these were precarious times.

The Reformation only made the country more vulnerable. In so far as the annulment of Henry VIII's marriage to Catherine of Aragon was a cause of it, the Reformation in England may be said to have been due to renewed anxiety about the succession. Catherine's failure to rear a son revived the old fears of what might happen if the crown had to pass to a woman, and it was principally for this reason that Henry cast her aside. Anne Boleyn failed in the same way, with even more disagreeable consequences, and Henry was over 45 before he had a legitimate male heir. In the meantime the religious changes of the 1530s had exposed the throne to Catholic and conservative opposition outside the country as well as within. Fortunately for Henry, Spain and France were distracted by quarrels of their own, and the Pilgrimage of Grace, the only serious rising of the reign, was eventually put down; but it was defeated only by temporisation followed by

[1] Henry VII tried hastily to add another string to his bow, but the Queen, now 38, died in childbed and the infant, a daughter named Catherine, 'tarried but a small season after her mother'.

treachery, and the Crown's success depended upon the loyalty of un-professional levies from the south. There was nothing permanently secure in the situation. If the Catholic powers should settle their differences, the Reformation had provided an excuse for foreign intervention to join itself with the latent discontent at home. Every Tudor Englishman knew that this was a threat that the country would some day have to face; and so far from leaving a settled dynasty to meet it, Henry passed his crown to three heirs, each born of a different mother. Two of them were disregarded daughters and the son was a minor. It remained to be seen how long he would be able to rule England from his grave.

The short reign of Edward VI saw two dangerous rebellions and a series of religious changes too swift and drastic to be immediately acceptable to the people. When the boy King fell mortally ill, the problem of a disputed succession rose once again. The Regent Northumberland produced a plot to disinherit Mary, and only his time-serving irresolution in the ensuing crisis averted a civil war that would have brought to violent issue the accumulated resentments of twenty years of change. Faction and the overmighty subject, spectres that Tudor government was thought to have laid to rest, had once again threatened the precarious peace. Moreover, with Mary 36 and still unmarried, a further crisis over the succession was inevitable, for at best there would have to be another regency. Her marriage to Philip of Spain meant that the crisis would probably be long and bitter. The accession of their son, if they had one, would certainly be contested by all earnest Protestants and by all Englishmen who put patriotism before religion; and if she died childless, Philip would not be likely to surrender his valuable footing in England without a struggle.

The ancient quarrel between Spain and France, which more than once saved England from foreign intervention during these difficult years, obligingly came to her aid once more, and with Philip engaged in war with Henry II, Elizabeth entered upon her dubious inheritance with surprising ease. Few sovereigns have succeeded to a more daunting task, and the public rejoicings at Mary's death spoke rather of relief at the ending of a nightmare than of confidence in the new dawn. Mary's religious fanaticism had further divided the nation and justified its deep-rooted forebodings about feminine rule. What was to be hoped from the rather shifty princess who had cautiously plotted against her half-sister and sacrificed her accomplices while piously protesting her innocence and affection? But the reign began fortunately. Philip was surprisingly civil in his approach when he found time to make one at all; and a Scottish rising, discreetly aided by Elizabeth, cleared the French faction from Scotland and relieved the hostile pressure from the north. This unexpected breathing-space gave Elizabeth time to make the first impact of her unique personal authority and to lay the flimsy foundations of the religious peace that was to 'make no windows into men's souls'. Elizabeth's settlement of religion, like the hesitant provisions that followed the revolution of 1688, was invested in time with a grandeur and completeness beyond its intrinsic merits. It was makeshift and temporising, because in the circumstances it could be nothing else. It represented only the highest common factor that could be agreed among the parties that procured or advised upon its making; and even then only one of the bishops, the pedantically Erastian Kitchin of Llandaff, would accept it. In an age of religious perfectionism it was doctrinally too compromising and ambiguous to satisfy anyone. But from the first it was an assertion of the English way of doing things, and men argued and eventually fought for it because it assured them of their independence. All Protestants, and even some Catholics, admitted the right of the sovereign to 'command for truth', that is, to lay down essential doctrine and see that it was observed. Against all pressure to amend, Elizabeth persisted that her Prayer Book and Articles contained all that was needful for salvation; things not prescribed were 'things indifferent'. When resisted on the ground of conscience, she laid claim to special insights, granted to herself in virtue of her office: all that was in the Prayer Book was of God. The extraordinary thing is that thousands of Elizabethan Englishmen accepted this, receiving as self-evident religious truths, derived from Scripture and conformable to reason, doctrines which their heart and mind rejected. At least until Bancroft initiated an Anglo-Catholic revival, there was hardly one Elizabethan bishop who believed that his office was divinely instituted: episcopacy was a thing indifferent, at the sovereign's discretion, not an article of faith. Many believed that their apostolic duty was to preach and teach, not to play the overseer; and most of them, Whitgift not least, had notions about predestination that were not to be found in the Thirty-Nine Articles. Yet they supported the Queen in holding the uneasy settlement of 1559 to be inviolate, defending the Church's doctrines and organisation against all the efforts of Puritan and Catholic apologists to have them altered. If there were errors, this was no time to have them expunged; Christian duty was to accept and obey. The religious settlement was the very heart of the Elizabethan 'Establishment', its invocation to unity, the symbol of its independence—and the inspiration of its historical writing.

Conservatism and independence, not always easy bedfellows, were the master themes of the reign. When we remember the vast energy and undisciplined curiosity of the Elizabethans, it is difficult to reconcile these with the almost monolithic conservatism of their official policy; but the Queen's obstinate adherence to the last detail of her religious settlement was typical of her attitude in everything else. Policy-making belonged to the royal prerogative. That was final, and Elizabeth yielded to no flattery or intimidation that tried to make her share it. Her personal instinct was to change nothing if she could avoid it, and all the agitators—warmongers eager to flesh their swords in Protestant-piratical crusades, religious innovators, champions of parliamentary privilege, visionaries with blueprints for an empire— were foiled in the end by her masterly equivocation and inactivity. Many were left vocal and dissatisfied, but in the main her undogmatic caution had the confidence of the people. It was not a revolutionary age. Even those who demanded changes in the Church were mostly conservative in spirit, proclaiming their willingness to 'tarry for the magistrate'; and in the constitutional field no one questioned the traditional theory that Crown and Parliament were partners, not rivals, in a harmonious body politic. The government's loudest critics in the Commons thought that they were only arguing from ancient precedents. The Elizabethans were proudly conscious of their nationhood, but their patriotism expressed itself in the feeling that this was a time for consolidation, for protecting the new Church and bureaucratic system that had been achieved in the revolutionary generation that now lay behind them.[1] In this task they were passionately loyal to the Queen who was 'mere English', the focus of their determination to defend their independence. Strength, unity and order were felt instinctively to be stouter sinews in the coming struggle than the larger designs of zealots who advocated change towards this or that perfection. Elizabeth's problems were in any case of a kind best handled flexibly. Watchfulness and adaptability served her better than a rigid policy based on theoretical principles.

Her course was bound to be dangerous, whatever she decided to do. The deceptive lull of the earlier years could not be expected to last, especially as Philip, rebuffed by Elizabeth, had married a French princess. Elizabeth's difficulties began in earnest when Mary, Queen of Scots, was dethroned by her subjects and in 1568 fled to England to demand her cousin's protection and English help in recovering her crown. As a great-granddaughter of Henry VII, Mary had a claim to

[1] See G. R. Elton, *England under the Tudors*, 295-8.

the English throne, and arguably a better one than Elizabeth, who had at one time been disinherited by her own father. Her presence in England stirred the Catholics into attempting their long-awaited stroke. Buoyed by Spanish promises, the Northern Earls marched to disaster behind the banner of the Five Wounds. Their failure contained nearly all the elements that Shakespeare was to discover in the rebellions against Henry IV—mismanagement, divided aims, mutual jealousies and failing nerve.[1] In Stratford, where Shakespeare was a child of five, the townsmen might feel themselves on the fringe of great events, for Mary was moved from Tutbury, the Earl of Shrewsbury's castle on the Dove, to the greater safety of nearby Coventry. If the rebels had ever managed to come so far south, the young William would have seen fighting in his own familiar streets; but the movement rapidly disintegrated, and in 1570 its last gesture failed when Leonard Dacre was routed on the banks of the Gelt by Lord Hunsdon, cousin to the Queen, who from 1594 until his death two years later was to be patron of Shakespeare's company, the Chamberlain's Men.

The Northern Rebellion was to prove the last feudal rising in England, but no one dared to hope it at the time. In 1570 the Queen's excommunication as a heretic freed the English Catholics from even nominal allegiance, and the almost hysterical phrases of the famous *Homily against Disobedience and Wilful Rebellion*[2] betrayed the government's deep anxiety for the future. As shock troops of the Counter-Reformation the Spaniards sent their agents to whisper treason in the manor-houses of the north and west where the old faith was still professed in secret, and Mary, although now kept in closer captivity, was the automatic focus of conspiracy. In the view of many of her subjects Elizabeth could best solve her difficulties by taking the open initiative against Spain and tossing Mary's head into the arena as a gage of battle. But Elizabeth always hoped to avoid an open declaration of war with Spain, and her relationship with Mary was even more complex and devious. In some ways she seems to have thought that Mary was less dangerous to her alive than dead. Alive, she could be used as a counter to ensure the good behaviour of the Scots, and it was possible that Philip would be discouraged from an invasion from which she stood to gain more than himself; dead, she was a martyr, crying to be avenged. But beyond any practical considerations the case of Mary

---

[1] The plan was that Norfolk, a Catholic and the only duke in England, should marry Mary and reign with her. In September 1569 the government summoned him to London and he meekly went, leaving his supporters without a leader.

[2] See below, pp. 37–41.

illustrates the striking potency of Tudor theories about rebellion and the duty owed to anointed rulers. Policy required Elizabeth to keep Mary under surveillance in England: she was much too dangerous to be allowed to go free. On the other hand, orthodoxy insisted that Mary was still Queen of Scotland and that the men who deposed her were godless rebels. Elizabeth was thus unhappily divided between the dogmas which, as a queen, she was herself bound to acknowledge, and the cold facts to which her own policy had contributed. Officially the Scots were still rebels, as were the Netherlanders whom Elizabeth occasionally and grudgingly assisted against their Spanish masters. Her indecision in dealing with Mary was the despair of her advisers, who had not the least doubt what she should do. Mary was a Catholic, a murderess, an adulteress, a plotter against the safety of the realm, and she should be sent to the death she deserved on each of these counts. But for Elizabeth the issue was never as straightforward as that, for once she admitted that subjects could lawfully proceed against an anointed sovereign, she abandoned her claim to the allegiance of her own people. It was one of the crucial issues of the age, and its complexity, as well as its urgency, made it particularly suitable for dramatic treatment. The hacks handled it as well as the greater writers, and the stage became a pulpit to urge the official dogma that rulers, however wicked, must be left to the vengeance of God. But it would not have been necessary to insist upon it so often if many Elizabethans had not felt in their mounting anxiety that there were times when official dogmas should yield to expediency.

When eventually Elizabeth did order Mary's execution, the decision was practically forced upon her by the people. Parliament and Star Chamber confirmed the verdict of a special commission set up to decide Mary's complicity in the Babington plot, and it only remained for Elizabeth to order the sentence to be carried out. When she hesitated, the Commons peremptorily pressed her to make up her mind. In vain she bade them accept 'an answer answerless' and begged them to find 'some other way'. Excusably frightened by Mary's ceaseless plotting with the country's enemies, Parliament wished for no other way. Elizabeth was in an agony of doubt. The international consequences of Mary's execution would be incalculable, but what really made Elizabeth hold back was the awfulness of the deed, the violation of the sacred law that protected crowned heads. In the end she signed the death warrant but then with characteristic vacillation held it back, trying instead to persuade Mary's gaoler to kill her in secret. Exasperated by the dangerous delay, the Council finally acted on their own initiative and despatched the warrant without the Queen's knowledge. Her rage and grief were not simulated, nor were they provoked simply by the explosive indignation with which the dreadful news was received at foreign courts. A fundamental law had been breached.

> Nay, if I turn mine eyes upon myself,
> I find myself a traitor with the rest;
> For I have given here my soul's consent
> To undeck the pompous body of a king.
> *Rich. II* IV i 247.

In the ensuing uproar Secretary Davison, who had let the warrant out of his keeping, was made the scapegoat. He was fined, deprived of his office and committed to the Tower.

This was in 1587, when Shakespeare may already have come to London and begun his apprenticeship in the theatre. Like any other thoughtful man, he was deeply affected by the tremendous implications of Mary's fate, in which one sovereign had dared to sit in judgment upon another. In *King John* he allowed no forgiveness to the monarch or his agent when they plotted the elimination of a rival to the throne, although the innocence of Arthur, and Shakespeare's curious insistence that John was a usurper, prevent an exact comparison with Elizabeth's treatment of Mary. He comes much nearer the bone in *Richard II*, where Exton, like Davison, receives no thanks for acting upon words that his sovereign meant and did not mean. 'They love not poison that do poison need.' Moreover, Mary, like Richard, was her enemy's 'buried fear'; dead but still potent, as much a threat to the government's security as ever she had been in life. Moral condemnation was only implicit, and Shakespeare was sufficiently capable of entering imaginatively into Elizabeth's difficulties to know that they were virtually insoluble. But he insists that killing was no solution. The Queen had scotched the snake, not killed it.

Her hesitation over killing Mary was something that all Elizabeth's subjects could with their different perceptions understand. No one could be insensitive to the awful quality of the deed.[1] What, on the other hand, they found incomprehensible was her sustained refusal either to marry or to nominate her successor. Her persistence in an attitude that seemed to her advisers to be wildly impolitic involved her in a running quarrel with Parliament that grew more bitter as the years

---

[1] Angels would plead trumpet-tongued against the deep damnation of this taking-off. In orthodox theory it made no difference that Mary had been guilty of conspiracy against the Queen, whereas Duncan was virtuous. Regicide was still a sin. And were not both victims their murderers' guests?

went by; and it meant, of course, that the old anxiety about the succession, already an embarrassment to the Tudor image of order and peace, was gratuitously protracted for another forty years.

Probably many reasons combined to keep Elizabeth single. She may have been physically deformed in the way that Ben Jonson and others lewdly conjectured; no doubt it pleased her to be, and to remain, the most eligible match in Europe; politically her position was stronger so long as the prize was dangled but never won; and certainly there was that in her temperament which forbade her to surrender her independence to any man.[1] Marriage, she once told the Commons, was an excellent state for a private woman but 'not meet for a prince'. Her instinct was sound, for it was safer and more profitable to keep a string of suitors in craftily animated hopefulness than by marriage to turn all but one of them against her. But this was not the view of her people. It was unprecedented and unthinkable that a queen should not marry, and subdue in wifely submission to the male the inborn capriciousness of woman. Her business was to raise a family, and to leave the mysteries of government to the sex traditionally capable of understanding them. Her first Parliament's address to her on this subject— for which they were rebuked—was no more than a hint to proceed with this necessary duty as rapidly as possible, and to be more careful in the choice of a mate than her predecessor had been. When they met again in 1563 and she was still unmarried, their protestations had a sharp edge of panic, for in the previous autumn Elizabeth had been seriously ill with smallpox and the problem of the succession loomed ominously large. As well as the Stuarts, both the Poles and the Greys had claims to the throne, and it was clear to everyone that until Elizabeth had a direct heir, the only hope of avoiding a disputed succession, and perhaps a civil war, was for her to make a choice between them.

But she never did. She was willing for the prospect of her eventual marriage to remain an enticing mirage, and as late as 1580, when she was long past an age for child-bearing, she beguiled many hours in kittenish coquetries with the pock-marked Duke of Alençon. But she resisted all inducements to name her successor. Her advisers frequently pointed out to her that if she were to choose a Protestant, she would rally the loyal sentiment that dreaded a Catholic succession in the person of Mary; or even by naming Mary she would put an end to Catholic plotting, for Mary's supporters would then be content to await her natural death. It was all to no avail. One may not, Elizabeth once said,

---

[1] 'I know your spirit cannot endure a commander,' Sir James Melville once said to her.

love one's own winding-sheet. Warier than her counsellors, she seems to have thought that to name an heir would be to sign her own death warrant, as the heir would have too strong a motive for wishing to hasten her departure. It were better that the future be kept as darkly uncertain as possible. This policy provoked angry disputes about parliamentary liberties and privileges, since the Commons refused to be warned off the subject by Elizabeth's assertions that marriage and the succession were matters pertaining to the prerogative, not to be chewed over by those ill-equipped to understand them. In 1566 the opposition saucily attempted to make the Queen's promise to marry and fix the succession a condition of their granting a subsidy bill: to which she answered that she knew no reason why 'any my private answers to the realm should serve for prologue to a subsidies-book'. The Commons' bitterness was aggravated by incomprehension of Elizabeth's motive, and for two or three angry, suspicious sessions they were ready to make a constitutional issue of her refusal to undertake her manifest patriotic duty. The quarrel lingered even into the nineties, and for attempting to discuss the succession in the parliament of 1593 Peter Wentworth was sent for the last time to the Tower. When Elizabeth died, England was still at war with Spain, the Dutch had not yet assured their independence, relations with France had been uncertain ever since Henry IV changed his religion; and still no successor had been named. Few Englishmen could dare to be hopeful of the outcome; and once they realised that it had really happened, the people greeted the peaceful accession of James as a miraculous deliverance. The preface to the Authorised Version (1611) is eloquent of their relief. 'For whereas', the translators say, addressing James,

> it was the expectation of many, who wished not well unto our Sion, that upon the setting of that bright occidental star Queen Elizabeth of most happy memory, some thick and palpable clouds of darkness would so have overshadowed this land, that men should have been in doubt which way they were to walk, and that it should hardly be known, who was to direct the unsettled state: the appearance of Your Majesty, as of the sun in his strength, instantly dispelled those supposed and surmised mists, and gave unto all that were well affected, exceeding cause of comfort.

The Elizabethans never really knew security, and it is particularly misleading to think of the last fifteen years of the reign as a period of calm after they had outlived the storm. The death of Mary and the defeat of the Armada, often seen as climactic events, began a new chain of dangers and frustrations. On the scaffold Mary disinherited her Protestant son and bequeathed her claim to Philip II; with the Jesuits and the seminary priests undaunted by persecution, Catholic intrigue did not suddenly cease. A great wave of relief and exultation greeted the scattering of the Spanish invasion, but 1588 in some ways marked a resurgence and new direction of Spanish sea-power. The enemy had slowly learned some important lessons, and thereafter their shipping routes and their more vulnerable outposts were better defended. The last heroic hours of the *Revenge* have passed into legend, but the incident was a significant success for the Spaniards' new convoy system. Although private buccaneering ventures, backed by wealthy merchants, often won substantial prizes, the large-scale, semi-official expeditions of the nineties were unrewarding. Essex's expedition in 1596 sacked Cadiz and forced Philip to repudiate his debts, but it failed to bring home the expected plunder, and all the other enterprises were in various ways unsuccessful. After the Armada, for example, some forty vessels had limped home to Spanish harbours, and a great opportunity was lost of sinking them before they could re-fit. Beguiled, as men of action often are, by the pathos of the disinherited, Drake persuaded the Queen to allow him instead to make an attack on Portugal in the name of the exiled Don Antonio. The expedition achieved no worthwhile result of any kind; while the Spanish galleons, now re-equipped, were available in the following years to foil English raids on the treasure fleets. By 1595 the three greatest Elizabethan sailors were dead, Frobisher in a minor operation in Brittany, Hawkins and Drake in a lame effort to revive old glories on the Spanish Main. These veteran commanders were now become too set in their habits to adapt themselves to the new vigour and resourcefulness of the enemy, and except in the raid on Cadiz their successors did no better. Essex set out again in 1597, but instead of attacking the storm-battered Spanish ships that lay in Ferrol and Corunna, he sailed to the Azores to intercept a treasure fleet. It eluded him, and he returned empty-handed to find the government in a state of near-panic because in his absence a Spanish fleet, composed largely of the ships he should have destroyed earlier in the year, had been sailing towards England's undefended shores. For a time both fleets had been converging on the Channel together, and the same north-east gales scattered them both. If they had met in battle off the English coast, the advantage must have been with the invaders, who were fresh and well equipped.[1]

[1] In 1595 the Spaniards grounded some ships in Cornwall, and in the following year Philip sent a considerable fleet to avenge the attack on Cadiz. It was wrecked in a storm off Cape Finisterre, but not before it had caused grave alarm in England. Later, Spanish ships achieved a certain nuisance value during the rebellion in Ireland.

Military action during these years was much more successful, and the help in protecting their flanks that Elizabeth gave to the French and Dutch contributed more usefully to the defeat of the Catholic League than any naval marauding could have done. But these campaigns were on a small scale and quite unspectacular. There were no processions of captured treasure through the streets, nothing to fire the imagination. Elizabethan soldiers, cadging reminiscently in St. Paul's, where Falstaff found Bardolph, were no advertisement for their profession, and the solid work done by the small English forces in the early nineties was not of a kind to mitigate the disappointment of the failures at sea.

We have to remember that these were the years when Shakespeare was writing his histories and urging the lesson that only by unity and integrity of purpose at home could England defeat her enemies. Naval reverses were not the only disappointments of these unhappy years, and the contemporary context of the histories was a decade of growing disillusion and anxiety. A spell of plague and ruined harvests made a sombre background to economic, political and religious uncertainties that would not rest. There is no need to try to ante-date Shakespeare's life in the theatre on the assumption that the sense of contemporary crisis that so evidently shadowed his histories must have belonged to the dangerous years of the Armada and Mary Stuart. In 1595 Englishmen felt that the great crisis of their age, so far from lying safely behind them, was still ahead. Something like an industrial revolution was taking place, creating problems of social readjustment reflected in the dark talk about 'undertakers' and 'projectors' in the comedy of Ben Jonson and the 'citizen' dramatists.[1] Moreover, after some fifteen years of commercial prosperity the nineties were a period of economic recession whose causes no one really understood. Its results, however, were inescapably evident in the aggravation of the old problem of vagrancy, the sixteenth-century term for unemployment, and in the existence of a near-famine which brought a sudden rise in prices. In religion, the Armada had given the answer to the question about Catholic loyalty, and the better men of the old faith, turning their back upon the scarifying activities of the lunatic fringe, asked only to be left alone. The Queen's firmness had also subdued, at least for the time, the Presbyterian element within the Protestant ranks, but those reformers who had been willing to tarry for the magistrate were now being succeeded by sectaries and separatists who spoke ominously of practising their spiritual nostrums 'without tarrying for any'. Giving an

[1] See *SWW* III-16.

edge to all other disputes was the long-drawn haggling over money.
Protracted war made it quite impossible for Elizabeth to run the country on the 'ordinary' revenues of the Crown, and from her wartime
parliaments she received something like £2,000,000 in direct extraordinary taxation: subsidies unprecedented both in their total amount
and in their persistent recurrence.

'All the fabric of my reign, little by little, is beginning to fail,'
Elizabeth lamented to the King of France. In both his surviving dramas
Fulke Greville examined the fate of countries ruled by an ageing
monarch.

> Where declining spirits
> To govern mighty sceptres God ordains,
> Order no basis finds; honour must fall;
> Where man is nothing, place cannot do all.
> Greville, *Mustapha* I ii 198.

In the same play Soliman himself wonders if it be not common knowledge that

> long life in the best kings discontenteth?
> That discontentment's hopes live in succession?
> *Mustapha* II ii 52.

Elizabeth was secure in her people's hearts, but that did not mean that
many of them did not wish her dead.[1] The fruits of her wilfulness would
be theirs to gather, and the mood of the nineties was at best one of
uneasy postponement. The Commons told James in 1604 that they had
refrained from pressing many matters 'in regard to her sex and age,
which we had great cause to tender'; in regard also, although they did
not say so, to her rage, which was still formidable. Only Burghley and
Whitgift now remained of the counsellors who had stood at her side in
the storm, and although she was as imperious and unpredictable as ever,
she was even less capable of making a decision. Policy tended to be
evolved in the tantrums of senility, and the great reign ended sadly in
the Irish rebellion, the quarrel about monopolies, and the tragedy of
Essex. In its very last hours the dynasty had to assert itself once again
to put down the sort of overmighty subject with whose elimination
the Tudor name is particularly associated. The reappearance of this
figure—no longer a territorial magnate, but still a 'king-maker' with

---

[1] For example, Sir Thomas Wilson's *State of England* (1600) mentioned as
many as twelve rival candidates 'that gape for the death of that good old Princess
our now Queen'.

a following of armed retainers recklessly exploiting faction—was a final realisation of sixteenth-century fears.

Only a century so persistently troubled by fears of rebellion and a disputed succession would have needed to evolve such a rigid theory of obedience and to proclaim it so frequently. Paradoxically it was the weakness of the Tudor state that forced it to its occasional displays of savagery and its almost hysterical reiteration of the duty of non-resistance. It is unnecessary at this time to multiply instances or to expound in detail the Tudor doctrine of 'degree'. It has been so fully illustrated in a number of recent works[1] that every student of the age is familiar with it, and it will suffice here to recapitulate the main arguments as shortly as possible.

In its need for order the sixteenth century insisted that political obedience was a religious duty. The idea was not new. Shakespeare belonged to a world in which the novel was still being silently absorbed into the familiar, and fusion was still more powerful than change. The continuity of intellectual belief had not yet been disturbed, for the Renaissance had accepted from the Middle Ages a vast bulk of ossified doctrine about man, his nature, and his place in the universe, a traditional amalgam of Christianity with pagan philosophy. It provided a cosmological system which, although complicated, inconsistent and even uncertain in its details, was definite in outline and purpose, and its core was the assurance of the unity and intimate correspondence of the whole of God's creation. This sytem had developed as a means of explaining and understanding life. It grew out of man's normal experience and his common needs, and it existed for his good. In assuring him of the interdependence of the spiritual universe, the physical creation (macrocosm), the body politic, and the individual soul (microcosm), it gave him the confidence that all his doings were of concern to God. When mortals sin, 'even heaven itself must see and suffer ill', and at a mother's incest

> heaven's face doth glow,
> Yea, this solidity and compound mass,
> With tristful visage, as against the doom,
> Is thought-sick at the act.
> *Ham.* III iv 48.

---

[1] For example, E. M. W. Tillyard, *The Elizabethan World Picture* and *Shakespeare's History Plays*; Theodore Spencer, *Shakespeare and the Nature of Man*; Hardin Craig, *The Enchanted Glass*; A. O. Lovejoy, *The Great Chain of Being*; *SWW* 113–15, 395, 457–78.

Man's conception of unity was unselective and various, after the mediaeval fashion, but it offered him a universe that answered God's great
plan, a tidy and comprehensive system in which everything had its
place and nothing existed in vain. As an explanation of life it was at
once Christian, rational and poetic. It was ethical, philosophical,
religious, physiological and political, and it could not so completely
have satisfied man's needs if it had excluded any of these main approaches to life. In fact, it drew its potency from the ability of the
mediaeval mind to embrace simultaneously various levels of knowledge and move almost unconsciously from one to the other, confident
that the divine unity of all things physical and spiritual would ultimately resolve all ambiguities.

The fundamental principle of the universe was order, the force that
held together what was constantly threatening to dissolve. The famous
speech of Ulysses in *Troilus and Cressida* (I iii 78–134) pictures in
detail the dreadful consequences that would follow if Nature were to
leave 'the observation of her own laws'. In this speech 'the speciality
of rule' is shown to have a more than merely political application.
Ulysses draws his analogies from the heavens, civil law, the elements,
the Law of Nature, ethics and psychology, all of which he reveals as
related parts of a single scheme. Disorder in the heavens produces a
reflexive disorder in the sublunary world, in the state and in the soul
of man; disorder in any one of these is the cause of disorder in all the
others, and the performance by all created things of their appointed
function is alone 'the stay of the whole world'.

The correspondence, or similitude, between all the planes of existence was the means by which men indicated the pervasive operation
of order in the universe and the interdependence of all its parts. They
believed in a Chain of Being which linked all created things in an
ascending scale reaching up to God and His angels. It at once distinguished and united all the levels of existence, and being both a
horizontal and a vertical chain, it could be invoked as a reminder that
as God is to the world, so is the sun to the heavens, the king to the
commonwealth, the lion to the beasts, the oak to the forest, justice to
the other virtues or the soul to the body. If one of these primacies was
overthrown, the rest must follow it to confusion: only let a subject kill
a king and the falcon will be hawked at by a mousing owl; if the jackal
overthrow the lion, rank fumiter will flourish where the rose once
bloomed. There could not be a single doom.

By such analogies, exuberantly and ingeniously multiplied, men kept
themselves in mind of the desperate truth that harmony, which was the

sole guarantee of the universal order, depended in every sphere upon the proper functioning of every part. In God's scheme nothing had been neglected. As in the physical creation He had prescribed for the celestial bodies the courses they were to follow; as to each individual He had given the four humours that might be blended in the perfect man; so in the commonwealth He had appointed the magistrate to bear His office on earth, and directed that all others should obey. *Obedience, respect, degree, status, calling* were the forms in which men stated their conviction that the speciality of rule, in all its far-reaching applications, must be preserved. In the state man's duty was to perform his function, directing those whom God had placed under him and never failing in his obedience to those who were set in God's place to rule him. A typical statement in Raleigh's preface to his *History of the World* might be found just as typically in a hundred passages in Hooker, Shakespeare or any educated Elizabethan writer:

> For that infinite wisdom of God, which hath distinguished His angels by degrees: which hath given greater and less light, and beauty, to heavenly bodies: which hath made differences between beasts and birds: created the eagle and the fly, the cedar and the shrub: and among stones, given the fairest tincture to the ruby, and the quickest light to the diamond; hath also ordained kings, dukes or leaders of the people, magistrates, judges and other degrees among men.

This—additionally compelling for its parade of the primacies and their opposites, and for its awareness of the correspondences between each level of being—is degree. One illustrative quotation leads easily to others, as contemporary literature contains so many assertions of the belief that reverence

> —That angel of the world—doth make distinction
> Of place 'tween high and low.
> *Cymb.* IV ii 247.

For Spenser degree was the means to the stability that would finally bring accursed Mutability to rest:

> I well consider all that ye have said
> And find that all things steadfastness do hate
> And changed be; yet, being rightly weigh'd,
> They are not changed from their first estate
> But by their change their being do dilate,
> And, turning to themselves at length again,
> Do work their own perfection so by fate.
> Then over them Change doth not rule and reign,
> But they reign over Change, and do their states maintain.
> *Fairy Queen* Book VII Canto vii 58.

At the beginning of *The Governor* Elyot praised order as that which 'in things as well natural as supernatural hath ever had such a pre-eminence, that thereby the incomprehensible majesty of God, as it were by a bright leme of a torch or candle, is declared to the blind inhabitants of this world'; and Hooker found in it the assurance of the essential unity of creation: 'We see the whole world and each part thereof so compacted, that as long as each thing performeth only that work which is natural unto it, it thereby preserveth both other things and also itself.' The preachers echoed the philosophers and poets. In his *Treatise of the Vocations* (c. 1599) the Puritan William Perkins demanded subordination on the ground that while 'God giveth diversity of gifts inwardly', He also imposes 'distinction of order outwardly'. Shakespeare's Bishop of Carlisle denounced rebellion against 'the figure of God's majesty, His captain, steward, deputy elect', Menenius more humorously vindicated the foreordained interdependence of all the body's parts, and the whole doctrine was summarised with appropriate unction by the Archbishop of Canterbury, using the hive as his term of reference:

> Therefore doth heaven divide
> The state of man in divers functions,
> Setting endeavour in continual motion;
> To which is fixed, as an aim or butt,
> Obedience.
>
> *Hen. V* I ii 183.

This sort of thing was, for many Elizabethan writers, part of the idiom of their thought, and the detection of subconscious examples lends a private zest and curiosity to the reading of their work. Time and again sickness or disorder on one level of being are instinctively related to like disorders upon another, and cosmic consequences are imagined for any act of weakness in the commonwealth or the soul of man. Another way of expressing the same dislocation in the universe was to hint at the overthrow of one of the primacies—sun, rose, lion, oak, cedar, diamond, pelican, eagle, falcon and many more.[1] The king

[1] There is an odd little collection in the anonymous *Woodstock*, where the parasitic Greene tells King Richard II that it is time he threw off the yoke of his domineering uncles:

> May not the lion roar, because he's young?
> What are your uncles but as elephants
> That set their aged bodies to the yoke?
> You are the oak against whose stock they lean.
>
> II i 18.

In one of Heywood's plays a falcon is solemnly put to death for having killed an eagle.

might be likened to any of these, and when Hotspur speaks of the dead Richard as 'that sweet lovely rose', there is a significant overtone that an Elizabethan audience would not have missed. The words generate emotion from the brief beauty of the flower, but they acquire a further and deeper meaning from the reminder that Richard was a king.

The doctrine of degree flourished in Tudor England through the special needs and anxieties of the age. Because rebellion was always imminent, it had to be denounced as the wickedest of all sins, the great 'puddle and sink', in fact, in which all other sins found their origin. This was a fundamental axiom for all the chroniclers and poets who turned their hand to history, and the doctrine was officially stated and amplified in the Homilies of the English Church. These Homilies, one of the first by-products of the Reformation, were compiled by the government to be read at divine service, in place of sermons, by beneficed clergy whose orthodoxy or learning might be unequal to the rather exacting necessities of their day.[1] In other words, they were a means to uniformity. The pulpits should speak with a single voice, and that the voice of the government. Homilies had long been used in Jewish synagogues for purposes of exposition after the reading of the law, and in the early days of Christianity they were useful in crystallising doctrine in the struggling outposts of the faith, but in England it was not until the sixteenth century that an official series of these dogmatic exhortations was issued. The first group, twelve in number, appeared in 1547; a further twenty were published in 1563, and the thirty-third, the famous *Homily against Disobedience and Wilful Rebellion*, was the government's panic-stricken reply to the Northern Rebellion of 1569.

The *Sermon of Obedience*, the tenth in the first series, is magnificent stuff, and we may see in the following extract how obedience is related to the whole scheme of God's creation.

> Almighty God hath created and appointed all things, in heaven, earth and waters, in a most excellent and perfect order. In heaven he hath appointed distinct orders and states of archangels and angels. In the earth he hath assigned kings, princes, with other governors under them, all in good and necessary order. The water above is kept and raineth down in due time and season. The sun, moon, stars, rainbow, thunder, lightning, clouds, and all birds of the air, do keep their order. The earth, trees, seeds, plants, herbs, and corn, grass and all manner of beasts keep them in their order. All the parts of the whole year, as winter, summer, months, nights

---

[1] Convocation declared in 1542 that Homilies were 'for the stay of such errors as were then by ignorant preachers sparkled among the people'.

and days, continue in their order. All kinds of fishes in the sea, rivers and waters, with all fountains, springs, yea, the seas themselves keep their comely course and order.

And man himself also hath all his parts, both within and without, as soul, heart, mind, memory, understanding, reason, speech, with all and singular corporal members of his body, in a profitable, necessary and pleasant order. Every degree of people, in their vocation, calling, and office, hath appointed to them their duty and order. Some are in high degree, some in low, some kings and princes, some inferiors and subjects, priests and laymen, masters and servants, fathers and children, husbands and wives, rich and poor, and every one hath need of other, so that in all things is to be lauded and praised the goodly order of God, without the which, no house, no city, no common wealth, can continue and endure. For where there is no right order, there reigneth all abuse, carnal liberty, enormity, sin, and Babylonical confusion. Take away kings, princes, rulers, magistrates, judges, and such states of God's order, no man shall ride or go by the highway unrobbed, no man shall sleep in his own house or bed unkilled, no man shall keep his wife, children, and possessions in quietness, all things shall be common, and there must needs follow all mischief and utter destruction, both of souls, bodies, goods and common wealths.

Bogeys to frighten the ignorant, perhaps, and with the Homilies we have always to remember that they were written to be delivered by unlearned men to unlearned congregations. They have the solemn exaggeratedness of public pronouncements. This passage contains none the less the substance of Tudor thinking and belief upon the subject of order in the state, the divine sanctions of government, the duty of obedience—and the terrible consequences of disobedience. It is important to realise that the Tudor Englishman was taught to regard his political allegiance as a religious act. His government was not put there for his convenience, to be removable at his pleasure; it was there because God had in His infinite compassion decreed it for his good, lest worse befall him. In a long passage demonstrating man's crucial position in the Chain of Being, midway between the angels and the beasts, Sir John Fortescue concluded with the simple reflection: 'So that there is nothing which the bond of order doth not embrace. And since God has thus regulated all creatures, it is impious to think that He left unregulated the human race, which He made the highest of all earthly creatures.' Having given to man the endowments of will and reason, through which he might aspire to heavenly grace, it was unthinkable that God should not have also made the necessary arrangements for his political existence. So it followed, as the same Homily said, that 'we may not, in any wise, withstand violently, or rebel against rulers, or make any insurrection, sedition, or tumult . . . against the

anointed of the Lord, or any of his officers; but we must . . . patiently
suffer all wrongs and injuries, referring the judgment of our cause only
to God.'

Only, we should note, to God; not to the Bishop of Rome. The
Tudor state made an energetic but not wholly successful attempt to
capture the conscience of man. In theory it would not allow religion
or any other scruple to deflect to remoter loyalties one jot of the allegiance that was claimed for the Crown. Circumstances favoured the
attempt, since the loss of the traditional Catholic ritual, with its intense devotion to the Virgin and the picturesque hierarchy of saints,
had left an emotional deficiency which the austerer pieties of the new
faith had not yet managed to satisfy. Simple folk found it much less
easy to venerate the written Word, even had it been possible to establish definitely which scriptures were indeed the true ones: the several
Bibles that circulated in sixteenth-century England were by no means
all the same Bible. So the instinct of adoration transferred itself to the
earthly sovereign, and found there a master reluctant to allow any
right of private judgment. There should be no division of loyalties
between God and Caesar, since Caesar was God's deputy on earth
and his commands were from God. The claim to obedience acknowledged no rival authority, and a man could not be a loyal Englishman
while maintaining that in spiritual matters his duty was to the Pope. In
practice, however, one important reservation established itself. A man
need not be compelled to an act which violated his conscience, even if
the sovereign expressly commanded it. The plea of conscience gave
no right of active resistance, and probably the refusal would be
punished; but at least a man could not be forced to commit what he
regarded as a crime.[1]

When in 1570 Elizabeth was excommunicated and proclaimed a
heretic, the loyalty of English Catholics was formally dissolved and it
became their duty to contrive her death or deposition. The particular
aim, therefore, of Homily 33, issued during 1571, was to demolish the
argument that rebellion could in certain circumstances be justified.
Obedience, it said, is 'the very root of all virtues, the cause of all
felicity'; it was God's first command to Adam, and Satan was the author
of dissension. Rebellion, on the other hand, was the greatest of all
mischiefs, the deadly sin that embraces and gives birth to all the other
seven.

---

[1] The issue between conscience and the command of the sovereign is debated
in several Elizabethan plays, notably by Clarence's murderers in *Richard III* and
by Hubert in the anonymous *Troublesome Reign of King John*.

He that nameth rebellion nameth not a singular or one only sin, as is theft, robbery, murder and such like, but he nameth the whole puddle and sink of all sins against God and man, against his prince, his country, his parents, his children, his kinsfolk, his friends, and against all men universally; all sins, I say, against God and all men heaped together, nameth he that nameth rebellion.

The Homily candidly faces the issue of a subject's duty if the sovereign should happen to be a tyrant,[1] and in these passages it is addressing itself directly to those Englishmen who denied that Elizabeth was their lawful queen. It was in the first place absurd that rebels, who are the worst of men, should make themselves judges of princes, 'to determine which of them be good or tolerable'. But even if 'a prince be indiscreet, and evil indeed, and is also evident to all men's eyes that he is so', rebellion is still 'an unfit and unwholesome medicine'. If rulers are evil, it is because God wills it so, as a punishment for past wickedness: 'God, saith the holy scriptures, maketh a wicked man to reign for the sins of the people.' It would be improper to allow any right of private judgment in these matters, and the duty of the subject is to submit himself to what God has ordained. His only remedy lies in prayer; or in 'sighs and tears', as James I was later to suggest.

Repeating all the scriptural sanctions of human government, the Homily concludes that if God sends a bad ruler as punishment for a people's wickedness, to rebel is to add a new sin to those not yet expiated. If occasionally rebellion has seemed to prosper, it is only because God, to whom alone vengeance belongs, has chosen to use rebels as instruments of His purpose, and in due time the usurper or his heirs will suffer for it. Having shown how nations and families and individuals have been brought to ruin by lending themselves to rebellion, the homilist paints a graphic picture of the disorder and civil war that are the inevitable consequence of this greatest of sins. Here, mirrored in the contemporary mind, is the horror that shadowed Elizabethan life. The misery wrought by pestilence, famine or foreign invasion

is nothing so great as is the mischief and wickedness when the subjects unnaturally do rebel against their prince, whose honour and life they should defend, though it were with the loss of their own lives: countrymen to disturb the public peace and quietness of their country, for defence

---

[1] Defenders of the monarchy were not altogether consistent here, some writers allowing a right of resistance if the ruler was proved to be a tyrant. Theory had somehow to accommodate itself to the deposition of Richard III by Henry VII, which was regarded as a righteous act, see below pp. 55–6, 64–5, 85.

of whose quietness they should spend their lives; the brother to seek and often to work the death of his brother, the son of the father; the father to seek or procure the death of his sons ... and so finally to make their country, thus by their mischief weakened, ready to be a prey and spoil to all outward enemies that will invade it.

CHAPTER THREE

The Tudor Historians

MEERCRAFT: By my faith, you are cunning in the chronicles, sir.
FITZDOTTREL: No, I confess I have it from the play-books,
And think they are more authentic.
Jonson, *The Devil is an Ass* II i 441.

THE role of the historian in the Tudor period was prescribed by
political necessity. History was not yet an objective study. It was less
concerned to discover historical truth, meaning events as they really
happened, than to proclaim the sort of truth that present times appeared
to need; and its function, as we saw in the opening chapter, was to
infer from the past universal principles and practical lessons that should
be of use to the writer's own contemporaries. It was impossible for a
historian to be uncommitted, to stand aside from his own age and bury
himself in a past that he conceived to have no relevance to the present.
There exists today, although with less authority than it had a generation ago, an academic purism which holds that a historian is a professional speaking only to professionals, and a writer may, without
prejudice to the dignity of his subject, occupy himself in some detailed
and specialised study without being expected to attend to its wider
implications. Such an attitude would have been impossible at the
Renaissance. Order and unity being the unchallenged imperatives of
the age, the duty of the Tudor historian was to discover the sort of
national and individual weaknesses that had endangered them in the
past, and so to make his work a practical guide to right action in the
present.

It is instructive to contrast the standard historical writing of the
sixteenth century, so uniformly official in tone, with the slightly earlier
Governance of England by Sir John Fortescue. Fortescue was Lord
Chief Justice of the King's Bench under Henry VI, whom he followed
into exile in 1461. He returned to England with the Lancastrians ten
years later but made his peace with Edward IV after Tewkesbury, and
it is uncertain, and immaterial, whether his famous work was written
for the better instruction of Henry VI or was designed as a practical
programme for his new master. Fortescue was a jurist rather than a

historian, but *The Governance if England*[1] was a strikingly mature and elaborate analysis of government, written by a man with first-hand experience of fifteenth-century disorder. Although his remedies tended to be authoritarian—'for certainly there may no greater peril grow to a prince, than to have a subject equipollent to himself'—the tone of his book is cool, detached and remarkably free of the mystical absolutism that coloured so many Tudor studies of the constitution. As in his earlier and more generalised work, *De Laudibus Legum Angliae*, he was careful to insist that England had a 'mixed' constitution, *dominium politicum et regale*, in which there could be no taxation without consent and the king governed by known and immutable laws that were not of his making.

But the new fashion in historical writing had already found its beginnings in the adulatory study of Henry V written by Tito Livio of Ferrara, who came to England in about 1430 and found a patron in Humphrey of Gloucester. His book was unusual in isolating a single brief reign from the flow of history, and his praise of Henry's heroism and piety was the first essay in the creation of a formidable legend. The firmness and integrity of Henry's rule were unmistakably to be seen as an example to his blundering successors. At exactly the same time another protégé of Gloucester, John Lydgate, a Benedictine monk of Bury St. Edmunds, was translating Boccaccio's *De Casibus Virorum Illustrium*. His *Falls of Princes*, solemn, copious and intolerably dull, was first printed in 1494 and re-issued by Richard Tottel sixty years later, and in Tudor England it was to be influential much beyond its literary or psychological merit. Lydgate had no useful explanation to offer of the reversals in men's fortunes that his halting verses so tirelessly recorded. In the Middle Ages the contemplation of the ups and downs of fortune's wheel, testifying to God's relentless way with mankind, merely supplied a repertory of lessons on the fickleness of fate and the inevitable punishment of sin. It was a harmless sort of didacticism, warning men against ὕβρις and cataloguing the virtues and vices that promoted prosperity or disaster in society. But society itself was changing, and when the Italian technicians revived the old classical preoccupation with statecraft, these moral *exempla* came to have an increasingly political application.[2] They became tables of instruction for the prince, and by the time the poetic narratives in *A Mirror for Magistrates* began to be written in the middle of the sixteenth century,[3]

---

[1] Originally called *De Dominio Regali et Politico*: which might be freely translated as, 'Of the Difference between Absolute and Limited Monarchy'.

[2] See Tillyard, *Shakespeare's History Plays*, 28.   [3] See below, pp. 62–5.

the largely meaningless *casus* recorded by Lydgate had become detailed studies of cause and effect in the history of states.

But in the main these were unconscious anticipations. The characteristic features of Tudor historiography, including the historical drama, were the deliberate creation of Henry VII and his advisers. We must not misunderstand this, for the methods of historical writing followed their natural development, and in England were not substantially different from elsewhere in Renaissance Europe. The contribution of the Tudors was to impose a special reading upon recent English history, representing the troubles of the fifteenth century as the prelude to a deliverance. A century of faction had been God's punishment for past crimes, all stemming from the deposition and murder of Richard II, and in final token of forgiveness He had brought Henry VII to the throne and sealed the country's peace in the symbolic marriage of Henry and Elizabeth, which united the warring houses of Lancaster and York. By claiming for his accession the direct agency of God, Henry sought to broach any allegation that he might be a usurper. His defeat of Richard III was not, in this special context, an act of rebellion, for he was a chosen instrument. 'God among men, no king but demi-god,' an Elizabethan poet would presently describe him,[1] unconsciously testifying to the success of the image he had created of himself; and it is in this image also that he appears in Shakespeare's *Richard III*, where he is not a man but a symbolic figure, a *deus ex machina*, moving with the calm assurance of one predestined.

Henry further sought to strengthen his position by maintaining through his Welsh ancestry a claim to the throne that should be independent of his Lancastrian descent or his Yorkist marriage. Through his grandfather Owen Tudor he claimed direct descent from Cadwallader, last of the British kings, and from this beginning he ventured upon the larger assertion that in himself and his heirs Arthur was born again. In giving this potent name to his elder son he evoked the patriotic sentiment that in the Middle Ages had gathered round the romantic legends of England's past. These legends had been remarkably persistent, largely because men like to believe in these things and are loth to abandon a good story, and the more critical historiography of the Renaissance took a long time to dispose of them. All good propaganda founds itself upon the things men want to believe. Legend prophesied that with the return of Arthur the Britons would at last defeat the Saxons and the golden age be born again; and

[1] John Davies of Hereford, *Microcosmos*.

much of the veneration which her people felt for Elizabeth sprang from the poetic belief that in her Arthur was reincarnated. It is absurd to us, but it was not absurd to Spenser. It was the sort of miraculous fulfilment that men with a providential view of history were conditioned to accept; and although this particular feature of the Tudor myth was not specifically endorsed by Shakespeare (he was strangely indifferent to Arthur, whose bosom the Hostess mistook for Abraham's), its influence is implicit in Cranmer's lines over the infant Elizabeth in *Henry VIII* (V v 15–56).

The Tudors deliberately encouraged the writing of history in a sense favourable to themselves. Bernard André, of Toulouse, an Augustinian friar who came to England with Henry VII and was made tutor to Prince Arthur, never completed his Latin life of the King, and the first important exercises in the new mode were More's study of Richard III and Polydore Vergil's *Anglica Historia*. Vergil was an Italian from Urbino who, after being chaplain to Pope Alexander VI, came to England in 1502 as a collector of Peter's Pence. He became a naturalised Englishman and was made a prebendary of Hereford and Archdeacon of Wells, holding these offices until his death in 1555, four years after he had returned to Italy for good. It was in about 1506 that Henry commissioned him to write his history. It occupied him some ten years, although none of it was published until 1534, and he later continued the story well into the reign of Henry VIII. In his own day Vergil was attacked for his sceptical disregard of the romantic inventions of Geoffrey of Monmouth, but his book was freely used by later sixteenth-century historians, and it is important in a number of ways. Unlike the general run of mediaeval historians, he scrutinised his evidence and was humane in judgment. An upbringing in the ecclesiastical courts of Italy had left him with no illusions about the mixed motives that underlie human affairs, and except on the occasions when he seems to be writing to a brief, he was capable of presenting both sides of a question with unusual tolerance and impartiality. He thought that the past was prone to repeat itself, and this gave a pattern to his work and saved it from being a catalogue of the overwhelming judgments of heaven. Methodically and patiently he attempted to discover the cause and effect of human events. Some of his conclusions may have been naïve and over-simplified, but Vergil had a genuine historical mind, balanced, critical and stubbornly interested in mankind.

His way of writing history was to have a strong influence on the Elizabethan dramatists, particularly as it was he who gave the first indications of what was to become the standard treatment of the stretch of English history preceding the accession of the Tudors. Whether it was his own conclusion or whether he was under pressure from the King, he wrote of the deposition of Richard II as a crime that brought misery to the country until God finally relented and was pleased to send a deliverer in the person of Henry VII. Here Vergil abandoned his customary urbane and humanist spirit and acknowledged the over-riding force of divine intervention. Certain individual misfortunes might be ascribed to individual follies and sins, but the Lancastrian usurpation had unloosed an inescapable sequence of events that would not end until heaven had been appeased. Even Henry V, the most glittering of Vergil's heroes, had to die young in expiation of the curse upon his house; and the humanly unaccountable good fortune of the Yorkists 'came to pass by reason of the infortunacy of the house of Lancaster, which wise men thought even then was to be ascribed to the righteousness of God; because the sovereignty extorted forcibly by Henry IV, grandfather to Henry VI, could not long be enjoyed of that family'. Vergil was too unimpressionable and level-headed to develop this theme with the passionate emphasis given to it later, nor was he constantly picking on rebellion as the prime mover of all a nation's troubles: he was aware that mankind had other failings. But the change of tone when he came to deal with the events of the fifteenth century indicates how successful the Tudors had been already in imposing their special interpretation of history.

More's fragmentary *History of Richard III* (c. 1513) was designed as a history of his own time, but after laying it aside to write *Utopia* he never returned to it. It was modelled in style and spirit on the ancient classical historians, even in the device of the invented speech which More borrowed from Thucydides and Livy. The tragic idea of Greek drama is evident in More's sense of an irresistible fate hanging over blind men who can see the danger to others but are unconscious of what is happening to themselves. With wry irony he follows his characters to their doom without revealing to them the sword which, as his readers know, is always suspended above their heads. Homely, aphoristic, jocular, alive with delicate and moving strokes of character, this was a remarkable book by a remarkable man, and in an aesthetic sense it was too special to have any immediate effect on the writing of history. More had unusual endowments in his great learning, high satiric intelligence and intuitive dramatic art; but the book's real quality is to be found in the man himself, in the extraordinary range of his affections and the breadth and independence of his vision. For two generations his fragment of history was a thing apart, and we have to wait until Shakespeare's *Richard III* before we find anything quite like it.

But in a possibly more important way More's *Richard* was one of the most influential books of the century, since it sealed the reputation of the central figure.[1] Although it is unlikely that More was consciously acquiescing in Tudor propaganda, he could not have done his work more thoroughly if it had simply been his intention to blacken Richard's name for a political purpose. He may have received facts or suggestions from Cardinal Morton, to whom he was page during the impressionable years from twelve to fourteen.[2] Morton was a career ecclesiastic, dependent for his safety and emoluments upon the survival of the new régime. Slandering the Yorkists was one of his professional duties, which he discharged so comprehensively that a hundred years later it was being said that he, and not More, was the real author of this *History of Richard III*. But William Rastell, More's nephew, printed it in his folio edition of More's works (even if it were not in any case rather beyond Morton's reach), and we shall misunderstand the book if we think of it only as an outburst of anti-Yorkist partisanship. More perhaps took little trouble to find out what really happened, but passages in the book show that he was not unremittingly hostile to the Yorkists as a dynasty. His history was a companion piece to *Utopia* in being a witty, imaginative, deadly serious condemnation of Renaissance statecraft,[3] an 'anti-Machiavel' written before Machiavelli's name was known. Richard does not exactly become a symbol—the character is too vivid and human for that—but he comes near to being the Vice of the morality play. While it is not a fair historical portrait, and perhaps would not have claimed to be, its truthfulness lies in the very real existence of the evils which More subtly attacked. The book is as much a protest against the harsh, competitive society of the early Tudors[4] as against the supposed tyrannies of Richard III. Just as in *Utopia* More removed his indignation to an imaginary island, so too in his history he set his scene at a discreet distance, in the reign of a monarch whom no one would wish to defend. His real targets were

[1] In this respect it resembles Buchanan's study of Mary, Queen of Scots. In the sense that each of these works seems to have irretrievably fixed a historical reputation, they may rank among the important books of all time.

[2] This has been freely surmised, but it is by no means certain. To what extent is the twelve-year-old page likely to have been in his master's political confidence?

[3] See R. W. Chambers, *Thomas More*, 117.

[4] Just occasionally criticism becomes overt, as when More says that unscrupulous taxation, 'gathering of money', is 'the only thing that withdraweth the hearts of Englishmen from the Prince'.

tyranny and misgovernment wherever they might exist, and he wrote as an artist whose bias could not be concealed. Shakespeare caught his spirit exactly. The Ratcliff and Catesby of the play are typical jackals of the Tudor state.

More the humanist was a shining ornament of the Tudor court, but in spirit no contemporary Englishman was farther withdrawn from it. His oblique reflections on the seamy side of life under the two Henries were confirmed at first hand in a curious book, *The Tree of Commonwealth*, written in prison by Sir Edmund Dudley in 1509. With Empson, Dudley was one of the two 'ravening wolves' who extorted money for Henry VII, and in an easy bid for popularity Henry VIII celebrated his accession by allowing charges of treason against them both. In essence *The Tree of Commonwealth* is a plea for clemency. In accepted allegorical form it recites the venerable doctrine that king and subjects should live together in harmony and mutual dependence, the aim of their joint endeavours being the reign of justice, truth and peace. Dudley's insistence on degree shows how deeply this conception was rooted in the mediaeval tradition, long before it was elaborated to serve the purposes of Tudor government. He shows the King and his nobility occupying their appointed places in the Chain of Being, and demands respect for the status that God has conferred upon them. His object, naturally, was to flatter the King, but it is none the less absurd to describe the book as a vindication of absolute monarchy. Dudley insists that the true foundation of prosperity in states is the love of God. There is no guarantee of harmony and order unless the prince and his advisers, particularly the clergy, set a good example, and the special interest of his book is its implicit condemnation of the sort of administrative despotism of which Dudley himself had such expert knowledge. When he refers to the 'lewd practices' which divide society from God, he ingenuously gives the game away, listing many of the petty tyrannies which Tudor England had to suffer as the alternative to civil war. The neglect of study at the universities, the worldliness and non-residence of the clergy, the promotion of ecclesiastics for their political services, are all exposed and condemned, and Dudley does not try to conceal the unsavoury financial and judicial expedients that the government sometimes employed. On the pretext of sending answers to local petitions the Privy Council would intrude upon the administration of justice in the provincial courts. Sometimes, abandoning pretence, they would issue a blunt directive; nor was it unknown for the King himself to intervene in matters thought to affect the interests of the Crown.

Indirectly More was writing of the same evils as Dudley, but these have received less attention than the grosser and more spectacular crimes attributed to Richard. It is always comforting to be assured that things have been worse in the past than they are now, and men liked to remember that they had been delivered from an ogre. More's book was probably the greatest single contribution to the Tudor myth. He could not be specific in his accusations, and anyway the malpractices of the Tudors, insidious and often cloaked in legalism, were not easy to define. So it is not surprising that his *Richard III* was taken at its face value as a dramatic account of the rise and fall of a monster, and its subtler reflections disregarded as being of no immediate application. More's purpose was to condemn injustice in all its forms and to assert his conviction that society is a partnership in morals. But he never finished the book, and it was only the terrible portrait of Richard that stayed in the mind. Ironically this was all that survived of his writings when anti-Catholic prejudice consigned him to temporary oblivion, and it passed intact and uncriticised into the work of nearly all the Tudor historians who followed him.

Robert Fabyan's *New Chronicles of England and France* was published in 1516, three years after the author's death. Fabyan was a wealthy clothier and alderman in the City of London, of which he was sheriff in 1493. Henry VII utilised his technical knowledge in employing him to negotiate a trade treaty with Flanders, and in 1497 he conducted the defence of Ludgate and Newgate against the Cornish rebels. His chronicle was a laborious compilation covering the history of England from Brut to Henry VII, but he was more interested in the affairs of London than in anything else. Hall and Holinshed found useful material in his work, and if Shakespeare consulted it at all, as he probably did, it was only in search of information.[1] Fabyan wrote in the owlish spirit of a mediaeval chronicler, gathering his facts largely for their own sake and presenting them from a naïvely providential point of view. He was quite indifferent to secondary causes in the behaviour of men, so that the only explanation he had to offer of a major event like the Norman Conquest was that God was on William's side. A poem in the *Mirror for Magistrates* aptly dismisses him in a damning couplet:

> Unfruitful Fabyan followed the face
> Of time and deeds but let the causes slip.

---

[1] According to John Bale, Wolsey ordered Fabyan's work to be destroyed because of its critical references to the wealth of the clergy. But Bale is not good evidence for anything to do with Wolsey.

He was not altogether unfruitful, as he provided a storehouse of facts for more imaginative men; and he does usefully remind us that this patient, uncritical style of chronicling was, and continued to be, one way of writing history. It was respectable, it had a long tradition behind it, and it did no one any harm. Many approaches to the past are possible. This was one that would still satisfy writers lacking any perception of the human drama behind events.

Like his father, Henry VIII encouraged the writing of history, and of history with a more positive attitude than Fabyan's. It was he who suggested to Berners that he translate Froissart and ordered Leland to pursue his antiquities. He approved, too, of the characteristic doctrines set forth in *The Governor* of Sir Thomas Elyot (1531), a courtly handbook for the training of a ruling class. Elyot was no egalitarian. His book was piously academic and humanist, soiled with no contemporary controversies, but it preached the sort of monarchical theories that Henry was anxious to encourage at the crisis of the Reformation. It said that monarchy was the best form of government because it was sanctioned in scripture; it was also the best because it was approved in Nature, bees using no other form. Elyot's devotion to degree was religious and ardent. Having established that a single sovereignty was the proper system of government, he occupied himself with the education of those inferior governors and magistrates who, coming under the king in the Chain of Being, yet had authority over humbler men. Theirs was to be a schooling in virtue, for Elyot had the optimistic, non-Machiavellian view that the qualities that make a good ruler are those which make a good man. In his curriculum he gives due place to history as an inspiration to wise and virtuous rule, and it was in *The Governor* that later writers found the story that Prince Hal was committed to prison by the Lord Chief Justice.[1] The practical benefits of history were also asserted by Sir John Cheke, tutor to Edward VI and first Professor of Greek at Cambridge, a man with unusual authority as a scholar and man of affairs. To Cheke all learning was useful in a severely pragmatic sense, and scholars had a duty to apply their knowledge in the service of the state. Roger Ascham's *Schoolmaster*, published posthumously in 1570 but rooted in principles acquired a generation earlier, shows intellectual discipleship to Cheke in taking it for granted that enlightened public service is the object of humane education, and here again is the assumption that a knowledge of history, and a readiness to apply its lessons to contemporary problems, help to form the character of a ruling class.

[1] See *2 Henry IV* V ii 68–71.

It often happens that dominant modes of thought express themselves most characteristically and completely in a writer of no personal distinction; the sort of commonplace mind that comfortably reflects the passions and prejudices of the time. Edward Hall was the historian laureate of the Reformation aristocracy, the 'new men' who came to power through the Tudor revolution and sealed their victory when Henry VIII gave them access at bargain prices to the lands and revenues of the Church. Coming of a Shropshire family which had given service to the House of York, he was born in the closing years of the fifteenth century and passed through Eton and King's to take up the study of law. He was made reader at Gray's Inn, common serjeant of the City and a judge of the sheriff's court, and for his uncompromising Protestantism was appointed a commissioner to enquire into supposed breaches of the Six Articles. He sat for Bridgnorth in the uneasy Parliament of 1542, and died only a few months after his hero, King Henry VIII.

Hall had no use for the compendious type of chronicling that started with Brut and plodded its patient way down the generations until it arrived at modern times. His very title, *The Union of the Two Noble and Illustre Families of Lancaster and York* (1548), proclaimed him a historian with a theme. He chose an isolated tract of English history to denounce the 'cankered crocodile' of sedition and manifest the blessings of unity, starting with Henry IV, 'the first author of this division', and ending with 'the reign of the high and prudent prince King Henry the Eighth', in whom the warring families found at last, by God's grace, their 'indubitate flower and very heir'. The treatment was highly selective, omitting, as the dramatists were to do, events that formed 'no part of my purpose', and it was through Hall that the historical pattern created by More and Polydore Vergil was transmitted to the writers of the Elizabethan age. Although his 'indenture English' and 'strange and inkhorn terms' were criticised by Ascham, these weird anticipations of euphuism were the price to be paid for Hall's consciously dramatic and rhetorical presentation of his theme. His chosen period unfolds in his hands as a great moral drama, with each event assigned to its appropriate causes and shown to bear its appropriate fruits. The method is characteristic of the new way of moralising the past, of forcing it into arbitrary patterns that point without any shadow of doubt the lessons to be learned from it. It is characteristic, too, in confining its scope to English affairs surveyed over a strictly limited period of time, and in rejecting even from this all matters not relevant to the author's dogmatic purpose. Compared with the aspiring universalism of mediaeval history, it is all very earnest and provincial. Humanist influences are further evident in the importance allowed to individual responsibility for events. Failure and suffering are traced to specific crimes, some offence against the moral or political order, and if this theory of causation had been worked out consistently, we might be justified in saying that Hall had a completely modern and secular approach to history. But he is most thoroughly typical of his time in somehow managing to combine these humanist attitudes with an exalted sense of the workings of providence. In some respects his work is naïvely theocratic. He has no doubt that God intervenes in the strangest ways: 'Whatsoever man intendeth, God suddenly reverseth, what princes will, God will not, what we think stable God suddenly maketh mutable.' The originality of Hall's contribution was to incorporate into a single coherent and dramatic pattern all the prevailing notions about history. He did this simply by identifying God's purposes with those of the Tudors. In this interpretation even the Wars of the Roses became a necessary part of a divine plan for England which culminated in the blessings of Tudor rule; and what the Tudors did was right because it was done in fulfilment of God's scheme. A providential view of history here merges with one secular and pragmatic. It was a marriage of the highest importance, since it consecrated the Tudor myth.

Shakespeare's debt to Hall was large, specific and often direct. It was still possible to go on having no particular philosophy of history, but every Elizabethan writer who thought at all deeply on the subject owed something, and most of them owed a great deal, to the Hall–More–Vergil reconstruction of the events preceding the accession of the Tudors. In Vergil this interpretation was only sketched, perhaps in perfunctory execution of a duty, by a man of wide and varied interests; in More it was concentrated into the brilliant and devastating portrait of Richard III; it was only in Hall that it was lovingly elaborated into a series of moral judgments and delivered in a fine spirit of oracular conviction. Bacon managed to escape the spell when he wrote his *Life of Henry VII*, but until his time one either accepted Hall's interpretation of these events or had no theories about them at all.

For Hall, as for the author of the Homilies, degree was the necessary bond of society and its defence against disruption. In 'disdain of superiority' he found (forgetting how grievously superiority had been disdained by the upstarts and innovators whose empire he was now seeking to preserve) 'that venomous worm, that dreadful dragon' that disturbs the inner peace of states, and the theme that he proposed for himself was to demonstrate how in England dissension had at length, by grace of God and the Tudors, given way to unity. Rome, Italy, France, Bohemia, Scotland, Denmark are all cited to show 'what mischief hath insurged in realms by intestine division', but when he comes to enumerating 'what misery, what murder, and what execrable plagues' had been brought upon his own country by the wars of York and Lancaster, Hall protests that 'my wit cannot comprehend, nor my tongue declare, neither yet my pen fully set forth' the enormity of the people's suffering. The difference is, however, that although elsewhere these tragic discords continue, in England

> the old divided controversy between the forenamed families of Lancaster and York, by the union of matrimony celebrate and consummate between the high and mighty prince King Henry the Seventh and the Lady Elizabeth, his most worthy Queen, the one being indubitate heir of the House of Lancaster and the other of York, was suspended and appalled in the person of their most noble, puissant and mighty heir King Henry the Eighth, and by him clearly buried and perpetually extinct. So that all men (more clearer than the sun) may apparently perceive, that as by discord great things decay and fall to ruin, so the same by concord be revived and erected.

To illustrate this progression from discord to harmony Hall propagated the special reading of history which Shakespeare was to adopt with only trifling variations in his two tetralogies. For that reason it is worth outlining here. It told how England's woe began[1] with Bolingbroke's perjury in breaking the oath he swore when he landed at Ravenspurgh. He vowed then that he wanted nothing but to recover his own estates, and he promised that no harm would come to Richard. Perjury, usurpation, tyrannicide were the crimes that set in motion a terrible train of suffering, and there would be no relief until God's anger was appeased. Its worst effects were not felt immediately. Henry IV was humbly penitent, and although he could not avert the inevitable punishment of a disordered, uneasy reign, full vengeance was deferred until a later day; and his son, the pious, heroic Henry V, was noble enough in the strength of his own virtue to persuade God to suspend the curse altogether for the few brief years of his reign. Henry was a model king. Although not himself a usurper, he acknowledged his father's crime by removing Richard's bones to Westminster; he was a true friend of the Church; he banished his evil counsellors and chose advisers whose wisdom and piety matched his own. But not even Henry could delay the reckoning for ever, and his

[1] In some versions, though not in Hall's, it began with the murder by Richard II of his uncle, Thomas of Gloucester.

own early death was a sign that it could be deferred no longer. The tragic reign of his infant son saw the triumph of avarice, pride and violent ambition, and their terrible culmination in the loss of France, caused by treachery and dissension at home, and the outbreak of the Wars of the Roses.[1]

The Yorkists had a better title to the throne, but their own crimes of perjury and murder delayed for another generation the final expiation of the curse. The worst was yet to be. In writing of Richard III, Hall touched with his own flamboyant rhetoric the unflattering picture he had inherited from More. His plangent moralising finds new stores of energy as he contemplates wanton evil. For most of his narrative Hall tempers the severity of his judgments upon erring statesmen by reflecting that their crimes are often contingent on the sins of others, but for Richard there is no such mitigation. Certainly Richard was involved in the collective penalty to be paid for the various crimes committed by his family. He could not have been a happy or successful king, and his ultimate ruin was inevitable. But Hall finds in him a capacity for wickedness not, as it were, required by the plot. He is the counterpart of Henry V, evil where Henry was good but sharing with him a certain independence of the tragic pattern in which both are involved. Each of them is in a sense author of his own acts.

Richard's murder of the two young princes was the abomination which induced God at last to pause in His anger. Providence directs the final stages of the story, and as he draws near to the battle of Bosworth and the mystical union that lies beyond it, Hall increasingly becomes the partisan spectator of his own drama. The vessel of providence is the Duke of Buckingham, who is inspired by the Holy Ghost to abandon his own shadowy claims to be the true Lancastrian heir and to work instead for the marriage of Richmond to the Yorkist Princess Elizabeth, the symbolic act that was to seal God's forgiveness and the promise of peace. So it comes about. Henry VII ruled wisely and well, but the final proof of the new order could only be the son who was the issue of the marriage. What Hall described as 'the triumphant reign of Henry VIII' brought the cycle to its close.

There are one or two awkward omissions in the story, and even in Hall's own day the critical reader must have wondered about Arthur. He, not Henry, was 'the indubitate flower and very heir' of the marriage

---

[1] Writing of the battle of Towton, Hall added the comment that may have suggested to Shakespeare his famous symbolic episode (*3 Henry VI* II v 55–124): 'This conflict was in a manner unnatural, for in it the son fought against the father, the brother against the brother, the nephew against the uncle, and the tenant against the lord.' But note how Shakespeare simplifies and heightens the drama.

that turned discord into harmony, and he bore a name that roused brave echoes of Britain's heroic past. A loyal subject of Henry VIII might ascribe his early death, not very convincingly, to Spanish witchery, but those more sceptical or less amiably disposed must have asked themselves why God brought this tragic fate upon the first-born of the symbolic union. This is not a large matter, and the poets of a later age got round the difficulty by presuming the legendary Arthur to have been reborn in their own Elizabeth. But Hall also omits, seemingly as one of the things that he regarded as not to his purpose, the delicate question of Richmond's right to come in arms against Richard, who was not merely king *de facto* but was also, once Edward V was dead, the lawful heir by succession. This issue was evaded by all Tudor writers, Shakespeare included; as indeed it had to be, for if they once admitted—explicitly—that there were circumstances in which a ruler might be forcibly deposed, the whole edifice so carefully erected against rebellion fell to ruins. Orthodoxy taught that all actual possessors of the crown, even if they were assassins and usurpers, must be suffered in patient obedience. But orthodoxy had somehow to reconcile this one all-important exception. Richard III was admittedly a tyrant; but the subject's duty towards tyrants, as declared by Latimer in the conventional piety of his age, was to 'tarry till God correct them'. The same piety should have indicated that Richmond was nothing more than a successful rebel; to be obeyed, perhaps, once he had seized the crown, since obedience to usurpers was a lesser evil than a series of risings to remove them, but in no sense the object of near-hagiography. His wickedness ought in theory to have been punished by crushing blows upon his people and his family, and the untimely death of Arthur might properly have been regarded as a step in this direction. But in this particular case rebellion, so far from being the ultimate wickedness, was the necessary prelude to a golden age. The 'cankered crocodile' has to be dressed in righteousness. Hall did not try to extricate himself from this difficulty by inventing sophistries to explain it. He managed at one and the same time both to pretend that it did not exist and to allow it to solve itself by implication. The implication was that both Richard and Henry VII were very special people; so special, in their opposing ways, that for a short moment of time the natural order of things was suspended. Richard was a monster,[1] a being so disruptive of the common morality of mankind that

[1] Cf. Shakespeare's constant references to Richard as various kinds of unattractive beast—hog, toad, spider, and so forth. Richmond's speech to his soldiers (V iii 237-71) takes the view that Richard was a tyrant and 'God's enemy', and so meet to be deposed.

the ordinary sanctions could no longer be invoked on his behalf. Henry too was no ordinary being. It was necessary to think of him as coming direct from God to end a tyranny so unnatural that it could never be repeated.

At a safe distance of time, when these once-vital issues have long been dead, it is easy enough to look with tolerant contempt upon such clumsy inconsistencies; forgetting that every society, our own included, has to rest itself to some extent upon illogicality in its attempt to reconcile the complexities of the human condition. To find an obvious flaw in Tudor political doctrine does not necessarily invalidate the whole system, nor does it give us the right to convict Hall and Shakespeare of mental dishonesty. Of course their reading of history will not bear objective analysis. If today we believe that the sins of the fathers are visited upon the children, we know in what sense we mean it, and it is no longer a religious conception. But the Tudors needed more intimate assurances of a watchful and in the long run kindly providence. They tried, as we have observed before, to hold simultaneously theories of history and society that were on the one hand practical and on the other hand providential.[1] These theories would not always be reconciled, and then the result was absurdity. The absurdity need not trouble us if we recognise that it occurred because the Tudors wanted to believe that God had England in His special care. They are not the only generation to have felt that way.

Unfortunately for historians and their neat little patterns, time does not stand still. Hall's book was the product of particular circumstances, and in the ordinary way it would have lost its appeal as different contemporary conditions called for a different evaluation of the past. It was in fact prohibited by Queen Mary, and no wonder. What kept it alive until the end of the century was the persistence of the menacing, uneasy climate in which it was written. England still needed to have faith in the Tudors. Northumberland's lawlessness, the Catholic reaction under Mary, the dangers that gathered round Elizabeth, all threatened to revive the ruinous dissensions against which, according to Hall, Tudor government had provided a more than human specific. Hall's history was, of course, a piece of special pleading, an interested

---

[1] Thus Hall writes of Henry VII taking the kingdom 'as a thing by God elected and provided and by his especial favour and gracious aspect compassed and achieved'. On the other hand, George Cavendish, who wrote his *Life and Death of Thomas Wolsey* later than Hall, during the reign of Mary, could still be entirely mediaeval in his account of Wolsey's fall. This came about because fortune at length 'thought she would devise a mean to abate his high port'; and in his sudden humiliation Wolsey is unprotesting and meekly acquiescent.

party's appeal to his opponents not to rock the boat. Things have undoubtedly been better recently, he is saying, so let us all be careful not
to endanger this new security by making too much of our differences.
If by any chance his book encouraged complacency, the two short
reigns that followed Henry's death were a rude shock to it; but at least
his interpretation of events appeared to offer some sort of emotional
anchorage in times of trouble. In the continuing crisis under Elizabeth
it became a matter of necessity to believe in Hall, to feel about the
Queen rather as he had felt about Henry VIII. A version of history
which presented the Tudors as past saviours of society seemed to offer
an insurance against the dangers of the present. To accept this version
was to assert one's enduring faith in the providence under whose hand
the dynasty had already achieved so much.

So Hall stood firm. Details were altered, amplified and glossed, and
Raleigh, writing after 1603, brought new perspectives to the now
familiar story. More than a hundred years had passed since the accession of Henry VII, and with the direct line now extinct, Raleigh was
free to take a more detached view of the Tudors. Although he drew
the customary lessons from the confusions of the fifteenth century, he
was no longer obliged to offer these events as the necessary prelude to
the Tudor deliverance. He disliked Henry VIII, whom he regarded as
unnaturally ruthless, and in seeking an explanation for the failure of
the Tudor line, he found it in the crimes of Henry VII in ordering the
execution of Sir William Stanley and the Earl of Warwick. The punishment invariably meted to kings who are guilty of crimes of this order
is that their dynasties shall fail with their grandchildren. It happened
to Edward III, it happened to Henry IV, and now it had happened to
Henry VII. But Raleigh found a new deliverer in James I, and it can
be seen that when he makes these rearrangements of the story he is
not abandoning Hall's method but is simply adjusting the pattern to
bring it up to date. The pattern itself, with its curious blend of providence and individual responsibility, goes on.

Hall's version of history was transmitted in the work of Grafton[1] and
of the hard-writing syndicate known as Holinshed. Raphael Holinshed

[1] Richard Grafton (c. 1513–72) was by trade a printer—he supervised several
issues of the Great Bible and received patents to print service books and primers.
He was interested in politics, being a member for London in two of Mary's
parliaments and for Coventry in 1562–3. He took to making his own additions
and emendations to chronicles issued from his press, and he wrote his own continuation of John Hardyng's fifteenth-century *Chronicle*, carrying it from
Edward IV to present times. Although he was only a compiler of the school of
Fabyan, Shakespeare occasionally used his work. It was he who published the
posthumous edition of Hall's *Union* (1548).

himself was at one time steward of Packwood Manor, near Stratford. He was employed by Reginald Wolfe, printer to Queen Elizabeth, to translate foreign chronicles and to assist him in his project for a 'universal cosmography'; but when Wolfe died in 1573, his successors restricted the scope of the work to the *Chronicles of England, Scotland and Ireland*, first published in 1578 and reissued, with additions, nine years later. The edition of 1587 was the one chiefly used by Shakespeare. It was prefaced by the Rev. William Harrison's celebrated *Description of England*, and its historical narrative, which extended from Noah to modern times, was written by Holinshed, Richard Stanyhurst, John Hooker and Francis Thynne. Sufficient of the chronicle has passed almost verbatim into Shakespeare's more perfunctory passages for the world to have discovered that Holinshed was not an exciting writer. He lacked Hall's dramatic power and Vergil's interest in humanity. Furthermore, he wrote of delicate matters at a time when censorship was prickly. Both editions of the chronicle were expurgated by the government, and on certain issues he had to be careful what he said. His pedestrian narrative managed none the less to convey the essence of Hall's treatment of the years so vital to Shakespeare and the Elizabethans, and his comments on rebellion, the duty of princes and their subjects were piously orthodox. Although not a man to attempt anything so majestic as a philosophy of history, he recognised the historian's obligation to moralise upon events, and on the whole he moralised in a practical way, his marginal observations underlining the sins and shortcomings of men and pointing to the disastrous consequences that followed. Holinshed faithfully reflects the dominant idea of his age that rebellion, with its inevitable train of discord and civil war, is the greatest of calamities, and he finds in the ample and varied lessons of history a means of educating men to avoid it.[1]

The same didactic impulse directed several Elizabethan poets in the choice and treatment of their epic themes. Closest in this respect both to Shakespeare and to Hall was Samuel Daniel, whose unfinished *History of the Civil Wars between the Houses of York and Lancaster* was probably in private circulation before Shakespeare began his second tetralogy. The first four books were entered in the Stationers'

---

[1] William Fulbeck, of Gray's Inn, wrote principally on legal matters, but in 1601 he produced *An Historical Collection of the Continual Factions, Tumults and Massacres of the Romans*, which had the object of revealing to contemporaries the perennial mischiefs of discord. Its cause, he said, was 'nothing else but ambition'; and, while making due allowance for providence, Holinshed would probably have agreed.

Register in 1594 and published early in the following year. Four
additional books had appeared by 1609, and in his introduction to the
edition of that year Daniel stated that his object in writing the poem,
begun when the succession to Elizabeth was cruelly in doubt, was to
show how conspiracy and rebellion endanger the country's safety
when there is no direct line to secure the throne. It is precisely the
theme of Shakespeare's histories; and from the safety of James's reign
Daniel looks back, as Shakespeare doubtless did, to the anxieties of
the recent past.

> And, whereas this Argument was long since undertaken (in a time
> which was not so well secur'd of the future, as God be blessed now it is)
> with a purpose, to show the deformities of civil dissension, and the miser-
> able events of rebellions, conspiracies and bloody revengements, which
> followed (as in a circle) upon that breach of the due course of succession
> by the usurpation of Henry IV; and thereby to make the blessings of
> peace, and the happiness of an established government (in a direct line)
> the better to appear: I trust I shall do a grateful work to my country, to
> continue the same, unto the glorious union of Henry VII, from whence
> is descended our present happiness.

Not that he ever did so continue it. By 1609 it had become less urgent
to preach the lessons of Tudor unity, and this may have been one of the
reasons, although a minor one, why Shakespeare too abandoned the
writing of history. If Shakespeare had ever had occasion to choose a
few lines in which to summarise his historical theme, he might justly
have used the very words of Daniel's dedication. Daniel did not have
it in him to be dramatic, and his diffuse, ruminative verse has none of
Shakespeare's penetrating power. But the resemblances are striking.
They both interpret events in the same spirit, have the same feeling
for the importance of history as a mistress of life, allow in the same
way the shadow of present uncertainties to stress the urgency of their
theme.

Michael Drayton's *Mortimeriados* (1596), heavily revised seven
years later as *The Barons' Wars*, deals with the troubles of Edward II
and therefore is less closely connected with Shakespeare, but here again
we find a poet taking very seriously the whole matter of history;
taking it too seriously for his poetic reputation, perhaps, and his own
comments on Daniel, in the *Epistle to Reynolds*, are at times equally
applicable to himself:

> Only have heard some wisemen him rehearse,
> To be too much Historian in verse;
> His rhymes were smooth, his metres well did close,
> But yet his manner better fitted prose.

In *Mortimeriados* and *The Civil Wars* the authors cared at least as much for history as for poetry, and their references, marginal comments and occasional weighing of the evidence indicate that they expected to have historians and statesmen among their readers. In their attempt to apply the epic form to the methods and aims of history, poems of this kind were not from the literary point of view very successful, but the interesting and important thing is that the effort should have been made. Drayton's passionate love of England, evident in every line of *Polyolbion*, overflowed into numerous ballads and 'legends'—*Agincourt*, *Matilda*, *Piers Gaveston*, *Cromwell*—in which, once again, present anxieties intrude upon the past.

This kind of poetry was very popular with the Elizabethans, if only for the immediacy of its themes. Ancient triumphs inspired the confidence that present emergencies could be overcome, and it was this mood which accounted for the huge success of William Warner's *Albion's England* (1586), a metrical history of Britain beginning with Noah and reaching, with the publication of the sixteenth book in 1606, the time of James I. Francis Meres bracketed Warner with Spenser as England's two great heroic poets, and Drayton paid him a tribute due rather to old friendship than to literary merit. His rhyming fourteeners do not make exhilarating reading. But despite his uncritical acceptance of all sorts of legendary matter, Warner too was in his way a serious historian, linking his episodic narrative with a certain amount of comment; and when he arrives at the Tudor period, he has no hesitation in discerning the hand of providence. Henry's pedigree is obligingly traced to King Cadwallader, and thereafter it is mere routine to find Arthur resurrected in the Tudor line. True, this is not what we would call 'serious' history, but as we have already seen, these conceptions were valid at the time, and were undoubtedly a source of strength to many people. Although not to be compared with Hall or Daniel, Warner was something more than a mere chronicler.

History thus being a weighty and pervasive matter, it is no surprise to find a slab of English chronicle, tendentiously related, in the middle of a grave moral and psychological poem, the *Microcosmos* of John Davies of Hereford (1603). What Davies thought is significant because, as Dr. Tillyard points out,[1] he knew everyone. Coming from the same sort of middle-class provincial background as Shakespeare himself, he won the acquaintance of the courtly and artistic world through his accomplished penmanship. He was the foremost scribe of his day, writing-master to many of the nobility and finally to the young Prince

[1] *Shakespeare's History Plays*, 10.

Henry, and the extent of his acquaintanceship is made apparent in the epigrams, unmistakably personal in their touch, that he addressed to many of the leading writers of the age. It is likely, from the warmth and particularity of his references, that he knew Shakespeare personally.[1]

Davies was neither a great metaphysician nor a great poet, but his literary and ethical interests soberly reflected the outlook of the intelligent and representative men with whom his work brought him into contact. His titles tell their own story: *Mirum in Modum, Summa Totalis, Wit's Pilgrimage, The Holy Rood, The Muse's Sacrifice.* They are verse tracts ranging over the eternal topics of God and His creation, the influence of the stars, man and his passions. Nothing is transmuted by the imagination, and a modern critic[2] has unkindly observed that his writings contain no answer to his own query:

> Busy invention, why art thou so dull
> And yet still doing?

On order and degree Davies was completely orthodox, and in the historical section of *Microcosmos* he rearranges English history to emphasise their importance. The kings to be imitated are those who were strong enough to hold the people under discipline, like William the Conqueror, Edward I and Henry V; or at least, like Henry IV and Edward IV, were successful and circumspect. Fortune never deserted these rulers, 'because they governed with due regard'. Most Tudor writers sought a pattern in events, and Davies found one in the frequency with which grandsons suffered for their forebears' sin, but the main purpose of his historical excursus is to proclaim the horrors of civil war and the providential miracle of the Tudor deliverance. Henry VII and his son were no less than demi-gods, and from their reigns, as from Elizabeth's, he deduces in the approved manner a number of important *exempla* for future generations.[3] His survey ends with some useful generalisations on political wisdom, his final advice

---

[1] His three references, two of them linking Shakespeare with Richard Burbage, are all genial and complimentary, see E. K. Chambers, *William Shakespeare*, ii 213–14.

[2] Douglas Bush, *English Literature in the Earlier Seventeenth Century*, 86.

[3] Davies's remarks on Elizabeth contain a sturdy defence of her equivocal policy that deserves to be pondered by historians inclined to dispose of her as a lucky and timorous amateur. Davies was, however, unorthodox in one respect. Unimpressed by the sixteenth century's championship of King John as the unhappy victim of Roman imperialism, he wrote of him as a usurper who was justly punished for being a bad king. He failed, it seems, to govern 'with due regard'.

to his contemporaries being that it is better to obey a bad king than to risk the dreadful consequences of rebellion.

This powerful strain of political didacticism in Elizabethan poetry derived from an earlier work, the composite *Mirror for Magistrates* that was begun by a group of earnest and reflective men in the middle of the century. In form the *Mirror* consists of verse monologues spoken to the authors by representative English statesmen who have been unfortunate in their public lives; and between the stories the authors take the opportunity to hold discussions in prose not only of the matter just revealed to them but of the political and ethical issues it has raised. The first nineteen stories, covering the period from Richard II to Edward IV, were printed in 1555, but publication was not permitted until four years later. In 1563 eight further stories were published, chiefly on the reign of Richard III, and subsequent additions, in 1578 and 1587, brought the story to Henry VIII.[1]

The leader, editor, and also the printer, of the enterprise was William Baldwin, but the most distinguished contributor was Thomas Sackville, Earl of Dorset, part-author of *Gorboduc*, who wrote on Buckingham and also produced the Induction which unified the second group of stories. Thomas Churchyard, sometime page to the Earl of Surrey, wrote on Jane Shore, and Baldwin's chief collaborator was George Ferrers, a lawyer but also a devious and versatile man of affairs, who wrote the verses spoken by such key figures as Humphrey of Gloucester, Thomas of Woodstock and Edmund of Somerset.

Two points about the *Mirror* stand out at once. First, it covered exactly the same stretch of history, from Richard II to Henry VIII, as Hall's chronicle; and secondly, the main contributors were men of moderate opinions and behaviour, since by the time of the edition of 1563 they had experienced the vicissitudes of four reigns. They were educated men, employed at court or on its fringes, and the *Mirror* is valuable as an expression of responsible opinion about politics and statecraft, and incidentally about literature, in the early part of Elizabeth's reign. The authors may reasonably be regarded as *politiques*, more concerned with the ways to achieve stability in times of change and stress than with advancing specialised theories about the state. If their views were substantially similar to those held later by Shakespeare, there is nothing surprising in that.

The work announced itself as a continuation of Lydgate's *Falls of Princes*, but that was only a selling point. The *Mirror* caught much

---

[1] The edition of 1587 incorporated stories written by John Higgins and Thomas Blennerhasset of an earlier period, from Brut to the Norman Conquest.

more faithfully than Lydgate the spirit of the stories he was translating, the *De Casibus* of Boccaccio, and introduced the element of
individual responsibility into the old-fashioned tragedies of men who
rose and fell at Fortune's arbitrary behest. Its purpose was to educate
the magistrate by showing him how to avoid error, the means being
the standard Renaissance device of the historical example. The dedication to 'the nobility and all other in office' advises them that 'here as
in a looking-glass you shall see, if any vice be in you, how the like
hath been punished in other heretofore; whereby admonished I trust
it will be a good occasion to move you to the sooner amendment'.
This is merely an enlargement of the objects more discreetly stated
by Elyot and Ascham, and whereas their rules for the training of
princes ranged over a wide field of activity, the *Mirror* confined itself
to the austerity of the historical parallel. It was an axiom of the
Renaissance that, as Baldwin wrote in his preface, 'the goodness or
badness of any realm lieth in the goodness of badness of the rulers';
and it was equally axiomatic that the lessons of history, if properly
digested, could teach the ruler how to be good.

The authors accordingly adopted the historical method of Polydore
Vergil and Hall. We have noted already what they thought of 'unfruitful Fabyan' and his way of doing things. The business of the
historian was to discover the underlying chain of cause and effect
and to moralise upon the conclusions to be drawn from it:

> Causes are the chiefest things
> That should be noted of the story writers,
> That men may learn what ends all causes brings.

Although they demand in theory that the facts shall be respected, the
poet-historians of the *Mirror* claim also the licence due to poetry: 'it
is lawful for poets to feign what they list, so it be appertinent to the
matter'. Thus it was legitimate to elaborate a forced correspondence, as
for instance that between Humphrey of Gloucester and the Tudor
Duke of Somerset, if thereby an 'appertinent' example might be
brought to the reader's notice. The method was to expound a contemporary situation by seeking an apt historical parallel, and in this
way to teach the necessary lessons. There was, of course, nothing new
in this; but its reiteration by this earnest-minded group of writers
shows how firmly it had taken root in the Tudor consciousness.

There was nothing new, either, in the sort of lessons they looked to
history to teach; but again we should not think these lessons unimportant simply because we have heard them all before. Human

society is a reflection of the larger and eternal polity that is God's; princes are to be obeyed because God has ordained the office they occupy and the justice they administer. It is the theme of the Homilies over again, stated with solemnity and passion. Baldwin argues that, since justice is chief of the virtues, the judge's is the supreme office.

> And therefore hath God established it with the chiefest name, honouring and calling kings, and all officers under them, by his own name, gods. Ye be all gods, as many as have in your charge any ministration of justice.

The magistrates whom God appoints as His deputies will be 'good when He favoureth the people, and evil when He will punish them'; rebels are sure of a wretched end, 'for God cannot but maintain His deputy'.

> Therefore was never traitor yet but missed
> The mark he shot at, and came to fearful end;

and this would be his fate even if God were using him as a divine instrument to punish a bad ruler. The *Mirror's* orthodox conclusion is that a Christian subject should 'obey his sovereign though he were a Jew'.

It was not, however, and never could be, an absolutely logical orthodoxy. We have already noted Hall's embarrassment over the deposition of Richard III by Henry VII, which he sought to escape by dodging the issue. The *Mirror* deals with this problem in a rather different way, conceding that when a ruler is so violent and wicked that he may justly be called a tyrant, then it is lawful to rise against him. Hall regarded Henry VII as the agent of providence and implied that this was sufficient to justify his rebellion. But the *Mirror*, altogether more sophisticated than Hall, will not make this concession to the Tudor myth.[1] Henry was not a providential visitant; it was explanation enough of his rebellion that Richard was a tyrant. Although the explanation is qualified by the warning that men must be careful to distinguish between the genuine tyrant and the bad king who has simply been sent by God to punish them, a solid wedge has been driven into the standard arguments about the wickedness and dreadful consequences of rebellion.[2] In the circumstances it could hardly have been

---

[1] The *Mirror* generally attributed less to providence than any comparable work of the period. Like Shakespeare, the authors sought for subtler methods of causation and conducted weighty ethical arguments to discover the real motives of human action. See Tillyard, *Shakespeare's History Plays*, 76–8.

[2] The *Mirror* also allowed that rulers need not be obeyed when they order a subject to commit a crime: an issue faced much more clearly in *The Troublesome*

otherwise, and the fact that the Tudor dynasty was founded on rebellion was not the only reason for it. Inevitably there were times when the encouragement of insurrection was sound Elizabethan policy. The career of Mary, Queen of Scots, overturned a good many comfortable theories in its time, and even Bishop Jewel of Salisbury, a stern apologist of the Elizabethan Establishment, found himself arguing in favour of certain forms of collective action that could not be permitted to individuals. What the Scots had done to Mary was justified, for clearly she was an enemy of God. There were times, Jewel said, when subjects might rise against their rulers 'by the common advice and by the public authority of the realm'. Granted this authority, and under the undoubted inspiration of God, they might lawfully combine to do what in a private man would have been a sin.

In other words, a sufficiency of private judgments may add up to a public judgment;[1] or, if treason prospers, men no longer call it treason; or, theory, then as ever, is the servant of necessity. Common sense demands that it shall be. Every system must be protected from its own natural tendency towards a self-destroying rigidity. Even Sidney's King Euarchus, the priggish embodiment of all the royal virtues as the age esteemed them, acknowledged a 'universal civility' that required the death of tyrants. By the same token, Elizabeth, who was godly, might aid the Netherlanders against Philip, who was not. This was only to recognise that the Tudor doctrine of non-resistance might, if pressed too far, lead to evils worse than those it sought to prevent. But to abandon it was a desperate remedy, and it would probably be a mistake to suppose that the theory was seriously weakened by a readiness in the last emergency to admit exceptions. Because—and not although—it was challenged, it remained the instinctive dogma of the age.

All of this—the doctrine, its reinforcement by historical example, and the accompanying doubts and contradictions—passed into the serious drama, where it found Shakespeare apparently somewhat to the right of centre. The matter of Renaissance historiography was the life of the state, and its methods penetrated alike into epic poetry and

Reign of King John than in Shakespeare's play. But this was standard doctrine, nearly all the religious writers of the age asserting the impregnability of conscience (and see below, p. 78). The subject's duty, however, was a merely passive resistance, a refusal to obey, even if this meant his own death.

[1] This had the sanction of Aquinas, who wrote in his *De Regimine Principium*: 'To proceed against the cruelty of tyrants is an action to be undertaken, not through the private presumption of a few, but by public authority.'

poetic drama. Reacting to the vitality and urgency of the subject, the dramatists appropriated the themes of history and chose their materials in the same way as the professional historians. The process was largely intuitive. Vergil, More and Hall had shown that events could be recorded in dramatic form, the historical 'plot' being shaped to have a beginning, middle and end. But they had done more than that. Their moralising on cause and effect, which amounted to a concern with personal responsibility, had directed attention to the purely human drama that governed great events. Treated in one way, this drama would be the material of tragedy; but wherever the serious political issue was allowed to dominate, it was the material of the history play, the play that was properly so called because it served the recognised purposes of history. Playwright and historian were equally conscious of their duty as moralists to hold up a mirror to the times, and in this *genre* the didactic functions of history and drama were congenially allied. In the Elizabethan history play we find at various times all the attitudes to history that have been illustrated in the foregoing pages. It may be used to exhibit the ways of providence or to demonstrate the working-out of a rational plan that affirms the wisdom and justice of God and His particular care for England; to glorify the nation by awakening memories of its heroic past; to recall great deeds as a spur to present emulation or to narrate the sufferings of former times as an incitement to fortitude against immediate calamity. The facts could be chosen and modified to serve all or any of these purposes, and most plays served two or three of them simultaneously. Moreover, certain notions were common to almost every Elizabethan historical play. It was axiomatic that every history, whatever its period or place, should throw light upon the contemporary situation; that its lessons and examples were to be studied for their immediate practical importance; and that its highest aim was the education of the ideal ruler.

There was a very common type of play, set in earlier times and dealing ostensibly with historical personages, that was not properly a history play at all. The real test is whether or not the purpose was didactic. The didactic element need not be especially ambitious; it may confine itself to the re-telling of an old story with the object of inspiring patriotic emulation or proclaiming the virtue of courage. So long as the material is shaped to serve a serious political theme, and individual characters, while seeming to have freedom of action, behave as history said they did, we have a genuine history play, and it does not matter if the dramatist takes certain liberties with the minor details of his story. Nor does it matter whether we call the result a 'chronicle' play or a 'history' play, and in this book it will be called a 'history'. The distinction is with the play that used the past merely for the sake of the story. Sometimes this sort of play was quite a faithful piece of chronicling. It based itself on the authorities and kept soberly to the facts. But the method was episodic and the total import nil; each act was likely to be devoted to an isolated event in the life of the central character, and there was no unifying theme to give the story significance. The result corresponded to the prose chronicle which, as though Hall and the *Mirror* had never been written, continued to assemble facts for their own sake. More often, however, the pseudo-history play was simply a popular extravaganza which exploited a well-known historical plot or character to give substance to a heterogeneous mass of comic and legendary matter. Robert Greene did this sort of thing most entertainingly. His *Alphonsus, King of Arragon* took a real historical person and involved him in fictitious battles and romantic entanglements. In *James IV* he dramatised a novel by Cinthio, and in order to attract an unlearned audience he gave some of the characters in the Italian fiction the names of real people, calling the result *The Scottish History of James IV, slain at Flodden*. Oberon, King of the Fairies, is one of the participants in this strange affair. *Fair Em*, a very popular romance of uncertain authorship, makes free with William the Conqueror, dispatching him to Denmark in search of a girl whose face he has seen on a knight's shield; and in *The Lovesick King* Canute finds himself infatuated with a nun. Plays of this kind show the persistent popularity of history as the subject-matter of drama, for there were evidently box-office advantages in dressing conventional romances in bogus historical trappings. But they have nothing to do with the history play proper. It is the difference between Shakespeare's *Cymbeline* and his *Henry IV*.

The history play developed naturally from the folk drama of the Middle Ages, the miracle and the morality.[1] In their most elaborate form the miracle plays told the Christian story from the Creation to the Last Judgment, each significant episode being given as a separate playlet within the complete cycle. They had begun in church, as part of the ritual of the service: simple dramatic representations to elucidate the subtleties of dogma for the better instruction of an unlettered congregation. Thus their method was a homely realism, uncomplicated by allegory. They aimed to interpret the Christian mystery by means of tableaux and simple actions, and the plotless structure gained

[1] *SWW* 43-51.

dramatic unity only from the presentation of the unceasing struggle of good and evil, with the ultimate victory of the goodness of God. In the more sophisticated drama of the Elizabethans their successors were the episodic plays in which a story was narrated in a series of incidents linked in a casual and insignificant plot. Once the religious theme had been first secularised and later forgotten, the miracle was not a form to produce memorable drama. It was suited best to those needy dramatists who, to satisfy the actors' relentless demand for plays, banded into groups of three of four to rough out a scenario and with-draw to their attics to write an act or two apiece.

The morality was a less rambling and potentially subtler type of entertainment. It developed out of the miracle in response to a need for plays which, while retaining an essential moral purpose, required fewer actors and less organisation. Mediaeval drama never forgot its origins as an offshoot of the liturgy, and the morality was a sort of personified sermon underlining the solemn lesson that the tomb is the end of all our journeys. It told man's story from the cradle to the grave, pro-claiming always that the toothless skull was the favour to which he must inevitably come, that his earthly goods were 'contrary to the love everlasting' and could not save him. During his mortal journey various personified abstractions struggled for possession of his soul. The usual pattern was for the 'hero' to forget the good advice received in youth from such characters as Temperance, Truth and Fortitude, and fall victim to the enticements of various of the Deadly Sins; until, after a timely repentance in the closing scenes, an embodiment of Mercy or Contrition or Good Deeds pleaded for him at the throne of judgment and achieved some success in mitigating the trials of pur-gatory. The best-known of the moralities was *Everyman*, a fifteenth-century translation of a Dutch play, in which Everyman is brought by Knowledge to recognition of his sins and the need for repent-ance, and then, after all his mortal powers have deserted him, only his Good Deeds accompany him when he is summoned by Death.

The chief agent in the gradual secularisation of the morality was the character of the Vice. Originally the Vice was introduced in order to bring Virtue into stronger relief, but his dramatic opportunities were so much greater that soon he was stealing the show. In the end he was carried off to hell, but not before he had diverted the audience with all the antics of which an expert clown was capable; at his hands the seduction of the hero into evil courses became less awe-inspiring than comic. The tutor and feeder of the prodigal's riots occurs in the folk literature of all peoples, and while his hour lasted he inherited the licence accorded to all jesters who attended the Lord of Misrule. No one exploited it more richly than Falstaff.[1]

The morality structure was ideal for the history play. It was already didactic, as history was required to be, and it dealt in allegory, which enabled the dramatist to preach his contemporary lessons under the cover of abstractions. For the historian, the abstractions would be the kings and statesmen of another age, whose remoteness offered him protection from the displeasure of the authorities: it was dangerous to be too openly contemporary. The form was easily adapted to new purposes, the state, *Respublica*, replacing man as the battlefield upon which good and evil counsellors waged their unending struggle. The change was not a drastic one. All political doctrines had a religious basis, and the old duty to God easily became the new duty to the king who was God's image; while the Vice was already present to give the seasoning of comedy that the popular taste demanded. The persistent mediaevalism of Tudor thought kept the morality pattern vigorously alive, while the Renaissance belief in human self-determination prevented its degeneration into a mere didactic charade.

The development was only gradual, and the first English play to use the new methods of history shows them imperfectly assimilated with the older habits of the morality. John Bale's *King Johan* was first written before 1536 and was revised more than once; it was acted in Cranmer's household during the Christmas festivities three years later, and it survives in the version given before Queen Elizabeth at Ipswich in 1561. Bale was a Carmelite friar who was converted to an extreme and polemical Protestantism. Cromwell protected him and encouraged his excesses, but after Cromwell's fall his views were too uncompromising to be acceptable to Henry and Cranmer and he was obliged to withdraw to the continent. Returning in the following reign, he was for a few months Bishop of Ossory before the accession of Mary sent him once more into exile. Under Elizabeth he did not regain his bishopric but ended his days, by now somewhat mellowed, with a prebend at Canterbury.

Bale was by no means the first Englishman to realise that history could be the instrument of partisan propaganda, but he was the first to see that drama might be a useful medium for presenting it. His purpose in *King Johan* was to depict John as the morning star of the Reformation. John had been given a bad reputation by the monkish

---

[1] Both Richard III and Iago inherit the Vice's jocularity.

chroniclers,[1] and Bale accordingly has a character named Verity who seeks to vindicate him against his traducers (who 'have raised up of him most shameless lies') and credit him with 'the beginning of the putting down of the Bishop in Rome'. The first part of the play ends with these lines:

> This noble King Johan, as a faithful Moses,
> Withstood proud Pharaoh, for his Israel,
> Minding to bring it out of the land of darkness,
> But the Egyptians did against him so rebel,
> That his poor people did still in the desert dwell,
> Till that Duke Josue, which was our late King Henry,
> Clearly brought us in, to the land of milk and honey.

In form the play was a morality, describing John's struggle to serve 'the widow Yngelonde' against the Church, but a more realistic method keeps on intruding, the abstractions finally turning into real people. Sedition becomes Stephen Langton, who is absurdly shown in conspiracy with a monk to poison the king; this monk, Simon of Swinstead, was originally Dissimulation, and likewise Usurped Power becomes the Pope, and Private Wealth becomes Pandulph. The play was chiefly an exercise in psychopathic Protestantism, with lewd exaggerations of clerical delinquency, but it had a serious contemporary purpose. Bale saw his country still threatened by sedition cunningly masked as religion, and *King Johan* has that undercurrent of proud and troubled patriotism found in later dramatic versions of the reign. It is important, despite its lack of artistic merit, because it was the first English historical play to use the past as a guide to the solution of contemporary problems, and indeed to offer an interpretation of the past which contemporary problems have inspired. Bale selected and manipulated the chronicles to support religious and political doctrines which he held to be to the present advantage of England, urging absolute obedience to the monarch who had restored the true faith. This was the proper use of history as the writers of the Renaissance understood it, and it does not seriously matter that Bale, who was frankly a propagandist, had no interest in the philosophical discussion of cause and effect. A few years later his polemic received endorsement in the Homilies of 1547 as the orthodox theory of the Reformed Tudor state: a practical illustration of the way in which historical drama might be written to serve the needs of the moment.

In *King Johan* morality and history were stranded in awkward

---

[1] And also by Polydore Vergil, against whom Bale directed his attack, claiming that Vergil had been misled by 'the malicious clergy'.

isolation by Bale's lack of literary skill, but the two forms were completely and artistically fused in *Gorboduc*, performed at the Inner Temple in 1561. The first three acts were written by Thomas Norton, translator of Calvin's *Institutes*, and the last two by Sir Thomas Sackville, an important contributor to the *Mirror for Magistrates*. The story, taken from Geoffrey of Monmouth, describes how Gorboduc, a descendant of Brut and King of Britain, decides in old age to divide his kingdom between his two sons, Ferrex and Porrex. Mutual suspicions inevitably arise between them, until Ferrex, the elder son, is killed by his brother, and Porrex is murdered in revenge by his mother, Queen Videna. The Duke of Albany tries to seize the kingdom, and all the chief characters are killed in the civil war that follows. The story is also told by Spenser (*Faerie Queen*, Book II, Canto X, 34–6), who laments

> the greedy thirst of royal crown,
> That knows no kindred, nor regards no right,

refers to the disastrous action of Porrex in assembling foreign help in pursuit of his ambitions, and concludes with a statement of the dreadful consequences of civil war:

> Here ended Brutus' sacred progeny,
> Which had seven hundred years this sceptre borne
> With high renown and great felicity:
> The noble branch from th' antique stock was torn
> Through discord, and the royal throne forlorn.
> Thenceforth this realm was into fractions rent,
> Whilest each of Brutus boasted to be born,
> That in the end was left no monument
> Of Brutus, nor of Britain's glory ancient.

The authors of *Gorboduc* chose this episode from early British history with a definite contemporary purpose, to demonstrate the dangers of a disputed or uncertain succession. Their message was directed expressly to the Queen herself. In abdicating his throne and sharing the kingdom in defiance of primogeniture Gorboduc was guilty of a terrible perversion of the natural order. (The play reminds us that Brut himself was similarly misguided, dividing the country into three. Much British blood had since been spilt 'to join again the sunder'd unity', and of the consequent disasters 'ruthful remembrance is yet raw in mind'.) From this sin others necessarily follow, until the stricken country finds itself with an empty throne. The play's closing speech moralises upon this dreadful state of affairs, when

> No ruler rests within the regal seat;
> The heir, to whom the sceptre 'longs, unknown,

and civil war cannot be avoided. Elizabeth did not have to be warned
of the perils of dividing the country among her children, since she had
no children; but the ancient fable of Gorboduc was employed to
inform her that, whatever might happen to be the reason for it, it
was a terrible thing if the sovereign died leaving the succession undecided. It was, in all circumstances, his duty to settle it while he
lived. Both the authors sat in Elizabeth's early parliaments, and they
wrote their play to reinforce the outspoken insistence of the Commons
that she prevent chaos by announcing the name of her successor. By
the last act of *Gorboduc* all the principal characters are dead, the story
is done, and it only remains to elaborate the lesson. The final scene
is purely homiletic, and Eubulus, the wise counsellor whose advice
has earlier been rejected, points out that it is not even sufficient that
there should be a rightful heir: his claim must be absolutely beyond
dispute, and the only certain heir is he who 'to the realm is so made
known to be'. If, as in the England of 1560, there was no candidate
likely to succeed unchallenged, then the authority of Parliament should
be used to buttress the Crown's nomination:

> The parliament should have been holden,
> And certain heirs appointed to the crown,
> To stay the title of established right
> And in the people plant obedience,
> While yet the prince did live; whose name and power
> By lawful summons and authority
> Might make a parliament to be of force,
> And might have set the state in quiet stay.
>   V ii 264.

The authors even hint at their own personal preference for one
candidate rather than another, urging that the chosen heir be 'one so
born within your native land', through whom the nation may avoid
'the heavy yoke of foreign governance'.

Seldom have playwrights, or indeed any unofficial advisers, so
forthrightly exhibited the past as mirror to a reigning monarch, and
Elizabeth could have had no doubt where, in their view, her duty lay.
In its fear of anarchy *Gorboduc* carries into drama the argument of Hall
and the Homilies. But the general conclusion was optimistic. The
political order was shown to be part of the divine and universal order,
which must finally reassert itself. The gods, 'who have the sovereign

care for kings', would in the end restore to the state the harmony that had been impiously broken by human error:

> Of justice, yet must God in fine restore
> This noble crown unto the lawful heir:
> For right will always live, and rise at length,
> But wrong can never take deep root to last.
> V ii 276.

The play's political doctrine was entirely orthodox, in spite of Norton's wish for parliamentary safeguards to correct the frailties and occasional irresponsibility of personal rule. Subjects have a duty to advise the monarch when he seems to err, but they have no right to rise against him:

> Though kings forget to govern as they ought,
> Yet subjects must obey as they are bound.
> V i 42.

In rebellion the wise Eubulus sees only the agony in which 'the father shall unwittingly slay the son'. Although punishment, bringing suffering in which the innocent too will be involved, must follow the outrage to the natural order, men must patiently endure until the crime has worked its expiation.

Morality influences are apparent in *Gorboduc* in the good and evil counsellors who besiege the principal characters with their warnings and enticements, but the play's conception of tragedy is not mediaeval. The natural order is good, and men suffer from their own folly and wickedness, not from the arbitrary turns of fate. Gorboduc could have averted his tragedy—just as, if she is wise, Elizabeth may avoid hers— and since he made a deliberate choice, we have to conclude that man is in control of his destiny. Once he has made his choice, the inexorable course of events involves the other characters in misfortunes that they can no longer prevent. Here, it is true, there is fatalism of a kind. These people are caught in a net. They are victims of Gorboduc's decision, even those who advised him against it, and, when the play shows one disaster inevitably following upon another, they have been deprived of their freedom of action. They do not even have the opportunity usually granted to characters in a morality to realise their errors in time to repent. But their helplessness is the consequence of Gorboduc's original choice, and he was not obliged to make it. The play presents a philosophy of history which affirms that God's plan for mankind is beneficent and good. It is only when this plan is arbitrarily and unnecessarily violated that men lose control of their subsequent fate.

With Hall, the *Mirror* and the Homilies, *Gorboduc* formed the matrix from which Shakespeare's sort of historical drama finally emerged. They all, in their various ways, gave artistic form to the ebullient didacticism that was the *raison d'être* of all Renaissance writing on political matters. The riches of *Gorboduc*, especially, were enormous. Its blank verse may seem unbearably ponderous and un-dramatic compared with what Marlowe and Shakespeare were to achieve with the medium only a generation hence; but once again it is the age-long difference between genius and competence, and *Gorboduc* was the pioneer, appropriating for drama the new, infinitely flexible rhythm first used in English in Surrey's translation of two books of the *Aeneid*, published in 1557. It is hard now to think of the play as exciting and revolutionary, but in its day it was nothing less: in the innovation of blank verse, in the fusion of the morality with modern conceptions of history and tragedy, in the mature handling of the political theme, and not least in bringing to historical drama a form that was to discipline the rambling incoherences of the chronicle mode. While commending the play's 'notable morality', Sidney found it 'very defectious in the circumstances', blaming it for occupying 'both many days and many places, inartificially imagined'. But Sidney was a severe critic, and *Gorboduc* observed the classical unities much more closely than most plays of the Elizabethan age. The regularity of its construction introduced classical form and precision into the con-temporary drama, and many of its devices—the five-act structure, the chorus to point and summarise the moral, the use of dumb-show to confine unseemly violence to the wings—had a lasting influence on playwrights who cared about the mechanics of their craft.

A few years ago Professor F. P. Wilson challenged tradition by wondering whether there were in fact any English historical plays before the time of Shakespeare and Marlowe. 'When we look for these early chronicle plays written before the Armada, where are they? . . . there is no certain evidence that any popular dramatists before Shake-peare wrote a play based on English history . . . if we look at the many comments on our popular drama before 1588, most of them made in abuse or defence of the stage, so far as I know we find the same absence of any evidence that the popular play on English history existed before 1588. . . . My conclusion is, though I am frightened at my own temerity in saying so, that for all we know there were no popular plays on English history before the Armada and that Shakes-peare may have been the first to write one.'[1] Wilson excepts *The*

---

[1] *Marlowe and the Early Shakespeare* (1953), 105–8.

Famous Victories of Henry V, in which Tarleton is supposed to have acted, and Tarleton died in 1588; he excludes the academic drama, of which Thomas Legge's *Ricdardus Tertius* (1579) is an example, justly observing that the academic playwrights, many of them writing in Latin, did not have to fear in the private theatres the censorship of the Master of the Revels; and he fairly claims that early popular histories like *Jack Straw*, *The Troublesome Reign of King John* and *Edward I* may well have been later than Shakespeare's *Henry VI*.

This spectacular hare will not be hunted here. If Shakespeare in *Henry VI* pioneered a new dramatic mode, it was the only time in his life that he did so; and that alone should give us pause. It is not a question that can be answered without more certain evidence for the dating of Elizabethan plays, the date of publication being no safe guide to the date of composition. Much depends, too, upon what we choose to mean by 'chronicle play', and we shall never all of us mean the same thing.[1] What cannot be disputed, however, is that long before *Henry VI* there existed a habit of using drama as a medium for historical anecdote and reflection. It would be surprising if it had not been so: drama was popular and history was popular, and their marriage was more than a convenience. Dramatist and historian had a common impulse, stimulated by the political anxieties of the age, to hold up a mirror to the present times. It is true that until about 1588 the dramatists' mirror was withdrawn to a discreet distance, preferring classical or legendary subjects to more recent history, and presumably that is what Wilson meant. It may have been the jingo enthusiasms aroused by the victory over the Armada that sent the dramatists to actual English history for their themes; more likely, as Tillyard suggests,[2] their inspiration came from the issue in 1587 of the second edition of Holinshed.

But the generation between *Gorboduc* and *Henry VI* contains ample evidence of the growing tendency to seek in drama a means to expound the lessons and examples of history. Men had already begun to write plays which mediated to their audiences the hard facts to be found in the prose chronicles, and it was already being assumed that audiences, for whatever reason, were interested in information of this kind. Many people probably learned it in the theatre who would have learned it nowhere else. That is really what Nashe is saying in the famous passage already quoted,[3] when he boasts that men would be ignorant of 'our

---

[1] The publisher of the 1608 Quarto of *King Lear* described the play as a 'true chronicle history'.

[2] *Shakespeare's History Plays*, 101.

[3] See p. 12.

forefathers' valiant acts' if the stage did not exhibit them. There was
no single way of gratifying this awakening interest: the variety of
Elizabethan drama always resists classification. Some plays simply
presented the facts for their own sake, as a certain type of prose
chronicle continued to do. These employed the episodic structure
of the miracle play and showed little inclination to make deductions
or teach lessons. But others, catching something of the serious moral
purpose of *Gorboduc*, adopted the form of the morality, whose simpli-
fied psychology not only permitted some elementary characterisation
but enabled the author to hint at a scheme of cause and effect underlying events. A further element was the native folk drama, secular
and non-didactic, in which the celebration of such heroes as Robin
Hood, Richard Whittington and Guy of Warwick ministered to local
and patriotic pride. Yet again, smatterings of history, and even of
political homiletic, occur incidentally in comedies and romances that
are not properly history plays at all.

The themes presented in these early works were mostly simple, the
appeal to patriotism being much the strongest of them. Anachronistic
tributes to Elizabeth may appear in a play about ancient Britain; any
reference to the foreigner is apt to digress into veiled defiance of Spain;
characters who in the context of the play are villains always recover
their virtue and dignity in the presence of national enemies. Politically,
the emphasis is on loyalty and obedience, and already Heywood might
have written that histories aimed 'to teach their subjects obedience to
their king, to show the people the untimely end of such as have moved
. . . insurrection, to present them with the flourishing state of such as
live in obedience, dehorting them from all traitorous and felonious
stratagems'.[1] Seldom, however, is there any implication that political
order is only part of a larger cosmic order, and except in one or two
plays that stand out of the ruck we find little evidence of mature
political reflection or an elaborated philosophy of history: which is
only a way of saying that English historical drama was still awaiting its
Shakespeare. On the other hand, the cumulative weight of the historical
matter found in the plays of this period, much of it occurring quite
casually in works of little merit, is quite impressive. It is instructive
to look briefly at some of the plays written between *Gorboduc* and, say,
the completion of Shakespeare's first tetralogy. Chronicle plays or not,
they indicate the beginnings of a native historical drama.

There is, for instance, the absurd *Cambyses* (1569): a dreadful
warning, perhaps, of what the English history play might have become

[1] *Apology for Actors* (1612).

if the Senecan *Gorboduc* had not given it form and discipline. The author was Thomas Preston: possibly a dramatist of that name of whom nothing else is known, or possibly the Thomas Preston who was Master of Trinity Hall, and Vice-Chancellor of his University, and later complained of the enormities of the popular stage. *Cambyses* could equally well have been written by a don in a mood of condescension or by a charade-writer anxious to be taken seriously. Its full title, *A Lamentable Tragedy mixed full of Mirth containing the Life of Cambyses, King of Persia*, tells us a good deal about it, and Falstaff has told us the rest.[1] Preston lavishly gave something of everything. His plot was a synopsis of the whole reign of Cambyses, and he crammed it full of violence, drunken orgies, lust and executions, providing comic relief in the person of the Vice Ambidexter and his three retainers, Huf, Ruf and Snuf, and even finding room for such morality abstractions as Cruelty and Murder. His play is none the less the occasion for a certain amount of serious political and historical reflection. Briefly summarised, it tells how on his accession Cambyses performs one good deed in removing the wicked judge Sisamnes, but is then led by Ambidexter into a series of crimes, including incest and murder, before he dies in the knowledge that he is being justly punished for his wickedness. This story is made to illustrate the chacteristic Tudor theme that bad rulers are to be punished by God and not by their subjects.

> If that a king abuse his kingly seat
> His ignomy and bitter shame in fine shall be more great.
>
> Prologue 11.

God will exact vengeance in His own way and time; subjects must merely endure, even to the extent, like the honourable Praxaspes in the play, of allowing a son to be murdered. But even in the worst of reigns God will occasionally relent and allow good deeds to be committed in order to demonstrate that the office of king is divinely ordained; and this explains Cambyses' virtuous action in removing the corrupt Sisamnes. To this extent the play teaches an important political lesson, and it concludes with a prayer that Elizabeth shall govern wisely. It illustrates also the gradual transition from allegory to direct historical narrative. Although Cambyses undergoes a conventional repentance, the morality action is not clearly insisted upon; the core of the plot is the relation of actual events.

Similar smatterings, and often more than smatterings, of serious

---

[1] *1 Henry IV* II iv 425.

political comment occur in other plays of the time. The academic *Ricdardus Tertius* (1579), by Dr. Thomas Legge, Master of Caius College, was a copious Senecan drama written in Latin, its fifteen acts being presented over a period of three days. Style and method were essentially classical, with no trace of the morality or heroic styles of the public theatre, but Legge founded his play on the chronicles of Grafton, Holinshed and Hall, all of whom incorporated More's view of Richard III, and it is not unlikely that this long-winded drama had some influence upon the serious dramatic treatment of history. Its political argument is that tyranny must inevitably fail—a combination of academic optimism with the more popular notion that England's prosperity is always within God's providential care. Legge also raises the important sixteenth-century issue of conscience. Ordered by Richard to commit a murder, two characters have a long discussion whether a tyrant should be obeyed when what he commands is contrary to the moral law. One of them is finally overcome by his moral scruples, but the other argues that the king's command is the supreme law. Shakespeare allowed the two Murderers to debate this issue in *Richard III*, but he curiously evaded it in *King John*.

Not long afterwards the reign was brought to the popular stage in *The True Tragedy of Richard III*, a Queen's Men's play printed in an imperfect version in 1594 but probably written four or five years earlier.[1] The political treatment follows More, Hall and Shakespeare, with Henry VII the humble instrument of providence and the blessings of the Tudor peace contrasted with the misgovernment of Richard. The play appropriately closes with praise of Elizabeth, 'that lamp that keeps fair England's light', and bids the grateful subject

> kneel upon thy hairy knee
> And thank that God that still provides for thee.
>   2206.

But it also seems to be trying in a clumsy way to marry history to the Senecan drama of revenge, and it reminds the audience with no little pomp that poetry is a legitimate means of furthering history's didactic purposes. In a peculiar prologue the Ghost of Clarence, ranging for revenge, talks with personifications of Truth and Poetry, and Truth makes the important claim that it is her function to add substance to Poetry's disquieting shadows. At any rate in its surviving version, this

---

[1] It has been argued by E. A. J. Honigmann ('Shakespeare's "Lost Source-Plays"', *Modern Language Review*, July, 1954) that the *True Tragedy* was a vamped version of Shakespeare's play made by the Queen's Men for provincial performance.

is not a very skilful play, and the chief advantage that Truth takes of her opportunity is to introduce in verse form a great deal of common-place chronicle matter; but the strange little episode does show how very solemnly the pretensions of history could be asserted.

Even when they were not asserted, they were freely assumed. Patriotic glorification made one part of the historical dramatist's duty, but he might also, even in the most trivial pieces, infer lessons in a way that left no doubt of history's didactic function. Chiefly, these lessons tended, as we should expect, towards the preservation of unity and the outlawing of rebellion. *The Misfortunes of Arthur*[1] (1588), acted before the Queen at Greenwich, shows, like *Gorboduc*, how a play set in legendary Britain might be relevant to contemporary issues. Denouncing rebels as 'the seminary of lewd Catiline, the bastard covey of Italian birds', it appeals to the country's internal enemies to close their ranks against the foreign invader:

> When Britain so desir'd her own decay,
> That ev'n her native brood would root her up:
> Seem'd it so huge a work, O Heavens, for you
> To tumble down?
>> Chorus at end of IV ii.

The play, incidentally, shows a sense of historical causation in tracing Arthur's misfortunes to the sin of Uther Pendragon when he seduced Igerna, but its particular interest lies in the implication that the lawyers of Gray's Inn endorsed Elizabeth's action against Mary Stuart in the previous year. The country was being threatened by Mordred, Arthur's son by his incestuous union with his sister Morgawse, and Arthur was reluctant to take up arms against his own flesh and blood. In this dilemma, similar in kind to Elizabeth's, his advisers tell him that ruthlessness is the only guarantee of the safety of the realm:

> No worse a vice than lenity in kings,
> Remiss indulgence soon undoes a realm.
> He teacheth how to sin, that winks at sins.
>> III i 62.

The anonymous *Life and Death of Jack Straw* (c. 1591) was an indifferent, unsophisticated play in the conventional morality pattern, but here again the author took pains to emphasise the wickedness and inevitable failure of rebellion. The scene is the Peasants' Revolt of 1381, in which Straw led the insurgents from Essex and was eventually killed at Smithfield. No man, the author seems to be saying, is naturally

---

[1] A play, Senecan in form, produced apparently by a collaboration of lawyers. The chief of them was Thomas Hughes, but Bacon may have helped.

a rebel, and Straw stands undecided between his tempters, the dema-
gogue John Ball and Nobs, the Vice, and on the other hand the leaders
of Church and State, his good counsellors, who condemn rebellion
and remind him that the King is under God's special protection. What
is interesting is to find that it is not only these props of the Establishment who believe that heaven has 'secret wreck' for the designs of
rebels. The disreputable Nobs has no illusions either. 'Swingledom
swangledom' is always the fate of traitors, and he predicts that there
will be work for the hangman to do. The peasant rising is carefully
insulated from the later events of the reign, and the uninformed
spectator would never guess that Richard II, who is presented in a
heroic light, would one day challenge the play's orthodox sentiments
by getting himself deposed. This was the characteristic way of didactic
history. Long views did not matter when they interfered with the
immediate intention, which here was to provide an oblique justification
for the Tudor government's attitude to social discontents.

Rebellion was rebuked with equal severity in several other plays of
the period, including *Sir Thomas More*, Marlowe's *Edward II*, the
anonymous *Troublesome Reign of King John* and Heywood's *Edward
IV*. *Sir Thomas More* is exceedingly difficult to date, and Shakespeare's
own hand has been suspected[1] in the scene where More reasons with
the May Day rioters:

> You shall perceive how horrible a shape
> Your innovation bears: first, 'tis a sin
> Which oft th'apostle did forewarn us of,
> Urging obedience to authority;
> And 'twere no error, if I told you all,
> You were in arms against your God Himself. . . .
> For to the king God hath his office lent
> Of dread, of justice, power and command,
> Hath bid him rule, and will'd you to obey:
> And, to add ampler majesty to this,
> He hath not only lent the king his figure,
> His throne and sword, but given him his own name,
> Calls him a God on earth.
>
> II iv 114.

In *Edward II* Marlowe was chiefly interested in the character of the
King, but while the political significance of the play is only inter-
mittent, it is not casual. Edward is a king, his failings are the failings
of a ruler, and the crisis of his reign is political; Marlowe recognises
that the sins of the man cannot be separated from the sins of his

[1] *SWW* 280–3.

government. The play presents no generalised theory of history. It
simply tells of one man's personal failure, and there is no sense that
this failure may be related to causes outside himself. Marlowe did not
conceive the existence of a divine plan in which the miseries of this
particular reign might in due time be forgotten in a restored prosperity;
and his explanation of the fall of Mortimer was not so much that he
deserved to suffer for his overweening ambition as that he had been
suddenly brought low by the turn of Fortune's wheel:

> Base fortune, now I see that in thy wheel
> There is a point to which when men aspire
> They tumble headlong down. That point I touch'd,
> And, seeing there was no place to mount up higher,
> Why should I grieve at my declining fall?
>
> V vi 60.

On the other hand, his attitude to rebellion was entirely orthodox. The
choric Edmund refuses to join the English lords in their revolt; and
when, later, he has been persuaded to withdraw his allegiance, he
swings violently back again to hysterical, self-disgusted loyalty:

> Edward, alas! my heart relents for thee.
> Proud traitor, Mortimer, why dost thou chase
> Thy lawful king, thy sovereign, with thy sword?
> Vile wretch! and why hast thou, of all unkind,
> Borne arms against thy brother and thy king?
> Rain showers of vengeance on my cursed head,
> Thou God, to whom in justice it belongs
> To punish this unnatural revolt.
>
> IV v 11.

Except for Mortimer, whose motive is ambition, the rebels are careful
to explain that they intend no harm to the King himself: their purpose
is only to retrieve him in his own despite from the unmanly toils of
Gaveston.

> Far be it from the thought of Lancaster
> To offer violence to his sovereign;
> We would but rid the realm of Gaveston.
>
> II iv 34.

In spite, however, of the purity of these sentiments, Marlowe gives
no hint of the historical patterning we find in Hall or Shakespeare. He
never suggests that the crime of rebellion against Edward may provoke
heaven to anger which future generations will have to expiate.

Whatever the exact date of Heywood's *Edward IV* (it was not
published until 1599), its composition was probably inspired by the

success of Shakespeare's *Henry VI*. It is a happy-go-lucky affair, with three quasi-historical themes interwoven with two stories from popular ballads and the facts cheerfully altered so as to fuse the historical and romantic plots into some sort of unity. In this play Heywood defined the limits of his royalism. One of his themes concerned the invasion of London by the Lancastrian Lord Faulconbridge to release Henry VI, who was being held prisoner in the Tower. Exulting in the defeat of the rising by the loyal merchants and shopkeepers of the City, Heywood by implication condemns Faulconbridge's brand of *de iure* allegiance, which held that Henry, the anointed of God, was the rightful king and Edward IV a mere usurper: 'Can that pure unction be wip'd off again?' Against this purism Heywood asserts the right of authority *de facto*: men's duty is to the king in possession. The robust Tanner of Tamworth declares that he will fight for his king whatever the niceties of his claim, and the cuckolded Shore likewise supports Edward despite the injuries done to himself. 'I'll not examine his prerogative.' On other occasions Heywood might write differently, but here he is manifestly looking beyond the immediate context to the political uncertainties of his own day and championing Elizabeth against those of her subjects who might be tempted into rebellion by the Popish doctrine that she was a usurper. What is more, he underlines the folly of rebellion by imagining the social confusion that might attend it. Three low-life characters, Spicing, Chub and Smoke, deriving from Shakespeare's Cade, are conventional archetypes of disorder, promising a régime in which maidenheads shall be no longer valued, bells rung backward, wine sold by the sallet (the headpiece in mediaeval armour) and gold and plate as plentiful 'as wooden dishes in the wild of Kent'.

The Troublesome Reign of King John (printed in 1591 but probably written soon after *Tamburlaine*), a much more thoughtful and consistent play, examines the Tudor quest for unity directly in the light of the conflict that most imperilled it, the issue with Rome. In view of its close connection with Shakespeare's study of the reign, the play will be more fully discussed below,[1] but it is useful to notice here a pre-Shakespearean play[2] that had among its most important purposes the clear relation of Elizabethan problems to a considered version of past events. The *Troublesome Reign* is an unequivocal assertion of royal supremacy against the counter-claim of the subject's right to depose. John thus addresses Pandulph:

Know, Sir Priest, as I honour the Church and holy churchmen, so I

---

scorn to be subject to the greatest Prelate in the world. Tell thy master so from me: and say, John of England said it, that never an Italian priest of them all shall either have tithe, toll, or polling penny out of England; but, as I am King, so will I reign next under God, Supreme Head over spiritual and temporal. And he that contradicts me in this, I'll make him hop headless.

Pt I sc v 73.

Arthur is made to say that it would be futile to expect surrender from a king of so high a temper, 'for questionless he is an Englishman'. Later, in acknowledging his own misdeeds, John appeals to native patriotism, urging that

> A mother, though she were unnatural,
> Is better than the kindest stepdame is.
> Let never Englishman trust foreign rule;
>> Pt II sc ii 139.

and Faulconbridge tries to clinch the argument by reminding the rebellious lords that vengeance belongs only to God:

> Why, Salisbury, admit the wrongs are true,
> Yet subjects may not take in hand revenge
> And rob the heavens of their proper power,
> Where sitteth He to whom revenge belongs.
>> Pt II sc iii 116.

The subsequent plot, with the English nobles in uneasy alliance with the French invaders, points to the central theme of the play and conveys to an Elizabethan audience the message that only through unity would England be strong and safe. Facts were altered to enforce the didactic aim. So long as the nobles were in league with the invader, the French were winning; but once they have returned to their allegiance, the Dauphin is compelled to acknowledge that unless the enemy has friends in the garrison, England is impregnable:

> It boots not me,
> Nor any prince nor power of Christendom,
> To seek to win this island Albion,
> Unless he have a party in the realm
> By treason for to help him in his wars.
>> Pt II sc ix 25.

With John living just long enough to receive the repentance of his contentious nobility, the new reign opens in a resurgence of national pride.

> Let England live but true within itself,
> And all the world can never wrong her state. . . .

> If England's peers and people join in one,
> Not Pope, nor France, nor Spain[1] can do them wrong.
>
> Pt II sc ix 45.

All in all, the play gives an unlikely account of the troublesome reign, but even the stupidest member of an Elizabethan audience would have been aware that the author was addressing him.

Unmistakably, then, the early Elizabethan dramatists, like the prose historians, were on the side of authority. On rebellion their doctrine was largely the official doctrine of the Homilies, that human government has been established by God, to whom alone belongs the right to condemn the wicked ruler. So most of them taught, and so most of them probably believed. But the unknown author of *Woodstock* (c. 1592)[2] was something of an exception. In a powerfully didactic and thoughtful play he confines the duty of obedience within much narrower limits than any of his fellows, and at the end he seems to be proclaiming that in certain circumstances subjects have the right to rebel. The early action is orthodox enough. Richard II, a weak and sensual king, is being misled by his upstart favourites, and, quite properly, it is against these parasites that the nobles, led by Gloucester (the Woodstock of the title), direct their opposition. Gloucester is always loyal. He says of the King:

> His youth is led by flatterers much astray.
> But he's our king and God's great deputy;
> And if ye hunt to have me second ye
> In any rash attempt against his state,
> Afore my God I'll ne'er consent unto it.
> I ever yet was just and true to him,
> And so will still remain: what's now amiss
> Our sins have caus'd, and we must bide heaven's will.
>
> IV ii 142.

Vengeance is God's alone, and men's present suffering is the consequence of past misdeeds: these sentiments are most correct, and even when he himself is doomed Gloucester writes to implore Richard to abandon the flatterers 'that hourly work the realm's confusion',

> That he forsake his foolish ways in time,
> And learn to govern like a virtuous prince.
>
> V i 186.

But once Gloucester has been murdered there is a weakening in this

---

[1] These are 'the three corners of the world' referred to in the closing lines of Shakespeare's *King John*. This speech was derived from three passages in the final scene of the *Troublesome Reign*, lines 25–9, 45–6, 53–4.

[2] See pp. 160, 229 n. for the relation of *Woodstock* to Shakespeare's *Richard II*.

sternly pious attitude, and Lancaster and York assure his clamorous Duchess, in terms that do not suggest that they intend to wait upon the divine act, that he shall be avenged. The author invents an unhistorical rising of the nobles that, whatever its face-saving formulae, is clearly directed against Richard's person. Here in dramatic action is the heterodox, Whiggish doctrine of the *Vindiciae*, Parsons and the Jesuit pamphleteers, that when a ruler is guilty of misgovernment, he may be resisted and, if necessary, deposed. Nor does the author suggest that this is a misdeed for which future generations will be punished.

Few dramatists dared, or probably wished, to go as far as this, but running through the plays we have been considering there is the suggestion, already asserted in *A Mirror for Magistrates*, that conscience may set its own limits to unconditional obedience. The sovereign need not be obeyed when to carry out his orders would be a breach of the universal moral law. If a man could be forced to violate his conscience, that would be to set up human law in place of the law of God. We saw this issue debated in Legge's *Ricardus Tertius*, when the King commanded a murder. It occurs again, in like circumstances, in both *Woodstock* and *The Troublesome Reign*, and also in the anonymous *Edward III*, where the occasion is the French King's order to his son to dishonour himself by violating a safe-conduct. In their various ways the dramatists suggest, too, that although obedience is, except in these extreme cases, a duty, kings nevertheless have an obligation to govern justly and humanely. *Jack Straw* expects the government to recognise its responsibility to the poor and dispossessed; in *The Misfortunes of Arthur* the good counsellor Conan warns Mordred that kings must respect the law and rule for the good of their subjects, and turns aside to praise Elizabeth as the embodiment of this basic principle of healthful government; Peele, in *Edward I*, uses the Castilian Eleanor as an example of a ruler too proud to seek her subjects' love:

> But if their sovereigns once gin swell with pride,
> Disdaining commons' love which is the strength
> And sureness of the richest commonwealth:
> That Prince were better live a private life,
> Than rule with tyranny and discontent.
> 276.

Although this was not his principal interest, Marlowe recognised the political faults of Edward II. A king who wishes to be strong cannot afford to be unaware of his subjects. He must choose good counsellors, respect their advice, and give his people justice.

Edward III, printed in 1596 but probably written three or four years earlier, shows more clearly than any of these early plays what the men of the Renaissance expected of their kings. It allows itself the customary liberties with the facts, lumping Sluys, Crécy and Poitiers into a single campaign and adding the submission of Scotland for good measure. So far it is just a patriotic invocation of a hero king, but its superiority lies in the author's careful examination of the stages by which Edward disciplined himself to perfection. For this purpose he drew upon a story by Bandello, translated in Painter's *Palace of Pleasure*, of the king's wooing of the Countess of Salisbury.[1] Infatuated with her beauty, he tries to seduce her; and when she resists him, he will do anything, even murder his own queen and the lady's husband, to gain his will. But, like Mark Antony, Edward is a fine enough man to be able to view his own behaviour with occasional detachment. He knows that what he wants is shameful, and he wonders if there be not some poison in the fair glances that so easily beguile him. In another mood he can sink low enough to order the Countess's own father, the Earl of Warwick, to break down her resistance, 'to bear my colours in this field of love'. She tells him that only tyrants violate the moral law, and marriage has a sanction older than monarchy itself:

> In violating marriage' sacred law,
> You break a greater honour than yourself:
> To be a king, is of a younger house
> Than to be married; your progenitor,
> Sole-reigning Adam on the universe,
> By God was honour'd for a married man,
> But not by him anointed for a king.
>   II i 260.

It is unnatural that a king should pursue adultery, the sin that would disrupt society, and in the end the sight of his young son 'corrects my stray'd desire' and fits him for his royal office.

> Shall the large limit of fair Brittany
> By me be overthrown? and shall I not
> Master this little mansion of myself? . . .
> I go to conquer kings.
>   II ii 95.

Reason has to master passion yet again when Edward, irked by Calais' long resistance, determines to make an example of some of

[1] In the source the Countess was a widow: which made Edward's wooing slightly less disreputable.

the citizens. Again it is a woman who tells him what is right to do. Pleading for the burghers' lives, Queen Philippa says that

> Kings approach the nearest unto God,
> By giving life and safety unto men;[1]
>
> V i 41.

and Edward at once agrees to make it known

> that we
> As well can master our affections
> As conquer other by the dint of sword.
>
> V i 50.

Edward has already displayed the positive virtues—courage, leadership, patriotism, the power of decision. Now that he has subdued the weaknesses in himself, he may stand for the model of a perfect king, and is fit to teach the kingly virtues to his son, whose valour he has already tested on the fields of Crécy and Poitiers. *Edward III* approaches history on a higher and more abstract level than the other plays we have considered. These mainly concern themselves with the practical lessons of statecraft—how to command obedience, how to deal with foreign and internal enemies, how to keep the country united and at peace. In *Edward III* these lessons are implicit in the many reflective passages which show the author's awareness of degree and the traditional cosmic correspondences. But the play's dominant idea is the Renaissance theme of *nurture*; the idea contained in Elyot's *Governor* and many similar works, that by a study of the right examples men may be educated in goodness and self-mastery. The education of a prince would be the controlling theme of Shakespeare's *Henry IV*.

We have now reached the point at which Shakespeare had begun to write historical drama. His influence is already apparent in some of the plays mentioned above, and it is certain that the best of them— *Edward II*, *Woodstock* and *Edward III*—would be lesser plays than they are if he had not already written *Henry VI*. But the debt is not all on one side. Because he is apt to feel dissatisfied when he can find no explicit references to the Elizabethan world picture, Tillyard has concluded that 'for any ideas on history . . . Shakespeare was indebted to the Chronicle Plays very little. He may have got his jingoism mainly from them but that is all': on the few occasions when the chronicle aspired to better things—schematic history, a sense of perspective, consciousness of the Chain of Being and cosmic correspondences—

---

[1] Cf. *Measure for Measure* II ii 58–63. Shakespeare has sometimes been regarded as the author of *Edward III*, or at least of the scenes in which the Countess appears. See C. F. Tucker Brooke, *The Shakespeare Apocrypha*, xx–xxiii.

these conceptions were mediated to the author through Shakespeare.[1] This is surely to make an unnecessary distinction between the 'history play', something written by Shakespeare and the top people, and the 'chronicle play', which was the work of journeymen. It is more useful to regard as a history play any that, however partially or inexpertly, handled past events in a serious political spirit. In philosophic sweep, perception and inclusiveness Shakespeare, of course, was unique, but we hardly need at this time to be reminded that he wrote better histories than anyone else. Genius has its own finality, often stultifying judgment. But when we look closely into the differences between other men's political plays and those that were written by Shakespeare, the distinction is rather one of quality than of kind. The historical ideas to be found in Hall and *A Mirror for Magistrates* were not just the property of an educated élite. They were more widely diffused than Tillyard supposes, and it is wrong to say that when they find their way into the popular drama, only Shakespeare was responsible for it. Nor were they *necessarily* the best ideas. They may only seem so because it was Shakespeare who used them.

What matters is that when Shakespeare came to London, there existed a clear recognition of the nature and purposes of history, and of the suitability of drama as a medium for their expression. Tillyard justly says that 'the bare habit of using drama was for Shakespeare of the highest moment. He was, as we shall infer, warmly interested in history from an early age. That there existed a form of drama ready-made into which he could infuse without violence the thoughts that were troubling his mind was a rare piece of luck.'[2] The various elements that composed the popular tradition left him free to handle historical or legendary subjects in any way he pleased. Potentially political stories of ancient Britain provided him in *Cymbeline* with a tragi-comic romance and in *King Lear* with the most inscrutable of his tragedies. But we are concerned here with the themes he took from more recent English history, and for this he found an existing tradition whose variety and comprehensiveness exactly suited his purpose. The interplay of moral forces; the nurse of statesmen and a mirror to contemporary life; a storehouse of examples; the study of the self-determining individual; a spur to patriotic emulation and endeavour; a demonstration of God's providence: Tudor history, dramatic and non-dramatic, could be all or any of these things, and the writer was free to alter the details to serve his didactic intent. Such, in the field of history, was Shakespeare's artistic inheritance.

[1] *Shakespeare's History Plays*, 98–124.   [2] *Shakespeare's History Plays*, 124.

CHAPTER FOUR

The Specialty of Rule

A power I have, but of what strength and nature
I am not yet instructed.

MM I i 80.

I. SHAKESPEARE'S SIGNIFICANCES

SHAKESPEARE'S plays, it is sometimes said, tell us nothing about his personal beliefs. 'Mine remains the unproffered soul': Browning's verdict is there to beguile us at those moments when we are tempted to think of artists as inscrutable people too deeply occupied with their inner perceptions to be concerned with life as ordinary men have to lead it. Aesthetic purists are always warning us, too, of the dangers of trying to reduce a work of art to paraphrase or summary. Art, they say, is not susceptible to re-statement in prose, and a writer's perceptions, as revealed in his creative work, cannot be formulated intellectually.

Admittedly Shakespeare's meanings are difficult to abstract, as he always preferred to express his conclusions enigmatically rather than by overt demonstration. He had, supremely, the dramatist's capacity for standing outside his own thoughts and viewing his creations with seeming detachment. His mind was too subtle, and perhaps too sceptical, to see human life in the reassuring tidiness of a preconceived pattern, and in certain moods it is possible to think of him as one who followed no doctrinal compulsion but created with the heedless fecundity of Nature itself, simply from the need to give birth to life. At such times his genius seems to consist in the matchless power of an imagination that rose superior to all moralising dogmas and systems of thought; and if he has any message to offer, it is simply that life is a magnificent and enthralling spectacle, too baffling to be analysed. His only concern, Mr. T. S. Eliot has said, was with 'turning human actions into poetry'. We are wrong, therefore, to regard him as a thinker or to look for meanings in his plays, except in so far as 'all great poetry gives the illusion of a view of life' and so leads us into the mistaken belief that we are looking at something that is capable of being expressed intellectually.[1] It was

[1] *Elizabethan Essays*, 47.

another Elizabethan, Sir Philip Sidney, who said: 'For the Poet, he nothing affirmeth.'

Writing not as an aesthetic critic but as a moralist, Dr. Johnson had a similar difficulty about Shakespeare's meanings. If the term had been current in his day,[1] he would have objected that Shakespeare's poetic universe offered no 'criticism of life'. Johnson believed that poetry should rise to 'general and transcendental truths', and that 'it is always a writer's duty to make the world better'. So it troubled him to find that Shakespeare's works 'support no opinion with arguments, nor supply any fashion with invectives'. He hated to see characters borne 'indifferently through right and wrong', their examples, which ought to have been consistently edifying, left to 'operate by chance'. At the back of Johnson's mind was the bogey, never long absent from Shakespearean criticism, of the philistine Elizabethan audience that was for ever tugging at the poet's heels and restraining him from the heights.[2] Because his first duty was to provide a flow of unexacting entertainment, Shakespeare's greatest glories were only occasional glories. Johnson complained that he was content to use trite, improbable plots, abandoned his characters to absurd and unmerited predicaments, sacrificed consistency to the entertainer's craving for an effective theatrical climax. So we look in vain for the coherent reading of life that we ought to expect from the greatest of poets. He is 'so much more careful to please than to instruct that he seems to write without any moral purpose'.

Such notions are valuable in reminding us that the sum of Shakespeare's work is ultimately an attitude that only poetry could express, but they hardly constitute a complete critical method. Art should not be absolutely explicit, and few artists try to be, Shakespeare least of all. His plays never mean just one thing only, his characters never embody a single fixed attitude, like a Jonsonian humour. He was too much of a poet to be at the service of any particular set of dogmas. Because he was imaginatively familiar with the whole range of human experience, he would not hold up a distorting mirror that showed only the beautiful and the good, or only what is evil and ugly. There is mingled yarn in all of us, and while he could find the soul of goodness in things evil, he knew too that virtue's steely bones may look bleak in the cold wind and

---

[1] It very nearly was. Fulke Greville held that drama should contribute to 'the use of life' by the ethical lessons that it taught, and he urged the spectator to 'look on that Stage wherein himself is an Actor, even the state he lives in'. He believed that his own plays offered 'a perspective unto vice, and the unprosperities of it'.

[2] *SWW* 314–27.

goodness itself, swollen to a plurisy, die of its own too-much. So the flickering perspectives of his world seem to end in a confused darkness. His awareness of the mixed elements in man's character muffles his conclusions, and if he sometimes appears evasive, it is because his view of life was complex. But it is equally wrong to say that he suspends judgment or that his judgments cannot be discovered.[1] His context is always the moral nature of man, and his way of expounding it is so to implicate his audience that they will be forced into awareness and an act of judgment. The issues that he raised are still with us, still awaiting the unambiguous answers that he never finally gave. We who come after him are merely, as Professor Harbage has called us, late arrivals at the Globe, faced with the same dilemmas and compelled, as his first audiences were, to make a choice. But Shakespeare always makes it clear where his sympathies lie. His own moral choice shows in various ways—perhaps in the slant of the narrative or the pervasively ethical quality of his imagery; sometimes in the twists and variations he imposes on the fables that were his sources, and sometimes, where there are basic facts that cannot be altered, in the deliberate process of selection and emphasis in the historical plays.

In the histories we may read his mind more clearly than anywhere else in his work. Broadly speaking, he adopted the view of history, and of man's duties in society, that has been outlined in the preceding chapters. He believed in the poet-historian's mission to interpret the past for the practical enlightenment of the present; and the lesson he chiefly taught was the old and familiar one that order means prosperity and bad or hesitant government means confusion. It makes a valid starting-point to say that he took his stand with Hall and the Homilies and the *Mirror for Magistrates*.

But this was not, for Shakespeare, a simple attitude. He was not by habit a man who thought in slogans, and there is a good deal more to his political ideas than a mere acceptance of Tudor propaganda and clerical commonplaces about degree—or than, as has sometimes been proposed, an aspiring *rentier's* surrender to the sheltering arms of government. The feeling for order and stability everywhere evident in Shakespeare's plays was an expression of his deepest moral convictions. The point to be made is that they were *moral* convictions, for society, as he and his age understood it, was a moral idea. He never divorced 'politics' (a word he did not use) from the larger context of society and human relationships, and his political philosophy was a part of

---

[1] See *SWW* 424–56 for a discussion of Shakespeare's values.

'that constant search for meanings that informs his work as a whole'.[1]

We must not over-rationalise, either. The Shakespeare who sat above the earthly pageant with distant, unseeing eyes, superbly uncommitted in all matters that did not affect the box-office takings, is no longer a credible figure. But that part of his work that can be paraphrased in terms merely comprehensible to intellect—the 'prose' Shakespeare—is only a fraction of his total meaning, only one of the ways in which he speaks to us. Through imagery, the ordering of the plot, the silent manipulation of the source material, the dramatic tensions developed between one key character and another, we become aware of layers and refinements of meaning so rich and subtle that the bare prose statement is seen to be no more than a partial revelation of Shakespeare's mind.

II. THE AMORAL STATE

> Dear friend, we must not be more true to kings,
> Than kings are to their subjects; there are schools
> Now broken ope in all parts of the world,
> First founded in ingenious Italy,
> Where some conclusions of estate are held
> That for a day preserve a prince, and ever
> Destroy him after; from thence men are taught
> To glide into degrees of height by craft,
> And then lock in themselves by villainy.
> But God, who knows kings are not made by art,
> But right of Nature, nor by treachery propp'd,
> But simple virtue, once let fall from heaven
> A branch of that green tree, whose root is yet
> Fast fix'd above the stars . . .
>   Chapman, *Biron's Tragedy* III i 1.

Many of the political complexities of Shakespeare's age are mirrored in the Elizabethans' strange love-hate relationship with the teachings of Machiavelli. In so far as they understood him, which was imperfectly, Machiavelli held them alternately appalled and fascinated: appalled because he defied all their cherished dogmas about order and natural law, and yet fascinated because everyday experience taught them that in many respects he might very well be right. He challenged the whole concept of a political society that thought of itself as part of a universal order existing at the express will of God; and yet, at least on a facile

[1] L. C. Knights, *Shakespeare's Politics* (British Academy Shakespeare Lecture, 1957), 2.

view, he seemed to point the way to a certain kind of success. Their failure honestly to make up their minds about him explains many of the emotional uncertainties of the age.

The Prince, written in 1513, had been known in England at least since 1534 (it is said to have been one of Thomas Cromwell's bedside books), but what Machiavelli actually said, either here or in the *Discourses on Livy*, came to be obscured in an extraordinary cloud of perversion and misrepresentation. What he said was bad enough. Life was Webster's suffocating 'mist of error', with treachery, cruelty, ingratitude and every sort of weakness lying at the root of human behaviour. Machiavelli was almost scornfully honest. As a consistent, dispassionate analysis of the limited world of fact and event, his theory of society has no equal in the history of political thought. 'I want to write something that may be useful to the man of understanding,' he said. 'I have thought it better to investigate the actual truth of the matter than what we imagine it to be . . . for there is such a distance between the way men do live, and the way they ought to live, that he who leaves what is done for the sake of what ought to be done sooner achieves his own ruin than his own preservation.'

'The actual truth of the matter,' as he proclaimed it, was that since man more often behaves like an untamed beast than a being endowed with godlike reason, the only way to govern him is by the tactics of the jungle. Man is naturally evil, divorced from grace and without hope of redemption; and so the prince, 'being obliged to know well how to act as a beast, must imitate the fox and the lion'. He need not keep faith, as his subjects will not think of keeping faith with him; he is a fool if he ever relies upon their loyalty; and the only point in his displaying virtues is that 'they are useful when you appear to have them: as, to appear compassionate, faithful, humane, upright and religious—and indeed to be such, so long as you have a mind so constituted that, when it is necessary to be the opposite, you may be able to change it'. In short, 'as every history illustrates, the man who founds a state and makes its laws must start by assuming that all men are bad and will try to display their vicious instincts whenever they find opportunity for it'. Law and humanity may have their occasional uses, but effective government is only to be founded on a cunning mixture of force and fraud.

These were terrible sayings. Machiavelli was writing as an Italian who passionately wanted his country to unite under a government strong enough to end the dominance of treachery, petty rivalries and foreign invasion. But the sixteenth century disregarded the powerful strain of patriotism—even, in a strange way, idealism—that dignified and justified his work, and fell with morbid horror upon those doctrines which seemed to substitute for God's watchful providence the least desirable practices of the animal kingdom. A society rooted in force and fraud could scarcely regard itself as a divinely-prescribed reflection of the celestial order. Withdrawn from God's protection, man might no longer feel himself to be even in his social activities responsible to the larger universe. Chaos was his natural condition, and the laws which governed him, mere creations of expediency, had no longer any connection with morals or ideals. The traditional system of closely interlocking hierarchies had no reality, and religion itself was the instrument which kept him abject and humiliated when he should have been strong and confident. If modern men lacked the robustness and stern passion for liberty found in classical antiquity, it was because of the debilitating influence of Christianity. 'Our religion', Machiavelli wrote, 'has glorified men of humble and contemplative mind more than men of action. It has in fact declared man's highest good to stand in humility and abjection, in contempt of human things; where the other [the religion of the ancients] placed it rather in greatness of soul and in all those other things that tend to make men valiant. And if our religion ever recommends strength, it demands rather that you should be strong in suffering than that you should achieve a valiant deed. This way of life seems to have weakened the world.'

Educated Englishmen knew Machiavelli, reviled him in public, and perhaps cherished him in secret. His political system, grounded on human inadequacy, would appeal most to weak men looking for protection or to aspiring men needing security in which to launch their private ambitions. But men are weak, are acquisitive, and Machiavelli seemed to have something to offer. The circumstances of sixteenth-century Europe, in England as in many other countries, were not of a kind to inspire confidence in traditional theories of society. These theories continued to receive at least a formal deference, for a man could be branded an atheist if he withheld it, but to progressive minds —perhaps to all minds, now and then—there might in practice appear to be certain advantages in the political approach recommended by Machiavelli. Even the honoured philosophers of Greece and Rome had discussed the techniques of getting and keeping power, and many of Machiavelli's little tricks of statecraft had been played in the courts of Europe for centuries. Any thinker influenced by the Renaissance would admit that there was an 'art' of politics, in which human reason was at the service of the natural impulses which draw men into society;

and Machiavelli, whatever else, was a deliberate political artist. Through cunning and ruthless calculation he showed a way to escape the capricious tyranny of Fortune or of God's unpredictable visitations. The man of strength could control events, manipulate his fellow-creatures, and make himself the master of his fate. Many times, in the recurrent crises of the age, Machiavelli's boldness and ingenuity must have seemed to promise short-cuts to effective action.

This does not mean that he ever became respectable. Rather, as we shall see, he provoked an angry reaction in support of accepted notions about order and natural law. Ultimately the moral and religious framework of society stayed impregnable.[1] But there was an undoubted sense in which some Elizabethan Harcourt might have remarked that 'we are all Machiavellians nowadays'. He bred a disturbing ambiguity in the Elizabethan mind. Men who were loud in their denunciation of the corrupting and materialist tendencies of his thought often wrote and spoke and acted in a demonstrably Machiavellian way. 'Admitted I am of those that hate me most.'[2] The confusion was presumably unconscious. The partial truth of his analysis of human nature and society coincided with the teachings of their own experience.[3] After 1580 there was scarcely an English writer of note who did not betray the marks of his influence. Shakespeare, Sidney, Spenser, Marlowe, Bacon, Greville, Chapman, Raleigh, Webster, were perhaps influenced more than any others, although of course in differing degrees and with noticeably different results. All of these met his challenge and evolved a response to it.

In the theatre the figure of the Machiavellian man was hopelessly distorted by exaggeration, but this was unfortunately the form in which it was chiefly represented to the public mind. Perhaps dramatic poetry was the wrong medium for the study of this sort of man. Faced with a character for whom, quite literally, the sky was the limit, a dramatist was inclined to surrender to the poetic opportunities of his theme, so that to travel hopefully became more exciting than to arrive. 'And ride in triumph through Persepolis': it is magnificent but it is not Machiavelli. This is sheer emotion, a contemplation of glory for its own sake; an activity which Machiavelli would have despised as merely part of 'the pleasing picture of things'. If Marlowe began with the object of

[1] In Shakespeare's time, that is. Later, when politics had become secularised, Machiavelli's ideas were effective or otherwise according to the psychological validity one chose to attach to them.

[2] Marlowe, *Jew of Malta*, Prologue 9.

[3] E.g. Bacon, *Advancement of Learning*, xvi 9: 'We are much beholden to Machiavelli and others, that write what men do, and not what they ought to do.'

enquiring how far Machiavellianism was a valid political analysis, his thundering heroes ran away with him. The same is true, to a smaller extent, of the less exuberant Chapman; and even Shakespeare's Richard of Gloucester, who promised to 'set the murd'rous Machiavel to school', was prey to destructive emotions and self-defeating ambitions that Machiavelli would have hated. Characters like these were studies in the nemesis of individualism, which is to have no more fields to conquer. That, if we like, is a comment on Machiavellianism, but it is only a partial comment, just as the characters themselves are only partly Machiavellians. They have the Machiavellian fervour, but not the tenacity, the emotional discipline, the impervious concentration. The serious drama exhibits surprisingly few characters whose authors had really understood the phenomenon they sought to represent.[1]

The lesser drama exhibits none at all, though it was not for want of trying. The playwrights knew what they meant by Machiavellian, and knew that he was an abomination. A 'politician' (Machiavellian) was 'one that would circumvent God'. The unanimity of their condemnation perhaps reflects an uneasy conscience born of secret flirtations with the monster. Professor Theodore Spencer has counted in Elizabethan drama 395 references to him as 'the embodiment of human villainy'.[2] But most of these personifications were just caricature. It was easy enough to gather up a few Machiavellian axioms and attitudes, wrested from their context and their proper meaning, and fashion them into a character bristling with aggressiveness and cynical ambition. Such a person was sure to gratify the appetite for melodramatic villainy which the playwrights shared with their audiences; and to label him a Machiavellian was to make certain of getting the right emotional response. It is simply a transmutation of the old-fashioned Vice into a new sort of popular villain, the comic Machiavellian.[3] He performed exactly the same dramatic function of entertaining the audience with his shameless knaveries and then attesting the final triumph of virtue. Shakespeare made his contribution to this sort of nonsense in *Titus Andronicus*. Without passing judgment on Shakespeare's feelings and intentions in this play,[4] one must believe that in the coal-black Aaron he was

---

[1] Shakespeare's Iago and Edmund, or Bosola, the Cardinal and certain other characters in Webster. The scope of Volpone's ambitions is limited, but he too had the proper Machiavellian outlook.

[2] *Shakespeare and the Nature of Man*, 44.

[3] It was from the Vice that the stage Machiavellian inherited his sardonic jocularity.

[4] It was the classic Elizabethan 'horror comic', but it also contains some serious political reflections in the spirit of the early histories. See note on page 120 n.

burlesquing the pseudo-Machiavellian villain of the public stage. The
tone is unmistakable:

> What signifies my deadly-standing eye,
> My silence and my cloudy melancholy,
> My fleece of woolly hair that now uncurls
> Even as an adder when she doth unroll
> To do some fatal execution?
> No, madam, these are no venereal signs:
> Vengeance is in my heart, death in my hand,
> Blood and revenge are hammering in my head.
> > II iii 32.

This is not the voice of the true Machiavelli, but it is what he had
become in the theatre. Again, when he has been captured and is urged
to repent his wickedness, Aaron's answer is to exult in the evil that he
has done:

> Even now I curse the day—and yet, I think,
> Few come within the compass of my curse—
> Wherein I did not some notorious ill:
> As kill a man, or else devise his death,
> Ravish a maid, or plot the way to do it,
> Accuse some innocent or forswear myself,
> Set deadly enmity between two friends,
> Make poor men's cattle break their necks,
> Set fire on barns and haystacks in the night,
> And bid the owners quench them with their tears.
> Oft have I digg'd up dead men from their graves,
> And set them upright at their dear friends' door,
> Even when their sorrow almost was forgot,
> And on their skins, as on the bark of trees,
> Have with my knife carved in Roman letters,
> 'Let not your sorrow die, though I am dead.'
> Tut, I have done a thousand dreadful things
> As willingly as one would kill a fly,
> And nothing grieves me heartily indeed,
> But that I cannot do ten thousand more.
> > V i 125.

Thus was Machiavelli diminished. After the first few lines this
declaration is only the small-change of wickedness. Both the matter
and the manner suggest Robin Goodfellow's catalogue of mischief,[1]
and the speech shows how in the public theatre Machiavelli's profound
seriousness had come to be prostituted for comic and melodramatic
effect. Alternatively, in the more thoughtful dramas written for the
private theatres, the Machiavellian would be depressed into the 'mal-
content', the fashionable melancholic. This dreary figure certainly had

---

[1] *MND* II i 32-57.

the master's unilluded vision of human baseness, but through glandular deficiency he was denied the cathartic properties of action. Few people are more pathetic than the morally impotent. But the immense popularity of the Machiavellian caricature as a dramatic type does show how deeply Machiavelli's view of life, albeit in a perverted form, had impressed itself upon the public mind. He was the great bogeyman of the age, the symbol of atheism, Jesuit intrigue, social disorder and even, through the displeasure he gave to God, of such lesser ills as plague, flood, famine and barrenness in women. Among more reflective men he was a main inspiration of the current of satire and verse tragedy that flowed so strongly at the turn of the century.

Shakespeare early studied Machiavellianism and found it inadequate for the individual man and therefore inadequate for society too. His Richard III is only a vulgarisation of the type, possibly because even at that early stage he found himself unable to take it very seriously. It is as though he decided to enquire into the amoral, high-aspiring character that was putting Marlowe into such a pother in the early nineties, and emerged with the immediate discovery that these immature people were not worth his trouble. Richard hardly sufficed him for a single play, and ever afterwards he showed a fixed dislike of individualism and the character who expresses himself in such phrases as 'I am myself alone'.[1] The Ghosts who visit the sleeping Richard symbolise the futility of that sort of moral isolation.

> Richard loves Richard; that is, I am I;

but also:

> There is no creature loves me;
> And if I die, no soul will pity me.
>> V iii 184, 201.

Iago is a much more authentic Machiavellian than Richard. 'Virtue! A fig!' He would profane his own 'gain'd knowledge' if he were to submit to the lusts of the blood and permissions of the will that most men allow to direct their lives. 'If the balance of our lives had not one scale of reason to poise another of sensuality, the blood and baseness of our natures would conduct us to most preposterous conclusions.' Iago has the true Machiavellian faculty of working to make himself master of the event, snaring his victims by means of the virtues and ordinary decencies for which he has nothing but contempt. But with

---

[1] A callous egotism that certainly included some of the attitudes associated with the modern 'I'm all right, Jack'.

his sudden perception of a 'daily beauty' in Cassio's life to which he cannot attain, he acknowledges the values that he has spent his life trying to deny. Iago has seen so clearly the hollow deceits of passion that he will never become their slave. But the superiority which this brings him denotes also an inferiority and a separation. It divides him from the common run of men, and his denial of blood and emotion is a denial of the normal attributes of a sentient being. It puts him in the company of Sir Andrew, in whose liver one would not find 'so much blood . . . as will clog the foot of a flea'; and Sir Andrew is something less than a man. Iago's failing, and the failing of the Machiavellian man, is the flaw in his psychological equipment which prevents him from comprehending not merely the innate goodness of people nobler than himself, but also the inconsistent and unexpected patches of virtue in those much his inferiors in capacity and intelligence. Othello's greatness of soul, the loyalty of Desdemona, even the dog-like decency of the fallible Cassio, are, as we should expect, virtues beyond his understanding. But in the end he finds himself judged also by Emilia and Roderigo, creatures whom he has deceived and despised. The failure of all that he stands for lies in the fact that he is finally revealed not as a frustrated schemer but as a wicked man; for he is therein submitted to a standard of judgment that he has dismissed as the froth of a deluded imagination. He learns that after all it is not merely in ourselves that we are thus or thus. There are universal laws of which even the abject Roderigo has some intimation; of which, indeed, in his successive attempts to conjure up a respectable motive for what he was doing to Othello, he has shown some fleeting awareness himself.

Through characters like Iago Shakespeare reveals his conviction that, in spite of its devastating successes, Machiavellianism is psychologically invalid. He feels that on the whole men do not behave like that; or when they do, they are not whole men. It is surely significant that he provides almost every one of his Machiavellians with some sort of pathological excuse for their behaviour. Perhaps it is only Iago whose malignity anyone should be able to describe as motiveless. Richard of Gloucester is deformed; Aaron is black and also, like Conrade, was born under Saturn, and saturnine men do not naturally 'apply a moral medicine to a mortifying mischief';[1] Don John and Edmund are humiliatingly conscious of their bastardy. The evil that these men do is presented as their deliberate wish for compensation. They demand revenge upon a world that injured them in some way when they were innocent and helpless to control it.[2] Machiavellianism,

---

[1] *MAN* I iii 13.   [2] See Una Ellis-Fermor, *Jacobean Drama*, 254.

in Shakespeare's view, is the creed of men who have been morally perverted by misfortune. Their twisted aggressiveness is not characteristic of ordinary human nature; and it is false to presume a universal egoism from a handful of isolated and exceptional instances.

If it fails as a creed for individuals, it fails too as a creed for society. No theory of the state can be valid if it is based on false assumptions about mankind, and the course of history has shown more than once that Machiavellianism is as bankrupt politically as it is morally. Marlowe, Shakespeare and Chapman all indicated—without much sympathy—the plight of the Machiavellian egoist at the peak of his bloody ascent.[1] He had 'no place to mount up higher', and none of the normal human satisfactions to console him then. The poets showed, too, how the schemes of these social wreckers foundered on the persistent decency of ordinary men. This decency, against all the odds, is the imponderable that has rescued society time and again from its fanatics and devourers; and the paradox of power politics is that by breaking the daily ties which bind man to man, ruler to subject, it ends in the very chaos it seeks to prevent.

> Then everything includes itself in power,
> Power into will, will into appetite;
> And appetite, an universal wolf,
> So doubly seconded with will and power,
> Must make perforce an universal prey,
> And last eat up himself.
>   *TC* I iii 119.

The consuming force is itself consumed, and the predatory self-interest which Machiavelli assumed to be the common condition of mankind proves to be only the high road to anarchy. While it is true that Ulysses in this same speech gives expression to Shakespeare's most powerful feelings about unity and order, the character is here speaking chorically. On other occasions in the play Ulysses thwarts degree by his ignoble scheming, and the whole bias of his thought and action is towards a dehumanised sort of statesmanship that is characteristically Machiavellian. His interest, as Professor Knights has said, is in the mere manipulation of men.[2] His coldly rational concept of society excludes all feeling, and he has no sense of the strange complex of loyalties and intimate relationships upon which political authority is truly based.

[1] Cf. Bacon: 'He doth like the ape that, the higher he climbs, the more he shows his arse.'
[2] *Shakespeare's Politics*, 5.

Kings are not made by art,
But right of nature.

But the real danger of Machiavelli's analysis is that we can so easily believe him to be right. The lucidity, the almost voluptuous cynicism, the candid disenchantment, the seeming completeness of his system are apt to create a dangerous illusion of truth, and put us in mind of the *Maxims* of La Rochefoucauld, those lethal little sentences that to a dispirited mind always seem to contain some melancholy but inescapable truth about mankind. The honesty and the realism commend themselves, and we are nagged into uneasy self-recognition. It requires a deliberate effort to give the lie to these specious assertions and to remember that while man no doubt might be endlessly aggressive, faithless and self-seeking, the facts of history and social organisation show that he is not—or at least that he is something else besides. Hope is perhaps the virtue best loved in heaven, and man is not content with a continuing vista of sin and struggle, ending in oblivion. The doctrine of the fall better fulfils his needs, because he prefers to think that he was formerly innocent and will one day be redeemed.

Machiavelli dismissed this as sentimental nonsense, holding that man was born into a condition of beastliness from which no fall was possible; and the persistence of his doctrines, even in perverted forms, was an important social and political fact of Shakespeare's age. It was one thing to reject them as immoral and blasphemous, and quite another to keep one's actions always free of their taint. Machiavelli does give an explanation of how all men behave at some time and how a man like Ulysses would behave all the time. He offers, too, a cynical resolution of the dilemma between public and private morality. Ideally these are one and the same, and in theory the Elizabethans believed that no one could be a good ruler who was not also a good man. But in practice they recognised that the public welfare sometimes compelled him to do things which as a private individual he would have thought unworthy; and here was Machiavelli to obliterate the possibly idle distinction by insisting that in public life the only morality was success. The danger of Machiavellianism was that it seemed to explain so many of the facts, not perhaps of life as it ought to be lived but of the actual events that men saw taking place around them. The Massacre of St. Bartholomew excited a universal horror far beyond its immediate political importance, for the reason that it seemed to represent the triumph of Machiavellian 'policy' in the cold-blooded adoption by a civilised and Christian government of a matured plan of treachery and violence. It was a symbolic event that released a new and incalculable force into the sphere of human relations. The dykes had broken in the night. By all that men held traditional this dreadful deed should have been followed by terrible reverberations in the planetary world and strange mutinies in the soul of man, and to thoughtful observers this is just what seemed to have happened. The massacre deepened a pessimism about man's true nature that had already been stirred by Calvinist determinism and the disturbing revelations of the new Copernican cosmology.[1]

Machiavellianism therefore compelled men to declare their moral allegiances. Let us remind ourselves again that the word was a label attached to a fairly large package into which they stored almost everything of which they disapproved, much of it not specifically Machiavellian. At other times and in other places Popery, Presbytery, Jacobin, atheist, Fascist, imperialist, Communist have served a similarly convenient purpose. So the package might contain anything from the grotesques of Elizabethan melodrama to studies like Iago or Webster's Cardinal; it included satanism and also the sleights of political *leger de main*, the 'conclusions of estate . . . first founded in ingenious Italy'. But fundamentally it asserted the sovereignty of the amoral, self-determining individual against the traditional assumption of an organic community observing status, authority and natural law. Mediaeval rulers had not, of course, been unaware of evil, of disruptive passions which it was their duty to subdue. What was new and outrageous in Machiavellianism was the open assertion that evil is the norm, that morality is as the prince decrees it and the state a mere erection of convenience.[2]

Shakespeare resisted all these doctrines, and that is the real significance of his continuous affirmation of order and degree, his mistrust of rebels and his acceptance of the crudities and falsifications of Tudor propaganda. The pattern of his history plays is often said to have been an enquiry into the nature of the ideal ruler, 'the true kingly type'. Obviously the character of the prince was of immense importance, but

---

[1] *SWW* 468–70.

[2] The dilemma of the ruler, torn between Machiavellian expediency and traditional reverence for God and justice, was thus expressed by the tyrant Soliman:

> The earth draws one way, and the sky another.
> If God works thus, kings must look upward still,
> And from these powers they know not, choose a will.
> Or else believe themselves, their strength, occasion;
> Make wisdom conscience; and the world their sky:
> So have all tyrants done; and so must I.
>   Greville, *Mustapha* IV i 38.

his quest was not as simple as that. He was seeking rather for the conditions in which might be realised the ideal society: no utopian fiction but a community based on eternal and immutable laws, wherein ruler and subject work together in ordered harmony and there is no place for Machiavellian self-assertion. It was an entirely conservative and orthodox conception, and all the more potent for being that. This was the well-governed state, the image of the divine order to which all human effort was destined to aspire; and Machiavelli stood for the uninhibited individualism that prevented its realisation.

By name Shakespeare mentioned him only three times, once in a jesting reference by the Host at Windsor, but Sir Andrew would as lief be a Brownist as a politician and 'policy', although it often means no more than the prudent management of affairs, appears sometimes with the special significance of intrigue, opportunism or low cunning. In this sense it is often contrasted with honour, and represents the sort of backstairs manoeuvring that causes the fragmentation of society and lays it open to its enemies. Pity and all ordinary virtues are of no account when 'policy sits above conscience'; policy, 'base and rotten', is contrivance which colours its working with elaborate deceits; it is the tool of Suffolk ('by devilish policy art thou grown great') and Aaron and Warwick. Shakespeare finds it in Richard II's insight into the motives and tactics of his enemies, in Prince John's treachery in Gaultree Forest, in Henry IV's advice to his son to busy giddy minds in foreign wars, in priests who consecrate commotion's bitter edge or propose war as a means to save the Church from taxation. He anatomises it particularly as Commodity ('smacks it not something of the policy?'), the vile-drawing bias which makes kings break faith and acknowledge gain as their only lord. Whatever its initial success, he always shows it as ultimately failing, as sterile, self-destructive and subversive of society. A true social order cannot be realised until both kings and peoples agree to renounce it.

The speech from *Biron's Tragedy* quoted above continues in this way:

> Religion is a branch, first set and blest
> By heaven's high finger in the hearts of kings,
> Which whilom grew into a goodly tree;
> Bright angels sat and sung upon the twigs,
> And royal branches, for the heads of kings,
> Were twisted of them; but since squint-eyed envy
> And pale suspicion dash'd the heads of kingdoms
> One 'gainst another, two abhorred twins,
> With foul tails, stern War and Liberty,[1]

---

[1] Liberty here means licence.

> Enter'd the world. The tree that grew from heaven
> Is overrun with moss; the cheerful music
> That heretofore hath sounded out of it
> Begins to cease, and as she casts her leaves,
> By small degrees the kingdoms of the earth
> Decline and wither; and look, whensoever
> That the pure sap in her is dried-up quite,
> The lamp of all authority goes out,
> And all the blaze of princes is extinct.
>
> > III i 25.

If for 'religion' in the opening line we understand a rather larger conception, embracing law and law-abidingness, justice, and all that
Shakespeare meant by *kindness*, this passage by another poet indicates
an important element in his social thought. Our corrupted wills forbid
us to achieve fully even those objects we propose to ourselves in our
better moments, and so society, marred with the imperfections of
fallen man, is a prey to his destructive selfishness. Without the aid of
some power beyond ourselves, the lamp of authority would not stay
alight.

In Shakespeare, as in the tragedians of Greece, the action has constant reference to a wider universe. When he urges obedience to
authority, it is not only through confidence in the individual ruler,
who is human and easily deluded by the seemings of power. His faith
is in the sanctified order of the world, a conception not specifically
Christian but corresponding more closely to the Roman idea of
numen, of a presiding genius, almost a genius of the race, whose spirit
is not hostile to man.

III. THE MEANING OF MAJESTY

> The single and peculiar life is bound
> With all the strength and armour of the mind
> To keep itself from noyance; but much more
> That spirit upon whose weal depend and rest
> The lives of many. The cease of majesty
> Dies not alone, but like a gulf doth draw
> What's near it with it; it is a massy wheel,
> Fix'd on the summit of the highest mount,
> To whose huge spokes ten thousand lesser things
> Are mortis'd and adjoin'd; which, when it falls,
> Each small annexment, petty consequence,
> Attends the boisterous ruin. Never alone
> Did the king sigh, but with a general groan.
>
> > *Ham.* III iii 11.

It is a grim and shabby context, with Claudius frightened of the dangers that hourly grow from his nephew's lunacies and Guildenstern finding the phrases of the eternal flunkey:

> Most holy and religious fear it is
> To keep those many many bodies safe
> That live and feed upon your majesty.

Then Rosencrantz weighs in with these lines that rise above the particular base situation to assert the true nature of society; and assert it although tainted with the speaker's insincerity. Shakespeare often betrays his characters through their verse, and this speech of Rosencrantz, so turgid and hyperbolic, pitilessly reveals the man. Chameleon courtier to the roots of his being, he ceased long ago to have opinions of his own. His essence is only to mouth dogmas that his betters will find agreeable. Here, however, he speaks with his own words and the mind of his creator. At first sight the passage merely seems, as Rosencrantz himself intended it, to announce the heavy responsibilities of personal rule. Henry V said much the same things, and the figure of the 'massy wheel' emphasises the highly centralised quality of Tudor thought. But the same figure, with the spokes of the wheel and the ten thousand lesser things mortis'd and adjoin'd, proclaims the interdependence of all levels of society. While the chief responsibility is undoubtedly the king's, 'majesty', as Shakespeare conceived it, does not belong to him alone.

Unless this be so, government is simply a matter of 'We' against a remote and nebulous 'They': at best a barren condition of mutual suspicion and indifference, at worst the cause of tyranny or rebellion. It implies a separation, whereas government should be a partnership. The partnership did not mean that every man was to take his share in ruling: Charles I was a true Elizabethan when he told his judges that king and subject are 'clean different things'. It meant recognition of one's particular responsibility, of the king's duty to govern, the magistrate's to exercise authority under him, the father's to rule the family, and every man's to obey the law and acknowledge the superiority of those set over him. Shakespeare believed that one must not expect to be allowed to 'contract out' of society. The Williams episode in *Henry V* is clearly directed at this issue. While every subject's soul is his own, his duty is the king's; and just as men 'have no wings to fly from God', they have no wings to fly from society either.

Separatism was one of the dangers of the age. It was the creed of impatient sectaries who would reform the Church—that is, secede from it—'without tarrying for any', and of Catholics who obeyed a foreign prince and whispered of tyrannicide. Subconsciously, but just as insidiously, it was the creed of the financiers and 'projectors' whose avarice resented the economic paternalism of the state. More damaging still were the defeatists. There are many reasons for wanting to abandon society, and one of the deadliest is the conviction that society has failed the individual.

> Oh wearisome condition of humanity!
> Born to one law, to another bound.
> Greville, *Mustapha* Chorus V.

Man will find no rest in Nature, which has made him a creature of conflicting impulses, reaching up to virtue but undermined by lust. He will not find it, either, in the dogmas of a man-made Church[1] or the common round of social duty. Greville here supposes a world-weariness, an erosion of soul, that abandons as hopeless the struggle between our fallen nature and the demands of God's law. Until he can be reunited with God, man must passively accept his inability to bear his earthly burdens. The pessimism that darkened the closing years of Elizabeth's long reign had certain practical causes that have been mentioned in the two previous chapters. But in the sphere of moral speculation it arose from the swift collapse of Renaissance aspiration or, more correctly, from the apparent diversion of that aspiration into paths of destructive egoism. Marlowe's intoxicating vision of

> Our souls, whose faculties can comprehend
> The wondrous architecture of the world,
> And measure every wand'ring planet's course,
> Still climbing after knowledge infinite,
>   *1 Tamburlaine* II vii 21.

turned to despair when man's aspiring mind seemed to challenge the very balance of the universe.

> Cut is the branch that might have grown full straight,
> And burned is Apollo's laurel bough,
> That sometime grew within this learned man.
> Faustus is gone; regard his hellish fall,

---

[1] It was often said that the clergy abused their spiritual authority to enforce obedience to tyranny, e.g. *2 Hen. IV* IV ii 16–22; Greville, *Mustapha* III v, called the clergy 'spiritual forges unto princes' might', and in the First Chorus of the same play the Bashas complain that in the name of conscience the priests rob men of the few freedoms the state has left them; see also Greville, *Alaham* III v 38–42, Fourth Chorus 49–52. These views illustrate the wide currency of Machiavellian scepticism.

> Whose fiendful fortune may exhort the wise
> Only to wonder at unlawful things,
> Whose deepness doth entice such forward wits
> To practise more than heavenly power permits.
>   *Doctor Faustus* Epilogue.

Daniel called the sciences 'gifts of grief' which bring every kind of knowledge but knowledge of what is right, and Sir John Davies's *Nosce Teipsum* was a plea for the rediscovery of fundamental truths. Seeking to 'know the moving of each sphere', we neglect the motions of the 'clock within our breasts', and after our journeyings in search of the fashionable wisdom

> When we come home, are to ourselves unknown,
> And unacquainted still with our own souls.
>   XXV.

When they opposed their new-won knowledge to their inherited beliefs about religion and society, men felt that their loss was greater than their gain. They seemed to themselves to 'confuse knowledge with knowledge', to pursue a wisdom that merely led them into error, so that, as Donne lamented, 'Prince, Subject, Father, Son, are things forgot.' Their rashness finally recoiled upon themselves when Bacon argued that their excessive worship of intellect was itself an obstacle to scientific advance. The human mind, he said, was a false mirror which distorts the true nature of things 'by mingling its own nature with it'.

Many correctives were proposed for this deflated optimism. Condemning the sort of man who hoped

> . . . the complete Universe might be
> Subject to such a rag of it as he,

Chapman took refuge in an Epictetan merging with the Creator. His Clermont proclaimed that no torture

> Can force me from my glad obedience
> To anything the high and general Cause,
> To match with his whole fabric, hath ordain'd:
> And know ye all. . . .
> That in this one thing, all the discipline
> Of manners and of manhood is contain'd;
> A man to join himself with th'Universe
> In his main sway, and make (in all things fit)
> One with that All, and go on, round as it. . . .
> . . . to consider great Necessity
> All things, as well refract as voluntary,
> Reduceth to the prime celestial cause.
>   *Revenge of Bussy d'Ambois* IV i 132.

Elsewhere in the play Clermont observed

> how dangerous it is
> For any man to press beyond the place
> To which his birth, or means, or knowledge ties him;
> For my part, though of noble birth, my birthright
> Had little left it, and I know 'tis better
> To live with little, and to keep within
> A man's own strength still, and in man's true end,
> Than run a mix'd course. Good and bad hold never
> Anything common; you can never find
> Things outward care, but you neglect your mind.
> God hath the whole world perfect made, and free,
> His parts to th'use of th'All; men then that are
> Parts of that All, must, as the general sway
> Of that importeth, willingly obey
> In everything without their power to change.
> He that, unpleased to hold his place, will range,
> Can in no other be contain'd that's fit,
> And so resisting th'All, is crush'd with it.
> But he that knowing how divine a frame
> The whole world is; and of it all can name,
> Without self-flattery, no part so divine
> As he himself, and therefore will confine
> Freely his whole powers, in his proper part,
> Goes on most God-like. He that strives t'invert
> The Universal's course with his poor way,
> Not only dust-like shivers with the sway,
> But crossing God in his great work, all earth
> Bears not so cursed and so damn'd a birth.
>   III iv 51.

If in this there is strength and consolation, it is only for rarer minds.
Others sought peace in Stoic resignation, a careful withdrawal from
the disappointments administered by fate or ignorance.

> Pox of your halting human knowledges;
> O death! how far off hast thou kill'd! how soon
> A man may know too much, though never nothing.
>   Chapman, *Biron's Conspiracy* III iv 110.

In men 'to whom the day and fortune equal are', the supreme virtue is
courage to endure our going hence.

But the insecurity of the times bred attitudes less heroic than these.
If it was no longer 'immortality to die aspiring', a safer anchorage in
doubt was fideism, which raised faith above reason and waited hopefully upon signs of grace. In society this proved a dangerous condition,
a disablement of soul in which order was valued for the wrong reasons

and obedience, not responsibility, was looked upon as man's highest civic duty. Other-worldliness was ready to acquiesce in the divorce of power from all considerations of right and wrong. Men of another character gave up the moral struggle altogether.

> Untruss your slaveries: you have height enough
> Beneath this steep heaven to use all your reaches.
> *Biron's Conspiracy* III, iv 139.

But heaven proved too steep for the assault, and the brave challenge to the universe perished in an abdication of individual judgment and responsibility. Despair soured into cynicism, and the obliquities of Machiavelli were able to enter the social body in the way that germs attack a man already weakened by emotional strain.

Polonius thought that 'to expostulate what majesty should be, what duty is', was as unnecessary as to go into the reasons why day is day and time is time. Majesty was Shakespeare's specific for the contemporary weakening of faith in the traditional bonds of religion, the family and society. By it he meant something more than 'power, pre-eminence, and all the large effects that troop' with kingship; Gaunt touched on its deeper meaning when he likened England to 'this earth of majesty', seat of Mars and other Eden. It was a common awareness, on all levels of society, of the worth and integrity of the whole community and the responsibilities of citizenship. It was the bond that holds men together against particularism, irresponsibility and faction. No one could be at times more pessimistic than Shakespeare in his analysis of the corruptions and delusions of government. In the bitter comedies and in *King Lear* he stripped authority of all its pretences; in *Troilus and Cressida* he supposed a concept of order that ironically questioned the common grounds of obedience; and in *Timon* he pictured all degrees, observances, customs and laws declined to their confounding contraries. But ultimately he reaffirmed the faith in the possibility of a healthy social order that had earlier guided the less penetrating exploration he made in the history plays. The Crown, which is the symbol of majesty, is the higher self of every subject, calling him to great deeds and sacrifice. If the heaviest demands are made upon the king himself, yet the royalism that is the final value of Shakespeare's political drama[1] recognises the common man's capacity to do uncommon things. The cease of majesty occurs when king and subject no longer realise their partnership in greatness.

Polydore Vergil quoted Cicero to the effect that 'it is not so great

[1] See G. Wilson Knight's examination of 'the Shakespearian Royalty' in *The Sovereign Flower*, esp. 28–32.

an evil that a prince should go astray, though that is indeed a big evil in itself, as that he corrupts others, and brings it about that as his own life is changed, so are the morals of his people'. Such is the specially heavy weight of royal responsibility. A prince's sins blemish all his people, and always in Shakespeare we find a relation between the character of the ruler and the moral condition, as well as the actual prosperity, of the governed: Gadshill and the Eastcheap stews are complementary to Henry IV's flawed, usurping title.[1] But it is a two-way relation, in which all may 'save the state by doing each their charge', and it is equally true that no ruler can be wise or effective if his subjects are indomitably bad. This interdependence, in rights and responsibilities, of all members of the community is finely stated in the fourth Chorus of Greville's *Mustapha*, where it is urged that 'spleen of the parts makes the universal smart'.

> So easy is it to bring states to death,
> By urging those powers to oppose, whose union gave them breath.
> 35.

> Thus, in disorder's chain, while each link wresteth other,
> Incestuous error, to her own, is made both child and mother.
> 55.

> In that noble work of public government,
> When Crowns, Church, soldiers, or the laws do overmuch dissent,
> That frame, wherein they liv'd, is fatally dissolv'd,
> And each in gulfs of self-conceit, as fatally, involv'd.
> 103.

We only bring confusion on ourselves if we forget the warning given by the author of the Tenth Homily, that 'every one hath need of others'. This was a vital sentiment in Shakespeare's conception of society.

> What is a man,
> If his chief good and market of his time
> Be but to sleep and feed?
> *Ham*. IV iv 33.

The whole universe was created 'with such large discourse' in order that we might use our God-given powers as moral and social beings, and without prejudice to our individuality we all have our share of responsibility for public acts. Montaigne's ideal commonwealth repelled Shakespeare by its utter lack of obligation and distinction, 'no

---

[1] The political health of the nation is always reflected in the images of Nature that Shakespeare uses in a given context. The countryside flowers or withers in correspondence with the ruler's fortunes.

name of magistrate . . . riches, poverty, and use of service, none . . . no occupation; all men idle, all.' There is no living together without duty.

IV THE SHAKESPEAREAN ORDER

This was the particular significance of the Shakespearean order; and it is surely a grave misunderstanding of his purpose to suppose that the great cycle of English historical plays was written just as a poetic exercise, as a concession in dramatic form to the Elizabethan taste for epic. It is doubtless agreeable to think of the young eagle flexing his wings and gradually becoming conscious of his strength, but the histories should mean more to us than that. Shakespeare was at all times a professional dramatist writing for commercial success, and an artist obedient to the deeper impulses of his own nature; and he was both these things before he was a political theorist. But he was also aware of his vocational responsibilities as historian and poet, and he chose deliberately to write of matters of consequence to his countrymen and himself.

The outcome was not just a piece of Establishment writing, demanding support for the government because this was the expedient thing to do. When Shakespeare demanded obedience, he showed the grounds for it and suggested limits beyond which it need not be pressed. Nor, on the other hand, were the histories an essay in antiquated idealism. Although substantially traditional, they did not invoke loyalties no longer applicable to contemporary facts. No detail in his picture of society was peculiar to himself, and it contained nothing with which educated Englishmen were not already familiar. What is uniquely Shakespearean is the depth and range of his penetration and the undogmatic balance of his conclusions. No one else realised so clearly that the social good depends not on the preservation of a certain set of laws and institutions but on every man's recognition of his moral duty. In this sense we may quite truthfully say that the real value of his theory of society derives from his poetic insight into the individuals who compose it.

Order as contemplated by the Elizabethan mind was much more than a political conception.[1] It was evident to Hooker that 'obedience of creatures unto the Law of Nature is the stay of the whole world', and if this obedience should fail at any point, the planets themselves would lapse into 'irregular volubility'. Chaos was the contemporary symbol of a very real dread of anarchy. Thus a concern for political

[1] See above, pp. 33–9.

order might be an alternative aspect of the quest for the steadfastness that lay behind the endless flux of Mutability; or again it might correspond in the realm of ethics to the individual's determination to be master of his own turbulent passions. The state being part of the larger cosmic order, any dislocation of the commonwealth was viewed as only a temporary departure from a divinely-established norm. Were it not so, men would have to believe that the universe itself was unhinged and the heavens constrained no longer to observe degree, priority and place 'in all line of order'. Order was, in fact, humanity's only right condition. Truth, self-mastery and justice were inaccessible without it.

In the state the focus of this impulse for unified authority was naturally the Crown. The king-subject relationship was universally felt to be a given relationship, plainly conformable with Nature, like the father-child relationship within the family. No other political arrangement was conceivable, and Elizabethan England was as queen-centred as a hive. In Tudor times the maligned and misunderstood doctrine of 'divine right' simply asserted the heavenly origins of human government. It was not a claim to sovereignty. Kings were under law,[1] and were as naught without their subjects' love, the possession which Elizabeth herself acknowledged as the greatest glory of her reign. Reverence was truly 'the angel of the world', since it was mankind's act of submission to the divine scheme of things. It is significant that even the stages on which the actors played out their earthly dramas displayed in visual symbols the fundamental doctrines of the age. The permanent structure of the open theatre was provided with the various tokens of degree, the throne, the altar, the tomb and the sky. God spoke from the 'heavens' above, angels and saints from the windows that overlooked the stage, the king from his throne on the main platform. The theatre was, quite deliberately, a miniature of the universe, a reflection of the archetypal pattern of human life. Its stylised structure projected the traditionally harmonious vision of an ordered creation and man's central position within the cosmos.[2]

This vision was not as artificial or foolish as we might suppose it. It was not foolish, because religious sanctions were a valuable reinforcement of authority when the hold of law was still precarious and obedience had not yet become the Englishman's habit. There were no police, and the Tudor state had testing problems to contend with. Nor, despite its formality, was it altogether artificial. Divine right is only a

---

[1] See below, pp. 128–35.
[2] See the article by G. R. Kernodle, *Shakespeare Survey XII*.

slightly elaborate way of stating the general conviction that the gods do act through man, and that the consequences are tragic when we try to resist their will. It is a belief which supplies a moral basis for government. Order, as Shakespeare and his age understood it, was an ethical conception which asserted the difference between right and wrong; and degree, although it may sometimes have seemed to curb ambition by insisting overmuch on 'mannerly distinguishment', protected a man in his possessions and guaranteed the sanctity of right against physical might. In his famous speech Ulysses made both these points. If degree is discarded,

> Strength should be lord of imbecility,
> And the rude son should strike his father dead:
> Force should be right; or rather, right and wrong
> —Between whose endless jar justice resides—
> Should lose their names, and so should justice too.
> Then everything includes itself in power.
>
> *TC* I iii 114.

Elizabethan notions of degree and correspondence do in fact make sense, and with the unhappy evidence of our modern specialisations and qualified allegiances, we ought to be increasingly aware of it. Science has confirmed mediaeval cosmology in proving that the universe depends on a balance of physical forces, one that is precarious and unlikely to be permanent. There are similar laws in the sphere of human society and morality. When today we recognise that the causes of disease may be mental, or that there may be physical reasons for moral delinquency, we are still inhabiting Shakespeare's world of correspondences.

Thus order and the observance of degree were closely linked by Shakespeare with his conception of *kindness*. The need for kindness, or the natural love which binds all human beings in distinction from the rest of creation, was the conviction which unified all his moral beliefs. It lies at the centre of his idea of virtue. Kindness relates to the specific function of man as man, to the continued exercise of the will and reason that are the attributes of his humanity: the attributes that keep him on two feet instead of four. Thus when Lady Macbeth tells her husband that his nature is 'too full o' the milk of human kindness' to murder his royal guest, she is not just using a pretty but empty metaphor. She is saying that he is too much of a man—too little, that is, of a beast—to carry out the dreadful plan at which he has hinted. She fears that he may be true to his nature, which would make such a deed impossible. From the compunctious visitings of such

a nature she herself asks terribly to be released. She would be unsexed
and the milk of her breasts should turn to gall. She means that she
would become 'unkind', or not human. It was the worst thing Shakespeare could find to say of anyone, implying as it did the abdication of
specific virtues and a surrender to the universal wolf of appetite. In
the form of *kindless* he uses it only of Claudius. As *unkind* (though it
often has only the shallower significance of modern usage, generally
with reference to the heedless lover) it adds a special layer of meaning
to certain sorts of behaviour, and particularly to behaviour that carries
the taint of treachery or ingratitude or betrayal of trust. It is Worcester's
rebuke to Henry IV for violating the pledges that brought him to the
throne; it is the word Desdemona uses of the breach between Cassio
and Othello; ironically, Lear uses it of Cordelia, only to find that it
would have been better applicable to his other daughters, of whom,
significantly, he scarcely speaks without likening them to savage
beasts. It strikes with terrible force in Antony's 'this was the most
unkindest cut of all', unkindest because delivered with the hand of
trust and friendship.

The penalty of unkindness is to be isolated from one's fellow-men.
He who has shown himself to be less than human is denied humanity's
special blessings,

> As honour, love, obedience, troops of friends.
> *Macb.* V iii 25.

Macbeth more than anyone deserved to suffer this deprivation, for it
was he who would

> Pour the sweet milk of concord into hell,
> Uproar the universal peace, confound
> All unity on earth.
> IV iii 98.

Concord is the harmony of the universe, the binding of one with
another by 'holy cords . . . too intrinse t'unloose'. Their dissolution is
the cease of majesty.

Machiavellianism, which denied men's compulsion to love and
virtue, was essentially unkind. Unkindness was not wholly, or even
particularly, a political evil. It might wear the mask of any of the
deadly sins, for sin was man's wilful surrender of the gifts and privileges with which God endowed him. In Shakespeare's moral scheme,
human suffering was never to be attributed to blind chance. The
planets would never fall into irregular volubility by their own unheeding motion. Always the cause would be found in human error,

in some act of kindlessness;[1] and politics and morals were so closely
entwined that it might be a non-political act which threw society into
confusion. Quite simply, sinners are those who 'vary from the kindly
race of men'. Albany says to one of them:

> I fear your disposition:
> That nature, which contemns its origin,
> Cannot be border'd certain in itself;
> She that herself will sliver and disbranch
> From her material sap, perforce must wither
> And come to deadly use. . . .
> If that the heavens do not their visible spirits
> Send quickly down to tame these vile offences,
> It will come,
> Humanity must perforce prey on itself,
> Like monsters of the deep.
> *Lear* IV ii 31.

It was in this moral context that Shakespeare viewed rebellion.
Rebellion was not, as we know, a subject on which Tudor England
thought dispassionately. Even in the untypically cool judgment of Sir
Thomas Smith, an objective commentator on the laws and customs of
the people, it was too 'doubtful and hazardous' to be recommended.
Experience showed that it was always inconvenient and seldom successful, and for seasoned politicians it was, on the whole, too drastic a
remedy to be risked against ordinary forms of misgovernment. The
more extreme and emotional view taken in the Homilies probably
expressed the general sentiment of the nation. The writers in *A Mirror
for Magistrates* echoed the Homilies in treating rebellion as the ultimate
sin, and even Greville came in the end to orthodox conclusions. In
his desperately serious and rarefied studies of political power he inclined at first to liberal slogans about reviving 'the old equality of
Nature', but he came round finally to the conventional pieties:

> Kings only are the rods or blessings of the sky:
> God only judge: He knows what they deserve.
> *Mustapha* V ii 319.

Since the king was God's instrument, the public lot was patiently to
endure: rebellion would destroy the state as well as the tyrant. Chapman's Clermont was only one of many characters in the literature of
the time who proclaimed that private acts of vengeance usurped the

---

[1] E.g. in the violent and unnatural consequences of regicide, *Macbeth* II iv
1–20, or of Montsurry's murder of his adulterous wife, Chapman, *Bussy d'Ambois*
V i 161–73. 'Even heaven itself must see and suffer ill.'

privileges of God.[1] That vengeance belonged to God alone, or at times to His appointed representative, was a concept that subdued faction and guaranteed the moral universe. It lies behind the very orthodox rebuke delivered to the rebel lords in *The Troublesome Reign of King John*:[2]

> Subjects may not take in hand revenge,
> And rob the heavens of their proper power,
> Where sitteth He to whom revenge belongs.
>   Part II Scene iii 118.

But Shakespeare went some way beyond orthodoxy. In *Richard II* and *King John* he discussed[3] the ethics of rebellion and the occasions, if any, when it might be justified; and Part One of *Henry IV* reinforced the implicit conclusions of these two plays by demonstrating (the mere existence of Falstaff being a large part of the demonstration) what happens to society when a rebellion has succeeded. Even rebellion itself is sick, and neither Glendower's incantations nor Hotspur's adolescent chivalry can bring it the glow of health. This theme, of the paralysing effect of rebellion on the rebels themselves, is developed by Shakespeare in the second part of the play, where the Percies and their allies are shown in every mood of futility, false optimism and despair. Rebellion is here presented as a form of unkindness, an offence against both God and man, and in a striking passage in the opening scene Shakespeare describes how the rebel forces, having by their own act made themselves less than men, found themselves incapable of summoning up their normal powers. Morton is telling Northumberland what happened to Hotspur's troops at Shrewsbury:

> My lord, your son had only but the corpse,
> But shadows and the shows of men, to fight;
> For that same word, rebellion, did divide
> The action of their bodies from their souls;
> And they did fight with queasiness, constrain'd,
> As men drink potions, that their weapons only
> Seem'd on our side: but, for their spirits and souls,
> This word rebellion, it had froze them up,
> As fish are in a pond.
>   *2 Hen. IV* I i 192.

---

[1] *Bussy's Revenge* III ii 117–27; and cf. *Richard III* IV i 220–8.

[2] Although this particular scene from *The Troublesome Reign* is not reproduced in Shakespeare's *King John*, the idea is clearly stated in his play, e.g. in Salisbury's speech, V iv 49–61. Salisbury's repentance follows his earlier emphatic ground for withholding his allegiance, that John by his wickedness 'hath dispossess'd himself of us'.

[3] 'Discussed' is used only for brevity and convenience. Shakespeare's dramatic method had no place for formal demonstration.

Thus by its effect on those who take part in it, rebellion is self-defeating. Shakespeare pursues this idea by indicating again and again throughout the play that this particular rising is doomed, by the sickness of its leaders, to continuous failure. When they are not torpid with despair, they are clutching nervelessly at straws. Thus in the same scene Morton tries to brace Northumberland's failing hopes by giving him the news that the Archbishop of York has brought spiritual influence to the cause.

> But now the bishop
> Turns insurrection to religion:
> Suppos'd sincere and holy in his thoughts,
> He's followed both with body and with mind,
> And doth enlarge his rising with the blood
> Of fair King Richard, scrap'd from Pomfret stones;
> Derives from heaven his quarrel and his cause.
>
> I i 200.

Followed 'with body and with mind': the Archbishop's presence will sanctify the cause and remove the doubts that paralysed the troops at Shrewsbury. The royalist Westmoreland's blunt challenge (why does York unlawfully presume to 'consecrate commotion's bitter edge'?) later puts this in proper perspective, but for the moment York's accession inflates the rebels' hopes. In I iii it is Lord Bardolph who looks back to Shrewsbury and blames Hotspur for risking battle on the mere promise of reinforcements:

> Who lin'd himself with hope,
> Eating the air on promise of supply,
> Flattering himself with project of a power
> Much smaller than the smallest of his thoughts:
> And so, with great imagination
> Proper to madmen, led his powers to death,
> And winking leap'd into destruction.
>
> I iii 27.

Bardolph warns that in an enterprise so critical

> Conjecture, expectation, and surmise
> Of aids incertain should not be admitted. . . .

> We fortify in paper, and in figures,
> Using the names of men instead of men.

But his infatuated colleagues pay more attention to the facile Hastings, who argues that

> It never yet did hurt
> To lay down likelihoods and forms of hope.

York utters some cynical platitudes on the fickleness of popular support, and the hopeless project, unplanned and ill-concerted, a mere rabble of little armies, duly goes forward with Hastings reflecting breezily that time bids them haste. Lady Percy's warnings (II iii) are as vain as Bardolph's, and in IV i, on the eve of disaster, Hastings is fatuously assuring the rebels that the King lacks instruments of chastisement. In this scene York introduces a deeper note when he reveals the true predicament to which the rebellion, and the Lancastrian usurpation that caused it, has brought everyone involved in it, whatever his party. The whole nation has become its victim.

> We are all diseas'd;
> And, with our surfeiting and wanton hours,
> Have brought ourselves into a burning fever,
> And we must bleed for it: of which disease
> Our late king, Richard, being infected, died. . . .
> I take not on me here as a physician,
> Nor do I as an enemy to peace
> Troop in the throngs of military men;
> But rather show a while like fearful war,
> To diet rank minds sick of happiness
> And purge the obstructions which begin to stop
> Our very veins of life. Hear me more plainly:
> I have in equal balance justly weigh'd
> What wrongs our arms may do, what wrongs we suffer,
> And find our griefs heavier than our offences.
> We see which way the stream of time doth run
> And are enforc'd from our most quiet sphere
> By the rough torrent of occasion.
>
> IV i 54.

The laboured, sonorous argument twists this way and that, but it has only one conclusion to reach: that in the sickness of the state men of both sides must now run wherever the torrent of occasion drives them. All are Time's fools. In the final analysis all the fluctuating attitudes of the rebels, from despair to reckless over-confidence, are shown to have been of no importance whatsoever. Being no longer men, they have long ago lost the power to direct their fate.

Rebellion, then, whatever its cause, disturbs the harmonious order in which alone men may move in their right relationships and fulfil their proper nature. When Caesar stated his ideal of personal government, it was stability that he named as the great essential.

> But I am constant as the northern star,
> Of whose true-fix'd and resting quality
> There is no fellow in the firmament.

The skies are painted with unnumber'd sparks,
They are all fire, and every one doth shine,
But there's but one in all doth hold his place:
So, in the world; 'tis furnish'd well with men,
And men are flesh and blood, and apprehensive;
Yet in the number I do know but one
That unassailable holds on his rank,
Unshak'd of motion; and that I am he. . . .
JC III i 60.

This stability, reflecting the measured movement of the celestial spheres, was for Shakespeare the specialty of rule. There would be time enough to explore the so-called 'kingly type', and the intricate responsibilities of power, when the fundamental values of obedience, authority and law had been made impregnable: for these alone kept the commonwealth 'unshak'd of motion'. Shakespeare believed in a universe created and made intelligible by God. It was doubtless true that

Had all been virtuous men,
There never had been prince upon the earth.
Chapman, *The Gentleman Usher* V iv 56.

Government was made necessary by the fall, and to that extent was marred by human error. But God's design assured its eternal righteousness, and this was a vital corrective of the Machiavellian view of the state as a man-made contrivance, existing only because human life was brutish and solitary, and incapable in itself of being a school of virtue. Society has to be protected from the relentless individualist 'that to himself is a law rational'. So government is God's remedy for human sin, not an opportunity for its indulgence; an organic growth, and not the artificial creation of the Renaissance prince. Although tyranny or weakness in the ruler are dreadful things, they do not destroy the idea of law; and political power, properly exercised, reconciles the conflicting passions of all sorts of men. To the naturally virtuous it brings the opportunity for discipline and service, through which they may build up the great stay of society, an anonymous tradition of restraint and good stewardship; and even the wicked may be made better by wise authority. To the countrymen who bade him identify himself by showing them his crown, Henry VI replied: 'My crown is in my heart, not on my head'.[1] The fulfilment of political life is the grace which individual action can bring to the lives of others.

[1] *3 Henry VI* III i 62.

V   POLITICS AND THE ARTIST

Shakespeare did not come to his conclusions all at once; nor did he
begin to write about English history with a matured theory of society
already shaped and demanding expression. His political ideas developed
with a broadening knowledge of life, and his early experiments in
comedy and tragedy obviously contributed to their making. Social
anxieties lie in the background to *Romeo and Juliet*, and it is possible
to find some oblique speculations on the nature of power in *A Midsummer Night's Dream*, where Theseus reveals himself as a rare
political sophisticate.[1] But Shakespeare must have had a starting-point,
and this is an appropriate time for a short digression on the artist's
instinctive outlook on political matters. A feeling for order is part of
his temperamental equipment.

Hazlitt, who decided that Shakespeare was 'a very dog to the
commonalty', attributed this inclination to the nature of poetry itself.
'The language of poetry naturally falls in with the language of power.'[2]
Aiming always at contrast and effect, it exists by excess, and its
principle 'is a very anti-levelling principle. . . . Poetry is right-royal.
It puts the individual for the species, the one above the infinite many,
might before right. A lion hunting a flock of sheep or a herd of wild
asses is a more poetical subject than they; and we even take part with
the lordly beast, because our vanity or some other feeling makes us
disposed to place ourselves in the situation of the strongest party.'

These fancies perhaps seemed truer when Hazlitt wrote them than
they do today, when we have had our share of the literature of the
hunted, but the main point is valid. The tendency of all art is centri-
petal. It is always seeking to bring diversity into unity, to make a
universe of separate worlds, and Shakespeare's 'leaning to the arbitrary
side of the question', which Hazlitt regretted, may have originated in

---

[1] Or again, in *Comedy of Errors* Aegeon is a model of the just, unimpassioned
ruler. He is not 'partial to infringe our laws' (I i 4) and he holds that an unbiased
justice is the only way to stop 'the mortal and intestine jars' between Ephesus
and Syracuse. *Titus Andronicus*, too, contains some interesting political issues.
The play argues for primogeniture, an uncontested succession, absolute unity; it
exposes personal ambition and speaks of the throne as 'to virtue consecrate, to
justice, continence, and nobility' (I i 14); and at the close Lucius comes as the
preserver to 'heal Rome's harms and wipe away her woe', after Marcus has
offered to teach the people

> how to knit again
> This scatter'd corn into one mutual sheaf,
> These broken limbs again into one body,
>   V iii 70.

[2] *Characters of Shakespeare's Plays*, on *Coriolanus*.

the compulsion to resolve personal and artistic dilemmas. The aristocratic tradition of Renaissance story-telling dealt exclusively with kings and nobles: for a writer that was an influence that he could hardly escape. But the writer has, too, his private struggle to master his own mental world, and it may be that for Shakespeare kingship emerged as a point of rest, and government became as important to him as composition and balance are to painters and musicians.[1] The office of king, magnified by the heroic imagination, was elevated into an order-symbol as much in tune with his artistic needs as with his social sympathies.

At any rate, his representation of royalty belongs rather to poetry than to prose. 'You have that in your countenance which I would fain call master,' Kent tells the fallen Lear. Shakespeare's royalty is an essence that clings inalienably to failures like Richard II and Henry VI, even when they have forfeited the right to rule, and it is never attainable by usurpers like Bolingbroke. It belongs naturally to Henry V, and likewise to the boy Arthur, who instinctively takes on his young shoulders the burden of Hubert's sickness (*King John* IV i). In a critical hour for England it is heroically assumed by Faulconbridge, because John has laid it down; and when the crisis is over it passes without question to the 'cygnet to this pale swan', the future Henry III. This royalty is not a quality we can precisely define, for it was a poetic idea incapable of being reduced to formula. Certainly it was not inconsistent with liberalism: Shakespeare never intended it as an alchemy to gild weakness or the abuse of power. Imaginative explorations of this kind are beyond rational analysis, and we must simply recognise that Shakespeare's kings have a style, a particular address to the world, that is unmistakably theirs.[2] But it is not theirs alone. It is the voice of a common consciousness of the mystery in the soul of state.

VI THE NECESSITY OF POWER

All political discussions arrive in the end at the many-sided question of power: its source and justification, its limits, the qualities needed in the men who have to bear it. For an Elizabethan this could only mean

[1] See G. Wilson Knight, *The Shakespearian Tempest* and *The Sovereign Flower*, and A. Sewell, *Character and Society in Shakespeare*.

[2] To understand what is uniquely Shakespearean in this conception of royalty, we may contrast it with Chapman's unfolding idea of the good king in *Biron's Tragedy*, e.g. III ii 31–55, IV ii 63–85, V i 49–65. This could be the creation of a political theorist, whereas Shakespeare's apprehensions of monarchy are essentially poetic.

an enquiry into the nature of monarchy. While every subject had his duties in the state, and there were several subordinate levels of authority, the ruler was the hub of the 'massy wheel', and on his character, and the justice of his claim to the throne, the welfare of the community principally depended. Although, therefore, Shakespeare's total theme was the whole question of man's social responsibility, it was inevitable that to a considerable extent the histories should be an extended examination of kings and kingship. The problem of power was the climax of his study of the political activities of man.

Power of course there had to be, and except for a few furtive Machiavellians (as it was not fashionable in England to be a Machiavellian openly) no one seriously questioned its origins in the laws of God and Nature. Certain Jesuit writers did argue a contractual relationship in civil society, but it was a theory designed for countries ruled by heretics, and its aim was to isolate royal power as a secular instrument limited to purely secular objects, thus claiming liberty of action within the state for the spiritual society. While it would, therefore, have considerably reduced the area of political obligation, its real purpose was to deny the Crown's supremacy in religion, and it was of a different spirit from the Whig theory of a social contract that emerged in the seventeenth century. With Protestant separatists also asserting the sovereign independence of religious communities,[1] Tudor government claimed, and was conceded, a much greater energy and concentration of power than had been thought necessary in the Middle Ages. It was no longer possible to accept the mediaeval notion that authority needed to be only occasionally exercised, since with God's help men would on the whole act virtuously in society.[2] Machiavelli had killed that comforting view of human innocence. Besides, the Tudor state was threatened with too many dangers for it to be safe to permit any weakness at the centre.

These dangers were described in the second chapter, and we must not lose sight of their importance in determining Shakespeare's theories of power. In reflecting the anxieties of his age he was a truly representative writer. In what was possibly his very first play, *Henry VI* Part II, he lingered in horror upon the moral and social anarchy implicit in the figure of Cade, who was the Elizabethan archetype of disorder. Cade's political expectations carry the theme of chaos to the point where the

[1] So that James I complained that Jesuits were 'nothing but Puritan-Papists'.
[2] The Middle Ages anyway could afford to be less concerned with the problem of power, as human government was only transitory and incapable of perfection.

habitual sanctions of society collapse and the irrational phantoms of desire walk unchecked.

The episode opens with the familiar resentments of the manual labourer towards the professional classes.

> GEORGE: O miserable age! Virtue is not regarded in handicrafts-men.
> JOHN: The nobility think scorn to go in leather aprons.
> GEORGE: Nay, more: the king's council are no good workmen.
>   *2 Hen. VI* IV ii 11.

This complaint leads to its own peculiar conclusion:

> It is said, 'Labour in thy vocation': which is as much as to say as, let the magistrates be labouring men; and therefore should we be magistrates.

Cade then enters and in a proclamation bids his followers be brave, 'for your captain is brave, and vows reformation'. The first item in this bravery is food subsidies: 'There shall be in England seven halfpenny loaves sold for a penny': as indeed they have been, and governments much applauded for it. In the quest for magnitude, regardless of quality or function, 'the three-hooped pot shall have ten hoops', and since only the best will do for the builders of the brave new world, 'I will make it felony to drink small beer.' Land shall be nationalised ('all the realm shall be in common'), and 'in Cheapside shall my palfrey go to grass'. If there is not room enough in Cheapside for everyone's palfrey, what then? It is a large question, but Cade's followers do not ask it. Overwhelmed by the splendour of his promises, they can only say, 'God save your majesty!'

The financing of these reforms is disposed of quite simply. 'There shall be no money; all shall eat and drink on my score; and I will apparel them all in one livery, that they may agree like brothers, and worship me their lord.' Shakespeare's satire is incisive and deadly. The inspiration of these rustic rebels is a muddled Utopianism, rooted in a not ignoble conception of the brotherhood of man. But the price of fraternity is shown to be the ubiquitous, intrusive presence of 'Big Brother' with his chuckling recommendation that all the little brothers should dress alike, the better to do him honour. In order to be free, we must be servile.

The good-humoured picture begins to darken. Cade has enough political instinct to know that prosperous Utopias are nourished on hatreds. The scapegoats of the new dispensation are men who can read and write, for learning is the power which keeps good men down. The rebels capture the Clerk of Chatham, a man not merely able to 'write and read and cast accompt' but guilty of the further iniquity of teaching boys to do these things, their passport into the ranks of the oppressors. He hangs with his pen and ink-horn round his neck. The indictment against Lord Say is still more formidable. First he is convicted of 'fellow-travelling', since he can speak French, the language of the national enemy.

> Nay, answer if you can: the Frenchmen are our enemies; go to then, I ask but this, can he that speaks with the tongue of an enemy be a good counsellor, or no?
>
> IV ii 179.

He too is stained with the treachery of learning,[1] and the worse treachery of spreading it.

> Thou hast most traitorously corrupted the youth of the realm in erecting a grammar-school; and whereas, before, our forefathers had no other books but the score and the tally, thou hast caused printing to be used; and, contrary to the king, his crown, and dignity, thou hast built a papermill. It will be proved to thy face that thou hast men about thee that usually talk of a noun or a verb, and such abominable words as no Christian ear can endure to hear. Thou hast appointed justices of the peace, to call poor men before them about matters they were not able to answer. Moreover, thou hast put them in prison; and because they could not read, thou hast hanged them; when indeed only for that cause they have been most worthy to live.
>
> IV vii 35.

Cade is magnificent in his assurance. He rewards one of his hard-fighting supporters, Dick, the butcher of Ashford, by giving him a licence to operate in the black market. 'The Lent shall be as long again as it is; and thou shalt have licence to kill for a hundred lacking one'; or, Lent, the period when eating of meat was prohibited, is to be extended by a further forty days and the conquering butcher will be able to double his under-the-counter traffic with those who cannot stomach fish. Arrived in London, Cade commands that 'of the city's cost, the pissing-conduit run nothing but claret wine this first year of our reign'. After a victory over the royal armies he proceeds to a final and comprehensive charter of liberties:

> The proudest peer in the realm shall not wear a head on his shoulders, unless he pay me tribute; there shall not be a maid married, but she shall pay me her maidenhead, ere they have it; men shall hold of me *in capite*; and we charge and command that their wives be as free as heart can wish or tongue can tell.
>
> IV vii 127.

---

[1] This mistrust of education was historically authenticated. In 1391 Richard II had to veto a parliamentary bill which aimed to make it illegal for villeins to receive instruction.

Dick begs him to tear up the statute-book, so that 'the laws of England may come out of your mouth'. Cade agrees:

> I have thought upon it; it shall be so. Away! burn all the records of the realm: my mouth shall be the parliament of England.
>
>   IV vii 15.

Falstaff, we remember, expressed the same hope, and it was not permitted even to him.

The interlude ends symbolically. The historical Cade died of wounds received in a battle at Heathfield in July 1450, but Shakespeare slightly altered the facts to suit his purpose. He turned Cade into a weary fugitive, deserted by his rabblement, climbing a garden wall in search of food. There he is found and killed by Alexander Iden, 'a Kentish gentleman'. It is Iden's immaculate normality that makes him the appropriate instrument of Cade's death. He is a complacent, unambitious ornament of the professional classes, perhaps a minor civil servant or local government officer, a family man with fixed habits and no ideas above his station.

> Lord! who would live turmoiled in the court,
> And may enjoy such quiet walks as these?
> This small inheritance my father left me
> Contenteth me, and worth a monarchy.
> I seek not to wax great by others' waning,
> Or gather wealth I care not with what envy:
> Sufficeth that I have maintains my state,
> And sends the poor well pleased from my gate.
>
>   IV x 18.

The perfect citizen and the embodiment of lawlessness are brought face to face.

In the Cade scenes we can only marvel at the timelessness of Shakespeare's imagination and the certainty and maturity of his political intuitions. While some of Cade's hopes and prejudices belong to any age,[1] others have become respectable only in our own time. But we must not be too modern in our appreciation of this episode, or lose sight of what Shakespeare was trying to do. Cade personified the contemporary dread of anarchy,[2] and we do not need to look before or behind that fact. This is what happens when government fails and

---

[1] They were soon to live again in the ranks of Cromwell's army.

[2] There are similar scenes in Shakespeare's contemporaries, as in Heywood's *Edward IV* or the anonymous *Sir John Oldcastle*.

the lamp of authority goes out. What Shakespeare did here, in this very early play, he never needed to do again. He has many other analogues of chaos, but when we read the mob scenes in later plays, we must remember that he has already explored through Cade what happens in the state when authority passes to the uninstructed multitude.

He is often charged with want of sympathy for the poor and under-privileged, the 'mutable, rank-scented many' that he seems to despise and dislike. But he has done his duty by the poor when he has re-minded us, as he always does, that they are human. He is indulgent to the mob as individuals, and Cade in himself is likeable in his insistence that politics have to do with human happiness. Although we may pity the simplicity of these people, pity is not the relevant attitude to what Shakespeare reveals about Cade and his kind: the animosity to learning the crude revenges, the nursery economics that expects a flow of benefits 'of the city's cost'; above all the view that the government of society is a usurping, antagonistic 'They', and when 'They' have been destroyed, there is no serious task remaining. Shakespeare is not here pleading against social injustice, nor is he recommending that it con-tinue. He is saying, with the authority of his moral and artistic insight, that this is the sort of thing that happens when power falls into the hands of those who have not been trained to bear it. Their innocence delivers them hand and foot to any adventurer with enough native wit to make the right promises and find a few appropriate sacrifices. 'Big Brother' has thrown a dark enough shadow on our own troubled century for us to be able to acknowledge the accuracy of the diagnosis. 'I will apparel them all in one livery, that they may agree like brothers, and worship me their lord.'

It is useful to look in some detail into this episode, because it answers emphatically one of the questions about power. Power may corrupt, it may be a greater responsibility than any one man is fit to bear, but it is necessary. There has to be authority, and it has to assert itself.[1] This was not just theoretical speculation. The social unrest that culminated in the Midland risings of 1607 was capable of producing its Cade at any moment, and possibly it was this disturbance that moved the Midland landowner to display such horror of the multitude in *Coriolanus*. An excessive concern for social justice is dangerous to the state, as it causes sensitive men to become confused between their

---

[1] Or else confusion predominates, as pictured by Northumberland, *2 Henry IV* I i 153–60, or in Chapman's vision of the collapse of authority in *Biron's Tragedy* I i 113–58.

generous human sympathies and their duty of allegiance to the Crown.

> . . . Liberty, that fair deceiving light,
> Turns mischief to an humour popular,
> When good men catch'd in nets of duty are.
> Greville, *Alaham* Prol. 116.

Religious zealots, exalting the search for spiritual truth above the need for social cohesion, were likewise 'catch'd in nets of duty' that made them politically dangerous. Their doctrine of parity within the religious community easily turned into an 'I'm-as-good-as-you' attitude in secular affairs. 'You must remember always that they hate Superiority,' Bishop Bancroft said of them. 'Equality, that is it which pleaseth them.' Talk of equality was a natural consequence, too, of the restless intellectualism of the age. The success of the Tudor 'new men' was an unassailable contemporary fact that ran counter to accepted notions about 'the primogenitive and due of birth' or the sanctity of degree. The existence of something like a 'career open to talent' was a heady stimulus to individualism and Machiavellian techniques of statecraft. There was a levelling spirit in the air, a scepticism that poisoned loyalty to old beliefs and found nothing to replace them. Hamlet, after philosophising on the equality that lies beyond the tomb, rounds on the Gravedigger for being so absolute. 'We must speak by the card'—precisely to the point—'or equivocation will undo us': equivocation being particularly the tricks by which Jesuits were believed to escape being pinned down in controversy, but in a more general sense the sort of hair-splitting and mental evasiveness that questions and unseats all values. 'These three years I have taken note of it,' Hamlet goes on. 'The age is grown so picked that the toe of the peasant comes so near the heel of the courtier, he galls his kibe.'

Without the exercise of power, to compel acknowledgment of law and the established instruments of government, all these disintegrating impulses will multiply and gain fresh energy. The king must bear the chief blame if he fails to restrain his subjects' potentiality for evil; or, to put it another way, if he fails, through lack of dedication or self-mastery, to release and direct their potentiality for good. It is, as always, a moral issue. There must be power, since political weakness allows men to lapse into sin and error. Henry VI acknowledged this when his comment on Cade's rebellion was simply: 'O graceless men! they know not what they do.' Greville's Sultan of Ormus, a weak and ageing ruler, reflects that all laws have lost authority through his in-competence; and in *Mustapha*, Greville's other surviving tragedy,

Acmat notes how the rule of a dotard king 'doth stain the public with ill managing', so that 'honour is laid asleep'. Authority is the earliest nurse of virtue.

> For what doth cherish weeds but gentle air?
> *3 Hen. VI* II vi 21.

VII THE LIMITS TO POWER

There must be power, but not an absolute power, free to do what it pleases. Shakespeare's two Richards are sufficient evidence of his dislike of arbitrariness, and Tudor England, at least in theory, had no use for this sort of thing:

> We are but subjects, Maximus; obedience
> To what is done, and grief for what is ill done,
> Is all we can call ours. The hearts of princes
> Are like the temples of the gods; pure incense,
> Until unhallowed hands defile those offerings,
> Burns ever there; we must not put 'em out,
> Because the priests that touch those sweets are wicked;
> We dare not, dearest friend, nay more, we cannot,
> —Whilst we consider who we are, and how,
> To what laws bound, much more to what lawgiver;
> Whilst majesty is made to be obeyed,
> And not inquir'd into; whilst gods and angels
> Make but a rule as we do, though a stricter,—
> Like desperate and unseason'd fools, let fly
> Our killing angers, and forsake our honours.
> Fletcher, *Valentinian* I iii 17.

Fletcher was a courtier poet, and *Valentinian* was written in about 1613, when sentiments were in the air that no one would have ventured to utter even ten years earlier. The play illustrates passive obedience in various excessive and unhealthy forms, and the tyrant Valentinian tells the woman he has ravished that she will cry in vain for justice.

> Justice shall never hear you; I am justice. . . .
> Know I am far above the faults I do;
> And those I do I am able to forgive too;
> And where your credit, in the knowledge of it,
> May be with gloss enough suspected, mine
> Is as mine own command shall make it: princes,
> Though they be sometime subject to loose whispers,
> Yet wear they two-edged swords for open censures:
> Your husband cannot help you, nor the soldier;

Your husband is my creature, they my weapons,
And only where I bid 'em, strike; I feed 'em:
Nor can the gods be angry at this action;
For, as they make me most, they mean me happiest.
                                    III i 41, 133.

In the sixteenth century no one really wanted to talk like this, and its occasional appearance in literature was a kind of complement to the Jack Cade episode, a picture of extreme misery that men prayed to avoid. We have to keep constantly in mind the paradox of the Tudor state, that the frequent assertions of sovereign power were made because in reality the central government was in many respects dangerously weak; and indeed was expected to be weak. Sixteenth-century discussions of power, Shakespeare's included, often seem to be using the language of modern theories of absolutism, but their real purpose was very different. The difference is that they took for granted the existence of legal and customary restraints that have largely disappeared in the highly centralised communities of the modern world.

The sixteenth century never overcame, or wanted to overcome, the strong classical and mediaeval tradition that government existed for certain specific duties and was limited by responsibility and law. It was handed down from Bracton[1] that 'the King is under no man, but he is under God and the Law'; he is under the law because it was the law that made him king. He was bound, too, to respect his subjects' sovereign humanity, to 'do them right in all things', and there should be no encroachment on conscience.[2] When Richard III bade 'Our strong arms be our conscience, our swords our law', everyone in an Elizabethan audience knew that he was branding himself as a tyrant by defying the traditional principles of Christian rule. The right principle is contained in the Duke's commission to Angelo:

Your scope is as mine own,
So to enforce or qualify the laws
As to your soul seems good:
                                    MM I i 64.

rule, that is, according to the dictates of your conscience. The same

[1] His *De Legibus et Consuetudinibus Angliae* (c. 1250) was issued in full by Richard Tottel in 1569.
[2] See *Richard III* I iv 101–64; although in practice many Tudor servants were doubtless obliged to take refuge in Brakenbury's 'I'll be guiltless of the meaning' of ambiguously-worded instructions that in fact intended the commission of a crime (I iv 94).

concern for justice and the affection of his people is illustrated in Chapman's model king, Henry IV, who would show his subjects

> how I never sought to build
> More forts for me than were within their hearts,
> Nor use more stern constraints than their good wills.[1]
> *Biron's Tragedy* III ii 45.

Henry will not execute his authority except 'by law's usual course', and he argues that subjects cannot be expected to keep faith if kings themselves prove faithless.

> If because
> We sit above the danger of the laws,
> We likewise lift our arms above their justice,
> And that our heavenly Sovereign bounds not us
> In those religious confines out of which
> Our justice and our true laws are inform'd;
> In vain have we expectance that our subjects
> Should not as well presume to offend their earthly,
> As we our heavenly Sovereign.
> V i 49.

Mediaeval tradition was so persistent that not even the Homilies gave permission for irresponsible government. They admit the occasional existence of bad rulers, whose badness lies in the very fact that they allow their own wills to supersede the law. Rebellion being, of course, a remedy worse than the disease—and even Bracton held that only God had power to punish kings—the bureaucratic authors of the Homilies could do no more than try to discourage misgovernment by dwelling on the sufferings undoubtedly endured by bad rulers in the past. The king's immunity from earthly sanctions makes more terrible his responsibility to God. It is impressive that these somewhat hysterical compilers of what today we should call 'handouts' from the central government should none the less reaffirm the supremacy of law and make no concession to tyranny. These public-relations officers were more concerned, as Shakespeare was, to protect

---

[1] Cf. *2 Henry VI* III ii 232:

> What stronger breastplate than a heart untainted!
> Thrice is he arm'd that hath his quarrel just,
> And he but naked, though lock'd up in steel,
> Whose conscience with injustice is corrupted.

The wicked Antonio admits that he has no conscience: 'I feel not this deity in my bosom' (*Tempest* II i 285); and in the Prologue to *Biron's Conspiracy* Chapman says that his play will show what happens to the state 'when men are great, not good'. See also *Bussy's Revenge* IV iii 51-72.

the whole social order than to make a particular case for monarchy.[1]
The exaggerated language of the Homilies is echoed in some of the
things said by and about Richard II. Richard declares that

> Not all the water in the rough rude sea
> Can wash the balm from an anointed king;
> The breath of worldly men cannot depose
> The deputy elected by the Lord.
> For every man that Bolingbroke hath press'd
> To lift shrewd steel against our golden crown,
> God for his Richard hath in heavenly pay
> A glorious angel.
>
> *Rich. II* III ii 54.

It is strangely ambiguous stuff, flawed by the personal weakness of
the speaker but dignified by the office that he holds. The emptiness
of these words is exposed in Carlisle's sharp reminder to Richard that
handsome is as handsome does and heaven first helps those who help
themselves. On the other hand, Richard is also speaking of something
that lies outside his personal predicament. For once he is not immediately thinking of his office as a means to indulge his private
whims (although there is something in the words by which Shakespeare would have us know that this is never far from his pettish mind:
the brash 'his Richard', perhaps); he is demanding the preservation of
the sanctified social order. This purpose comes through much more
clearly in Carlisle's speech in the abdication scene (IV i 114–49),
because here it is stated by a man who has no personal involvement
beyond his membership of the community. Carlisle is no career-
ecclesiastic: a careerist would long ago have joined the other side.
The force of his speech is that he looks beyond the immediate consequences—which Richard seldom does—to give the warning that
the violation of majesty is an act to make future ages groan. In purpose,
and even in language, his words come very close to the spirit of the
Homilies. Yet—and it is important to remember this—nothing that
he says excuses Richard. Richard has acted wantonly and unpredict-
ably, without respect for his people or the law. He is one of those bad
rulers for whom the heavens reserve their penalties.

The English constitution was dominated by the concept of the Law
of Nature, that basic, unchanging law which was the ground of
all other laws and the pattern of all justice.[2] Aquinas called it 'the

---

[1] See C. Morris, *Political Thought in England: Tyndale to Hooker*, 76–7.
[2] The idea of the Law of Nature underlies all Shakespeare's observations on
law, government and justice. It is explicit in the great debate at Troy (*TC* II ii),
where Hector 'in way of truth' says that Helen ought to be restored to the

unrevealed law of God'. It was the means by which man, in the exercise of his God-given reason, might discover God's mind and will and participate in the law that stands outside all changeableness. This law was binding on everyone who had to legislate for human societies, and Hooker even argued that it was binding on God Himself, who was at once the author of law and its voluntary subject. Human law, therefore, was merely declaratory. The business of kings and parliaments was not to make law but to say what the law is, to provide working interpretations, adapted to local and temporary needs, of the divine law that is universal and unchanging. There was no such thing as a sovereign law-making power free to enact what it pleased. Statutes that conflicted with fundamental law were not laws at all but mere declarations of policy, and they were not binding. This is well illustrated in the famous story told about More and Richard Rich. More had appealed to fundamental law in denying that a parliamentary statute could make the king supreme head of the Church, and at his trial Rich told of a conversation which he alleged had taken place between them. Rich said: 'Admit that there were an Act of Parliament that all the realm should take me, Richard Rich, for King; would not you, Master More, take me for King?' More admitted that he would, but went on to put 'a higher case; how if there were an Act of Parliament that God should not be God?' [1] It was a *reductio ad absurdum* of what, in More's view, Parliament was then engaged in doing. His conception of an eternal and unbreakable law survives today in the existence of the American High Court, which has the power to invalidate acts of the legislature deemed to be contrary to the principles of fundamental justice.

Faith in an eternal and immutable law survived the crisis of the Reformation, by which it might easily have been extinguished. It was difficult to maintain, for example, that the whole process of the Reformation in England, with its various acts of revocation and dispossession, was in accordance with the Law of Nature. In official preambles and proclamations much eloquent ingenuity was devoted to making the people believe that this had been a conservative revolution, a mere resumption by the Crown of ancient moneys, rights and privileges which the foreign Bishop had usurped. Thomas Cromwell, at least, knew differently, and from the constitutional standpoint the Reformation was an act of sovereign power. Statute had not declared

Greeks, since by 'these moral laws of nature and of nations' she is wife to Sparta's king. His orthodox exposition stands out in contrast to the over-subtle 'policy' of the Greeks or the emotional, self-centred arguments of Troilus, who sets up his will as the proper standard of action.

[1] R. W. Chambers, *Thomas More*, 337.

law, it had made it; and the logic of these proceedings was to accept the revolutionary notion that henceforth statute was omnicompetent and that law, no longer the unchanging manifestation of divine will, was whatever the sovereign King-in-Parliament said it should be.

In fact this did not immediately happen, and at any rate until the end of Shakespeare's lifetime the harmonious body politic of the mediaeval world managed to co-exist with the germ of the modern autonomous state. A continuing belief in the Law of Nature, which regulated the universe and was the inspiration of all man-made law, made it impossible to recognise any human form of sovereignty. A meeting of parliament was still an exceptional event for an exceptional occasion—there were only thirteen sessions in the forty-five years of Elizabeth's reign—and law-making of any kind was therefore rare. The functions of the Tudor state were mainly administrative. It kept order, fought the Queen's enemies, established and defended the true religion, and collected what taxes it could. It had no inclination, and no particular need, to pass new laws, and so the potentialities of the Crown-in-Parliament remained untested and undefined.[1]

Eternal law also survived the anxious period when, under the threat of rebellion and invasion, government became potentially despotic.[2] Stern measures were necessary if order and a show of unity were to be maintained, and the reformers, bringing theory to the service of necessity, produced some astonishing exaltations of monarchy. Tyndale's *Obedience of a Christian Man* declared that 'the King is in this world without law and may at his own lust do right and wrong and shall give accounts to God only', and with much emphasis being placed on scriptural texts denoting apostolic submission to the secular arm, royal rights were upheld more strenuously than for centuries past. The godly prince had the right and duty to 'command for truth', which meant to define the faith as well as to compel its decent observance.[3] An important prerogative that for centuries had belonged to the Popes was transferred to the Crown; and in the area of practical politics the Reformation brought the monarchy an enormous accession of power in jurisdiction, patronage, possessions and wealth.

But the picture of overwhelming strength may be misleading. Once the first shock of resistance had been weathered, the naturally

---

[1] G. R. Elton, *England under the Tudors*, 398–404.

[2] See above, p. 33.

[3] This was not just a form of words. It explains Cranmer's changes of belief under successive monarchs and his final (although retracted) submission to Mary. Cranmer was neither a time-server nor a faint-heart. He was an orthodox and consistent upholder of the Tudor theory of society.

disintegrating tendencies of Protestantism began to weaken the sudden and alarming power of Henry VIII's unitary state. This power had always been qualified by the explicit assumption that in defining the truth the Crown must be obedient to God's word: which was merely to reassert the old supremacy of fundamental law in a slightly different form. It only needed a ruler who was ungodly (Mary), or insufficiently enthusiastic (Elizabeth), for the appeal to the prince to be replaced by an appeal to private conscience against the prince proved to be unworthy. Only in its initial stages, or in very small communities where there was no opposition, was Protestantism despotic. Ultimately, by its very nature and origins, it demanded freedom of conscience. Theories of resistance developed all over Europe and either won considerable concessions or provoked authority into gestures of repression that could not be sustained. In Shakespeare's England Protestantism worked in the long run for the weakening of the prerogative. While it undoubtedly stimulated the doctrine of non-resistance, and enjoined passive submission to public injuries, it did not offer much encouragement to active co-operation. Paradoxically, the spread of non-resistance enlarged the area reserved for private conscience, the area where authority might command but need not be obeyed.

If for a few critical years the emergency measures of the Reformation did overlie the supremacy of law, it was only a temporary interference with an age-long tradition that quickly reasserted itself. The true purpose of the reformers was to evolve a proper theory of church government: a theory of the state, as such, was not a thing they knew about,[1] and the emergence of the sovereign law-making state was delayed until long after Shakespeare's death. The religious faith that demanded obedience to the godly ruler was an implied attack on rulers who held different beliefs, and this ensured that the impregnability of conscience, and in extreme cases the right to resist,[2] should develop side by side with any tendencies towards absolutism. Where royal absolutism did eventually prevail, as in France, this was through the previous collapse of public order. But nothing of the kind happened in Tudor England, where Bodin's tentative sovereignty and the ideas of Roman jurisprudence never took root. The constitutional quarrel of the seventeenth century followed the specialisation of theories that had earlier been complementary, but in this does not concern us here. When Shakespeare debated questions of power, he accepted his age's

[1] C. Morris, *Political Thought in England*, 40–7.
[2] In England this was chiefly maintained by Catholic writers like Parsons, but it did have its Protestant advocates, notably Knox, Buchanan and Ponet.

belief in the mysteries of birth and royalty, but he equally assumed the limitation of authority by law and conscience.

> Dear friend, we must not be more true to kings,
> Than kings are to their subjects.
>> Chapman, *Biron's Tragedy* III i 1.

VIII. WHERE THE ANTIC SITS

The discussion of power becomes finally a discussion of individual worth. Ultimately a society will be good or bad as the people who compose it are good or bad, and Shakespeare's drama sometimes shows how occasions may conspire to destroy a ruler who to the limits of his responsibility has been honourable and efficient: it is not within the scope of princes to command success. But there comes a time when all political philosophy turns from theorising about the community to examine the intimate and crucial question of the individual exercise of power. At this point the general enquiry into the moral nature of man —and all political philosophy is that—narrows itself into a special enquiry into the moral nature of the ruler. It may well be, too, that at this point the enquiry comes to the highest peak of value and interest, for many of the noblest and most enduring theories of society—like Shakespeare's own, or Hooker's or Augustine's, or Plato's in *The Republic*—have been incidental offshoots of larger speculations about man and his relation to the universe.[1] The dehumanised history that became fashionable in the nineteenth century wrote of man as a creature blindly acted upon by various external 'forces', scientific, economic, ethnic, and so forth, all of them impersonal and irresistible. The laws of mechanistic science were thought to operate in human affairs, and for a while history and sociology ceased to be written in the light of the historian's own notions about human nature and the world in which he lived. But with Shakespeare we are back in an age which believed a man's social relations to be, next to his relations with God, the most important thing about him; which, in fact, found the value of the state in the value of the individual. A man was most intensely himself when moving and acting in society; and to the eye of a poet, public life might be only a symbol of the private life, an enquiry into government merely a way of describing a man's efforts to order his own nature.[2] What power does to a man, and what a

---

[1] C. Morris, *Political Thought in England*, 3.
[2] See Rebecca West, *The Court and the Castle*, 57, 69-70.

man does with power, were for Shakespeare the natural conclusion of
his investigation of society and the state.

> No man's worth can be justly judged
> But when he shines in some authority. . . .
> Great vessels into less are emptied never.
>   Chapman, *Bussy's Revenge* II i 142.

As Ulysses said,

> No man is the lord of any thing
> —Though in and of him there be much consisting—
> Till he communicate his parts to others:
> Nor doth he of himself know them for aught
> Till he behold them form'd in the applause
> Where they're extended.
>   *TC* III iii 115.

It is only in society, where his deeds are reflected in the response of
other people, that a man can discover his true worth.[1]

When Shakespeare contemplated power, there were times when it
frightened him so much that he could not believe that anyone was
either fit to hold it or virtuous enough to resist its corrosion. Many
passages in his work seem to show him bitterly mistrustful of authority.
The three so-called 'problem' comedies all question the wisdom and
justice of the leaders of the people;[2] in *Timon* society itself dis-
integrates,[3] in *Coriolanus* soldier-hero, senators, tribunes and people
have all lost understanding of brotherhood and degree. Shakespeare
hated beadledom, the insolence of office, the self-assertiveness of 'every
pelting, petty officer' and small-time bureaucrat, and Lear's 'great
image of authority' is a terrible indictment:

> A dog's obeyed in office.
> Thou rascal beadle, hold thy bloody hand!
> Why dost thou lash that whore? Strip thine own back;
> Thou hotly lust'st to use her in that kind
> For which thou whipp'st her. The usurer hangs the cozener.
> Through tatter'd clothes small vices do appear;
> Robes and furr'd gowns hide all. Plate sin with gold,
> And the strong lance of justice hurtless breaks;

---

[1] Cf. *AWW* II iii 132–48, especially 142–4: a man's true honour is derived
from his virtuous acts in society.

[2] E.g. *MM* II ii 117–22.

[3]   The learned pate
> Ducks to the golden fool: all is oblique;
> There's nothing level in our cursed natures
> But direct villainy.   IV iii 17.

Arm it in rags, a pigmy's straw doth pierce it. . . .
                    Get thee glass eyes;
And, like a scurvy politician, seem
To see the things thou dost not.
                                        Lear IV vi 164.

It is to this that Commodity may come, and the strange prologue to *Henry VIII*, Shakespeare's final play, seems to indicate a crowning disillusion with political life. It was a festival play, written for the celebrations at the wedding of James I's daughter to the Elector Palatine, and true to the spirit of such an occasion it glorified England through Henry and the infant Elizabeth. But it has unmistakably pessimistic undertones, and although Henry himself escapes censure, the people near to him—Buckingham, Wolsey, Queen Katharine, Anne Bullen—are all victims of public necessity. Anne sadly concludes that

'tis better to be lowly born,
And range with humble livers in content,
Than to be perk'd up in a glist'ring grief
And wear a golden sorrow.
                                    II iii 19.

The Prologue warns the audience of the heavy theme.

I come no more to make you laugh: things now,
That bear a weighty and a serious brow,
Sad, high, and working, full of state and woe,
Such noble scenes as draw the eye to flow,
We now present. Those that can pity, here
May, if they think it well, let fall a tear;
The subject will deserve it. . . .
                            Think ye see
The very persons of our noble story
As they were living; think you see them great,
And follow'd with the general throng and sweat
Of thousand friends; then, in a moment see
How soon this mightiness meets misery:
And if you can be merry then, I'll say
A man may weep upon his wedding day.
                                    Prol. 1, 25.

Power, at best, is a grievous burden, its glitter tarnished by a sense of personal inadequacy, and the figure of the puny ruler weighed down by responsibility is a dominant symbol of the history plays. 'The milkmaid's lot is better than mine, and her life merrier,' Elizabeth is reported to have said when rusticating at Woodstock, and the presumed desirability of the 'life exempt from public haunt' inspired the fashion for pastoral which is always liable to be the self-indulgence of busy minds. Even in *Richard III*, a play whose theme is the concentrated pursuit of power, the choric Brakenbury reflects upon the anxieties of public life as he watches over Clarence, his sleeping prisoner.

> Sorrow breaks seasons and reposing hours,
> Makes the night morning, and the noon-tide night.
> Princes have but titles for their glories,
> An outward honour for an inward toil;
> And, for unfelt imaginations,
> They often feel a world of restless cares:
> So that, between their titles and low names,
> There's nothing differs but the outward fame.
>> *Rich. III* I iv 76.

It is the plaint of Henry VI at Towton, when the hawthorn bush gives

> a sweeter shade
> To shepherds, looking on their silly sheep,
> Than doth a rich embroider'd canopy
> To kings, that fear their subjects' treachery.
>> *3 Hen. VI* II v 42.

Henry IV, mocked by the chances which fill the cup of alteration with divers liquors, leaves his son a crown that is only a golden care and polish'd perturbation; and this same son, a man truly dedicated to his kingly responsibility, has his hour of doubt and bitterness when he knows

> what infinite heart's ease
> Must kings neglect that private men enjoy!
> And what have kings that privates have not too,
> Save ceremony, save general ceremony?
> And what art thou, thou idol ceremony?
> What kind of god art thou, that suffer'st more
> Of mortal griefs than do thy worshippers?
> What are thy rents? what are thy comings-in?
> O ceremony! show me but thy worth:
> What is thy soul of adoration?
> Art thou aught else but place, degree, and form,
> Creating awe and fear in other men?
>> *Hen. V* IV i 256.

But for ceremony, the peasant, following the ever-running year with profitable labour, is happier than his master, and he never knows 'what watch the king keeps to maintain the peace'.[1] In very similar words

[1] This is a recurrent theme in Shakespeare, cf. Henry IV on sleeplessness (Part Two III i 4–31), or Richard II's plangent dissertation on the sad fate of kings (III ii 144–77).

Richelieu, who was a true Machiavellian in his conscious artistry of power, warned Louis XIII in his *Political Testament* that rulers must 'sleep like the lion, without closing our eyes'. They will be deprived of all rest and contentment, 'except that which they receive in seeing many sleep quietly, relying on their watchings'.

> He should be born grey-headed that will bear
> The sword of empire.
> Chapman, *Biron's Tragedy* IV ii 72.

It is, Henry V reflects, the hard condition of monarchs that, 'twin-born with greatness', they are subject to the breath of every fool who is conscious of nothing but his own wants and sufferings. Shakespeare was aware of the paradox that kings, on whom so heavy a responsibility lies, are not exempt from the pains and errors of fallen humanity. Will itself, by which the best men aspire to the condition of God, is a part of our corrupted nature, and we are all of us, kings and subjects, members of an imperfect society in whose evils we necessarily participate. The hand that reaches for responsibility is only mortal, and it is the irony of power that the man whose duty is to rule the state is himself tainted with the weaknesses of those he has to govern. Thus power, whose best reward may be only the delusive glitter of the idol ceremony, is at worst an evil that may destroy the man who wields it. Its lusts and temptations are potent enough to change a man's character and purpose. It may find him weaker and wickeder than he would have been if he had never borne it. 'It is the bright day that brings forth the adder.' What moved Brutus to join the Roman conspiracy was his fear that power would corrupt a nature of which himself he knew nothing but good. He admits he has 'no personal cause' to spurn at Caesar, nor ever knew the time 'when his affections sway'd more than his reason'. But

> He would be crown'd:
> How that might change his nature, there's the question. . . .
> Crown him?—that!
> And then, I grant, we put a sting in him,
> That at his will he may do danger with.
> *JC* II i 12.

Although he never puts his thoughts into precise terms, the opening scene of *Measure for Measure* similarly leaves no doubt that the Duke expects power to have a destructive effect on the character of the virtuous and disciplined Angelo.

> Thou art, if thou dar'st be, the earthly Jove:
> Whate'er the ocean pales, or sky inclips,
> Is thine, if thou wilt ha't.
>
> *AC* II vii 74.

Such is the vision of the glory of the world, and Shakespeare knew how seductive and solid-seeming it could be. In the opening scene of the second part of *Henry VI*—which conceivably could have been the first scene he ever wrote for the theatre—York speaks of the crown as 'the golden mark I seek to hit', and his own son reminds him, a little later,

> How sweet a thing it is to wear a crown,
> Within whose circuit is Elysium,
> And all that poets feign of bliss and joy.
>
> *3 Hen. VI* I ii 29.

Shakespeare never denied this fascination, and he may even, in his active imagination, have experienced it. Scornful as he is of ceremony, and knowing that 'the world is still deceived with ornament', he will always let his verse take wing when he writes of the panoply of power. The richness of these evocations altogether exceeds the visual requirements of his theatre, where admittedly the gorgeousness of festival, processions and obeisances was one of the few concessions made to the spectator's eye. (Was it not one of these spectacular occasions that caused the destruction of the original Globe?) There is more than dramatic necessity in such lines as these:

> Know'st thou not
> That when the searching eye of heaven is hid
> Behind the globe, and lights the lower world,
> Then thieves and robbers range abroad unseen,
> In murders and in outrage bloody here;
> But when, from under this terrestrial ball,
> He fires the proud tops of the eastern pines,
> And darts his light through every guilty hole,
> Then murders, treasons, and detested sins,
> The cloak of night being pluck'd from off their backs,
> Stand bare and naked, trembling at themselves?
>
> *Rich. II* III ii 36.

Poetically, of course, these are not particularly good lines. They merely elaborate the well-known king-sun correspondence, and rhetoric blurs the effect with something of Richard's own uncertainty. But there is no mistaking the assertion of royalty, of the grandeur and potentiality of power; almost, one might say, its divine mission.

It is all the worse, then, when power betrays the holder.

> The abuse of greatness is when it disjoins
> Remorse from power:
>
> *JC* II i 18.

when, that is, a king slips the restraints of law and conscience and uses his strength to indulge the very human emotions of pride, revenge and callousness. This same Richard shows a sensual relish of power for its own sake—in his sour, impatient jesting with the dying Gaunt or the almost lascivious rhythm of the lines in which he announces Mowbray's banishment:

> The sly slow hours shall not determinate
> The dateless limit of thy dear exile.
> *Rich. II* I iii 150.

Malice here jostles with a poet's gift; and with four years suddenly remitted from his own punishment, Bolingbroke presently remarks upon this intoxicating sovereignty.

> How long a time lies in one little word!
> Four lagging winters and four wanton springs
> End in a word: such is the breath of kings.
> I iii 213.

With time this bright capriciousness stales into the weary routine of evasiveness and corruption that is Commodity's daily bread; into a spurious conception of 'order' that, as in Menenius's homily to the Citizens (*Coriolanus* I i 101–52) or even in certain aspects of the famous speech of Ulysses, represents the determination of the propertied classes to preserve the existing structure of society in their own interest. Fuller than any of Shakespeare's expositions of greatness disjoined from humanity is the picture of brazen amorality given by Ben Jonson in *Sejanus*. The soliloquy of the time-serving Macro is worth quoting in full, as it is the ultimate of political cynicism and Machiavellian statecraft.

> I will not ask why Caesar bids do this;
> But joy that he bids me. It is the bliss
> Of courts to be employ'd, no matter how;
> A prince's power makes all his actions virtue.
> We, whom he works by, are dumb instruments,
> To do, but not inquire: his great intents
> Are to be served, not search'd. Yet, as that bow
> Is most in hand, whose owner best doth know
> To affect his aims; so let that statesman hope
> Most use, most price, can hit his prince's scope.
> Nor must he look at what, or whom, to strike,
> But loose at all; each mark must be alike.

Were it to plot against the fame, the life
Of one with whom I twinn'd; remove a wife
From my warm side, as loved as is the air;
Practise away each parent; draw mine heir
In compass, though but one; work all my kin
To swift perdition; leave no untrain'd engine,
For friendship, or for innocence; nay, make
The gods all guilty; I would undertake
This, being imposed me, both with gain and ease:
The way to rise is to obey and please.
He that will thrive in state, he must neglect
The trodden paths that truth and right respect;
And prove new, wilder ways: for virtue there
Is not that narrow thing she is elsewhere;
Men's fortune there is virtue; reason their will;
Their licence, law; and their observance, skill.
Occasion is their foil; conscience, their stain;
Profit, their lustre; and what else is, vain.
If then it be the lust of Caesar's power,
To have raised Sejanus up, and in an hour
O'erturn him, tumbling down, from height of all;
We are his ready engine: and his fall
May be our rise. It is no uncouth thing
To see fresh buildings from old ruins spring.

> Jonson, *Sejanus* III iii 96.

Here, made explicit—too explicit for Shakespeare's inclination: the speech is undramatic—is the morality of all those Shakespearean characters for whom power was simply an object in itself. Shakespeare had no illusions about the dangers and corruptions of political life. He feared, like Bacon, that 'all rising to great place is by a winding stair', and he could wonder whether in mortality there was any virtuous enough to carry such dreadful responsibility. What is to stop men abusing their authority? What, save force, will induce them to obey? Royal caprice (like the obsessive folly of Leontes), or aristocratic intrigue, or 'the yea and no of general ignorance' may at any time destroy society, and Shakespeare's artistic detachment was fascinated— just as his pity was aroused—by the spectacle of ordinary men drawn by destiny into great events. Power brings little happiness, and for any man who is not innately gifted it is tragic to be called to high responsibilities. Even ambition, which Shakespeare regarded as the indispensable driving-force in public life, may dissolve into illusion, 'for the very substance of the ambitious is merely the shadow of a dream ... of so airy and light a quality that it is but a shadow's shadow'.[1] Or, if it should be crowned with wordly success, it will

---

[1] *Hamlet* II ii 267.

probably be at the expense of the individual's virtue. We seem to be led inescapably to Imogen's sad conclusion:

> Most miserable
> Is the desire that's glorious: bless'd be those,
> How mean so'er, that have their honest wills,
> Which seasons comfort:
> > *Cymb.* I vi 6.

or to the agony of the man who beyond any other in these plays found royalty precious, its cates as well as its sacred essence:

> Within the hollow crown
> That rounds the mortal temples of a king
> Keeps Death his court, and there the antic sits,
> Scoffing his state and grinning at his pomp;
> Allowing him a breath, a little scene,
> To monarchise, be fear'd, and kill with looks,
> Infusing him with self and vain conceit,
> As if this flesh which walls about our life
> Were brass impregnable; and humour'd thus
> Comes at the last, and with a little pin
> Bores through his castle wall, and farewell king!
> > *Rich. II* III ii 160.

IX. LOVE STANDS HUGELY POLITIC

Shakespeare's misgivings about power, which in some moods he saw only as a siren calling men to misery and self-betrayal, reflect his steady awareness of the darker aspects of human nature. A heroic tradition of historical writing could not, any more than the romantic convention that he inherited in comedy, prevent him from looking on men as they usually are. But these anxieties do at the same time suggest that power is a trust so precious that its betrayal is as much a tragedy for the individual as for the society that is involved in his ruin. Shakespeare would have understood the sentiment of Greville's character who thought that 'faults to the state all other faults exceed';[1] just as service of the state exceeds all other virtues. Power is a means, possibly the highest of all means, to self-perfection.

So through the kings and statesmen who crowd the histories Shakespeare searches for the ideal public figure: the man, himself uncorrupted by power, who is the ruler of a healthy, harmonious society. It is a composite portrait, for the total requirements are not to be found in any single man. Talbot, the brave, single-minded soldier, is

[1] *Alaham* I i 208.

a political innocent; so too is Humphrey of Gloucester, who cannot even prevent intrigue and self-delusion within his own family. These two are helpless in the jungle. York, a man not without a patriotic vision of a strong and united country, has a necessary will to power but he is a rebel and violent and ruthless in his methods. He is an early sketch of Richard III, the archetypal tyrant who cares only for the getting and keeping of power and is indifferent to the use he might make of it. The mild and saintly Henry VI lacks the qualities that his situation needs. A distant love of humanity is not, in his England, a substitute for leadership, and he has the fatal defect of being afraid of power. In the first tetralogy we must not forget the strange figure of Cade, a political 'irregular' who, despite his ignorance and irresponsibility, has the common touch and knows that a warm heart is an essential ingredient in a good society. In *King John*, where John himself is regal only when he is defying the Pope, the idea of royalty is momentarily embodied by a man for whom Commodity has been the mainspring of political life. Richard II's exalted sense of office is diminished by his inadequacy in meeting its obligations; while Henry IV, sober, tenacious and desperately conscious of his responsibilities, is never allowed to forget the base means by which he won his crown, and his notion of statesmanship is therefore a series of Machiavellian expedients.

In Henry V we find most of the right qualities. He is a natural leader, brave, disciplined and dedicated, neither greedy for power nor frightened of it. But he is not perfect. Even without looking too closely behind the bright façade, we sense something lacking in this too-flawless man. Perhaps it is Henry VI's real feeling of kinship with the peasant; or Cade's uninhibited vitality; or the limitless human understanding possessed by the Falstaff whom he banished. Shakespeare's final conception of the public figure demanded qualities to which all these men contributed: Henry V's leadership and dedication, his father's anxious stewardship, the personal piety of Henry VI, the uncomplicated patriotism of Faulconbridge, Richard II's intuitive grasp of the mystical element in kingship, Richard III's driving-force, even perhaps the earthiness of Cade. From this composite figure there emerges a vision of power rightly held and rightly administered that tells us what Shakespeare believed majesty to be. Power does not necessarily corrupt. Restrained by law and private conscience, it enriches its possessor and those who are bound to serve it. When Carlyle wrote a hundred years ago that 'liberty requires new definitions', he was really looking back to older definitions, to the classical and mediaeval heritage of an ordered freedom that was the basis of Shakespeare's political thought. Burke, writing on the eve of the revolutionary age in Europe, insisted that the state was something more than 'a partnership agreement in a trade of pepper and coffee, calico or tobacco . . . it is not a partnership in things subservient only to the gross animal existence of a temporary and perishable nature'. In revolt against the egalitarian dogmas of their time, Carlyle and Matthew Arnold were even more positive than he. Carlyle preached that our higher selves want to be guided by the best that the greatest men can show us, and so we should ask to be led by heroes, for that is in itself a heroic thing to do. Arnold said that *culture*, the best that has been thought and said about mankind, should be allowed to set a standard in public life; the alternative being *anarchy*, or a chaos of individual wills, passions and interests. Culture is a standard of authority outside and above ourselves, an assertion of our collective right reason and our higher will to be ruled for the betterment of society and ourselves.[1] But what are this right reason and higher will if not that God-given disposition to virtue which Hooker and Shakespeare knew as the Law of Nature? Between Elizabethan and Victorian there is a vast difference in the context and in the terms employed, but the doctrine is essentially the same. Wise authority is a means to the realisation of what is best in us.

So one of the first things Shakespeare teaches us about power is that we should not belittle it. It is an enormous admission when we remember how often he portrayed the misery that follows upon its abuse, and the condition of its exercise is, of course, that the ruler shall first be master of himself, able to harness not only his political ambition but also the passions, such as jealousy, lust and vengefulness, that might deflect him from his duty to the state. Othello cannot govern Cyprus if he cannot govern himself; Angelo, Leontes, Macbeth, Antony, Lear (whose fault was that 'he hath ever but slenderly known himself') all undermine their service of the state with personal weaknesses more proper to lesser men, and other examples can be found among Shakespeare's English kings. Angelo, who was to fail under the test, significantly asked for further trial of his self-control to be made before he was entrusted with power.

> Let there be some more test made of my metal,
> Before so noble and so great a figure
> Be stamp'd upon it.
>
> *MM* I i 48.

---

[1] Cf. Lord Radcliffe, *The Problem of Power*, 113–17.

The request did him credit, for at least he recognised that rulers are men sorely tried, and if this knowledge does not excuse his later fault, it may make us more sympathetic to it. Here was a man who realised how deeply he had failed.

The importance attached by Renaissance writers to self-mastery is evident from their preoccupation with nurture, the training necessary for public life. In the drama a striking example is the anonymous *Edward III*,[1] and the two parts of Shakespeare's *Henry IV* describe the apprenticeship of the future Henry V in the discipline of his office. But granted this self-control, there is nothing dishonourable in the pursuit of power. Ambition, rightly directed, was a steely virtue which Shakespeare regarded as necessary for the sort of ruler he admired. Politics is not an occupation for the over-scrupulous or the chicken-hearted, and when the alternative to strong government is the probable disintegration of society, there is no place on the throne (always saving his title) for a monk *manqué* like Henry VI. Men like Brutus, who want to be gentlemen, should not try to be statesmen, for, as 'Trimmer' Halifax observed, 'State business is a cruel trade; good nature is a bungler in it.' Within the limits of law, power has its own special morality. This is not a permission for Machiavellian deceits and ruthlessness, although the distinction is obviously fine-drawn: which is why it is so important that virtuous men should have power, and that those who have power should be virtuous. But it does acknowledge the simple truth that kings and subjects are required by their function to have different values.

> Power hath great scope; she walks not in the ways
> Of private truth: virtues of common men
> Are not the same which shine in kings above.
> Greville, *Mustapha* I ii 5.

At Southampton Henry V has to put to death a dear friend whose ingratitude and betrayal he might as a private individual have pardoned. The fault against the state all private faults exceeds:

> Touching our person seek we no revenge;
> But we our kingdom's safety must so tender,
> Whose ruin you have sought, that to her laws
> We do deliver you.
> *Hen. V* II ii 174.

To refuse this kind of kingly duty is unheroic and disastrous. It only leads to misrule and rebellion, until the ensuing anarchy is ended by

---

[1] See above, pp. 85–7.

the sort of Machiavellian statesmanship that is ruthless without being scrupulous. Shakespeare has only contempt for men who refuse power when they are called to it or fail to guard it with all their sinews. It is a French prince who reminds his sovereign that

> Self-love, my liege, is not so vile a sin
> As self-neglecting.
> *Hen. V* II iv 74.

Richard II is justly rebuked for cushioning himself upon the angels (III ii 178 sq.), and the Duke tells Angelo that those who have political capacity must be ready to use it:

> Thyself and thy belongings
> Are not thine own so proper, as to waste
> Thyself upon thy virtues, they on thee.
> *MM I* i 29.

But this admonition comes ill from a man who confesses that he has himself 'ever loved the life remov'd' and has allowed his city's laws to sleep for fourteen years. Even Prospero is implicitly censured for

> neglecting wordly ends, all dedicated
> To closeness and the bettering of my mind,
> *Temp.* I ii 89.

and Shakespeare suggests that these withdrawn and precious spirits are, in their contrasted way, just as much individualists, and so just as culpable politically, as men of violence like Richard III. Henry VI, who is one of them, cannot understand why his people do not love him.

> My need hath got me fame:
> I have not stopp'd mine ears to their demands,
> Nor posted off their suits with slow delays;
> My pity hath been balm to heal their wounds,
> My mildness hath allay'd their swelling griefs,
> My mercy dried their water-flowing tears;
> I have not been desirous of their wealth;
> Nor much oppress'd them with great subsidies,
> Nor forward of revenge, though they much err'd.
> Then why should they love Edward more than me?
> *3 Hen. VI* IV viii 38.

It is an excellent thing to fear and honour God, but it avails little to fear God if one is frightened of everything else. Henry's inward-looking piety was disastrous for the nation, and the weak man's refusal is terribly indicted by the dying Clifford.

O Phoebus! hadst thou never given consent
That Phaethon should check thy fiery steeds,
Thy burning car never had scorch'd the earth;
And, Henry, hadst thou sway'd as kings should do
Or as thy father and his father did,
Giving no ground unto the house of York,
They never then had sprung like summer flies;
I and ten thousand in this luckless realm
Had left no mourning widows for our death,
And thou this day hadst kept thy chair in peace.
For what doth cherish weeds but gentle air?
And what makes robbers bold but too much lenity?
3 Hen. VI II vi 11.

A second requirement of the good ruler is patriotism. From brave Talbot down to the final affirmation of England's destiny at the close of *Henry VIII*, pride of country is never far absent from Shakespeare's thoughts. The great Marquess of Halifax lived in the last exhausting days of a struggle that had substantially altered men's conception of monarchy and the value of government generally. By that time Selden had observed that 'Never king dropped out of the clouds. A king is a thing men have made for their own selves, for quietness' sake, just as in a family one man is appointed to buy the meat': a view that is something less than Shakespearean. Halifax too lived in a disenchanted world where few are good and few are wise. 'As mankind is made, the keeping it in order is an ill-natured office', he wrote; and his conclusion was that 'the Government of the world is a great thing, but it is a very coarse one too, compared with the Fineness of Speculative Knowledge'. But his detached and cynical mind was warmed by a passion for liberty ('the only seasoning that giveth a relish to life') and a passion for his country. Shakespeare would not have wished to write anything finer than the Trimmer's confession that he is free of all idolatry, excepting only that 'his country is in some degree his Idol; he doth not worship the Sun, because it is not peculiar to us, it rambles about the world and is less hard to us than others; but for the Earth of England, tho' perhaps inferior to that of many places abroad, to him there is Divinity in it, and he would rather die than see a spire of English grass trampled down by a Foreign Trespasser'.

Shakespeare's patriotism often has the same air of deprecatory boasting, the same half-mocking seriousness. We will not apologise 'for wearing our own noses', and the Gravedigger is allowed to establish the English quiddity by laughing at it.[1] It is only our deepest

---

[1] Cf. *Tempest* II ii 29–34, *Merchant of Venice* I ii 72–81.

and most cherished emotions that can be brought to the test of this sort of laughter, and Shakespeare teaches that love of country, as an instinctive and overwhelming feeling that in the final analysis has little to do with safety or expediency, must burn fiercely in nations that would keep their strength. There is a primitive strain in the histories that simply exalts the acts of Giant Albion.

> I' the world's volume
> Our Britain seems as of it, but not in 't:
> In a great pool, a swan's nest.
> *Cymb.* III iv 140.

Gaunt's great speech and the Bastard's apostrophe at the end of *King John* have become ossified as anthologised set-pieces, but Shakespeare's patriotism turns up in less expected places. The cruelty of their banishment is that it deprives Mowbray and Bolingbroke of English air, and there is small consolation in Gaunt's kindly suggestion that

> All places that the eye of heaven visits
> Are to a wise man ports and happy havens.
> *Rich. II* I iii 275.

In Richard himself it is hard to distinguish true feeling from affectation, but there does seem to be a redeeming sincerity in his tears of joy

> To stand upon my kingdom once again.
> Dear earth, I do salute thee with my hand,
> Though rebels wound thee with their horses' hoofs;
> III ii 5.

or, again, in his apprehension of England's suffering when Bolingbroke comes to open 'the purple testament of bleeding war':

> Ten thousand bloody crowns of mothers' sons
> Shall ill become the flower of England's face,
> Change the complexion of her maid-pale peace
> To scarlet indignation, and bedew
> Her pastures' grass with faithful English blood.
> III iii 96.

We even have to admire Richard III when in a hopeless hour he finds the noonday courage to rally his troops to 'lash hence these over-weening rags of France'.

> If we be conquer'd, let men conquer us,
> And not these bastard Bretons; whom our fathers
> Have in their own land beaten, bobb'd, and thump'd.
> *Rich. III* V iii 333.

Spirit of this kind is a necessary sinew of statesmanship, and it often amuses Shakespeare to see its reflection in the eyes of England's enemies: as in the deluded over-confidence that pervades the French camp before Agincourt or in Chatillon's tribute to

> all the unsettled humours of the land,
> Rash, inconsiderate, fiery voluntaries,
> With ladies' faces and fierce dragons' spleens,
> Have sold their fortunes at their native homes,
> Bearing their birthrights proudly on their backs,
> To make a hazard of new fortunes here.
> In brief, a braver choice of dauntless spirits
> Than now the English bottoms have waft o'er
> Did never float upon the swelling tide,
> To do offence and scathe in Christendom.
>
> *KJ* II i 66.

Shakespeare's passion rises far above contemporary Elizabethan anxieties when he writes of

> that pale, that white-fac'd shore,
> Whose foot spurns back the ocean's roaring tides
> And coops from other lands her islanders. . . .
> That water-walled bulwark, still secure
> And confident from foreign purposes.
>
> *KJ* II i 23.

Of any man who holds office there he demanded leadership worthy of a people whose

> discipline
> —Now winged—with their courage will make known
> To their approvers they are people such
> That mend upon the world.
>
> *Cymb.* II iv 23.

Thirdly, Shakespeare demanded of the ruler dedication. He recognised what was due from kings, who must understand the sources of their power and the nature of their responsibility. But it is not enough that they should simply acknowledge moral right as the only basis of their power. Power is itself a privilege so tremendous that it demands the sacrifice of everything else, and the ruler has to sink himself in his office.

> While these do labour for their own preferment,
> Behoves it us to labour for the realm.
>
> *2 Hen. VI* I i 182.

Authority is first, as Bacon described it, 'the vantage and commanding ground' for doing good: a compulsion acknowledged, for instance, by Henry IV in his unavailing determination to lead a crusade. When the ruler is so minded, he can then, and only then, establish a proper relationship with his subjects. The due of obedience becomes an act of co-operation, and membership of the community avoids the twin evils of ill-governed states, on the one hand a blind submission that surrenders personal responsibility, on the other a restless dissatisfaction that shows itself in a foolish resentment of authority and a desire to opt out of society. The people are only the image of those who govern them.

> We are the glass of power, and do reflect
> That image back, which it to us presents:
> Greville, *Alaham* Fourth Chorus 43.

so that the cease of majesty dies not alone. The emphasis, therefore, is on service, and Shakespeare, like Plato, contemplates the ruler as a man who assumes the burden he has not sought, simply because his duty compels him to it. Shakespeare is ambiguous about Bolingbroke's motives and he seems quite deliberately to leave the character opaque. But if we accept the man's own subsequent account of his actions ('Necessity so bow'd the state That I and greatness were compelled to kiss'), we have a not ignoble picture of one who took power because a disintegrating society needed him.

When we look at the contrasted characters of Henry V and Coriolanus, both dedicated men, we realise that what Shakespeare's ideal of service supremely requires is the repudiation of pride, and in particular the sort of pride that denies our common humanity. Coriolanus has a noble and disinterested conception of service. This and associated words are often on his lips, or others use them when they speak of him, and it is clear that his quest for power is never selfish. His deeds are sufficiently rewarded in the doing of them; nor does he desire praise and thanks for carrying out his simple duty.

> He had rather venture all his limbs for honour,
> Than one on's ears to hear it.
> *Cor.* II ii 85.

If courage is the greatest virtue, then, Cominius says, this Caius Marcius 'cannot in the world be singly counterpois'd'. The quality of his courage, and the sheer animal force of his leadership, shine in the account which Cominius gives of his military apprenticeship and astonishing deeds at Corioli (II ii 87–127).

Here we seem to have the very pattern of a hero. He is brave, he

C.M.—L

exercises a natural authority, he wants no higher privilege than to serve the state, and he has the thrust for power which men need if they are to realise their potentiality. But it early proves to be a cold and lonely virtue. Coriolanus lacks a dimension.

> Know, Rome, that all alone Marcius did fight
> Within Corioli gates.
>
> II i 181.

It is characteristic; and it is evident from the report given by Cominius that this was very much a one-man victory. He was a man who would breach the walls to make a gap for his men to enter; but except in so far as all great deeds are inspiring by example, his was not the sort of courage that breeds courage in others. His leadership is wanting in all that is evoked in the mind by 'a little touch of Harry in the night'. He speaks of his soldiers as 'boils and plagues . . . you souls of geese, that bear the shapes of men', and this disdainfulness, a bad enough defect in a general, is fatal to him when he is called upon to make the daily face-saving compromises of a political career. Shakespeare took Plutarch's hint that Coriolanus was a man of 'haughty stomach', so coldly distant that the Romans 'could not be acquainted with him, as one citizen useth to be with another in the city'. He is too proud to ask the 'bisson multitude' for their love and trust, for he assumes that they are his right by virtue of his deeds. Even his ideal of service, which is his noblest quality, is flawed by the presumption that service is something that only the chosen few can render. 'What do you prate of service?' he says contemptuously to the tribune Brutus. He exhibits a kindless self-sufficiency,

> As if a man were author of himself
> And knew no other kin,
>
> V iii 36.

that for all his splendid gifts marks him as a man unfit to rule.

Both his greatness and his failure are analysed by his enemy Aufidius.

> I think he'll be to Rome
> As is the osprey to the fish, who takes it
> By sovereignty of nature. First he was
> A noble servant to them, but he could not
> Carry his honours even; whether 'twas pride,
> Which out of daily fortune ever taints
> The happy man; whether defect of judgment,
> To fail in the disposing of those chances
> Which he was lord of; or whether nature,

Not to be other than one thing, not moving
From the casque to the cushion, but commanding peace
Even with the same austerity and garb
As he controll'd the war; but one of these,
As he hath spices of them all, not all,
For I dare so far free him, made him fear'd,
So hated, and so banish'd: but he has a merit
To choke it in the utterance.

IV vii 33.

Academically, Coriolanus is right to insist upon a single unified authority.

When two authorities are up,
Neither supreme, how soon confusion
May enter 'twixt the gap of both and take
The one by the other.[1]

III i 108.

If the rabble were to seize power, this would only 'throw forth greater themes for insurrection's arguing'. But patrician upbringing and an unstable temperament have perverted his values, and he looks upon the people merely as 'things created to buy and sell with groats'. He thinks he needs a 'harlot's spirit' to beg their vulgar wisdoms for support, and when at length he does agree to address them, his stiff and cliché-ridden utterance betrays his discomfort.

The honour'd gods
Keep Rome in safety, and the chairs of justice
Supplied with worthy men! plant love among us!
Throng our large temples with the shows of peace,
And not our streets with war!

III iii 33.

The tribunes justly tell him that he speaks of the people 'as if you were a god to punish, not a man of their infirmity', and he is exposed as a man who, though ready and able to serve the state, will serve it only upon his own terms and without offending his fastidiousness. Although outwardly a traditionalist, he would 'o'erleap that custom' that stands in his way, and when precedents inconvenience him, he dismisses them as the unswept 'dust on antique time'. At heart he knows only one solution for all difficulties, and he wishes that the senators would 'lay aside their ruth, and let me use my sword'. His departure to the Volscians is the petulant action of a frustrated child who has never

---

[1] Cf. *1 Henry IV* V iv 65:

Two stars keep not their motion in one sphere,
Nor can one England brook a double reign.

grown up, and at the end Aufidius finds exactly the right phrase for him: 'thou boy of tears'. Coriolanus boasted that he could not be 'such a gosling to obey instinct', but in fact he never did anything else.

It is Volumnia who acts virtuously in this play, for when she is forced to choose between the destruction of the city and the loss of her son, she sacrifices the son. Coriolanus himself is the tragic ruin of fine qualities that could have benefited the state; and the more tragic because he might have done so much. Pride, choler, self-will—all facets of his immaturity—undid him, and he stands in the long line of Shakespearean rulers who failed because they lacked knowledge and mastery of themselves. An emotional contempt for one's fellow-men is no foundation for political success.

Henry V, by contrast, deliberately schooled himself into humility and self-awareness, and he tells the audience all about it when he is left alone on the stage after his first meeting with Falstaff (*1 Henry IV* I ii). For this soliloquy Henry has been taxed with hypocrisy and priggishness and Shakespeare with want of art, so we must try to realise its true significance. The speech adopts a recognised convention of the morality play, in which a character may step outside himself and inform the audience of his creator's intentions. Henry is here supplying a programme note. It comes at the end of a scene in which degree has seemed to be called in question and the heir to the throne has lent himself to a scheme for a highway robbery in disreputable company. In its context the soliloquy is therefore Shakespeare's assurance that in reality all is well with England and the audience may enjoy the play without anxiety. The image of the sun, potent in cosmic implications, promises that Henry will come to his throne without dishonour, and in the meantime we may indulge Falstaff to the full, as Henry himself intends to do. When the time comes, he will pay the debt he never promised, but for the moment he asks to be left free of the burdens that he knows he must one day carry. It is our first intimation of this kingly man's attitude to the problem of power. He will assume it when he must, and something in his words suggests that then he will assume it gladly. But he is young and human, his tide of blood yet runs in vanity and he is unapt for the cares of formal majesty. His present disinclination for responsibility only convinces us of his ultimate dedication. He is shirking nothing. It is precisely because he knows how heavy the burden will one day be[1] that he asks to be spared it now.

---

[1] When he takes the crown from his sleeping father's pillow, he thinks of it, even then, as the symbol of anxiety and watchful nights, *2 Henry IV* IV v 20–36.

The speech is integral to the play, which takes its special character from the promise that he will make the right decision. If that were ever in doubt, the whole balance of the play, and with it our understanding of Henry, would be disturbed. We should no longer be free to laugh with Falstaff, and the civil wars would so disturb the action that we should find no comfort in the picture of the calm and permanent English countryside. But once Henry has identified himself with the stability of society, everything is for our pleasure. The comic theme may develop its own glorious irresponsibility and the market price of bullocks receive the grave attention that is due to it when no dark clouds hang above the world. 'I know you all'; and we must be glad that he knows.

We must not think of it as an easy decision, for nothing that a ruler does is easy. Always 'there is a world elsewhere',[1] tempting him to seek refuge from his cares. Shakespeare seems to come to the conclusion that this is the hardest temptation the ruler has to overcome. He feared the abandonment of power more than he feared its tyrannical exercise, and it may be significant that the first crisis Henry has to meet on coming to the throne is the Dauphin's accusation that England is 'idly king'd', her sceptre fantastically borne by a self-indulgent playboy. The mocking gift of tennis-balls, an explicit reminder of 'our wilder days', gives further urgency to the war that Henry has already decided to fight. He does not invade France out of personal pique because he has been insulted. The proper inference is that the world shall realise that England is now ruled by a man who will keep his state, be like a king and show his 'sail of greatness'. Although not to our taste a particularly agreeable incident, it is a necessary demonstration of the new king's calibre and an assurance that he means to devote himself to the common weal.

In this respect he never fails (witness his refusal of mercy to the Southampton conspirators, although one of them has been his dearest friend; the severity to Bardolph's church-breaking, the desperately earnest apologia to Bates and Williams, the final clumsy wooing as an act of state[2]), and Shakespeare finds in Henry's absolute dedication a fusion between the man and the office that he has sought in vain in his previous studies of monarchy. In other reigns the mystery of

---

[1] *Coriolanus* III iii 133.

[2] Richard III's proxy wooing of the Princess Elizabeth (IV iv) has mixed motives, including the shoring of his own dynastic safety and also, perhaps, some relish for 'the sweet silent hours of marriage joys'; but he shows a public motive similar to Henry's when he claims that the match would 'infer fair England's peace'.

the royal office is shown to be greater than the man who holds it. It must be so, for the principle of royalty has to survive the personal failure of kings like Richard II and John, who might fatally degrade it.

> The saint we worship is authority;
> Which lives in kings, and cannot with them die.
> Greville, *Mustapha* IV iv 17.

At one time when it seems to die—

> How easy dost thou take all England up!
> From forth this morsel of dead royalty,
> The life, the right and truth of all this realm
> Is fled to heaven; and England now is left
> To tug and scamble and to part by the teeth
> The unow'd interest of proud swelling state.
> *KJ* IV iii 142.

—it survives through the momentary genius of Faulconbridge. He briefly personifies England until the repentant nobles once again run on in obedience 'even to our ocean, to our great King John' and there is no doubt of the answer to Prince Henry's grief-stricken question,

> What surety of the world, what hope, what stay,
> When this was now a king, and now is clay?
> *KJ* V vii 68.

The surety is the 'mended faiths' of the recent rebels and the recovered majesty of England. Likewise, although this time the process takes longer, the country recovers under Henry V from the blemished rule of Richard II. It is true that there are times when the crown seems to be diminished to the unworthiness of its wearer. Thus Gaunt tells Richard,

> Thy death-bed is no lesser than thy land,
> Wherein thou liest in reputation sick;
> *Rich. II* II i 95.

and Richard's misfortune is that he has no Faulconbridge. 'Where man is nothing, place cannot do all.'[1] A country cannot be saved just by its institutions and its laws, which under slack rule become a scarecrow for the birds to perch.[2] But Shakespeare's conclusion is optimistic. Even in the long agony of the fifteenth century the forms of kingship never wholly lost their potency, and always there would appear the deliverer, a Henry V or a Richmond, the rare and dedicated man in whom crown and wearer are perfectly matched.

---

[1] Greville, *Mustapha*, I ii 201.   [2] *MM* II i 1–4.

A just ambition, patriotism, dedication: if there is a final requirement, it is what we may call humanity, although Shakespeare would have called it love. Politics, we must again recall, is a matter of morals, and there is more to government than the exercise of power. In Shakespeare's tradition the ruler was a responsible and ethical being, granted authority for the pursuit of recognised moral objects. The state was not the conscious construction of art (that was the Machiavellian heresy); it was rather the creation of mutual needs,[1] and was raised to its highest function when it was the source of justice. Society therefore demands more of the prince than a schooling in the techniques of government, which was Henry IV's conception of his office. Majesty regards the uniqueness of every man, and loves what it finds. In the long run Shakespeare discovers that contemporary dogmas about order and degree provide an incomplete explanation of society, because they fail to penetrate to the roots of man's social activity. Political sufficiency is dangerously liable to stunt the full flowering of humanity.[2]

Coriolanus is one who does not understand the true nature of society.

> I go alone,
> Like to a lonely dragon, that his fen
> Makes fear'd and talk'd of more than seen.
>   IV i 29.

It is not just his banishment that establishes his monstrous isolation. He has been cut off all the time, and his arrogant 'I banish you' announces a relationship that has never been any different. When for a ceremonial occasion he needs the people's regard, he knows nothing better than to 'mountebank their loves'. It is very different with Henry V. Henry is politically efficient in a way that Coriolanus is not, and the reason is that he knows and understands the people that he has to rule. In a war against crushing odds he generates a comradeship that turns disaster into victory, and leadership of this quality cannot be achieved without an immense human understanding. But not even Henry is the complete king.[3] Many have found him too relentlessly and flawlessly official. The responses to every situation are politically immaculate, and it is only on rare occasions, as in the few words of prayer before Agincourt, that the official manner relaxes to show the naked man, dubious of his title and confessing to the dreadful strain

---

[1] See L. C. Knights, *Shakespeare's Politics*, 9–12.   [2] See Chapter VI.
[3] See above, p. 144. But the defect in Henry's character was perhaps not intended by Shakespeare. *Henry V* is cast as an epic, which is chiefly concerned to celebrate the hero's more public virtues. See below, pp. 320–2.

that this involves. In Henry the human instinct has been frozen beyond the admitted needs of royal discipline. Only his son, in all other respects a failure, possesses the sustained humanity that is the final attribute of kings. He pities Cade ('O graceless men! they know not what they do'); and the famous speech at Towton (*3 Henry VI* II v 1–54) breathes a love and fellow-feeling for the homely swain and the shepherds 'looking on their silly sheep' that Henry V clearly does not experience for

> the wretched slave,
> Who with a body fill'd and vacant mind
> Gets him to rest, cramm'd with distressful bread.
> *Hen. V* IV i 288.

We cannot fail to notice the difference in tone or to be aware of the emotional gulf that it represents. In kings love is 'the glorious sun' that

> Stays in his course and plays the alchemist,
> Turning with splendour of his precious eye
> The meagre cloddy earth to glittering gold.
> *KJ* III i 78.

> It fears not policy, that heretic,
> Which works on leases of short number'd hours,
> But all alone stands hugely politic.
> *Sonn.* CXXIV 9.

CHAPTER FIVE

Shakespeare's England

It is a kind of history.
TS Ind. ii 144.

I. THE HISTORIES

THE period of English history stretching from Richard II to Richard III provided Shakespeare with the material he needed for his speculations about power and his illustration of contemporary problems and dangers. Moreover, it was safe to write about the fifteenth century, as it would not have been safe to write about the Tudors. 'I might have been more pleasing to the Reader, if I had written the story of mine own times; having been permitted to draw water as near the well-head as any other,' Raleigh said in the preface to his *History of the World*. 'To this I answer, that who-so-ever in writing a modern History, shall follow truth too near the heels, it may happily strike out his teeth.'

Men had to be very careful what they said. All historical writing was understood to be to some extent allegorical, even when the subject was Persia, Rome or ancient Britain, and since the historian's avowed purpose was to instruct his own age, he could not be surprised if people sometimes made identifications that he would have preferred them to avoid. Raleigh took pains to protect himself from such identifications.

> It is enough for me (being in that state I am) to write of the eldest times: wherein also why may it not be said, that in speaking of the past, I point at the present, and tax the vices of those that are yet living, in their persons that are long since dead; and have it laid to my charge? But this I cannot help, though innocent. And certainly if there be any, that finding themselves spotted like the Tigers of old time, shall find fault with me for painting them over anew; they shall therein accuse themselves justly, and me falsely.

The most alarming of these identifications was that between Richard II and the Queen herself. According to a reasonably authenticated anecdote, Elizabeth was examining a parcel of records brought to her by William Lambarde, her Keeper of the Tower, when she 'fell upon the reign of King Richard II, saying, "I am Richard II. Know ye not that?"' When Lambarde loyally demurred, she observed rather obscurely, 'He that will forget God will also forget his benefactors'; adding that 'this tragedy was played forty times in open streets and houses'. In essentials there was little resemblance between Richard and Elizabeth, for Elizabeth's mind was the servant of no man's and she did not waver in doing her duty as she conceived it. But her people, who could not always follow her tortuous policies, sometimes felt differently about her. In her feminine wiles and tergiversations she could be an exasperating woman, and there were times when she seemed to bring the country to the edge of disaster by sheer wanton irresolution. Superficially there were flaws in her character grave enough to disturb men who already had the fate of Richard heavily on their minds. Her more sober advisers were painfully conscious of their equivocal position, and they earnestly disclaimed any resemblance between themselves and the favourites of Richard II. In a letter written to the Queen in 1578 Sir Francis Knollys excused himself for giving advice that he knew would be unwelcome to her. He would not, he said, 'play the parts of King Richard the Second's men'. In almost the same words the first Lord Hunsdon declared that 'I was never one of Richard II's men'. Evidently it was a current phrase; and if her most loyal servants were aware of supposed similarities between Elizabeth and Richard, it can never have been far absent from their minds that she might suffer the same fate.

Richard's reign was therefore a dangerous theme for writers, and probably the more so after the acting of *Thomas of Woodstock* in the early nineties.[1] Perhaps the anonymous author showed deliberate caution in stopping short with the death of Gloucester, for he had been frankly hostile to Richard and one wonders what he would have made of the abdication if he had reached it. The orthodox cannot have found *Woodstock* reassuring. Although Gloucester himself continued to profess his loyalty, his brothers closed the play by swearing to avenge his death; and if Gloucester's death cried for vengeance, did not Mary's too? Many of the charges brought against Richard might at this time have been brought against Elizabeth herself. In unfriendly eyes his sentimental pacifism might correspond to her thrifty reluctance to press the war against Spain, his dependence on favourites to her doting on the unstable Essex, his neglect of his senior counsellors to her hectoring way with the Commons.

At any rate, when Shakespeare's play was printed in 1597, and twice re-issued in the following year, it was printed without the deposition scene (IV i 154–318). This scene had almost certainly been acted in

[1] See above, pp. 84–5.

the original performances, for the version printed for the first time in 1608 was apparently based on some kind of memorisation, and it may be that the public acting of a king's deposition had so much alarmed the authorities that they had forbidden it to be printed. The reign of Richard had become a topic that wise men did well to avoid. In 1599 a sober and well-intentioned historian, Sir John Hayward, disregarded the omens and ran head-first into trouble by publishing a *History of Henry IV*, which he was further unwise enough to dedicate to Essex. Hayward's theme was the familiar one of the disasters following upon the treatment of Richard and the country's final redemption in the accession of Henry VII. In fact he went farther back than most historians in suggesting that the collapse of the fine hopes embodied in the seven goodly sons of Edward III may have originated in Edward's own part in the deposition of his father. But in detail he devoted most of his book—some 135 pages out of 150; so it is not altogether surprising that the authorities, already sensitive on this subject, misunderstood him—to reviewing the causes of Richard's fall. His conclusions were entirely respectable, for he decided that the people have no right to depose their sovereign, whatever the provocation, and that the heir should peaceably await the death of his predecessor without trying to force the event. The dedication to Essex was possibly cautionary, to remind him of the wickedness of rebellion, but the government decided otherwise and Hayward went to prison.

The last episode in the curiously linked story of Elizabeth and Richard is the most remarkable of all. In 1601, on the eve of the Essex rebellion, some members of his faction (two Percies among them) approached Shakespeare's company and asked them to give a special performance of *Richard II*: the idea apparently being that the spectacle of a royal deposition would incite the Londoners to fall in with Essex and his nebulous designs. The actors objected that the play was 'so old and so long out of use that they should have small or no company at it', but the conspirators guaranteed their losses by promising them forty shillings above their usual fee, and the performance was accordingly given. Augustine Phillips was later summoned before the Privy Council to make an explanation, and he appears to have satisfied the authorities that the players had no knowledge of the intended rising, for there is no record of their being punished in any way. Instead they were commanded to give a performance at court on the night before Essex died on the block; but we do not know the name of the play with which the Queen consoled herself.

Daniel was another playwright who found himself in trouble for

having supposedly given support to Essex. His *Philotas* was thought
to be seditious, and he published the play in order to vindicate himself
and show that this was not his intention.[1] Greville cautiously adapted
the sources he used for *Alaham*, so as to escape any suspicion that his
Mahomet might be intended to represent Essex come to purify the
state after the misgovernment of an old and feeble ruler. Another play
he even thought it prudent to destroy altogether. It was about Antony
and Cleopatra, whose irregular passions he condemned in 'forsaking
empire to follow sensuality', and he destroyed the manuscript because
the characters had 'some childish wantonness in them, apt enough to
be construed, or strained to a personating of vices in the present
Governors, and government'. He feared that some might judge the
play 'in the practice of the world, seeing the like instances not poetically, but really fashioned in the Earl of Essex then falling'.

Such were the dangers besetting all who wrote on historical subjects,[2]
and Shakespeare had always to expect the accusation that he was
glancing at living persons. That, so far as we know, he escaped this
suspicion is an unconscious tribute to an artistic tact that knew how to
generalise upon immediate experience. None the less the theme of his
histories is Elizabethan England, and modern historians have few
better sources to preserve them from misunderstanding this anxiety-
ridden age. Although his genius transcended his theme, to give his
exploration of government a universal value, the histories have an
inner consistency that distinguishes them from all his other work.

Serious political reflection occurs everywhere in his drama—even a
knockabout farce like *The Taming of the Shrew* moralises upon the
duty of obedience—and Shakespeare never ceases to remind men of
their social obligations. In a sense, therefore, it is true that the histories
by themselves do not contain the full scope and variety of his political
thought; and since with the doubtful and uncharacteristic exception of

---

[1] This was in 1605, after both Essex and the Queen were dead; and Philotas
was only a Macedonian general who was executed for conspiracy against
Alexander the Great. After the misfortunes of Hayward, the publisher of a quarto
of *2 Henry IV* in 1600 thought it prudent to delete references to Richard II and
his abdication, as well as part of the Archbishop of York's speech in support of
rebellion. Many years later the authorities were still touchy about the theme. The
hymn-writer Nahum Tate produced a characteristic adaptation of *Richard II* just
at the time when the fabrications of Titus Oates had again made deposition a
dangerous topic. With 'exclusion' in the air, the government were in no mood
for a production of *Richard II*. The hopeful Tate altered the setting and the
names of the characters and re-christened the play as *The Sicilian Usurper*; but
no one was deceived, and the second version, like the first, was suppressed.

[2] Cf. the instruction of the Master of the Revels on the *MS.* of *Sir Thomas
More*: 'Leave out insurrection wholly, and the cause thereof, at your perils.'

Henry VIII, he wrote no further histories in the last dozen years of his professional career, it may also be argued that they do not present his final conclusions on the great questions of state upon which as a younger man he had brooded so earnestly. But the distinguishing quality of the English histories is that here, and here alone, political virtue is the only standard of reference. The characters exist in a single dimension and are judged solely by the dramatist's overriding conception of the welfare of society. Admittedly there are occasional relaxations of this austerity, but these exceptions to the prevailing mood are seemingly casual and quite astonishingly few. Sentimental misunderstandings about the rejection of Falstaff occur because his admirers (who perhaps would like him less if he lived next door) choose to ignore his real function in Shakespeare's story of England. His very existence, or the sort of existence he was allowed to develop, certainly raises questions to which the history plays give no direct answer:[1] Shakespeare made the same mistake with Shylock, and did not make it with Malvolio. But the only pertinent question at the end of *Henry IV* is whether Falstaff would be a suitable companion for a king newly dedicated to 'mock the expectation of the world'. Nor has there ever been any doubt about the answer. As the embodiment of a certain political attitude he stands condemned. Within the limits of a history play he has no need of private emotions like shame or grief, and so he does not ask for pity.[2]

Parolles, an infinitely lesser Falstaff, could say, when he was humiliated: 'Simply the thing I am Shall make me live.' Falstaff could not have said it, and that is the irreconcilable difference between them, and the difference, too, between the histories and all the other plays. The histories lie uniformly within a comprehensive vision which determines plot, argument and characterisation in sole reference to the safety of England and the political qualities that minister to it. Outside this, the characters have no individual life whatever—or if they do, it is a superfluity, an irrelevance or an artistic blunder. The private essences which many of them do in fact develop are an overflow of Shakespeare's creative energy, and an admission of his inability to write strictly to a formula. But he never loses sight of his main structural purpose, and from time to time he brings us up short, as with Falstaff, puts an end to indulgence and thrusts his characters back into the play. If for a moment they have seemed to feel and bleed, it was only an illusion.

[1] See Chapter VI.
[2] See Arthur Sewell, *Character and Society in Shakespeare.*

Parolles, then, had that in him which would let him live; but Falstaff, politically discredited, could only die. Outside the histories, the characters have inner lives and they are free from the constant pressure of a particular judgment that lies so heavily on the kings and statesmen of the histories. In spite of the wealth of political reference elsewhere, only the histories may truly be described as political plays. *Coriolanus*, with its picture of class division and competing sectional interests, is in some ways the most elaborate as well as the subtlest of Shakespeare's political studies, but at its climax it is focused upon an individual's decision in an issue that has ceased to be political at all. There is the feeling, too, that all the decisions that Coriolanus makes in the play are for him the right ones; and we should not feel that about him if these things had happened in sixteenth-century England. Antony and Cleopatra throw away an empire, but they are not judged, as they surely would be if the play were political. In other plays—*Measure for Measure, Troilus and Cressida, The Winter's Tale, The Tempest* and all the great tragedies—political situations, with their attendant judgments, are implicit but do not develop, or just develop sub-ordinately to something larger and more important. Shakespeare will often open a play with a political issue and then let it be absorbed in a much wider examination of human behaviour.[1] In this less constricted atmosphere his characters enjoy a freedom and fullness of growth that remain inaccessible in the histories. It means that they are admitted to a complex of judgments and sympathies in which political conduct is only incidental. Respect for the social order may not always be the most sustaining of the virtues, nor rebellion the greatest of crimes.

This requires an important qualification of the political sentiments to be found in the plays written after about 1600. Once he had com-pleted his historical cycle with *Henry V*, Shakespeare never again wrote a play whose values were exclusively political. He seems to have found this a liberation, and henceforth his political comment operates in a much wider context. It is noticeably coloured by the scepticism that pervades his so-called tragic period, and on a narrow view he seems to have lost his optimism about society. One after another, his heroes are politically disastrous, and sin so darkens the world that power is only possessed to be abused. The ugly spirit of Thersites dominates the scene. 'Lechery, lechery; still wars and lechery; nothing else holds fashion.' Power seems inevitably to corrupt the possessor, and the leaders of men are 'incontinent varlets' all. Nevertheless we should be

---

[1] Notably *Measure for Measure*, which opens as though it were to be a play about government but soon breaks off into other themes.

wrong to forget the very different terms of reference and suppose that all this invalidates the conclusions of the histories. The histories show clearly enough what Shakespeare thought power and office could do to a man, and in the tragedies and the 'bitter' comedies he chose to examine their consequences in, apparently, a mood of total disillusion. The abuse of power is often the complement, and sometimes the mainspring, of disorders much more serious. But we have to see Shakespeare's values in the right perspective. Politics are no longer the main issue, and Macbeth, Lear, Hamlet, Othello, Troilus, Angelo, Leontes, Prospero and others are political failures only because they have other and more destructive defects. Shakespeare's apparent pessimism about the state is here only a minor aspect of a much more comprehensive pessimism about mankind generally. He is not condemning majesty. These later plays simply show a series of situations in which, for various evident reasons, majesty is not able to operate: Angelo's lust, Othello's personal immaturity, Hamlet's paralysing scepticism, Lear's want of self-knowledge, and so on. It is important to remember that the social and personal values stated in the histories are not impugned. Shakespeare's later heroes demand to be judged by different standards, and the earlier standards stay intact. Dedication, discipline, kindness, love of country are still the cardinal political virtues, and Shakespeare nowhere suggests that where these are found, society will not be happy.

II. 'HENRY VI'

The three parts of *Henry VI* make an episodic survey of English history from the funeral of Henry V in 1422 to the final defeat of the Lancastrians at Tewkesbury in 1471. The plays have something of the epic sweep of the prose chronicles, but Shakespeare[1] takes a dramatist's licence to condense the narrative, switch the order of events, and even alter the ages of the characters, wherever these changes will assist his homiletic purpose. The sequence is essentially didactic. It offers a straightforward moralising of the Tudor pattern of history, with only an occasional glimpse of real people and recognisable human predicaments. In its extreme earnestness it is perhaps the standard example of

[1] The difficult questions of the date, authorship and order of the plays will not be discussed here. It is possible that Part One was written later than the two other parts, and that Shakespeare did little more than revise and add to someone else's original play. But in matters of this kind there are dogmatists who will never yield and discussion is inevitably inconclusive. To accept Shakespeare's responsibility for the three parts is convenient and not necessarily wrong.

a poet-historian using drama to teach lessons appropriate to his own times.

Shakespeare here attempts the orthodox reconciliation[1] between a providential view of history and the conviction that man, while not the total author of his fate, does by his own actions co-operate in his destiny, however slightly or obscurely. Thus the unhappy story of fifteenth-century England originated in the dethronement of Richard II, described by Hall as 'the beginning and root of the great discord and division'. Shakespeare makes the point quite clearly when Mortimer encourages Richard Plantagenet (later Duke of York) to recover the crown that belongs to him by right:

> Henry the Fourth, grandfather to this king,
> Depos'd his nephew Richard, Edward's son,
> The first-begotten, and the lawful heir
> Of Edward king, the third of that descent.
> *1 Hen. VI.* II v 63.

After this crime everything was in a sense foredoomed. France must be lost and England suffer civil war; while within this scheme the fate of individuals would be determined by the ups and downs of Fortune's wheel, with the added implication that Fortune itself was God's agent in demanding the expiation of a crime. But the dramatist's attitude is not wholly fatalistic. Henry himself marvels 'to see how God in all his creatures works',[2] and the suffering in these plays can be traced to direct human action. Personal wickedness is part of the penalty that God inflicts, and so the erring individual is at once an agent of God's purpose and a man aware of his own evil and capable of at any rate an illusion of choice. The plays present an ominous cycle of sin and retribution, with every crime brought terribly home to its author and its consequences made evident in misery to himself and those he loves. It is an arrangement which makes effective characterisation impossible, as all the characters are victims of their own unruly natures and also of the disasters to which the whole country is fated. They are imprisoned in various kinds of anti-social attitude, and in spite of their noise and energy they are men without personal authority. They speak, too, in the plangent, undifferentiated language of an apprentice poet as yet overweighted with classical memories and admiration for Marlowe. The sonorous blank verse, the rhetorical exuberance and the episodic structure are all in some degree the legacy of *Tamburlaine*.

Shakespeare is not particularly concerned in these plays to study the effects of power or look for kingly types. He is writing of an England

---

[1] See above, pp. 8-9.   [2] *2 Henry VI* II i 7.

where majesty has entirely ceased and kings, prelates, statesmen and people will be unable to restore it until God decides that the Lancastrians' crime has been expiated and sends Henry of Richmond as deliverer. This largely accounts for the strident monotony of *Henry VI*. For the length of three plays the poet has nothing but violence and calamity to write about, and it was not until *Richard III* that he found a way to make this sort of catastrophe interesting. So any inferences we care to make about royalty and power are only casual, and at the time they may have been unsuspected by Shakespeare himself. In Part Two he dislikes Henry, and contemptuously dismisses him as the sort of weak, self-centred ruler—a Richard II without the *panache*—under whom states will never prosper. In the third part he comes to value Henry as a man, but he has already decided that in kings it is the public virtues that matter. In the heat of battle Henry sits upon a molehill, satisfied that 'to whom God will, there be the victory'. His fatalism and surrender to despair are tantamount to abdication.

Shakespeare also exposes the essentially destructive ambition of York and the young Richard of Gloucester, but beyond this he has little to say about the specialty of rule. His concerns here are more primitive. *Henry VI* is a prolonged morality, with England as its central character, betrayed by a long line of evil and selfish men. These egotists overwhelm the few faithful servants who point the way to better things, and although the plays get their undoubted momentum from the energy of the sinners, it is Shakespeare's anxiety about his own times that gives them their real significance and interest.

> Oh, England! Model to thy inward greatness,
> Like little body with a mighty heart!
> What mightst thou do, that honour would thee do,
> Were all thy children kind and natural!
> *Hen. V* Second Chorus 16.

The Tudors had put an end to civil war, but there were conditions in which it might recur. The whole of *Henry VI* is a long-drawn demonstration that internal dissension, caused by a factious nobility, is the greatest scourge that a nation can suffer.

> 'Tis much when sceptres are in children's hands;
> But more, when envy breeds unkind division:
> There comes the ruin, there begins confusion.
> *I Hen. VI* IV i 192.

The child here is Henry VI, but in the uncertainty of the immediate

C.M.—M

future even this misfortune might return when Elizabeth died. The three plays therefore embody the standard Tudor warning against rebellion, and Shakespeare insists that, however bad or weak the ruler, he must be obeyed. He must be obeyed even if his title is not impeccable. The genealogical argument, strenuously conducted, is on the side of York against Lancaster, but that does not justify York's rebellion. Nothing justifies the risk of civil war.

If Part One of *Henry VI* was the '*Harey the vi*' which Henslowe presented at the Rose in March 1592 for a triumphant run of fifteen performances within three months,[1] we may wonder what made it so popular. According to Nashe, who may have had something to do with its composition, it would comfort 'brave Talbot' to know that his bones had been 'new embalmed with the tears of ten thousand spectators (at several times)', and the play must have touched some nerve that needed the assurance that an England undivided had no one to fear. Otherwise it was a strange play to have won such popularity on the public stage, with its hero defeated and slain by the traditional enemy. It has been often said that the defeat of the Armada released a patriotic fervour that demanded for its gratification a series of poems, plays and chronicles setting forth the past and present glories of the country. In this exalted mood the play about Talbot must surely have proved somewhat disillusioning. It is true that Talbot's struggle against 'a world of odds' was evocative of Grenville's *Revenge* ambushed by the galleons of Spain. Such a struggle was a splendid thing in itself, and the dramatist, who was clearly moved both by its honest courage and by its uses as an *exemplum*, never doubted that a major conjunction of hostile stars and internal treachery was needed to make it unavailing. Otherwise there is little in the play's long record of dissension and failure to arouse patriotic enthusiasm.

It is primarily a play about the French wars, showing how Talbot, a rugged, selfless warrior, lost the English provinces in France because his simply loyalties were powerless against the witchcraft of Joan of Arc and the dissensions of his principal lieutenants. These dissensions, which will grow later into the Wars of the Roses, provide the secondary theme of the play.

The story opens with his captains sadly gathered about the bier of King Henry V, untimely dead in France. They fear that 'the bad revolting stars' have robbed them of their leader as only the first in a series of crushing blows from Fortune, and their forebodings are at

[1] *SWW* 195–6.

once borne out as one messenger after another interrupts their council with tidings of cities lost and armies scattered in defeat. One of these messengers offers an explanation:

> Among the soldiers this is muttered,
> That here you maintain several factions;
> And, whilst a field should be dispatch'd and fought,
> You are disputing of your generals.
>
> I i 70.

In the following scene this explanation is complemented by another. The French have been granted supernatural aid by the arrival of Joan la Pucelle, complacently certain of her destiny:

> Assign'd am I to be the English scourge.
> This night the siege assuredly I'll raise:
> Expect Saint Martin's summer, halcyon days,
> Since I have entered into these wars.
> Glory is like a circle in the water,
> Which never ceaseth to enlarge itself,
> Till by broad spreading it disperse to nought.
> With Henry's death the English circle ends;
> Dispersed are the glories it included.
>
> I ii 129.

Thereafter the English armies fight as men foredoomed. They have their momentary successes, because the dramatist is anxious to show that courage and leadership in themselves can accomplish much. Thus they take Orleans, audaciously, after Joan has raised the siege, and retrieve Rouen on the very day the French have captured it.[1] But these victories are won at a heavy price, with Salisbury killed by a chance cannon-shot at Orleans and John of Bedford left to die at Rouen of sickness and 'crazy age'. All the time, too, their strength is being undermined by faction, quarrels begun at home in England leading to jealousy and recrimination in the field, until at last Talbot is left to struggle on alone. In effective contrast to these paralysing divisions we see Joan twice rallying the French when their confidence has been shaken by defeat, twice restoring their broken unity and carrying them forward with her to new and successful projects. It is almost as a predestined sacrifice that Talbot meets his death in a fruitless attack on Bordeaux, voluble, angry and unafraid, clasping his dead son in his arms. The rhyming verse of these final battle-scenes seems to give a symbolic significance to his fate.

---

[1] This is dramatic licence. Orleans was never captured after Joan had relieved it. Nor was Rouen lost and recovered in a single day. In fact it was not lost until 1449.

Although assisted by some remarkable violations of fact,[1] the play's opening is constructed with dramatic skill and concentration. In 177 lines the first scene manages to introduce all the significant issues. French witchcraft is immediately suggested as a cause of Henry's early death:

> Or shall we think the subtle-witted French
> Conjurers and sorcerers, that, afraid of him,
> By magic verses have contrived his end?
> I i 25.

The anxious dialogue contrasts the blaze of light, which was Henry while he lived, with the pervading gloom and blackness now that he is dead. Sustained imagery of this kind is never accidental.[2] It springs from a poet's secret contemplation of events, and the process which creates it is more than intellectual. The same idea develops more elaborately in *Romeo and Juliet*, where the shining happiness of the young lovers lights a brief trail of brilliance across the darkness to which they will presently be sacrified. In *Henry VI* the outward image —of comets, sun and stars in conflict with the enveloping blackness of the heavens—reflects the emotions of Henry's captains as they mourn his loss. Their minds are still dazzled by the splendour of his 'brandish'd sword' and the flashing eyes which blinded his enemies like 'mid-day sun fierce bent against their faces', and they grope to find their way in a world suddenly darkened by his death. The image runs through the scene until, at line 57, the bad news brought by the first of the messengers shows that the planets, already several times invoked, have indeed imported change of time and state. Bedford is speaking of his fear that civil war is inevitable now that Henry's strong hand has been removed:

> Posterity, await for wretched years,
> When at their mothers' moist eyes babes shall suck,

---

[1] In this opening scene the dramatist wants to show the overwhelming consequences of the death of Henry V. So Guienne is lost, the messengers cry, and Champagne, Rheims, Orleans, Paris, Gisors, Poitiers, Rouen. In cold fact Henry's death was followed by no such general doom. He died in 1422, and immediately the English won victories at Crévant and Verneuil. It was not until 1429 that Joan relieved Orleans and won the battle of Patay. Rheims fell in the same year, Paris in 1436, Rouen in 1449, Guienne not until 1451. To concentrate these losses within a few weeks is a legitimate device for starting a play, since actual history, being sprawling and untidy, is unkind to the dramatic unities. But the spectator will be surprised to find, later in the play, Henry being crowned in Paris, whose loss had been reported in the first scene; Orleans still under siege; and Rouen still in possession of the English. The same scene transfers to 1422 the crowning of the Dauphin and the defeat and imprisonment of Talbot, both of which occurred seven years later.

[2] The star image is effectively resumed in I ii.

Our isle be made a marish of salt tears,
And none but women be left to wail the dead.
Henry the Fifth! thy ghost I invocate:
Prosper this realm, keep it from civil broils!
Combat with adverse planets in the heavens!
A far more glorious star thy soul will make,
Than Julius Caesar, or bright—

                                            I i 48.

Here, dramatically in the middle of the sentence, a messenger breaks in
with the first news of military disaster, and soon we learn that only
'some petty towns of no import' are still held by the English. The
speeches of the messengers at the same time establish the heroism and
great reputation of Talbot, who

                    above human thought
        Enacted wonders with his sword and lance.

The messengers stress the need for reinforcements, but the incipient
faction that will leave Talbot friendless is declared in the bickering
between Gloucester and the Bishop of Winchester, and again in the
closing lines of the scene when Winchester is left alone to speak his
private intents:

        The king from Eltham I intend to steal,
        And sit at chiefest stern of public weal.

The reason for the stars' defection is stated in II v, where Mortimer
recalls the act of usurpation whose memory still haunted Henry V on
the eve of Agincourt. But Talbot, whose simple virtues[1] are innocent of

---

[1] These virtues are naïvely illustrated in the invented episode of the Countess
of Auvergne, who has the notion to play Delilah to Talbot's Samson (II iii).
He contemptuously evades her trap, surprised that she could ever have thought
that the scourge of France was to be taken in human weakness of this sort.
Probably the scene is purely symbolic, to proclaim that the true champions of
England are proof against fleshly lures; but it may have been written with topical
intent, to warn some unknown Elizabethan captain of the dangers of combining
war with amorous dalliance. The dramatist takes surprising liberties with Talbot's
career. He was not really the prime antagonist of Joan that the play makes him
out to be. Joan's actual fighting career was very short, lasting little more than a
year. She appeared in 1429, was taken by John of Luxemburg in 1430, and put
to death by the English in 1431. Talbot's career, on the other hand, was very
long. In Henry V's time he was Lieutenant of Ireland, and the Talbot who was
present at Agincourt (*Hen. V* IV iii 54) was his elder brother, Gilbert, who died
in 1419. But he fought at the sieges of Melun and Meaux in the last years of the
reign and again distinguished himself at Verneuil in 1424. After another campaign
against the Irish he was back in France in 1427 and was made Governor of
Maine and Anjou. He took part in the siege of Orleans, but soon afterwards he
was captured near Patay and held prisoner until 1431; so he did not attend
Henry VI's coronation in Paris, where in the play he makes such dutiful speeches.
Finally, in 1452, at the age of 64, he was put in command of an expeditionary

political calculation, never realises what is happening. He cannot account for the irresolution of his soldiers.

> My thoughts are whirled like a potter's wheel;
> I know not where I am, nor what I do:
> A witch, by fear, not force, like Hannibal,
> Drives back our troops and conquers as she lists:
> So bees with smoke, and doves with noisome stench,
> Are from their hives and houses driven away.
> Hark, countrymen! either renew the fight,
> Or tear the lions out of England's coat;
> Renounce your soil, give sheep in lions' stead:
> Sheep run not half so treacherous from the wolf,
> Or horse or oxen from the leopard,
> As you fly from your oft-subdued slaves.
>
> I v 19.

Talbot is a tragically helpless figure, for he is the champion of a cause which the higher powers have already destined to defeat. His trust in the fighting qualities of the English soldier is inevitably confounded; and so, in the end, is his trust in God, whom he had come to know as England's unfailing ally in the field. The conventional pieties are often on his lips. 'God is our fortress', he tells his men, and past victories have justified him in thinking so. It is first to God that the faithful soldier will ascribe 'the glory of his conquest got'. When, therefore, he faces the triumphant Joan, he pathetically enquires of the heavens how they can 'suffer hell so to prevail'. His helpless incomprehension is revealed in his references to his soldiers as men surrounded and ensnared, 'girdled with a waist of iron', walled 'from the liberty of flight', or, like deer, 'park'd and bounded in a pale'.

Talbot's eyes are further sealed because he has not been present at the scene in the Temple Garden (II iv) where the faction is born—York, Warwick and Vernon aligned against Somerset and Suffolk—which is to condemn his cause in France and breed two generations of civil war.

> And here I prophesy: this brawl to-day,
> Grown to this faction in the Temple garden,
> Shall send between the red rose and the white
> A thousand souls to death and deadly night.
>
> II iv 124.

---

force to Aquitaine. After recovering Bordeaux and the surrounding district, he was defeated and killed at Châtillon in the following year, and the Hundred Years War was at an end. But in the play the dramatist matches him against Joan of Arc, who is present to mock him at his death, which in fact occurred 22 years after her own, and in another place. The two great feats attributed to him in the play, at Orleans and Rouen, are imaginary.

It is a key scene, not only for this play but for the whole historical sequence, and it may well be a later addition. We are for the moment in a different world, with the change of climate declaring itself in an apparent change in the calibre of the men who are speaking. Sheerly by the urgency with which they are here imagined, Warwick and Somerset and the rest of the jarring nobles come to life. They are suddenly formidable. The menace behind their words is suddenly significant, and they are not, as elsewhere in the play, just posturing rhetoricians.

The scene gets its unity and impact from the metaphor of the garden, seen in growth and decay, that runs all through it. In Shakespeare's histories the garden, with its good husbandry and bad, its cankered blossoms and the plants that through the ever-running year ripen and wither and die, becomes a symbol of the commonwealth of man. Where the gardener is thrifty, his blossoms are not blasted, nor is his ordered estate overrun by pests and weeds; but where he is neglectful, destruction and decay 'choke the herbs for want of husbandry'. This dominant theme of the histories comes to full expression in another garden scene, *Richard II* III iv, where the King's ruin is imaged in the technical language of the two gardeners who discuss his fall.

In the Temple Garden this theme is stated for the first time. As yet it is not developed very far, but this is a scene of infinite suggestion, as though the writer's mind had fastened lovingly on a complex of images which promised a rich flowering when he had tended them better. *Grow, crop, wither, flourish, ripen*, all words of the garden, are here used with multiple significance as the roses are plucked and the quarrel becomes more furious. York would prove the justice of his cause 'were growing time once ripened to my will', and he identifies his fortune with the growth or withering of a flower:

> And, by my soul, this pale and angry rose,
> As cognizance of my blood-drinking hate,
> Will I for ever and my faction wear,
> Until it wither with me to my grave
> Or flourish to the height of my degree.
>   II iv 107.

Other words are used in a double sense. *Colour* occurs often in the scene in its ordinary uncomplicated meaning, but it occurs too in its subsidiary sense of *reason, pretext* or *semblance*; and the *red* of the roses at once links itself with the blushing cheek and with the blood that will stain the earth—and so choke its natural fertility: thus returning to the original image of the garden. This sort of writing is characteristically Shakespearean,[1] for any word which contained within itself a double potentiality seems to have had a compulsive effect on his imagination.[2] It was almost impossible for him to say one thing at a time. There was a constraint upon him to use double meanings when he could, to extract from any thought or object the full implications of its being. He could never think of a rose without remembering, as here, the thorn which makes it dangerous or the canker which untimely kills its beauty.

Talbot's defeat and death at Bordeaux do not end the play. The dramatist, who does not like Joan, is at length able to indulge his insular impulses by sending her, her work accomplished, to a degrading death; and he also occupies his final Act by starting a theme that is to be important in the later parts of the trilogy. Gloucester here urges the young King to marry the daughter of the Earl of Armagnac, a nobleman 'near knit to Charles' and 'of great authority in France'. In reply Henry shows all the right attitudes. He protests that he is young and studious, at better ease with his books than in 'wanton dalliance'. But he will do as his counsellors advise and as his responsibilities call him.

> I shall be well content with any choice
> Tends to God's glory and my country's weal.
> V i 26.

It is all so seemly that we are reminded of Malcolm's self-examination before Macduff. But unfortunately for these fine sentiments, the Earl of Suffolk, sent to France to arrange a truce, falls in love with Margaret, the fair young daughter of Reignier, Duke of Anjou and titular King of Naples and Jerusalem. Suffolk works swiftly. He woos Margaret in Henry's name, wins her father's consent to a royal marriage, and hurries home to persuade Henry and the council to ratify the contract which he has had no warrant to make.

His account of Margaret's charms is so beguiling that the virtuous Henry feels the sting of brutish desire ('I am sick with working of my

---

[1] The scene has other evidences of Shakespeare's maturer presence, as when Somerset declares himself 'a truant in the law' and Warwick echoes him by disdaining 'these nice sharp quillets of the law'. Somerset and Warwick are forerunners of other and greater characters who will level their ambition with the lawful authority of the state. Shakespearean, too, is the truth so evident that it 'will glimmer through a blind man's eye': a complement of the lover's eye that will gaze an eagle blind.

[2] For Shakespeare's use of puns and double meanings, see *SWW* 519-24.

thoughts'), and it is in vain that Gloucester reminds him of his earlier pledge to Armagnac's daughter:

> How then shall we dispense with that contract,
> And not deface your honour with reproach?
> V v 28.

Gloucester eventually retires in dark foreboding and Suffolk is left to end the play in prospect of Margaret's secret favours and his own rise to pre-eminence in England:[1]

> Margaret shall now be queen, and rule the king;
> But I will rule both her, the king, and realm.
> V v 107.

The episode is significant in various ways. Suffolk is cast for his future role as an ambitious intriguer, and Gloucester, who has come forward as the guardian of the King's conscience, is now 'the good Duke', pledged to maintain firm and honest government. For him it is a change in character, as earlier in the play he has been a loud-mouthed brawler pursuing a feckless quarrel with Cardinal Beaufort. Again, the King is shown to have some personal responsibility for the misfortunes he will have to bear in the next two plays. Primarily, of course, he was a victim of the curse that lay upon his House. No deed of his could have turned it aside, and saintly, passive suffering was to be his destiny. But as the providential view of history did not exclude personal responsibility, Shakespeare shows Henry guilty of actions that did to some extent contribute to his ruin. He listened to the evil counsellor rather than the good, a momentary surrender to passion involved him in a broken pledge, and the marriage thus ill begun was doomed to disaster.

Moreover, the disaster would not be his alone. The whole kingdom would have to share the affliction that Margaret would bring. From the first she is fatal to England. Attached to the marriage treaty is a humiliating clause which permits her father to possess Anjou and Maine in his own right, with no fealty owed to his son-in-law of

---

[1] This is another invention. It is true that Suffolk supported this marriage and opposed Gloucester's scheme for a union with Armagnac. He finally brought Margaret to England and for some years they had similar aims. But Suffolk's motive was to build a lasting settlement with the French, whereas Gloucester was merely seeking diplomatic advantages for the renewal of the struggle. There is no historical foundation for the amorous intrigue with Margaret. Suffolk, who was married to a grand-daughter of the poet Chaucer, was 49 when Margaret came to England in 1445, and she was a lovely, high-spirited girl of 16. Suffolk's wife even accompanied him on his embassy to France. The invention is typical of the devices the dramatist uses to darken his picture.

England. She comes, without love or regard for her husband, to be
the mistress of Suffolk; and in her person she incarnates a broken
promise and a stain on England's honour. The suggestion is not made
explicitly, but we feel that to her have passed the familiars, 'charming
spells and periapts' with whose aid Joan la Pucelle had already begun
to work the doom of England.

As if the meaning of his play were not clear enough, Shakespeare
employs certain characters to underline it. Sir William Lucy is there
to typify the qualities of loyalty, patriotism and singleness of purpose.
When treachery weakens England's fighting strength, he is on hand to
make the conventional observations about it. To Somerset, whose
private feud with York has delayed their coming to the assistance of
Talbot, he says:

> Whither, my lord? from bought and sold Lord Talbot;
> Who, ring'd about with bold adversity,
> Cries out for noble York and Somerset,
> To beat assailing death from his weak legions:
> And whiles the honourable captain there
> Drops bloody sweat from his war-wearied limbs,
> And, in advantage lingering, looks for rescue,
> You, his false hopes, the trust of England's honour,
> Keep off aloof with worthless emulation.
> Let not your private discord keep away
> The levied succours that should lend him aid,
> While he, renowned noble gentleman,
> Yields up his life unto a world of odds.
>
> IV iv 13.

It is dissension, Lucy says on another occasion, that has lost all the
conquests Henry V had made:

> Thus, while the vulture of sedition
> Feeds in the bosom of great commanders,
> Sleeping neglection doth betray to loss
> The conquest of our scarce-cold conqueror,
> That ever-living man of memory,
> Henry the Fifth: whiles they each other cross,
> Lives, honours, lands, and all hurry to loss.
>
> IV iii 47.

Our scarce-cold conqueror has been dead a number of years by now,
but no matter. Whenever in Shakespeare the public good is betrayed
by private ambition, a faithful Lucy is standing by to make sure that
no one shall miss the point.

Often, too, there is an Exeter. This nobleman, in life the third illegitimate son of John of Gaunt and Catherine Swynford, has a role entirely choric. In himself he has no existence, but his comments on the wavering health of *Respublica* show the strength of morality influences and remind us that England is the real hero of the play. He is a barometer that indicates whether the good or evil counsellors are in the ascendant.

Thus it is he who stays behind to speak the uneasy epilogue to III i, a hot-blooded scene in which Gloucester and Winchester pursue their private quarrel in the presence of the King. Henry's first words in the play are, significantly, a prayer for internal peace:

> Uncles of Gloucester and of Winchester,
> The special watchmen of our English weal,
> I would prevail, if prayers might prevail,
> To join your hearts in love and amity. . . .
> Civil dissension is a viperous worm,
> That gnaws the bowels of the commonwealth.
>
> III i 65.

Some sort of truce is then patched up, although it is obviously impermanent and insincere. The fated King has no real command over his subjects. Then, in the atmosphere of false amity that has been momentarily established, another mistake is made. Richard Plantagenet, who has just been privately advised by Mortimer to make a bid for the crown, is restored to the full inheritance of the House of York, of which his family had been deprived after his father's treason in the previous reign.[1] The council of state then withdraw, Henry credulously happy to have turned a quarrel into fair words, Gloucester oozing naïve optimism, and the others concealing dark thoughts behind a display of back-slapping bonhomie. But uncle Exeter is not deceived.

> Ay, we may march in England or in France,
> Not seeing what is likely to ensue.
> This late dissension grown betwixt the peers
> Burns under the feigned ashes of forg'd love,
> And will at last break out into a flame:
> As fester'd members rot but by degree,
> Till bones and flesh and sinews fall away,
> So will this base and envious discord breed.
> And now I fear that fatal prophecy
> Which in the time of Henry, nam'd the Fifth,
> Was in the mouth of every sucking babe;
> That Henry born at Monmouth should win all;

---

[1] *Henry V* II ii.

And Henry born at Windsor should lose all:
Which is so plain that Exeter doth wish
His days may finish ere that hapless time.
                                    III i 186.

In IV i the smouldering quarrel between York and Somerset breaks
out to mar the dignity of the King's coronation in Paris, a ceremony
designed to impress the French with the undiminished strength and
confidence of the invaders. York manages to conceal his anger and
ambition, but once again Exeter, lingering behind a pillar, comes
forward to tell the audience not to be misled by fair appearances. In
a speech predicting that when France is lost, the English will turn to
fighting one another, he establishes York as a man dangerous to the
nation. Exeter has only two more speeches to make, and both are in
character. He gloomily fears the sharpened ambition of a Winchester
now 'call'd unto a cardinal's degree', and he speaks a dutiful couplet
in favour of honouring the contract made with Armagnac and turning
down the new proposal to marry the King to Margaret.

The prominence given to these choric intrusions denotes Shakespeare's technical immaturity, and he would presently learn to convey
his intentions in more dramatic ways. Immaturity of a different kind is
evident in the verse. To write like Marlowe was a pardonable ambition
in an aspiring dramatist at that time, but much of the verse is rather
sonorous than significant and, since copiousness was a quality much
admired, there is a good deal of conscientious straining after the simpler
rhetorical effects. Often there is more clamour than sense, and much of
the imagery is lacking in taste and precision. The opening lines of the
play feature comets with long hair which they are invited to use as
whips; so it is not surprising, a few lines later, to come upon mothers
who suckle babes with their tears. The author also has a fancy for
ornament drawn from a commonplace store of classical and other
learning. To speak of Talbot as 'the great Alcides of the field' is well
enough, for the comparison is apt and brief, but mostly these classical
demonstrations occur in contexts where they are tasteless and inappropriate. The Dauphin thus addresses Joan:

Was Mahomet inspired with a dove?
Thou with an eagle art inspired then.
Helen, the mother of great Constantine,
Nor yet Saint Philip's daughters were like thee.
Bright star of Venus, fall'n down on the earth,
How may I reverently worship thee enough?
                                    I ii 140.

Elsewhere the same speaker celebrates Joan in lines that echo the similitudes and cadences of Marlowe:

> And all the priests and friars in my realm
> Shall in procession sing her endless praise.
> A statelier pyramis to her I'll rear
> Than Rhodope's or Memphis ever was:
> In memory of her when she is dead,
> Her ashes in an urn more precious
> Than the rich-jewell'd coffer of Darius,
> Transported shall be at high festivals
> Before the kings and queens of France
>
> I vi 19.

When Tamburlaine spoke like this, the setting was oriental and the woman he addressed was Zenocrate, his wife; or Faustus, suspended somewhere between earth and outer space, was lost in a dream of all fair women. Their words were dramatically appropriate and did not much offend decorum. But it is another matter to find such language on the lips of a feudal prince, not as a knight laying the gauds of victory at his lover's feet but simply in otiose admiration of a country girl who has done some fighting for him. Such was the unfortunate and short-lived fashion set by the bookish gentlemen who condescended to the public stages. Classical allusiveness is at its most oppressive when Talbot vows to avenge Salisbury's death by setting fire to French cities. Apparently the cliché is inescapable. He will exult in his revenge

> and like thee, Nero,
> Play on the lute, beholding the towns burn.
>
> I iv 95.

For the sake of dragging in even so jaded a comparison as this, the dramatist is reckless of the impropriety of suggesting that the Talbot of his play, whose normal language is of the sword and the beasts of forest and field, would ever have known how to put his scarred hands to the lute.[1]

But these inexperienced follies are only an incidental weakness of a serious and mainly effective play. *1 Henry VI* has an earnestness which distinguishes it from most of the rather turgid and meaningless entertainments offered on the public stages at the time of the Armada. It is far from being a rumbustious glorification of England such as the audiences of the early nineties are supposed to have enjoyed, and its

---

[1] In the speech which opens IV vii, where Talbot mourns the death of his son 'in a sea of blood', the hackneyed metaphor similarly brings to mind the death of Icarus, who also was a son who died by falling into the sea.

purpose, with an unmistakable eye upon contemporary uncertainties, was to underline the evils of disunity. Elizabethan England is here being reminded that disunity was the means which God formerly chose for the terrible fulfilment of the curse brought upon the nation by the usurping House of Lancaster. The stars had revolted and the French were receiving unnatural courage from the aid of sorcery, but the English co-operated in their doom by the sin of disloyalty. Shakespeare divides the responsibility between fate and individual weakness. At times he regarded the quarrelling noblemen as helpless victims of the Lancastrians' curse, which compelled them to act as they did; but he could not think of them as wholly free from blame, and at times he seems to forget the stars and simply lay the guilt upon those evil counsellors of the king who neglected the common weal for their own feuds and ambitions. Even their enemies, themselves united in an unfamiliar discipline by Joan's witchery, comment wonderingly upon it:

> Had York and Somerset brought rescue in
> We should have found a bloody day of this.
> IV vii 33.

The play makes the same appeal as *King John*, imploring the English to close their ranks and forsake the divisions through which alone they are vulnerable.

The events of Part Two cover the years 1445–1455, from Margaret's coming to England, after the peace negotiations at Tours, to the first battle of the civil war at St. Albans.[1] The theme is still to show the wickedness of dissension, the implicit consequence of the Lancastrian usurpation, and it is here embodied in the ambitions of York, whose success is made possible by the weakness of the King and the overthrow of Humphrey of Gloucester, the conventional good counsellor. The whole of the action takes place 'in various parts of England', reported events in France[2] merely being used to furnish the 'good' characters with occasions to urge the importance of national unity, and in this play Shakespeare introduces Cade and other characters to show the effect of the prevailing disorder on ordinary people. For the first time he warns us that majesty dies not alone.

---

[1] The fall of the Duchess of Gloucester strictly belongs to 1441, but Shakespeare quite legitimately includes it among the events leading to the overthrow of her husband.

[2] The references are surprising. No mention whatsoever is made of Talbot, and it is implied (I i 84 sq.) that the English champion against Joan had been the Duke of Bedford.

2 Henry VI still adopts in the main the structure of the morality, with *Respublica* threatened by the various personifications of Lust, Pride and Ambition; and the special political lesson that Shakespeare wishes to use for the instruction of his contemporaries is that pre-scriptive right—York has a better claim to the throne than Henry—does not justify an attack on the *de facto* possessor. York is not, except in flashes, the sort of hero he so easily might have been. In the opening scene he identifies himself plainly as Ambition:

> Cold news for me, for I had hope of France,
> Even as I have of fertile England's soil.
> A day will come when York shall claim his own. . . .
> And, when I spy advantage, claim the crown,
> For that's the golden mark I seek to hit.
> I i 238.

These are the flat, conventional tones of *Respublica's* commonest and most easily recognisable enemy, and they indicate York's normal way of speaking and thinking. Only once does he catch the accents first of Macbeth and then of Marlowe's favoured heroes:

> Now, York, or never, steel thy fearful thoughts,
> And change misdoubt to resolution:
> Be that thou hop'st to be, or what thou art
> Resign to death; it is not worth the enjoying.
> Let pale-fac'd fear keep with the mean-born man,
> And find no harbour in a royal heart.
> Faster than spring-time showers comes thought on thought,
> And not a thought but thinks on dignity.
> III i 331.

For the rest of the speech a brain 'more busy than the labouring spider' weaves plots in the spirit of an acknowledged Machiavellianism. This is the high-aspiring man for whose own good 'all causes shall give way', the compelling master of events. Men of this sort engaged Marlowe's imagination and inspired his finest writing. For him, as for them, it was passing brave to be a king, whether of slaughtered Persians or the secret books of knowledge or 'golden poesy' itself. Shakespeare was evidently impressed by these intoxicating displays, and there must have been a temptation to realise such a character in York. But with remarkable self-discipline he gives no more than occasional hints of what York might have been if he had wanted to catch the fashion that Marlowe had made popular in the theatre. *2 Henry VI* is something more complex than an analysis and celebra-tion of this type of man; it was not to be a play in which all the light and heat would blaze about the person of a single character. Shakespeare's handling of York shows his real preoccupations at this time. In discovering the causes of weakness and disunity, the history play was to be a serious instrument of political education, and for this purpose the important thing was to expose the effects of York's egoism on other people. Shakespeare was much more concerned with this than with the effects on York himself. The rise and fall of a particular individual meant less to him than the disaster he brought to England.

> I will stir up in England some black storm
> Shall blow ten thousand souls to heaven or hell;
> And this fell tempest shall not cease to rage
> Until the golden circuit on my head,
> Like to the sun's transparent beams,
> Do calm the fury of this mad-bred flaw.
>
> III i 349.

This is York's usual manner, and his destructiveness will not ensure the promised calm. Like all the principal characters in this trilogy, he is, despite his energy, strangely passive. They commit their crimes because they are victims of a sickness that is endemic.

But if York is no Mortimer or Guise, he does appear as an embryo of Bolingbroke. By the time he came to write *Richard II*, Shakespeare was able to divest his drama of all that encumbered its main purpose, and he presented a clear issue between the ethics and expediency of rebellion. Purely in terms of statesmanship, Bolingbroke would make a better king than Richard—if there were no more to be said than that. Although subordinate to the simple morality theme of the state attacked by various evil personifications, the same issue occurs intermittently in *2 Henry VI*.

Thus it would have been sufficient for York to base his claim to the crown on the acknowledged principle of legitimacy. He was heir to the dethroned Plantagenets, and the restoration of his lost estates and titles[1] left him with only one more step to take. Alike for the purposes of history and of drama, this hereditary right would have been a respectable cloak for the ambition which York does not hesitate to reveal. But Shakespeare also provides him with more practical excuses, allowing his patriotism to be sincerely wounded by the King's misgovernment. In this play Henry is drawn with a surprising lack of charity. He can no longer be acquitted with the fatalistic reflection that it is always thus when sceptres are in children's hands. He is a man

[1] *1 Hen. VI* III i 163-4.

now, and a responsible king, and the insipid pieties with which he greets misfortune are no substitute for good government; nor, which would have partly redeemed them, do they bear the mark of a truly Christian resignation. His failures are many. Although he weeps for Gloucester's death, he has already abandoned him to his enemies; and he grieves just as much when the wicked Beaufort dies. When his subjects quarrel in his presence, he is just a feather puffed to and fro upon their angry breath. In IV ix, which is only a short scene, he begins by wishing that he were no longer king and ends with a resolve to 'learn to govern better'. After the military failure at St. Albans he immediately wants to give up the struggle altogether: 'Can we outrun the heavens?' A man so conscious of his own unfitness and disinclination to rule cannot hope to inspire either loyalty or achievement.

These weaknesses are not lost on York. His picture of Henry 'surfeiting in joys of love' is just a smear (the Queen's affections are directed elsewhere) but he has two trenchant phrases about Henry's 'churchlike humours', unsuitable in the occupant of a throne, and the 'bookish rule' that has 'pull'd fair England down'. York knows that he would make a better king:

> Let them obey that know not how to rule;
> This hand was made to handle nought but gold.
>
> I am far better born than is the king,
> More like a king, more kingly in my thoughts.
> V i 6, 28.

As soon as the crown is his, he will wipe out the disgrace of the long defeats in France. These are not idle boasts, and his ability is not in doubt; for the moment we may even forget his ambition and accept his good intentions. In capacity for leadership Shakespeare deliberately contrasts him with Henry and so foreshadows the theme of *Richard II*.

But the idea is only casually introduced and we should not make too much of it. In so far as reality intrudes upon the conventional pattern of the play, it is a source of artistic weakness, and anyway it made no difference to Shakespeare's conclusions. Supreme rights were vested in the king *de facto*, even if his rival had a better claim by inheritance. Shakespeare's dread of civil war was too strong to be qualified by extenuations of any kind, and ultimately his recognition of Henry's failure, or of York's patriotism and political abilities, was less significant to him than his determination to reveal York without sympathy as a monster of ambition. But he has already realised that power is a trust which it is sinful to refuse. If there could be a political crime

C.M.—N

graver than rebellion, it would be the failure of a king to do his duty.

When the play begins, England's hopes rest upon Humphrey of Gloucester. He is Protector of the realm and the good counsellor through whose efforts disaster might still be averted—the morality convention required that the victim should always appear to have a chance. Gloucester's overthrow occupies the first three Acts, and as in Part One, the opening scene skilfully establishes the theme. Employing patriotic arguments which at once mark him as a 'good' character, Gloucester opposes the marriage alliance with Reignier which had been proposed at the end of the preceding play. Margaret, who is Reignier's daughter, will therefore be Gloucester's enemy, and so will Suffolk, Margaret's paramour, who has negotiated the marriage. Cardinal Beaufort is an enemy whom Gloucester takes over from Part One, so the alignment of most of the principal characters has been demonstrated in a single economical stroke. When animosities of this kind threaten the state, tradition demands that there shall be some guileless by-stander, like Exeter in Part One, to announce the claims of duty and unselfishness, and this is punctually performed by the Earl of Salisbury. Warwick, his son,[1] echoes him:

> While these do labour for their own preferment,
> Behoves it us to labour for the realm. . . .
> Join we together for the public good,
> In what we can to bridle and suppress
> The pride of Suffolk and the cardinal,
> With Somerset's and Buckingham's ambition;
> And, as we may, cherish Duke Humphrey's deeds,
> While they do tend the profit of the land.
>
> I i 182.

So the good counsellor still has his supporters, and when, later, the Nevilles side with York, their action is the more significant after their display of orthodoxy in the opening scene. It shows how far the poison

---

[1] These men are not the Salisbury and Warwick of Part One, although Shakespeare evidently thought they were. The Salisbury killed in France in 1428 was Thomas de Montacute, the fourth Earl, whose only child married Richard Neville. In 1429 Neville became Earl of Salisbury in the right of his wife, and although he did spend a short time with the King in France, he did not achieve anything of note. His son, also Richard, was not born until 1428, and he did not fight in France in Talbot's time. The 'victorious Warwick' of whom Gloucester speaks (I i 87) was Richard de Beauchamp, the Warwick of Shaw's *St. Joan*, who died at Rouen in 1439. The younger Neville married this Warwick's only daughter, in whose right he succeeded to the earldom in 1449.

of sedition has already spread. Meanwhile, York the dissembler professes to agree with these hopeful sentiments, but as soon as he is alone he reveals his personal ambition. He has seen enough to realise that he need not come into the open to destroy Gloucester, who has enemies enough already. When these enemies fall out among themselves will be his moment to strike and win the throne.

There remains the King. His unwisdom is shown immediately when, against Gloucester's advice, he accepts the marriage treaty, with its humiliating conditions; and then, unprovoked, deprives York, who has not yet spoken, of his regency in France. Ingenuously throwing more fuel on to the fire, he goes on to raise Suffolk to a dukedom. The man who should have been royal enough to be guided by his good counsellor has already shown himself to be a political imbecile. Gloucester is clearly doomed.

Subsequent events reinforce the pattern which this scene has made. Gloucester's good qualities, which he wears with a certain smugness, receive further demonstration in the casual episodes of Horner and Simpcox and in his rebukes to his own Duchess for the dangerous thoughts she communicates to him. The Duchess tries to play Lady Macbeth[1] to a husband who will not 'catch the nearest way', and his reproofs are uttered in the unmistakable tones of political virtue.[2] But it is often the weakness of good counsellors to be too politically innocent, too tightly immured in their own righteousness, to make a correct estimate of their enemies. Gloucester seems never to know what is gathering about him, and we should recognise that his blindness is just another symptom of the sickness from which the whole country suffers. He is himself discredited when the Duchess fails in her reckless hope 'to play my part in Fortune's pageant', but he does not heed her warnings that the nobles are plotting his fall. They have all, she tells him,

> lim'd bushes to betray thy wings;
> And, fly how thou canst, they'll tangle thee:
> But fear not thou, until thy foot be snar'd,
> Nor never seek prevention of thy foes.
>   II iv 54.

This image is significantly taken up by Suffolk later, when he says that any trap may be used to catch a fox:

---

[1] Cf. I ii 1–16, 61–7 with *Macbeth* I v 16–31. The drift and arguments are remarkably similar.

[2] In a significant phrase he urges her to 'banish the canker of ambitious thoughts' (I ii 18). For other examples of his orthodoxy, see II iii 15–16, 32–8.

And do not stand on quillets how to slay him:
Be it by gins, by snares, by subtilty,
Sleeping or waking, 'tis no matter how,
So he be dead.

III i 261.

Meanwhile York is quietly working out his schemes. He uses the lightweight Buckingham to unmask the Duchess of Gloucester, and then, in a scene which is totally undramatic but would have conveyed a good deal to an Elizabethan audience, he wins the support of the Nevilles. Dutifully prompting him with questions that allow him to amplify his long-winded disclosures, they listen patiently while he details his pedigree and proves that the crown lawfully belongs to him. The sacred principle of legitimacy, set aside by the Lancastrian usurpation, brings York the support of the only two noblemen who have hitherto been neutral observers of the struggle. They are not, nor do they ever become, enemies of Gloucester, whom they regard as the King's shield against the treachery of Beaufort, Suffolk and the Queen. But they too, in their honest, blundering way, are struck with the general blindness. Without properly realising it, they are committed to a plot which will be much more damaging to the country's peace than the other schemes that are overwhelming Gloucester. Warwick already has his feet on the path that will lead him to be the maker and un-maker of kings.

Act III assures York of success by removing most of his rivals from the scene and showing yet again that Henry will be incapable of resisting his designs. In III i York is able to stand aside while the conspiracy against Gloucester comes to a head and he is accused in full council at Bury St. Edmunds. The wretched Henry makes no effort to save him.

My lords, what to your wisdom seemeth best
Do or undo, as if ourself were here;

III i 195.

and his inaction becomes the more ignoble when he goes on to admit that he knows Gloucester to be innocent. The news of Gloucester's death brings the Nevilles rushing to accuse Suffolk and the Cardinal of his murder; and when their protests are made more dangerous by murmurings of popular discontent off stage, the irresolute King is moved to order Suffolk's banishment. On his way out of the country Suffolk is seized and killed by pirates; and as for the Cardinal, 'suddenly a grievous sickness took him' and he dies in no little torment of soul and body. It is nearly a clean sweep; and York, for whose ultimate advantage it all happens, is not even on hand to witness these latter events, as he has been sent to quell a rebellion in Ireland. He does not fail to note that the troops so employed will be useful for another purpose later on.

Significantly, the sequel to the good counsellor's fall is the episode of Cade, which throws the dark shadow of chaos. Cade is just an instrument of York, and his rebellion is part of a softening-up process, to probe the strength of the government's resistance and discover how much support may be expected for a more strongly mounted enterprise. The historical Cade, a rather enigmatic figure, did play some such part as this, but in Shakespeare's play he is the incarnation of disorder, a symbol of the corruption that is rotting the country's soul.[1] In the final Act, with York returned from Ireland, the parties are aligned for the struggle that will occupy the following play. Over the unambitious countryside round St. Albans they fight the first great battle of the civil war, and with Somerset's death in action the Queen is left for the moment the solitary champion of her unroyal husband's cause.

> Oft have I heard that grief softens the mind,
> And makes it fearful and degenerate;
> Think therefore on revenge, and cease to weep.
>   IV iv i.

Left friendless by the death of Suffolk, who 'rul'd like a wandering planet over me', she is ripe for the terrible destiny that will be hers for the rest of the story. In certain circumstances it would be possible to pity her or admire her spirited defence of the crown, but Shakespeare will not gild her motives. She is devoid of political virtue. The country's peace, the restoration of strong and orderly government, do not concern her; she is simply the embodiment of revenge and general destruction.

Shakespeare does not end the play on any particular climax but he ends it tidily, with the assurance of more to come. For the Lancastrians he finds a bonny fighter in Young Clifford, who is determined to avenge his father's death; and on the other side he introduces York's two sons, Edward and Richard, who will lead the Plantagenet cause when he is dead. It is interesting to make Richard's acquaintance for the first time and to watch Shakespeare coming to realise his possibilities. Already he is a master of sardonic insult—'You shall sup with Jesus Christ to-night', he tells Young Clifford on the eve of battle—

---

[1] See above, pp. 122–7.

but he observes that weapons will achieve what words cannot. 'Priests pray for enemies, but princes kill.' The short closing scene of the play celebrates his outstanding courage in the battle, where, it is said, he three times rescued Salisbury from death. Actually he was only two and a half at the time, having been born at Fotheringay in October 1452.

2 Henry VI is not a good play but it achieves the effect that Shakespeare intended, of a society ravaged by mortal disease. The victims cannot help themselves, and when they speak of the normal human virtues, it is in a sense of something unattainable and not perfectly understood. They know themselves to be the victims that they are. The play is remarkable in the Shakespeare canon as the only one that has no single character with a redeeming vision of an uncorrupted society and the possibility of virtue. Gloucester and the Nevilles are better than the rest but there is no depth in them. They are no more than conventional attitudes of goodness, easily deceived, and their very simplicity is a vice. Shakespeare is at pains to show how the contagion of evil has spread to the least of men. Cade and his followers are the gullible architects of anarchy; Horner and his man Peter play out the political feud in miniature; the Duchess of Gloucester's familiars seem to be the twisted fancies of a brain tormented by ambition; and the episode of Simpcox, while it enables Gloucester to prove his superiority to elementary impostures, shows how easily the simple affections of ordinary folk have been corrupted by credulity and deception. Although the King is much to blame, the play pictures a society wholly incapable of virtue. It is a grim illustration of the total cease of majesty.

Inevitably the verse reflects the savage passions of those who speak it, and even the rare passages of tenderness are fretted with restlessness and violence. In their parting at the close of III ii Suffolk and Margaret momentarily find language that seems to come from the heart. She silences the 'bitter-searching terms' in which he has been cursing his enemies and bids him go,

> that I may know my grief;
> 'Tis but surmis'd whiles thou art standing by,
> As one that surfeits thinking on a want.
>   III ii 346.

Just for a few lines he catches her gentler mood:

> 'Tis not the land I care for, wert thou thence;
> A wilderness is populous enough,

So Suffolk had thy heavenly company:
For where thou art, there is the world itself,
With every several pleasure in the world,
And where thou art not, desolation.

This is the language of genuine emotion, but they cannot sustain it. Suffolk is soon lost in a tortured image in which he supposes his soul being taken into heaven

As mild and gentle as the cradle babe,
Dying with mother's dug between its lips;

Margaret likens parting to 'a fretful corsive' applied to 'a deathful wound', and Suffolk ends the matter by seeing their separation in terms of the sundering of 'a splitted bark'. Violence of this kind is the natural language of the play, and it is the accompaniment to violent deeds. At the sight of his dead father Young Clifford is moved to sudden tenderness:

Wast thou ordain'd, dear father,
To lose thy youth in peace, and to achieve
The silver livery of advised age,
And in thy reverence and thy chair-days thus
To die in ruffian battle?

V ii 45.

But once again the gentle mood does not last, and he flings himself into characteristic threats of vengeance:

Even at this sight
My heart is turn'd to stone: and while 'tis mine
It shall be stony. York not our old men spares;
No more will I their babes: tears virginal
Shall be to me even as the dew to fire:
And beauty, that the tyrant oft reclaims,
Shall to my flaming wrath be oil and flax.
Henceforth I will not have to do with pity.

In the main Shakespeare has to look to the animal kingdom to find similitudes apt for the savagery of his humans, and the reiterated references to foxes, curs, kites, wolves, lions and other beasts of prey invest the action with an atmosphere of noisy, naked violence. The characters can scarcely speak without baring their teeth in a snarl.[1] In

[1] If they do happen to smile, it is in deception.

Seems he a dove? His feathers are but borrow'd,
For he's disposed as is the hateful raven:
Is he a lamb? his skin is surely lent him,
For he's inclined as is the ravenous wolf.
Who cannot steal a shape that means deceit?

III i 75.

Act III the enemies of the throne are pictured in a continuous image of snakes and scorpions, and by contrast the unguarded innocence of chicken, dove or lamb suggests the helplessness of the victims of conspiracy. The same theme is alternatively presented in Henry's symbol of the butcher and the slaughter-house.[1] For the men who have banished him Suffolk wishes

> Their chiefest prospect murdering basilisks!
> Their softest touch as smart as lizard's stings!
> Their music frightful as the serpent's hiss,
> And boding screech-owls make the concert full!
> III ii 324.

The mood of unchained brutishness is deepened by the dramatist's habit of crystallising these reflections on animal behaviour into quasi-proverbial *sententiae*. The Senecan aphorism was a device much studied by literary men, especially by the Euphuists, who consulted the animal and vegetable creation for generalisations to illuminate every facet of human activity. In a single scene, III i, we find these examples:

> Small curs are not regarded when they grin,
> But great men tremble when the lion roars.

> The fox barks not when he would steal the lamb.

> The ancient proverb will be well effected:
> 'A staff is quickly found to beat a dog.'

> And Gloucester's show
> Beguiles him as the mournful crocodile
> With sorrow snares relenting passengers.

> My brain, more busy than the labouring spider,
> Weaves tedious snares to trap mine enemies.

As a further symbol of disorder Shakespeare uses the well-known image of storm and tempest. Professor G. Wilson Knight has taught us that the tempest is 'Shakespeare's intuition of discord and conflict',[2] and that all his drama revolves round the distinction between the storm as discord and music as harmony. Tempests project the soul's unrest, music its cherished attainment of harmony and grace. This distinction is commonly mirrored in the sea, which in tempest has a tragic suggestion of death and chaos, and in calm is to be interpreted as a symbol of peace. The familiar dualism of order and chaos in the state is only a

---

[1] See C. F. E. Spurgeon, *Shakespeare's Imagery*, 228–9.
[2] *The Shakespearian Tempest*, especially Chapter I.

statement in political terms of the larger dualism in which all human life is lived.

Wilson Knight finds each of these two representative symbols to be associated with a wealth of subsidiary images which are interchangeable and always carry a similar meaning. Thus the tempest may be associated with tears, water, shipwreck, winds, rocks, wild beasts, battle, untuned instruments or any other presage of violence and disorder. With music, perhaps because it is the rarer state, the associations are fewer, but sunshine, moonlight, jewels, love and the whole range of the kindly affections stand as symbols of that harmony and order whose archetype is God's plan for the universe. The polarity is concisely stated by Adonis:

> Love comforteth like sunshine after rain,
> But Lust's effect is tempest after sun.
> *VA* 799.

The statement is seldom so direct, and as Shakespeare's art matured, the full range of associative imagery became a kind of shorthand in which any one of the key words was capable of suggesting all its complements and all its opposites.

In an early play like *2 Henry VI* Shakespeare's poetic apprehensions were struggling against the rhetorical devices which the age demanded, and the image of the savage beast, stiflingly conventional though it was, had to serve him as the prevailing symbol of disorder. But the storm is the symbol he uses at one of the most significant moments of the play, when the Queen describes her coming into England and chides Henry for spurning the love she brought him:

> Was I for this nigh wrack'd upon the sea,
> And twice from England's awkward bank
> Drove back again unto my native clime?
> What boded this, but well forewarning wind
> Did seem to say, 'Seek not a scorpion's nest,
> Nor set no footing on this unkind shore'?
> What did I then, but curs'd the gentle gusts
> And he that loos'd them forth their brazen caves;
> And bid them blow towards England's blessed shore,
> Or turn our stern upon a dreadful rock?
> Yet Æolus would not be a murderer,
> But left that hateful office unto thee:
> The pretty vaulting sea refus'd to drown me,
> Knowing that thou wouldst have me drown'd on shore
> With tears as salt as sea through thy unkindness.
> III ii 82.

As the sky darkened she took a jewel from her neck 'and threw it towards thy land: the sea receiv'd it'. The jewel is frequently a symbol of
love, and the picture of rich merchandise scattered on the ocean-bed
tells of love that has been shipwrecked by the world's storms. Suffolk
revives the image at the climax of his parting from her. Her heart will
go with him on his banishment,

> A jewel, lock'd into the woefull'st cask
> That ever did contain a thing of worth.
> III ii 409.

The opposition of storm and music is stated in the King's words when
Gloucester and the Cardinal are quarrelling:

> The winds grow high; so do your stomachs, lords.
> How irksome is this music to my heart;
> When such strings jar, what hope of harmony?
> II i 55.

Finally, as the divisions widen, the storm naturally becomes the symbol of civil war. York threatens that

> I will stir up in England some black storm
> Shall blow ten thousand souls to heaven or hell;
> And this fell tempest shall not cease to rage
> Until the golden circuit on my head,
> Like to the glorious sun's transparent beams,
> Do calm the fury of this mad-bred flaw;
> III ii 349.

the sun here taking the place of music as the instrument of harmony.

2 Henry VI is not a play that greatly moves us. Shakespeare is still
observing life from a distance, writing a play rather than living it, and
his true poetic intuitions are smothered by the demands of literary
fashion. The swift, tangy prose of the Cade scenes is better than anything he manages in the way of verse. But this is not to say that the
poetry is wholly undramatic. Still overburdened with classical ornament[1] and still (in Greene's sense) bombastic,[2] it comes much nearer

---

[1] For instance Young Clifford ends the speech already quoted by summoning
to his aid the merely conventional decoration lent by the familiar names of Medea,
Aeneas and Anchises. And see IV i 97–9.

[2] Writing on his deathbed, Greene warned his fellow-dramatists of the university that there was an upstart actor-playwright (Shakespeare) who thought
himself 'as well able to bombast out a blank verse as the best of you'. These
were not words of contempt. Bombast, literally, was the cottonwool used to stuff
and pad clothing, and to bombast out a blank verse was to stuff it out with
copious variations of style and meaning, to pack it with artifice and so make it
more impressive. 'Artificial' was a word of praise, and Greene wrote in grudging
admiration of Shakespeare's ready mastery of the arts of Rhetoric which he so
well deployed in *Henry VI*.

than the verse of Part One to sustaining the disheartened mood of a play in which not a single character has vision or memory of better days.

Part Three carries on the story in a gathering crescendo of destruction. The sea and the wind become the most potent images of these final episodes of the trilogy, as if it were only by means of this symbol that Shakespeare could realise the horrors which civil war had brought upon the kingdom. The images already familiar in the preceding plays, of the axe wantonly laid to the fruitful tree and England become a jungle and a slaughter-house, still have some force but they are now subordinate to the dominant symbol of the destructive, unheeding storm. To emphasise their helplessness, the characters are conceived as ships struggling against the tide or carried inertly before the gale, and the storm thus appears as the arbitrary instrument of the chaos which men's actions have created. Chaos, to Shakespeare, was never a passive condition. It was always a compulsive force, a ravening wolf or universal appetite, devouring and destroying. In *3 Henry VI*, where statecraft is stripped of its modest pretences and even the common decencies of war give place to acts of monstrous cruelty, the winds are fierce with the savagery and capriciousness of Fortune's wheel itself. The tide in men's affairs is no longer one which their own choice and energy will bring on to success. It will throw them on the rocks, try how they may.

If anyone in the play, Richard of Gloucester is the man with power to ride the winds, and it is significant that even he dreads the uncertain, estranging ocean when he feels the distance that separates him from the crown.

> Why then, I do but dream on sovereignty;
> Like one that stands upon a promontory,
> And spies a far-off shore where he would tread,
> Wishing his foot were equal with his eye;
> And chides the sea that sunders him from thence,
> Saying he'll lade it dry to have his way.
>
> III ii 134.

To the King, as he sits on the hillside watching the struggle on the plains below, the battle at Towton sways

> like a mighty sea,
> Forc'd by the tide to combat with the wind:
> Now sways it that way, like the self-same sea
> Forc'd to retire by fury of the wind:

> Sometime the flood prevails, and then the wind:
> Now one the better, then another best;
> Both tugging to be victors, breast to breast,
> Yet neither conqueror nor conquered:
> So is the equal poise of this fell war.
>
> II v 5.

So equal; and so arbitrary, and in the long run so unimportant, for there will be no victors, only vanquished. All the combatants are the sport of the winds. Later, Edward ominously warns Warwick that, 'sail how thou canst, have wind and tide thy friend', the capricious elements are about to desert their favourite and 'wind-changing Warwick now can change no more'.

As in the previous play, the most elaborate expression of the tempest image is given to Queen Margaret. After the defeat at Barnet, where Warwick has been killed and the King made prisoner, she compares her cause to a ship whose mast has been blown overboard, its cable broken, its anchor lost and half its sailors drowned. But in the young Prince Edward 'lives our pilot still', and

> Is not Oxford here another anchor?
> And Somerset, another goodly mast?
> The friends of France our shrouds and tacklings? . . .
> We will not from the helm, to sit and weep,
> But keep our course, though the rough wind say no,
> From shelves and rocks that threaten us with wrack.
>
> V iv 16.

Margaret's courage is always admirable, but here she is only rallying her followers with the energy of despair. The real significance of the voyage she proposes to them is its hopelessness. Continuing the metaphor, she likens Edward to 'a ruthless sea', perjured Clarence to 'a quicksand of deceit' and the deadly Richard to 'a ragged fatal rock'. Since any one of these would destroy them if they abandoned ship, they can only continue their journey with what feeble strength they have.

> There's no hoped-for mercy with the brothers
> More than with ruthless waves, with sands and rocks.
> Why, courage, then! what cannot be avoided
> 'Twere childish weakness to lament or fear.

How many characters in *Henry VI* go to their ruin with such sentiments as these. Courage and resignation are all that remains of their manhood.

The men and women of this trilogy do not inhabit a withdrawn world of hints and shrugs and oblique allusions. The amplification which encumbers their heavier speeches is without nuance or hidden meaning. Even when they are most long-winded, they are deafeningly downright. In Part Three their voices howl more shrilly than elsewhere, as if they were trying to outshriek the competing winds. It often leads them into absurdities, as when Queen Elizabeth fears that her weeping and 'blood-sucking sighs' may blast or drown the infant she carries in her womb, but it expresses their sense of helplessness in a world become infinitely violent and dangerous. Desperation is their only pilot, and each sea-sick weary bark is destined to founder on the rocks.

The reiteration of this idea[1] gives imaginative coherence to a play which is a continuous record of perjury, bloodshed and destruction. It covers the years 1455 to 1471,[2] a period so much occupied with fighting and intrigue that Shakespeare had no room for anything else. His canvas is therefore smaller than in Part Two. He has no space to show in detail the impact of the war upon the common people. Two keepers, a huntsman and a group of watchmen, briefly introduced for the sake of the story, leave no impression behind them. This does not mean that Shakespeare has lost interest in them. The storm that envelops England is a general doom, and in the ritualistic scene at Towton he wrote a suitable epitaph for those of its victims who were innocent.

In the opening scene he is once again swift and skilful in getting the story moving. He immediately takes up the threads from the previous play, and York's occupation of the throne seems to follow the battle we saw him win at the end of Part Two. Henry once more displays his futility. After calling upon his supporters to take revenge upon the 'sturdy rebel', he proceeds to weaken the effect of these militant observations by refusing to make a shambles of the parliament-house and announcing that 'frowns, words, and threats' will be his weapons

---

[1] E.g. in Edward's fatalistic

> What fates impose, that men must needs abide;
> It boots not to resist both wind and tide.
>   IV iii 57.

In this play even the sun is the enemy of man. Instead of generating life, it parches and shrivels, dazzles the eye, breeds swarms of flies, attracts gnats, pierces at midday, sears, is clouded, brews a shower. Summer breeds no increase, but is associated with scalding heat, flames, fire, the parching of the entrails. The few favourable references to the sun are mostly heraldic.

[2] Or perhaps from 1460. The dramatist seems to confuse the first battle of St. Albans with the Yorkist victory at Northampton in 1460, after which York went to London to claim the throne. There are various simplifications introduced to speed the action, but on the whole the play is reasonably faithful to the facts. That Edward is made to march from York to Coventry by way of London is a point that is likely to escape notice in the theatre.

in the sort of war he means to conduct. Renewed bluster ('First shall war unpeople this my realm') is followed by another collapse when he admits the weakness of his title, got by his grandfather's violence: an early reminder to the audience of the curse upon his House. The appearance of soldiers in arms then frightens him into disinheriting his son on condition that he himself may rule for the rest of his natural life. Margaret, ever strong in purpose, enters to denounce this betrayal of their son, and the scene ends with Henry fatuously writing a letter to beg for the renewed allegiance of three lords who have abandoned him in pardonable disgust.

York is at once persuaded by his son Richard of Gloucester to break his promise that he will wait until Henry's death before taking the crown, and the battle of Wakefield follows. In a grisly little scene Clifford slays the Earl of Rutland, York's twelve-year-old son,[1] who, pert as all Shakespeare's juveniles, dies with a Latin sentence on his lips; and then York's defeat and execution are moralised as a commentary on the just deserts of unprincipled ambition. Margaret stands him on a molehill, sets a paper crown on his head and jests upon his fallen state.

> What! was it you that would be England's king?
> Was it you that revell'd in our parliament,
> And made a preachment of your high descent?
> Where are your mess of sons to back you now?
> The wanton Edward and the lusty George?
> And where's that valiant crook-back prodigy,
> Dicky your boy, that with his grumbling voice
> Was wont to cheer his dad in mutinies?
>
> I iv 70.

It was not yet considered bad form to gloat over a man when he was down, but modern sympathies, unused to such exhibitions, are all with York when Margaret tells him of Rutland's death and hands him, to dry his tears, a napkin reddened with the boy's blood. Yet the language in which Margaret speaks, the sharp idiom of a village scold, is an implicit comment on the man who

> Raught at mountains with outstretched arms,
> Yet parted but the shadow with his hand.
>
> I iv 68.

This is the play's epitaph on York. But before his enemies are done playing with him, he hits back in a speech (111–49) full of Shake-

---

[1] This is historically accurate. Rutland, York's second son, really was killed at Wakefield at the tender age of 12.

spearean sentiments and forms of expression.[1] It contains the raging wind of anger that blows up showers of grief; a characteristic adage ('beggars mounted run their horse to death'); an animal image (the wolf 'whose tongue more poisons than the adder's tooth'); and, of especial interest, York's wonderment that Margaret's face, 'visor-like, unchanging, made impudent with use of evil deeds', does not mirror the cruelty of her heart. Like Hamlet, he does not expect that one may smile and be a villain, that the appearance may be so much at odds with the reality. He asks if she can really be a woman at all, as 'women are soft, mild, pitiful and flexible'.

York's dying curses are prophetic, for the rest of the play shows how his family take their revenge. All the salient incidents of Wakefield are re-enacted in reverse. Like York in an earlier scene, Henry is persuaded into perjury, revoking his promise that the Plantagenets shall succeed him, and immediate defeat in battle is his punishment, just as it was York's. At Towton, while the battle rages at his feet, he draws aside to meditate upon the emptiness of wordly ambition; and in a nasty little pendant to the battle York's sons mock the body of Clifford, who at Wakefield slew their father and their brother. After certain minor fluctuations of fortune, brought about when Warwick and Clarence change sides, the pitiless story comes to an end at Tewkesbury. Here the young Prince Edward, son of Henry and Margaret and so the Lancastrian heir, dies with the same fatalistic courage as Rutland, and it is Margaret's turn to exclaim in grief and beg for death. More refined in their cruelty than she had been, her enemies refuse her request. Fortune's wheel has come full circle, after the accepted pattern of Tudor historiography, and the Lancastrians have had to suffer in defeat all the cruelty and humiliation they had inflicted when they were riding high. Prevailing notions of poetic justice have been nicely satisfied.

Of course the pattern was largely artificial, and in his insistence upon it Shakespeare was deliberately organising a crude, episodic story to an artistic purpose. As yet his art was self-conscious and over-didactic. He saw certain things more simply then than he was to see them later, and he had no need of ambiguities. Ambition and civil war were unmitigatedly evil. To make others feel the horror of his story as deeply as he felt it himself, he employed the consistent formality of art: a stylised balancing of the plot and a narrative method that had the tidiness of fable.

Thus in the central scene of the play, at Towton, the horror of civil

[1] It contains the line 'O tiger's heart wrapp'd in a woman's hide' which Greene parodied in drawing attention to Shakespeare's precocious skill, see *SWW* 91–2.

war is taken up into pure symbol. The King's speech in envy of the shepherd's lot is entirely conventional in spirit and content. An imagined rustic bliss was the salve monotonously applied to minds weary of the life of court and city. The coveted simplicities of milk-pail and maypole formed the basis of the pastoral vogue, and Towton was no occasion for Touchstone to intrude with the suggestion that 'in respect of itself it is a good life; but in respect that it is a shepherd's life, it is naught'—and did not Jane Shore have chapped hands from too much pressing of the dugs? Henry's soliloquy established a mood that the audience would recognise and would not probe too deeply. It is followed by the parallel episodes in which a Son finds that he has killed his Father, and a Father finds that he has killed his Son: 'sad-hearted men, much overgone with care', and yet, since their grief is only personal and private, much less woeful than their king. Shakespeare did not invent this particular symbol. It was already familiar from the chronicles and *A Mirror for Magistrates*, where it epitomised the blind wastefulness of civil war, but familiarity does not diminish its effect. The characters stiffen into the rigid attitudes of figures in a stained-glass window as their emblematic language echoes with the horror of those 'erroneous, mutinous and unnatural' days.

With this, Shakespeare had virtually said all that he needed to say upon this particular theme. He still had half a play to write and he continued dutifully on his way, but he seems to be losing interest. He is obviously perfunctory in observing the moral law that for every disaster there should be a precedent crime, usually perjury. This oath-breaking, already compelled into service before Wakefield and before Towton, becomes less effective with each repetition, and there are many repetitions. Edward of York throws over a French marriage because he is infatuated with Lady Grey; perjured Clarence changes sides twice; and Edward again, after being admitted to the city of York on the understanding that he is only come to claim his dukedom, is urged by Gloucester not to heed 'nice points' and agrees to declare himself king. Overworked to this extent, it is revealed as merely a device to keep the plot moving. Shakespeare seems to have felt it so, for he adds a fresh and individual touch by suggesting that Edward's main offence is not perjury but lust.

This oblique emphasis on a personal frailty touches upon the favourite Renaissance theme of *nurture*, which taught princes to be master of themselves before they attempted to rule others.[1] It is important here because for almost the first time Shakespeare turns his attention

[1] See above, pp. 85–7.

to the personal qualities of a king, something particular to the man himself and distinct from his predestined lot in a disastrous age. We met something of the kind at the end of Part One, where Henry broke his pledge to marry Armagnac's daughter because Suffolk's description of Margaret had stirred him to 'passion of inflaming love'. There it was quite out of character, and it was not seriously suggested that the priggish boy was overwhelmed by desire for a girl he had never seen. Its repercussions are only political. If Henry obtained any sensual satisfactions from his young bride, we are left to imagine them. Whatever his failings, lust is not one of them. But it is otherwise with Edward. His swift passion for Lady Grey is laid bare to the innuendoes of Gloucester and is lightly suggested as an indulgence of which a king should not be guilty. His acts of perjury are sins, but it is Gloucester who makes him commit them and they seem to lie only on the surface of his character. They are just a piece of the story-teller's mechanism. But his sensuality, prompting him to throw over a diplomatic marriage for the sake of a pretty face, belongs to himself, and it tangles his kingliness. Retribution, in Warwick's desertion and the temporary loss of the throne, comes too pat and copy-book to be convincing, but when he is restored, with his wife and her relations all about him, a doubt has been raised. His fitness has been called in question, and we can already see ahead to the haunted, ineffectual creature that he becomes in the earlier scenes of *Richard III*.

We must not insist too much on this, for Shakespeare himself is indirect in his handling of it. He is not particularly interested in Edward anyway. But it does point the way to a change of the highest importance. It is clear that as the play proceeds, Shakespeare begins to tire of the chronicle form, with its mechanical motivation, and to concern himself rather with the human problems of kingship. He never loses sight of his main purpose, which was to teach the same lessons he had already made evident in Part Two, but in the second half of *3 Henry VI* he is feeling his way towards something much more original and striking.

This is his changing conception of the character of the King. In Part Two Henry was not an individual. He was just a symbol of unfitness to be a king, wearing his piety and vacillation like a concealing mask. York, too, was incarnate ambition, not a man. Shakespeare made no attempt to consider either of them as a human being; he was content for them to express an attitude. He seems to have started Part Three in a similar frame of mind, and it is not until he has mastered his material and organised the plot within its conventional framework that he begins to find certain people interesting for what they are. He wants to look behind the mask and examine the fascinating idea that the man who is called to rule is a man as well as a king. He seems to realise that he will presently have to start his examination from the other end: not with the king but with the man.

He begins to discover new potentialities in Henry. There has been an earlier intimation of it in a short scene in Part Two (III iii), when his attitudinising piety seems for a moment to be the expression of an inner strength and conviction. Gloucester has just been murdered. Suffolk, one of the contrivers of the act, has been sent into banishment and word is brought that another, the Cardinal Beaufort, is mortally ill. Henry would have been only human if he had watched the Cardinal's last agonies with a certain satisfaction, but in genuine distress he asks for heaven's mercy on his enemy:

> O thou eternal Mover of the heavens!
> Look with a gentle eye upon this wretch;
> O! beat away the busy meddling fiend
> That lays strong siege unto this wretch's soul,
> And from his bosom purge this black despair.
>
> III iii 19.

When Warwick sanctimoniously suggests that an ugly death is a fit conclusion to an evil life, Henry tells him to 'forbear to judge, for we are sinners all'. It is to be his verdict on all his enemies. But elsewhere in Part Two his religiosity is too good to be true. Either it is a cover for his irresolution, a series of phrases brought out to disarm rebuke; or, if it is sincere, it provokes the sort of dislike that certain critics of *Measure for Measure* have felt for Isabella's chastity. In the first half of the following play, he is just as ineffective. If he had had his wish to be a shepherd, he would certainly have lost his sheep.

The change is first evident after Towton, when Shakespeare seems at last to discover what may be made of him. His mind has achieved a new discipline when the keepers find him wandering, a fugitive from Scotland, in the northern forests. Reflecting on his predicament, he reaches the conclusion—so different from the merely facile self-criticism of earlier scenes—that the king who cannot help himself is powerless to help his subjects, and he welcomes 'sour adversity' as a tonic, 'for wise men say it is the wisest course'. When the keepers accost him, he can even speak in riddles:

> More than I seem, and less than I was born to:
> A man at least, for less I should not be;
> And men may talk of kings, and why not I?
>
> III i 56.

His voice has never before carried such a note of maturity and confidence; and to the observation that he is speaking as if he were a king, he makes what is, considering his outward state at the time, a remarkable reply: 'Why, so I am, in mind; and that's enough.' His kingdom is in his mind:

> My crown is in my heart, not on my head;
> Not deck'd with diamonds and Indian stones,
> Not to be seen: my crown is called content;
> A crown it is that seldom kings enjoy.
>
> III i 62.

Henry has found himself, and found at the same time the unique place that he occupies in Shakespeare's histories. Outwardly the least fortunate of his kings, he is the only one who is able to say that he is content. Hallowed by suffering and his calm acceptance of it as his worldly lot, no one henceforth can harm him. Self-knowledge has set him free.

A man who is king cannot be otherwise than as he is. Once he has ceased to aspire to the sort of royalty that he could never command, Henry is free to display his true qualities of patience, humility and love. These are what he is and what he has to offer to his troubled age. At other times they might have prevailed, for they are qualities proper to a king. They will not prevail now, but at least Henry can leave them as a gracious memory to times when they will, and it is right that he should be the man chosen to speak prophetically of the young Richmond:

> Come hither, England's hope: If secret powers
> Suggest but truth to my divining thoughts,
> This pretty lad will prove our country's bliss.
> His looks are full of peaceful majesty,
> His head by nature fram'd to wear a crown,
> His hand to wield a sceptre, and himself
> Like to bless in time a regal throne.
> Make much of him, my lords; for this is he
> Must help you more than you are hurt by me.
>
> IV vi 68.

These are not great words—Shakespeare did not fully rise to his opportunity—but Henry is looking to the day when mildness and dignity will again be valued in a king, and this vision of a happier future is the source of his content. He has no illusions about his present unfitness and, when Warwick has released him from prison, he wants to abdicate,

> That the people of this blessed land
> May not be punished with my thwarting stars . . .

> I myself will lead a private life,
> And in devotion spend my latter days,
> To sin's rebuke and my Creator's praise.
>   IV vi 21, 42.

This is something different from his former irresolution, for the principles he now expresses are positive ones. His charity and forgiveness cast a benediction on the disordered scene and remind his generation that chastisement is not heaven's only task. He gives his own account of his stewardship:

> I have not stopp'd mine ears to their demands,
> Nor posted off their suits with slow delays;
> My pity hath been balm to heal their wounds,
> My mildness hath allay'd their swelling griefs,
> My mercy dried their water-swelling tears;
> I have not been desirous of their wealth;
> Nor much oppress'd them with great subsidies,
> Nor forward of revenge, though they much err'd.
>   IV viii 39.

The plays have supplied little practical illustration of these benefits, but Henry offers a recognisable ideal of kingship at which no one else in the trilogy has even hinted. It is disregarded, since his supporters simply treat him as a factor in the political struggle, useful because the monarchy will always command certain resources of loyalty and prestige. They seem to feel, too, that his sanctity lays on ordinary men a burden heavier than they should be expected to endure: which is an effect that sanctity often produces. But even if the characters on the stage are blinded to it, Henry's ideal of kingship prevails in the promise that the young Richmond shall one day be the sort of king that Henry himself would have liked to be. Henry has taught that he who would be master of a kingdom must first have settled his own estate. The whole trilogy is proof that other qualities are necessary too, but Henry has won the victory that all kings must win, and with it his peace of mind. That it contained the seeds of a still larger victory is hinted in Edward's words to Margaret in this play:

> For what hath broach'd this tumult but thy pride?
> Hadst thou been meek our title still had slept,
> And we, in pity of the gentle king,
> Had slipp'd our claim until another age.
>   II ii 159.

These are words that lay an enormous responsibility on a reigning king. They suggest that ambition would have been content to wait, that even the claims of legitimacy would have been allowed to rust, if the man on the throne had had the qualities to inspire loyalty. With reference to Henry VI, this idea is, as we know, specious and disingenuous. For causes beyond himself, Henry was fated. But if we will allow the lines as a marginal gloss, written outside the context of the play, we may sense Shakespeare moving towards a less fatalistic conception of royal responsibility.

The ideal that Henry represents is illuminated by the contrast with the aims of Richard of Gloucester, whose development runs parallel with his own. Even in Part Two Gloucester's sardonic realism has set him apart from the other combatants. He seems to have been born disenchanted, with a ruthless steely intransigence that scorns accommodation. 'Honour, love, obedience, troops of friends' are ethical perquisites in which he is simply not interested. His sword and speech are so readily turned to war that Shakespeare knew what he was about when he brought him to the battlefield at the age of something over two.

> Teeth hadst thou in thy head when thou wast born,
> To signify that thou cam'st to bite the world.
> > V vi 53.

At first his very considerable courage is at the service of a much-vaunted clannishness. The young Richard is a good Yorkist, vehement in his father's and his brother's cause. It is he who, playing for the highest prize, urges his father into the fatal perjury that precedes the rout at Wakefield; and in the scene (II i) that follows the battle it is his leadership that cheers his broken party and gives them confidence to change their fortunes.[1] His own grief at his father's death is a spur to action:

> To weep is to make less the depth of grief:
> Tears, then, for babes; blows and revenge for me!
> > II i 85.

Warwick, beaten at St. Albans, has to be cajoled and mocked and flattered out of his pessimism at the Yorkists' double defeat:

> 'Tis love I bear thy glories makes me speak.
> But, in this troublous time what's to be done?
> Shall we go throw away our coats of steel,
> And wrap our bodies in black mourning gowns,
> Numb'ring our Ave-Maries with our beads?

---

[1] Even in this he was exceptional, for it was customary to accept rebuffs from Fortune as part of the scheme of things and wait stolidly for the next revolution of the wheel.

Or shall we on the helmets of our foes
Tell our devotion with revengeful arms?
II i 158.

At Towton it is Richard again who rallies his brothers and Warwick when they would leave the field for rest or retreat.

But this clannishness presently proves to have been no more than the instinct which says that it is safer to keep with the pack while the jungle is dangerous. With Edward crowned and Richard himself raised to the dukedom of Gloucester, he reveals himself as the solitary hunter that at heart he has always been. The claws show as he spits out his hatred of Edward:

Would he were wasted, marrow, bones, and all,
That from his loins no hopeful branch may spring,
To cross me from the hopeful time I look for!
III ii 125.

From his earliest appearance he has always been the member of his family that the Lancastrians have hated and feared the most, and the audience will not forget the caressing, seductive words in which he has spoken to his father of the crown:

And, father, do but think
How sweet a thing it is to wear a crown,
Within whose circuit is Elysium,
And all that poets feign of bliss and joy.
I ii 28.

So far the practised Machiavel has kept his ambitions hidden, but in the second half of the play, as a complement to the growing importance of the King, the character is given greater room for deployment. A comparison between his long speech at III ii 124–95 with the similar speeches of his father in the previous play (I i 215–60 and III i 331–83) will show how much more skilful Shakespeare has become, and how his interest has shifted from the formal narration of the chronicle story, with its moral embellishments, to the sort of problem indicated in his maturer treatment of Henry VI. The sin of perjury, the seemingly capricious motions of Fortune's wheel, the inescapable doom of the House of Lancaster were all time-honoured mechanisms that helped to unfold the plot at a certain level. More than that, they were the drama-tist's means of ensuring that his didactic intention should not be mis-taken. But there are signs that Shakespeare was already looking for a more satisfactory explanation of human affairs, and he seems to have found it in moral conceptions rather different from the straightforward,

eye-for-an-eye morality of the chronicles. He found it superficial and
inadequate to go on seeking the causes of events in men's outward
actions, since their actions are only a consequence of the sort of men
they are, their response or resistance to the forces working on them.
The real causes are to be found in their minds, for being is as important
as doing, and what a man is will in the long run matter more than what
he does. Civil war is ultimately the product of disorder in the soul.
York's massive declarations of ambition are only mechanical and formal. They have no real significance, as York is not in the least a human
being. But it is otherwise with his terrible son, lost in the thorny wood
of his bloody imaginings. Where York conventionally absorbs himself in visions of cosmic upheaval, Richard is breezily practical in his
revelations. Here is one who will smile and murder while he smiles,
and frame his face to all occasions, and add colours to the chameleon.

Thus the play's interest is withdrawn from the lesser men and their
predestined doings[1] and is concentrated upon the two who stand at
opposite extremes of good and evil. Henry lacks the power of action,
but his saintliness and serenity shed their own illumination; Richard,
the man of deeds, is sheerly wicked. The play moves to its climax
under the shadow of their conflict. In so far as it is still a morality, they
have something in common with the Fairy Queen and Demon King
who contend in fable for possession of the hero—in this case England.
These roles never quite desert them. But there is a very real difference
between York and Gloucester, on the one hand, and on the other between the Henry of Part Two, with his church-like humours and bookish rule, and the man whose crown is called content. It is the difference
between characters who are merely the embodiment of moral attitudes
and characters who are struggling towards individuality and life.
Henry's new-found insight gives him a self-contained strength which
works upon men who hold him of no account as a political factor.
Gloucester, though naïvely theatrical (Shakespeare was not to learn
everything at once), is a master of wickedness who may contaminate
a nation.

The two men meet at the end of the play, when Gloucester hurries
from the field at Tewkesbury to his mission at the Tower. 'What scene
of death hath Roscius now to act?': Henry knows for what purpose he
has come. Unlike Richard II, he meets his death without resistance, for
he has long ago come to terms with himself and has no need to convince himself that he is brave. Rather it is Gloucester who has to seek
relief in action, drawing his sword to silence for ever his victim's

[1] Even Margaret is comparatively subdued. Her character does not develop.

prophecies of the misery he will bring to England. Henry dies with a pardon for his murderer and a prayer that his own sins may be forgiven.

Armed with the strength of the lion and the cunning of the fox—true Machiavellian attributes—Gloucester has been too powerful for this innocent enemy, and the scene lays conventional emphasis on the fact that the murder was foreordained. But so powerful is the force of Henry's virtue that the audience should feel that it will ultimately prevail. In the endless search for animal characteristics to denote the quality of human beings, the Middle Ages taught men to admire the pelican. From its fabled habit of suckling its young with its own blood, the pelican became the symbol of disinterested and self-sacrificing love.[1] This is a life-creating quality, and strength and cunning, when used to bad ends, must finally yield to it. Transmitted from Henry to the dedicated Richmond, it will one day cleanse England of the evil that Gloucester represents.

Left alone with Henry's body, Gloucester blusters like a man with a bad conscience. Before he silenced them, Henry's words had hit their mark, and he shows the reactions of a guilty man. He gloats over the body, brutally describing the blood on his sword as tears shed 'for the poor king's death'. The further, needless wounds that he then inflicts upon the corpse are his revenge for the inner wounds inflicted on himself, and the bloody gesture restores his good humour, for he finds some grim satisfaction in the contemplation of his own moral and physical deformities.

> I, that have neither pity, love, nor fear . . .
> I have no brother, I am like no brother;
> And this word 'love', which greybeards call divine,
> Be resident in men like one another
> And not in me: I am myself alone.
> V vi 68, 80.

Gloucester's intrigues and threats are commonplace, but his sense of isolation, of a moral perversity as remote from the minds of ordinary men as his twisted body from their clean, straight limbs, is not commonplace at all. His awareness of his own nature distinguishes him from all the other characters in *Henry VI* save the King himself. He has chosen the lonely, kindless road which will bring him one

[1] To his good friends thus wide I'll ope my arms;
And like the kind, life-rendering pelican,
Repast them with my blood.
Hamlet IV v 144.

day to Bosworth, where his words recoil on him with shocking force:

> Alack! I love myself. Wherefore? for any good
> That I myself have done unto myself?
> *Rich. III* V iii 188.

Gloucester is first a villain of melodrama, one of the most eloquent and exuberant there has ever been, but through him Shakespeare divined that separateness—the awful 'I am I' that begins as a boast and ends as a cry of pain, the badge of the lonely Caesars and emotional eunuchs like Iago—which is the most pitiable affliction of truly wicked men.[1]

Gloucester is the dominating figure in the ironic little scene that ends the trilogy: ironic because his very presence makes fatuous the optimistic platitudes uttered by King Edward at the christening of the baby prince.

> Young Ned, for thee thine uncles and myself
> Have in our armours watch'd the winter's night;
> Went all a-foot in summer's scalding heat,
> That thou might'st repossess the crown in peace;
> And of our labours thou shalt reap the gain.
> V vii 16.

Once arrangements have been made to dispose of Margaret (Edward plans to 'waft her hence to France')

> now what rests but that we spend the time
> With stately triumphs, mirthful comic shows,
> Such as befit the pleasure of the court?
> Sound, drums and trumpets! farewell, sour annoy!
> For here, I hope, begins our lasting joy.
> V vii 42.

These vapid expectations are typical of the delusion which grips all the characters in the trilogy, and a glimpse of Gloucester's face will send the audience home anticipating a sequel of a different sort.

III. 'RICHARD III'

In *Richard III* Shakespeare completes his study of the Wars of the Roses. The play clinches its arguments by frequent references back to *Henry VI*, and although its production may have been held up by the

---

[1] In contrast, Henry's goodness made him weep for sorrows that were not his own. He drew his peace of mind from his feeling that all men were his brothers and might be the stronger for the tears he shed for them.

plague,[1] it must have been written not long afterwards, while the character of Gloucester still held Shakespeare's imagination. It is a verse play (all but some 80 lines in 3600), and Senecan influences, which diminish rapidly as Shakespeare found his way to a dramatic style of his own, appear in its rhetorical devices and its controlling pattern of Nemesis and revenge. The structure is severely formal, almost ritualistic. In the action each successive blow of fate is the ful-filment of a curse, until at last the bleeding country is rescued by its foreordained deliverer. The language, vituperative and extravagant, seems to be pitched deliberately high in acknowledgement of these solemnities, and the element of formality is sustained by a number of stylistic tricks, such as recurring patterns of line structure, internal balances within the line, stichomythia, antiphonal voices, and the subtle repetition of emphatic words and phrases. Shakespeare is still very much in earnest. He is duly conscious of poetry's high office, and he still believes that the gravity of its message requires to be matched by an appropriate gravity of utterance and exposition. But the charac-ter of Richard himself gives the play the boisterous energy of the con-temporary *Comedy of Errors* and *Taming of the Shrew*. His incisive, intensely personal utterance looks forward to a more dramatic style of writing, and the main difficulties of the play arise from Shakespeare's failure to harmonise the two styles and the vastly different dramatic conceptions that they represent.

The theme is as elaborately patterned as the verse, and it rounds off the view of history taken in *Henry VI*. In *Richard III* curses are ful-filled that were uttered in the earlier plays, sometimes in the very lan-guage in which they were spoken. In their darkest hours the Wood-villes, Hastings, Buckingham and Queen Elizabeth all refer back in specific terms to the threats made to them by Margaret of Anjou. 'Remember Margaret was a prophetess'; and she herself is brought unhistorically on to the scene—she left England for France in 1475 and died there seven years later—as an embodiment of the Destiny, or Nemesis, found in early English drama. In I iii she breaks into the quarrel between Gloucester and the Woodvilles, 'wrangling pirates', to plague the House of York and all its collaterals and dependencies, warning them that Gloucester will be the destruction of them all. By IV iv, when the young Princes are dead and Richard has seized the throne, she is able to remind them that several of her baleful predictions have already come true. Then, because 'sorrow can admit society',

---

[1] Between June 1592 and June 1594 plague closed the London theatres except for three or four short seasons of only a few weeks.

she sits on the ground with her two old enemies, Queen Elizabeth and the Duchess of York, and the three of them rock in an ecstasy of grief and malediction.

Their lamentations take in review most of the history of the two preceding plays:

> MARGARET: I had an Edward, till a Richard kill'd him;
> I had a Harry, till a Richard kill'd him:
> Thou hadst an Edward, till a Richard kill'd him;
> Thou hadst a Richard, till a Richard kill'd him.
> DUCHESS: I had a Richard too, and thou didst kill him;
> I had a Rutland too, thou holp'st to kill him.
> MARGARET: Thou hadst a Clarence too, and Richard kill'd him.
>
> IV iv 40.

These caterwaulings continue for 135 lines, and modern performances considerably reduce them, but these two scenes, and others in which the women lament (II ii, IV i), serve for Shakespeare an important purpose. They provide a formal setting for Richard's crimes and epitomise the Elizabethan reading of history. The hour of deliverance is near and the flawless Richmond is already waiting in the wings. Meanwhile Gloucester concentrates within himself all the evil and suffering which the country has borne since the Lancastrian usurpation, and all the crimes that flowed from it. Vituperation outruns sorrow, and in violent declamatory language the women denounce him as the troubler of the poor world's peace, slave of Nature and son of hell, foul defacer of God's handiwork, hell's black intelligencer, bottled spider, foul hunchback'd toad, and much else in the same kind. Even his mother declares that the womb that bore him was a 'bed of death'. The emphasis throughout is on Richard as a wild, destructive animal, a creature not of Nature's fashioning. Elsewhere he is stigmatised as dog, hell-hound, the 'elvish mark'd, abortive, rooting hog' who preys on the peaceful garden, and this ubiquitous condemnation is crowned in Richmond's picture of him as

> The wretched, bloody, and usurping boar,
> That spoil'd your summer fields and fruitful vines,
> Swills your warm blood like wash, and makes his trough
> In your embowell'd bosoms.
>
> V ii 7.

This is More's Richard,[1] already mediated to the Elizabethans by Holinshed and Hall. Aided by Tudor propaganda, Richard's reputation had practically passed into folk-lore, and rustic mothers would

---

[1] See above, pp. 46–9. The same view of Richard was taken in a play written a year or two after Shakespeare's, Heywood's *Edward IV*.

descant upon his deformity to discipline their children. Shakespeare borrowed more than the general outlines of More's unfriendly portrait. More had already indicated how Richard's rise and fall might be handled dramatically, and Margaret and Henry Tudor were easily cast to share the role of Destiny. Shakespeare has caught, too, More's irony and his relish of the human situation, with its sidelong reflections on the human gullibility which Richard exploited so merrily. Translation to the stage has somewhat coarsened the subtlety of the picture and broadened the comic effects, so that Shakespeare's Richard perhaps has less of Cesare Borgia than of Captain Hook; but in essentials the character is still faithful to More's original, with its astringent flavour and habitual self-command.

In some respects Shakespeare has insulated us from the true impact of Richard's wickedness. Richard's deployment of his diabolic arts is a spectacle seen from far off, literally as in a theatre. We do not have to feel much sympathy for his victims, as our moral attitude has already been determined by the conventional structure and the nature of the action. The play is most significant when it is most formal, and our ultimate judgment of Richard is inescapably fixed in those scenes which are hardest to endure on the stage. As always when Shakespeare's text is cut in deference to modern tastes, we lose much that was of the greatest importance to the audiences of his own day. We misunderstand *Richard III* if we see it only as a study, in Marlowe's manner, of a gigantic, misshapen individual. Shakespeare put all his seriousness into the emblematic Richard, the figure who gathered into himself two generations of ambition, treachery and grief. The inspired Machiavellian was only for light relief.

Thus the antiphonies and archaic incantations of the wailing women are introduced to recall at timely intervals that Richard is the author of a world in which a mother may terribly declare that, through him, her name is ominous to children. He is 'one that hath ever been God's enemy' and made the happy earth his hell. These symbolic episodes are multiplied beyond the possibility of misunderstanding. A little group of citizens, hurrying about their business, pause to whisper their forebodings. In their conversation the truisms of the countryside are reiterated with choric effect:

> When clouds are seen, wise men put on their cloaks;
> When great leaves fall, then winter is at hand;
> When the sun sets, then who doth not look for night?
> Untimely storms make men expect a dearth.
>
> II iii 32.

The same speaker sees nothing for it but to put his unsure hopes
in God.

> All may be well; but, if God sort it so,
> 'Tis more than we deserve, or I expect. . . .
> By a divine instinct men's minds mistrust
> Ensuing danger; as, by proof, we see
> The waters swell before a boisterous storm.
> But leave it all to God.
>   II iii 36.

Despite its gloomy reservations, the citizen's trust is not misplaced,
for in the end it is indeed God who comes to the rescue of the ravaged
people. But first all Richard's enemies are struck down through his
agency, although they themselves feel it to be the operation of Nemesis. The pattern is several times repeated, of men who think themselves
secure suddenly brought down by a sharp turn of Fortune's wheel.
Clarence is the first, and after him the Greys and Woodvilles. Deluded
by an insincere truce with their enemies, the Queen's family greet
King Edward's death as the prelude to new prosperity and advancement: until at Pomfret they find that 'now Margaret's curse is fall'n
upon our heads'. It is the turn of Hastings next, who 'too fond, might
have prevented this'. 'Too triumphing', he has boasted

>   how mine enemies
> To-day at Pomfret bloodily were butcher'd
> And I myself secure in grace and favour.
> O Margaret, Margaret! now thy heavy curse
> Is lighted on poor Hastings' heavy head.
>   III iv 88.

Although innocent in themselves, the young Princes were heirs of
a father who won the throne by force; and they strutted precociously
in their royal dignities before a heedless fate visited his sins in them.
The final victim was Buckingham. Always the open-eyed partner in
Richard's plans, he thought he could 'grow circumspect' when the
throne was won. Besides, he claimed his reward when the King was not
in giving vein.

Except the Princes—and their doom was really their father's—all
these people had lived by treachery and violence, and many silent
victims were avenged in the fall of each. Richard, the agent of their
destruction, was wickeder than any of his victims, but it was orthodox
mediaeval doctrine that fate might use bad men as the instrument of its
purpose. Following the original crime which set the whole tragic
sequence into motion, history is seen as a scheme of retribution, with

a recurring pattern of victors following vanquished to destruction. Because each blow is the direct fulfilment of a prophecy, it seems to be fate; and with every victim admitting that he deserved his punishment, Nemesis appears to be upholding a moral order of government.[1]

All the time Nemesis has been pointing at Richard as its final prize. For this last act of expiation it is no longer personified in Margaret, so 'well skill'd in curses', who disappears from the scene, presumably somewhat hoarse, while Richard is still in possession of his crown. To dispose of any awkward questions about the morality of rebellion, Shakespeare adopts the conventional view that at this point God himself intervened on behalf of the stricken country. His agent was Henry of Richmond, to whom Dr. Johnson laconically referred as 'a man who put an end to the civil war of the two houses, but not otherwise remarkable for virtue'. It is unlikely that Shakespeare had any illusions about the Tudors. He could recognise power politics when he saw them and, when he gave dignity to the watery visions of Clarence, he cannot have been unaware of what the Tudors did to Clarence's descendants.[2] But in this play he gave Richmond the flat, unimpassioned utterance proper to symbolic persons, a tone as conventional in its different way as Margaret's. In its context the lifelessness of the character shows how seriously Shakespeare took him. There was a language for these occasions, colourless, rhythmically flat, and pious in phrase. The Ghosts in Richard III use it too, and all through his life Shakespeare resorted to it, or something very like it, at the times when a dramatist needs a form of speech that will raise certain characters above the accidents of personality.[3]

Historically, Richard and Henry were probably rather similar people. Both were good administrators, and both seem to have developed the grasping, suspicious natures often to be found in successful careerists. But in Shakespeare's play they inhabit different worlds. Thus Richmond:

> O! thou whose captain I account myself,
> Look on my forces with a gracious eye;

---

[1] See the discussion of the play in R. G. Moulton, *Shakespeare as Dramatic Artist*.

[2] His son, Edward Plantagenet, Earl of Warwick, was executed in 1499, his daughter, Margaret, Countess of Salisbury in 1541, and his grandson, Baron Montague, in 1538. Their crime was to be dynastic alternatives.

[3] Sir Edmund Chambers suggests (*William Shakespeare* i 303) that 'the extremely ineffective speeches' of the Ghosts were a later theatrical addition. But it is dramatically fitting that they should use the language they do. It gives them the proper symbolic quality by helping us to forget the sort of people they were when they were alive.

> Put in their hands thy bruising irons of wrath,
> That they may crush down with a heavy fall
> The usurping helmets of our adversaries!
> Make us thy ministers of chastisement,
> That we may praise thee in thy victory.
>
> V iii 109.

These lines, the last two especially, skirt the difficulty that in orthodox thinking vengeance was the prerogative of God. God is here asked to delegate His powers to a chosen vessel. In a later speech, addressed to his soldiers on the eve of battle, Richmond argues that there are times when subjects are justified (contrary to the doctrines set forth in the Homilies) in taking arms against a tyrant:

> Then, if you fight against God's enemy,
> God will in justice ward you as his soldiers;
> If you do sweat to put a tyrant down,
> You sleep in peace, the tyrant being slain.
>
> V iii 254.

In earlier scenes, Dorset, Buckingham, Morton and other characters have all struck unavailing blows at Richard's crown. The assured, conventional rhythms of Richmond's speech tell the audience that he is armed with more than human powers; and it is the only time that Shakespeare explicitly excuses rebellion.[1]

After the battle, in the speech which ends the play, Richmond says all the right things. He pays tribute to degree ('inter their bodies as becomes their births'), promises mercy to enemies who submit, gives suitable thanks to God, and pledges himself to the symbolic marriage which will unite the warring families. He closes with a prophecy that is really a reminder to an Elizabethan audience that violent men are still in their midst:

> And let their heirs—God, if thy will be so—
> Enrich the time to come with smooth-fac'd peace,
> With smiling plenty, and fair prosperous days!
> Abate the edge of traitors, gracious Lord,
> That would reduce these bloody days again,
> And make poor England weep in streams of blood!
> Let them not live to taste this land's increase,
> That would with treason wound this fair land's peace!
> Now civil wounds are stopp'd, peace lives again:
> That she may long live here, God say amen!
>
> V iv 45.

---

[1] The sting is further drawn by the implication that Richard himself was a divine instrument in a scheme which required the fullest punishment before forgiveness could be expected.

In opposition to this sanctified figure, Richard is in essence no more than the traditional Vice. To leave no doubt, he says so:

> Thus, like the formal Vice, Iniquity,
> I moralise two meanings in one word.
> III i 82.

Frequent images of the garden, with the royal House seen as a tree of which the members are the leaves or the fruit, indicate Richard as the storm which shakes it or the poison which makes it wither. 'When great leaves fall, winter is at hand,' the Citizen says, and the young Duke of York would not grow too fast, since 'sweet flowers are slow, and weeds make haste'. Richard knows himself to be the force that destroys the healthy growth of plants and trees. 'They that stand high have many blasts to shake them,' he reminds Queen Elizabeth. He has been 'a weeder-out' of his enemies, and has 'cropp'd the golden prime' of young Prince Edward. In another image of destruction the Queen says to him,

> My tongue should to thy ears not name my boys
> Till that my nails were anchor'd in thine eyes;
> And I, in such a desperate bay of death,
> Like to a poor bark, of sails and tackling reft,
> Rush all to pieces on thy rocky bosom.
> IV iv 231.

But we miss the full significance of the play if we think of Richard as the only agent of evil. In so far as he is the author of his actions—and Shakespeare continues from *Henry VI* the rather unsatisfactory ambivalence between men who are inherently bad but are at the same time victims of a situation in which virtue is impossible—he is obviously wicked; but his wickedness should not blind us to the complicity of many other people. No crime escapes its penalty, and crime and punishment are so fastidiously matched that the play is almost an Aeschylean exercise in the justification of God's ways to man. There is no one who does not get precisely what he deserves, either for what he now is, or for what he has been in a previous play, or simply for what he represents. Even the self-righteous Lady Anne is moved by flattery, if not, at an even deeper level, by the stirrings of desire; while the other women—Margaret, Richard of York's widow, and Elizabeth Woodville—have small excuse for their recriminations if one remembers their earlier contributions to the general misery. Obliquely Shakespeare makes the point that evil such as Richard's could only exist in a world already habituated to it; and through a variety of characters he creates a frightening picture of the conditions in which tyranny becomes possible. Ratcliff, Catesby, Tyrrell and Lovel are typical lackeys of despotism; Clarence's murderers may bear a conscience, but they do their killing none the less for that; even the honourable Brakenbury takes refuge in the pretence that he does not know what his orders mean. We are in a world where citizens whisper to one another for fear of being overheard, where men may be 'sent for to the justices' without quite knowing why. In the dozen lines of III vi the Scrivener, an unregarded civil servant, hints at the fears which all men have but dare not express. 'When such ill dealing must be seen *in thought*': because they will not *do* anything about it, these smaller fry are in some degree accomplices in the misgovernment they half-heartedly condemn. More so, then, the greater ones: Anne, who lets herself be talked into marriage with the usurper; Stanley, who feebly equivocates until his belated desertion has the stamp of treachery; Hastings, a light-weight but morally null; and Buckingham, who misguidedly thinks that he can be a fellow-traveller in wickedness for just so long as it suits him, and then call a stop. When Clarence, the arch-deceiver, calls to mind the sins 'that now give evidence against my soul', he is speaking for many others beside himself. This England is a land without majesty, and Richard is its appointed scourge.

Such is the official Richard; and having determined our official attitude to him, we are free to enjoy his company as he seeks a world to bustle in. The artistic weakness of *Richard III* is that Shakespeare has chosen a potentially tragic situation for the creation of his first great comic character. In his own day this would not have meant that the play failed in its purpose. Elizabethan audiences were familiar with the large liberty permitted to the Vice, and in the immense care that he took over the formal structure and the rhetorical patterning of the verse Shakespeare left no possibility of misunderstanding. Richard's monstrous tyranny is the terrible climax of generations of misrule. But it is rather different with us. In performance we cut most of what would have mattered to an Elizabethan and relish the great virtuoso role of Richard.

Probably Shakespeare relished it too. The pungency and sharp definition of Richard's speech, with almost every line creating a little cameo of movement, is a great advance on anything he has ever done before. Characters with a strong histrionic streak in them were always congenial to him as a dramatist, and to Richard it is second nature to

> counterfeit the deep tragedian,
> Speak and look back, and pry on every side,

> Tremble and start at wagging of a straw,
> Intending deep suspicion: ghastly looks
> Are at my service, like enforced smiles;
> And both are ready in their offices,
> At any time, to grace my stratagems.
>
> III v 5.

The words are Buckingham's but it is Richard that they describe. The drive of his ruthlessness is sustained by the conscious delight he takes in his psychological penetration. He wins the crown by a series of triumphant impersonations, entered upon with such exuberance that we forget the consequent suffering. For his victims we have no more pity than we feel for gulls who are hoodwinked in a comedy. The blood is only greasepaint.

At the start of the play Richard admits the audience to his intentions, telling them of the character he means to bear. This speech should be compared with those he has made in III ii and V vi of the previous play, for there is a difference in content as well as in the crispness and fluency of the language. In the theatre, actors playing Richard are sometimes tempted to incorporate passages from *3 Henry VI* into 'Now is the winter of their discontent'. This is a mistake, as Richard is no longer quite the same person. The speeches in *3 Henry VI* are violent assertions of ambition:

> Then, since this earth affords no joy to me
> But to command, to check, to o'erbear such
> As are of better person than myself,
> I'll make my heaven to dream upon the crown;
> And, whiles I live, to account this world but hell,
> Until my mis-shap'd trunk that bears this head
> Be round impaled with a glorious crown . . .
> Torment myself to catch the English crown:
> And from that torment I will free myself,
> Or hew my way out with a bloody axe.
>
> III ii 165, 179.

> The midwife wonder'd, and the women cried,
> 'O! Jesus bless us, he is born with teeth.'
> And so I was; which plainly signified
> That I should snarl and bite and play the dog.
> Then, since the heavens have shap'd my body so,
> Let hell make crook'd my mind to answer it.
>
> V vi 74.

But the opening of *Richard III* finds him in a milder, more philosophic vein. It is true that he says that he has laid plots and admits to being 'subtle, false, and treacherous', but in forty lines he does not actually mention the crown. His theme is that, with Edward firmly settled on the throne, peaceful diversions have replaced the ruder fashions of war and there is scant employment for a military man ill fitted for the pleasures of court and chamber. 'Adieu, valour! Rust, rapier! Be still, drum!' Always a connoisseur of language, he rolls ironically on the tongue such phrases as 'lascivious pleasing of a lute', 'amorous looking-glass', 'strut before a wanton ambling nymph' or the 'weak piping times of peace'. Since Nature has not made him for these sports, he has

> No delight to pass away the time,
> Unless to see my shadow in the sun
> And descant on mine own deformity.
>   I i 25.

It is largely because he is bored that he is now 'determined to prove a villain', and his pursuit of the crown becomes an exercise to occupy his unwilling leisure. Shakespeare has unmistakably pitched him in a lower key of villainy. We are not to think of him in terms of Iago or Macbeth. Shakespeare has only just emerged from *Titus Andronicus*, and genuine tragedy is still a long way off. He seems to feel that the horrors of the play will be endurable only if their contriver is thought of as a comic intriguer and the victims are heard only through the symbolic voices of the wailing women. Thus there is a deliberate dissipation of the mood which Shakespeare was seeking to create in the second half of *3 Henry VI*, where Henry and Richard stand at the poles of good and evil. In this sense the one play is not an exact sequel of the other. The moral tension slackens, and *Richard III* is, from a purely political point of view, a less interesting play than *3 Henry VI*. Richard himself is too much of a monster—perhaps too much of a grotesque—to be taken altogether seriously. He is so obviously not the sort of man who ought to be a king that no serious political or moral discussion can arise from his behaviour.

But this will not diminish our pleasure in him as an entertainer. The entry of Clarence allows him to demonstrate his histrionic abilities, and at once the play is afoot. Blithe and euphoric, Richard sweeps to the throne in a dazzling sequence of audacities and improvisations.[1] The first Act is designed to show off his powers, for Shakespeare invented most of it. Henry VI died in 1471, and his body was taken from London to Chertsey, but there is no warrant for Richard's wooing of Anne

---

[1] We have to be quick-witted to follow him at times, as when in the opening scene he says he will do anything to have Clarence freed—even 'were it to call King Edward's widow sister' (I i 109).

at that particular place and time. On Henry's death Anne was being kept in safe hiding by Clarence, her brother-in-law, and she did not marry Richard until three years later. Clarence himself was not imprisoned until 1478. The Yorkist family reconciliation, and Richard's presence at it, is another invention, but all these episodes give an energetic picture of Richard's character.

> Simple, plain Clarence! I do love thee so
> That I will shortly send thy soul to heaven,
> If heaven will take the present at our hands.
> > I i 118.

> And thus I clothe my naked villainy
> With odd old ends stol'n forth of holy writ,
> And seem a saint when most I play the devil.
> > I iii 336.

The touch of self-mockery is disarming. This is deception practised as an art, and Richard has an artist's satisfaction in it. He glows with the radiance of one who has a good digestion, a prosperous career and an easy conscience. His attitude to his victims is one of genial contempt that the world could hold so many fools, and his frequent asides are warmed by his pleasure in the contest. If he has no pity for those whom he destroys, he does not hate them either; nor are his triumphs accompanied by the self-righteous gloating which in *Henry VI* greets every turn of the wheel. When he exults, it is in admiration of his own skill. It reflects, no doubt, the obsessive vanity of the born criminal, but in the theatre it is difficult not to be on his side.

Hazlitt notes that when he undertakes the wooing of Anne, Richard approaches her like the first Tempter, confident of his prey. He woos her not in the humble spirit of a lover but as an actor joyously intent upon his own performance. Like the serpent he despises mankind, for there is no one whom he cannot deceive. He knows all the tricks, from the sanctimonious rebuke,

> Lady, you know no rules of charity,
> Which renders good for bad, blessings for curses,
> > I ii 68.

to the witticism that puts a new, deceptive gloss upon the facts:

ANNE: O! he was gentle, mild, and virtuous.
GLO: The fitter for the King of heaven, that hath him.
ANNE: He is in heaven, where thou shalt never come.
GLO: Let him thank me, that holp'd to send him thither;
 For he was fitter for that place than earth;
> > I ii 105.

and finally to the declaration, hard for any woman to resist, that his deeds were all for love of her. Her beauty has drawn tears from eyes that scorn to weep (he says), and he goes down upon knees that have never sued to friend or enemy. His final gesture is to bare his breast and bid her kill him—and so 'let the soul forth that adoreth thee';

> Nay, do not pause: for I did kill King Henry;
> But 'twas thy beauty that provoked me.
> Nay, now dispatch; 'twas I that stabbed young Edward;
> But 'twas thy heavenly face that set me on.
> > I ii 180.

This technique carries him through all his outrageous impositions. Just as Falstaff liked to recall the days when he sang anthems, Richard revels in the impersonation of a holy man whose devotions have been untimely interrupted by the 'vehement instigation' of the Londoners who wish him to be king.

> He is not lolling on a lewd day-bed,
> But on his knees at meditation;
> Not dallying with a brace of courtesans,
> But meditating with two deep divines;
> Not sleeping, to engross his idle body,
> But praying, to enrich his watchful soul.
> > III vii 71.

At length he appears, standing between two bishops, 'to stay him from the fall of vanity'; and after a display of winning modesty he agrees to be enforced to 'a world of cares'. He does not vary his methods, but good comedians seldom do.

The opening Act having taken us to 1483, Shakespeare thereafter follows the sources fairly closely until, for legitimate dramatic effect, he rushes events after Richard's crowning. Clarence's son, whom Richard 'pent up close', was only three in 1483; and his daughter, said to be meanly matched in marriage, was not in fact married for another ten years. There is a further telescoping of history in the following scene, IV iv, to give the impression of an unbroken series of risings against the usurper. None of this matters; and the references to Doctor Shaw and Friar Penker show that Shakespeare was well enough acquainted with the chronicles when he chose to be. But what, as readers and spectators, we are likely to regret is the change in Richard once he has received the crown. Roughly at the point where More's history stops, the comedian loses his zest and becomes a man heavy with suspicion and self-doubt.

> I have not that alacrity of spirit,
> Nor cheer of mind, that I was wont to have.
>   V iii 73.

The change is necessary to Shakespeare's purpose, for he has to show that a crown won by violence is not to be worn with comfort. After the infectious high spirits of the chase, Richard finds the prize curiously unsatisfying. For one thing, he may not be able to keep it.

> But shall we wear these glories for a day?
> Or shall they last, and we rejoice in them?
>   IV ii 5.

No longer will he have the joy of getting; and he knows, as tyrants always must, that his companions henceforth will be 'iron-witted fools and unrespective boys'. Men like him flinch from eyes that consider, and this is the torturing uncertainty that drives him to test the dutiful Buckingham, to see if he be 'current gold'. Eventually he has to kill the two young Princes—an unpromising risk, but he can no longer help himself:

> Uncertain way of gain! But I am in
> So far in blood, that sin will pluck on sin.[1]
>   IV ii 63.

A meeting with the women, still 'copious in exclaims', still nurses to one another's grief, seems to rally his spirits. He bids the trumpets shriek to silence their protestations, and with a flash of the old sardonic wit he says to his mother, as she recalls the agony of his birth, 'And came I not at last, to comfort you?' But when he pleads with Queen Elizabeth to mate him with her daughter, his touch has gone. He cannot find again the Satanic advocacy which on an earlier occasion had overwhelmed the reluctant Anne. You killed my children, the Queen reminds him, and he answers,

> But in your daughter's womb I bury them:
> Where, in that nest of spicery, they shall breed
> Selves of themselves, to your recomforture.
>   IV iv 424.

It is the highest flight of his impudence but it does not persuade her. She promises to inform him later of her decision: the phrase that unmistakably means 'no' to any pedlar that still has his wits about him.

---

[1] Cf. *Macbeth* III iv 136:

> I am in blood
> Stepp'd in so far, should I wade no more,
> Returning were as tedious as go o'er.

The words that he throws after her as she withdraws virtually admit his
failure. His 'relenting fool, and shallow changing woman' is just idle
abuse, far removed from the apt and pithy comment with which he has
celebrated his genuine victories.

As the tide sets against him, he confuses his followers with rebuke,
suspicion and contradictory orders. A feeble 'My mind is chang'd' is
his only explanation of a sudden revision of his plans. His collapse is
theatrically disappointing but it is necessary to Shakespeare's overriding theme. With the entry of Henry Tudor, Richard must cease to
be his outrageous self and make his contribution to a given reading of
history. The Ghosts utter their comminations, and there follows the
uneasy, unconvincing episode of 'the conscience of the king'.

> Alack! I love myself. Wherefore? for any good
> That I myself have done unto myself?
> O! no: alas! I rather hate myself
> For hateful deeds committed by myself.
> I am a villain. Yet I lie; I am not.
> Fool, of thyself speak well: fool, do not flatter.
> My conscience hath a thousand several tongues,
> And every tongue brings in a several tale,
> And every tale condemns me for a villain.
> Perjury, perjury, in the high'st degree:
> Murder, stern murder, in the dir'st degree;
> All several sins, all us'd in each degree,
> Throng to the bar, crying all, 'Guilty! guilty!'
> I shall despair. There is no creature loves me;
> And if I die, no soul will pity me:
> Nay, wherefore should they, since that I myself
> Find in myself no pity to myself?
> V iii 188.

These uncharacteristic lines revert directly to *3 Henry VI*. Blame has
the due of blame, and these are the broken mutterings of a man who
has knowingly married himself to evil, scorned pity, love and fear and
all that greybeards call divine. He slinks away to creep about the camp
with his ear to the tents, 'to hear if any mean to shrink from me'.

But daylight scatters his fears, and with the need for action he is himself again. 'Come, bustle, bustle.' He draws up his line of battle with
all his old decisiveness, and he will die, as he has lived, confident in his
creed of hell.

> Let not our babbling dreams affright our souls;
> Conscience is but a word that cowards use,
> Devis'd at first to keep the strong in awe:
> Our strong arms be our conscience, swords our law.
> V iii 309.

His speech to his soldiers before Bosworth plays on their contempt for foreigners,

> A sort of vagabonds, rascals and runaways,
> A scum of Bretons and base lackey peasants,

who are led by

> A milksop, one that never in his life
> Felt so much as cold over shoes in snow.

They are creatures whom our fathers have 'beaten, bobb'd, and thump'd', and he shrewdly invokes the safety of hearth and home when he asks,

> Shall these enjoy our lands? lie with our wives?
> Ravish our daughters?
>
> V iii 317, 326, 337.

The speech is true Richard. Its appeal is directly to the lower emotions of fear and a disdainful sort of patriotism, but it glows with a zest absent from Richmond's pious exhortations and finally he urges his men into battle in the accents of a born leader:

> A thousand hearts are great within my bosom:
> Advance our standards! set upon our foes!
> Our ancient word of courage, fair Saint George,
> Inspire us with the spleen of fiery dragons!
> Upon them! Victory sits upon our helms.
>
> V iii 348.

Presently he will offer his kingdom, so hardly won, for a horse: which was one of the corniest jokes of the Elizabethan theatre. He dies without remorse, drunk, as Hazlitt says, with his wounds.

That is how we may most appropriately remember him. The 'timorous dreams' to which his wife refers are unnatural to Richard as we habitually see him, and Shakespeare only introduces them out of respect for the truism that bad men do not sleep. The morality method was always at odds with psychological realism, but there was no escaping the unwritten law that after entertaining the audience for an hour or more, the Vice should undergo an awkward five minutes before the end. The interlude of Richard's conscience means no more than this; and it is only right that the moral intention of the play, which is to reveal Richard's crimes against England, should have for its full effect a belated recognition by the villain himself that his wickedness has earned him nothing. The creed of kindlessness has to be disavowed.

Shakespeare avoids any hint of personal tragedy in Richard's predicament. His physical deformity—believed at that time to mirror the twisted soul within—sets him outside the ordinary run of mankind, and we are watching the headlong career of a monster, not the withering of a human soul. *Richard III* is an unremittingly earthy play. True recognition of a higher power is found only in Richmond, who is a visitant from another world. For the rest, it is surprising how mundane is the vision even of the wailing women, whose function is to expound the play's significance. In an exceptional moment Margaret calls him 'cacodemon', and there is a general tendency to speak of him as an enemy of God; but for the most part Richard's enemies denounce him as a poisonous and destructive animal, and the pains and curses they wish upon him are in kind. They are indifferent to his immortal soul. What they demand for him is physical torment here and now, an eye for an eye, exact requital of all the suffering he has caused. This insensibility shows how low these women themselves have fallen. Except in an emptily rhetorical way, they are not touched by the finer issues. We are reminded of Caliban, who invoked on Prospero the merely terrestrial discomforts that lay within his own experience, 'all the charms of Sycorax, toads, beetles, bats'.

'God' and 'heaven' are frequently on Richard's lips, but always it is in expletive or mockery, or in cynical exploitation of the weaknesses of the simple-minded. When Queen Elizabeth mourns her sons, he offers for her consolation the idea that 'at their births good stars were opposite', and 'all unavoided is the doom of destiny'. This 'unavoidable' destiny was, of course, contrived by Richard himself, and he is a man who thinks of fate as just a word that greybeards use, like love or fear. If we are weak and unsuccessful, the fault is in ourselves, not in our stars; and in thinking so, Richard belongs to the dark company of Iago, Cassius and Edmund.[1] In the absence of any character with a wider vision, the result is to narrow the universe of the play. Richard bustles about his intrigues in a tight little world which, until Richmond enters it, seems to stand in a morally indifferent void. The man himself never rises to the level of great poetry, for he never has feelings that are incommunicable. His deeds create no sense of tragic waste. The mechanical Nemesis which strikes him down never makes contact with his innermost being, and he seems to exist just to fulfil unequivocal prophecies to which he pays no heed. There is no tragic power in that, since he has never been valued by us as a man.[2]

[1] See above, p. 9.
[2] Comparison with Macbeth, favoured by some critics, only shows the gulf that divides them. Macbeth is not morally indifferent, nor is the universe that

Except for its comic inspiration, Shakespeare seems to have found *Richard III* a dead end, and for the time being he abandoned history. He was to complete his two erotic poems and write a number of comedies and an apprentice tragedy before turning to it again, and by then there would be certain differences of approach. He would never write another play, not even *Hamlet*, with the same intense concentration on a single figure, and none of his later heroes would be so flat and one-dimensional. In *Richard III* he uses a crude symbolism to fix a central character in a setting that protests against his every thought and action. It was a resourceful adaptation of morality technique, to be admired for its virtuosity, but Shakespeare does not seem to have been sufficiently pleased with it to think it worth repeating. Symbolism and the primness of morality are always present in his historical drama, and he never discards the reading of history which shapes these early plays; but in the future these elements will be deployed with much greater subtlety. Having at last put the Wars of the Roses behind him, Shakespeare finds it possible to begin to individualise his characters. He begins, as it were, to pass beyond the history of the chronicle and the classroom and enter the company of living men and women. In *Henry VI* and *Richard III* almost everyone is clamorous and nasty. Their collective voice swells into a din of hatred and recrimination, and they survive in the memory as the animals to which they are so ready to compare each other. In his later histories Shakespeare is better able to express his delight in the variousness of men.

From the standpoint of the future, the comedian Richard is the most significant feature in a play which otherwise is only a complement to *Henry VI*.[1] It lacks political interest, for its main thesis—that usurping tyrants like Richard are intolerable—is too obvious for so much elaboration; and the ultimate deliverance by Richmond is a foredoomed event for which, when it at last happens, we seem to have been waiting for a very long time. Only Clarence's murderers find themselves in any sort of moral dilemma, and the action

he inhabits. The evil that he does has cosmic repercussions (II iv 5, 12). Macbeth has a soul that would cry out to magnify the Lord, and because we care for him, we care for his victims too. But Richard never has regrets for what he has done, and it would be impossible to say of him, 'What thou wouldst highly, That thou wouldst holily.'

[1] One of the minor curiosities in its history is that in 1633 it was performed at court by the special order of Charles I. It is fascinating to speculate what emotions it may have aroused in that removed and solitary spirit, who extracted Malvolio and Parolles as the significant characters in their respective plays. Another curiosity is a performance in Scotland in the middle of the last century, in which a different actor played Richard in each Act.

develops no serious conflicts of loyalty or principle. The exploration of royalty apparently foreshadowed at the end of *3 Henry VI* is not pursued; we just have to be content with the pasteboard Richmond. Yet the play has always, and deservedly, been popular, and in the theatre it is splendid entertainment. That is because Shakespeare has relegated the political argument to the periphery of the action. It is no less important, but it leaves the centre of the stage to the seminal character of Richard.

IV. 'RICHARD II'

Richard II always occupied a special place in the Elizabethan mind. Until he relinquished his crown of thorns to Charles I, he was the archetypal English martyr; no other mediaeval king aroused such compassion for his fate, not even Edward II, who like himself was deposed and cruelly murdered. That he was the last of the Plantagenets, the last direct descendant from the Conqueror, gave him a particular sanctity. The unbroken line that was severed in his fall has never been restored.

Nor did it seem that the harshness of his fate was merited by the sum of his misdeeds. Like Henry VI, he was the peace-loving son of a father whose glory had been to scourge the French, and the Black Prince's memory was a heavy burden to him. His enemies saw him in an image that was not his own. After the fair beginnings when he rode out to face Wat Tyler, his councillors expected of him things that he was unfitted to perform, so that there was always a conflict between his own inclinations and other men's notions of his royal duty. He was neither a bad man nor an outstandingly bad king. The most frequent charge against him is that he was content to be flattered and misled by light-minded favourites. The chroniclers are almost unanimous about this. Hall says that in himself he was 'not of the most evil disposition, was not of so simple a mind, nor of such debility of wit, nor yet of so little heart and courage, but he might have demanded and learned good and profitable counsel, and after advice taken, kept, retained, and followed the same: But howsoever it was, unprofitable counsellors were his confusion and final perdition'. Holinshed thought that he was 'of nature good enough, if the wickedness and naughty demeanour of such as were about him had not altered it'. He was vain, 'being desirous enough of all honour, and more ambitious than was requisite', and so he listened too easily to flattery. This was the view of Richard generally accepted in the sixteenth century. His story in *A*

Mirror for Magistrates is introduced with the suggestion that he was
'a King that ruled all by lust' and

> alway put false flatterers most in trust,
> Ensuing such as could my vices claw:
> By faithful counsel passing not a straw.

In *Woodstock* we meet the same complaint:

> Shall England, that so long was governed
> By grave experience of white-headed age,
> Be subject now to rash unskilful boys?
>   II ii 169.

Shakespeare's Bolingbroke says to Bushy and Green,

> You have misled a prince, a royal king,
> A happy gentleman in blood and lineaments,
> By you unhappied and disfigur'd clean:
>   *Rich. II* III i 8.

and later, in a long analysis of Richard's public failings, Bolingbroke
remembers how

> The skipping king, he ambled up and down
> With shallow jesters and rash bavin wits,
> Soon kindled and soon burnt; carded his state,
> Mingled his royalty with capering fools,
> Had his great name profaned with their scorns,
> And gave his countenance, against his name,
> To laugh at gibing boys and stand the push
> Of every beardless vain comparative. . . .
> So, when he had occasion to be seen,
> He was but as the cuckoo is in June,
> Heard, not regarded.
>   *1 Hen. IV* III ii 60.

This attitude has to be regarded with caution, since it was the practice of rebels to clear themselves of treason by professing that they were
only trying to rescue the king from counsellors who had led him into
evil ways, but in Richard's case it seems to have been something near
the truth. Holinshed, not a friendly reporter, says that 'if there were
any offence, it ought rather to be imputed to the frailty of wanton
youth, than to the malice of his heart'. His faults came from a fundamental instability of character. He had exalted notions of his prerogative, and his vanity was further nourished by the personal beauty to
which all pay tribute.[1] So long as things were going his way, he would

---

[1] His mother was the admired 'Fair Maid of Kent', Joan, daughter of Edmund
of Woodstock, youngest son of Edward I.

be self-satisfied and self-indulgent; but when he was crossed, darker qualities revealed themselves and he was liable to the frightening explosions of passion that were a legacy of Plantagenet medical history.[1] However, his worst crimes were not disastrous politically, for the elimination of enemies like Arundel and Gloucester was a necessary concession to the iron laws of survival. If he had always been able to bring himself to that pitch of resolution and cunning, he might not have lost his throne. The fatal blunders were things petty, needless and exasperating, the actions of one who was not so much a tyrant as a political child. Viewed from a distance, they do not seem to have added up to very much, and Richard, who was only occasionally vicious, was deposed because his incalculable vacillations and moodiness were, in a king, more serious faults than a bloody mind.

But time and martyrdom washed away the traces, and only the charm and the pathos stood in people's memory. In two generations of misrule the whole nation had atoned for the wrong done to the Lord's anointed, and in the Tudor mind Richard was a sacrificial victim. The fault seemed so trivial, the penalty so unaccountably large, that these events were explicable only through the action of Fortune's sightless wheel, in whose motion consisted the mediaeval idea of tragedy. Much of Richard's fascination for succeeding generations lay in the rapidity, suddenness and magnitude of his fall. So much more painfully than he deserved—for his were not the abominations of Edward II—he plunged from greatness, while his rival just as swiftly climbed on high.

Thus it was not altogether an accident that the reign had acquired a particular significance in English history. In some respects the Middle Ages may be said to have ended with Richard, and although they would not have used those terms about it, the men of the sixteenth century were able to perceive that something had passed which they would never know again. A new order came in with the Lancastrians, a dynasty launched in blood. For some historians, as Hall, Daniel and Shakespeare himself, Richard was the natural starting-point of their exposition.

> In this man's reign began this fatal strife
> (The bloody argument whereof we treat)
> That dearly cost so many a prince his life,
> And spoil'd the weak, and ev'n consumed the great.
> Daniel, *Civil Wars*, i 23.

---

[1] His father sacked Limoges in an epileptic fury. Richard himself ordered the complete destruction of the palace of Sheen because his first wife died there; and at her funeral he assaulted the Earl of Arundel.

Even in the chroniclers who covered a much longer stretch of history—
Holinshed, for instance, and Polydore Vergil and Warner—the usurpation and its consequences were treated with a new intensity and a
marked insistence on pointing the moral. Richard was the prescriptive
sovereign driven from his inheritance; the proud man suddenly
'dejected' by Fortune's arbitrary motions; and the king whose reign
initiated a sequence of events, initially tragic, which turned eventually
to joy. To quote Daniel again:

> Yet now what reason have we to complain,
> Since hereby came the quiet calm and joy,
> The bliss of thee, Eliza? Happy gain
> For all our losses, when no other way
> The heav'ns could find, but to unite again
> The fatal sever'd families: that they
> Might bring forth thee; that in thy peace might grow
> That glory which few times could ever show.
>
> 13.

All these attitudes are implicit in Shakespeare's play; and no writer
who chose to handle this reign can have been unaware of the contemporary immediacy of his theme. 'I am Richard II. Know ye not that?' [1]
In 1595, when the play was written, deposition was practical politics.
Richard was a king who had been turned off his throne. That was an
unassailable fact, and no one could write about it without giving some
indication whether in his opinion it had been rightly done. No subject
that Shakespeare ever touched was on a workaday level more urgent:
the use to which his play was later put is proof of that. The judgment
that he passed on Richard and his supplanters must in some sort be a
judgment on the Queen and her office, and also on all those men who
for a variety of reasons would have been willing to see her removed.
He was giving a verdict on a contemporary situation upon which,
for all that anyone knew in 1595, the future peace of the country might
depend.

Shakespeare's answer (if we may use so crude a word about an
argument conducted in strictly dramatic terms and with matchless
artistry) is that Richard's fate was settled before the play began. The
crucial question forced upon the audience in the opening scene is this:
who was responsible for Gloucester's death? Various hints and indications, here and in later scenes, put Richard's complicity beyond all
doubt. He has been guilty of an unroyal crime and his just punishment

[1] See above, pp. 159–60.

is assured.[1] If that punishment should be deposition and death, it will not be too severe; but, since majesty dies not alone, his guilt is a stain on all his people. Thus the question about the rights and wrongs of rebellion is already answered. Bolingbroke may be a better man than Richard—in some respects he obviously is—but his cause is tainted from the start. He is touched by the general sickness, of which his rebellion is just a sympton. He cannot escape being corrupted by the low and selfish motives of men like Northumberland, and the immediate judgment upon his actions is that they have not prospered: by the end of the play his reign is set towards disaster.

This reading of the play is supported by Shakespeare's repeated suggestion that Bolingbroke was not the author of his actions.[2] It has often been noted that the play lacks a central climax, that the actual transference of power from Richard to his enemy is bloodless and perfunctory. In effect Richard is defeated while he is absent from the stage; and on his return he accepts his fate with the petulant resignation of a child of Fortune whose guardian angels have mysteriously deserted him. His guilt has robbed him of the power of action. Bolingbroke, meanwhile, seems to be the passive instrument of fate. When at a critical moment in the play York reminds him that 'the heavens are o'er our heads', he meekly answers,

> I know it, uncle; and oppose not myself
> Against their will.
>> III iii 18.

There is irony in this, for neither of them yet knows that the will of heaven will turn out to be the opposite of what at that moment they have in mind. York's later comment on the whole affair is that 'heaven hath had a hand in these events', and Bolingbroke himself would always protest that he did not deliberately seek the throne.

> Though then, God knows, I had no such intent,
> But that necessity so bowed the state
> That I and greatness were compelled to kiss.
>> *2 Hen. IV.* III i 72.

---

[1] In adopting this reading, Shakespeare carries straight on from *Woodstock*, which ends with Gloucester's murder at Richard's command. In their search for moral causation, other writers, including Hall and the *Mirror for Magistrates*, attributed Richard's fall to this act, but historically it was not a very plausible interpretation. Gloucester was a violent, disloyal and unpopular man (Holinshed calls him 'the chief instrument of mischief'), and his death was not unjustified by the morality of the age. There were many other reasons for Richard's fall.

[2] Cf. *2 Hen. IV* IV i 54–8: the whole country was in a fever of which Richard, 'being infected, died'.

To a large extent this is also admitted by the hostile Percies, who at the time were his accomplices. Northumberland

> heard him swear and vow to God
> He came but to be Duke of Lancaster;
> *1 Hen. IV.* IV iii 60.

and Worcester says that, after Henry had sworn at Doncaster 'that you did nothing purpose 'gainst the state',

> in short space
> It rain'd down fortune showering on your head,
> And such a flood of greatness fell on you.[1]
> *1 Hen. IV.* V i 46.

Shakespeare is implying that the rebellion succeeded because Bolingbroke was the chosen instrument of Richard's predestined fall. But he does not mean that the rebellion was therefore justified. It was the diseased product of a diseased condition. Personal ambition was a prominent part of it, and it contained its own nemesis in the subsequent rivalry of the accomplices. The argument of the play is that rebellion is always wicked; and when the ruler is a guilty man, rebellion is one of the consequent manifestations of his guilt.

Fortunately that is not all that the play is about. Determinist patterns of this kind do not make good drama unless the characters are men of feeling and seem to possess some freedom of choice and action. Character and destiny co-operate in Bolingbroke's ruthless drive towards the crown: Shakespeare does not deny either the self-interest or the superior capacity which hastened its accomplishment. York is human enough to display all the hesitations of a commonplace but conscientious man on the edge of intolerable uncertainty. His dilemma is real and is one of the cruxes of the play; its significance is not diminished because we know what the result is going to be. So too with Richard. The end may be known and inescapable, but his every action shows that he is a man unfit for power. Once this is established, the play's mood insensibly changes. We must not say that it ceases to be political, as Richard's adherence to his inalienable royalty is a political fact of the highest importance. But there is a shift of emphasis

---

[1] Lines 41–56 give a complete retrospective summary of what happened in 1399. It does not, of course, matter that the Percies are now saying that his usurpation was deliberately planned: they are no longer on his side. What is significant is their repeated witness that he *said at the time* that he was only coming to recover his family estates. On the other hand, Henry made a different admission when speaking frankly to his son. See *2 Hen. IV* IV v 182–4.

from an England made sick by disloyalty and misrule to the personal predicament of the King. The play is also a drama of character.

In the opening scene Richard establishes his exalted conception of the crown he wears. He receives the two disputants with remote detachment and remains strangely cool and silent throughout their angry exchanges. His display of disinterested royalty is all very proper and correct. Bolingbroke's blood relationship with the King will not earn him any favours, for 'impartial are our eyes and ears' and nothing shall 'partialize the unstooping firmness of my upright soul'. But dissembling is over when Bolingbroke raises the question of Gloucester's death and the soul which 'from the tongueless caverns of the earth' cries out for justice. This so nearly touches Richard that he can no longer impose a dispassionate solution of the quarrel. He pleads for a bloodless settlement but weakens the effect by a half-hearted, self-conscious little joke, 'Our doctors say this is no time to bleed.' Although he reminds them that he is a lion to tame leopards, and that kings are not born to sue but to command, ultimately he has to allow the two enemies to fight it out. Already the high conception of the royal prerogative is at odds with the event.

We know the worst about Richard by the time that Gaunt is dead. The brief I ii tells the audience beyond doubt that he was the cause of Gloucester's murder—'correction lieth in those hands which made the fault'. Gaunt's orthodoxy during this episode is significant. He offers the importunate Duchess no hope of instant vengeance, bidding her place her trust in God, ever the widow's champion and defence. 'God's is the quarrel.' If wrong has been done (and even this qualification is important: Gaunt knew things about Gloucester that the widow did not), God will avenge it in His due season. Gaunt is the spokesman of the traditional order, and his assumptions are the same as Richard's. Kings may sometimes err, and it is the duty of their counsellors to give rebuke: a duty which he will shortly exercise with no small eloquence. But rebuke will always stop short of sedition. Gaunt will never 'lift an angry arm against [God's] minister'.

In the lists at Coventry the hollow deference of the combatants builds up Richard's image of himself, but their presence there in arms says something different. Once he had failed to impose a peaceful settlement of their quarrel, there was no easy solution to be had. In a later play Mowbray's son was to declare that

> When the king did throw his warder down,
> His own life hung upon the staff he threw.—*2 Hen. IV* IV i 125.

Perhaps this was being wise after the event. The decision that Richard
made, after a show of consultation with his council, at least had the
merit of getting both men out of the country. But the manner and the
method were at fault. Richard's vanity and love of drama needed the
colour and bustle of the lists, the pomp of the heralds, the valedictions
and mounting tension, broken at the climax by the theatrical gesture of
intervention. Thus does the sun shrivel lesser luminaries. There is
malice in the lifelong banishment of Mowbray and a typical offhand
insensitivity in the King's remark to the stricken Gaunt, 'Why, uncle,
thou hast many years to live.' He is credulous to suppose that a promise
exacted in his presence will necessarily prevent the two men from meeting and conspiring in the years to come. It is ingratitude and folly
to inflict the heavier sentence on Mowbray, who has been waging
Richard's quarrel as well as his own. Finally, it is fatal weakness, a
mere sentimental gesture, to reduce the sentence on the dangerous
and popular Bolingbroke, who at once judges the concession at its
true worth:

> Four lagging winters and four wanton springs
> End in a word: such is the breath of kings.[1]
>   I iii 214.

In the next scene two veteran statesmen, York and the dying Gaunt,
ruminate sadly upon the disgrace of the kingdom under Richard's
feckless rule. York says that the King will hear no good advice,
only flattery and the venom sound of lascivious metres, and his
time and treasure are wasted in empty imitation of foreign fashions.
Perhaps there is little more in these strictures than old age's dislike
of pleasures it is no longer able to enjoy, but Gaunt's indictment
is conceived on a larger scale. His matchless invocation of 'this
other Eden' creates an idealised picture which he sets in contrast
with the actuality of an England dying from misrule.[2] It is a plea for
the vanished majesty which even now, if it is not too late, may cure
the country's fatal ills. But when Richard enters, his obdurate callousness provokes Gaunt to words that 'hereafter thy tormentors be'.
Twice (II i 105, 127) he directly accuses Richard of contriving
Gloucester's death, and in their wry jesting about health and sickness
warns him that he is no less sick than himself.

---

[1] In view of what is to come, it is ironical that Richard's declared reason for
stopping the duel is that the country's soil shall not be stained 'with that dear
blood which it hath fostered'.
[2] See D. A. Traversi, *Shakespeare from 'Richard II' to 'Henry V'*, 20–2.

> Now, he that made me knows I see thee ill;
> Ill in myself to see, and in thee seeing ill.
> Thy death-bed is no lesser than thy land
> Wherein thou liest in reputation sick:
> And thou, too careless patient as thou art,
> Committ'st thy anointed body to the cure
> Of those physicians that first wounded thee.
>   II i 93.

Richard may know that what he says is true, but his illness is indeed past cure. He receives the news of Gaunt's death with a perfunctory couplet and a curt 'So much for that'. Then he announces the decision that must have been already in his mind, to seize the dead man's property to finance his Irish wars. This is too much even for York's deep-rooted loyalty, and he reminds Richard that to deprive Bolingbroke of his rightful inheritance is to bring into question the principle of 'fair sequence and succession' to which his own crown is due:

> You pluck a thousand dangers on your head,
> You lose a thousand well-disposed hearts,
> And prick my tender patience to those thoughts
> Which honour and allegiance cannot think.
>   II i 206.

But Richard has scarcely been listening.

> Then all too late comes counsel to be heard,
> Where will doth mutiny with wit's regard.
>   II i 27.

In this scene Richard is given one last chance. If he had risen to the idea of duty that Gaunt, and even York in his fumbling way, had indicated to him, at least it could not have been said of him that his fall was the just desert of an incurably frivolous mind. But in fact he has paid so little attention to York's warnings that he casually leaves him as regent during the campaign in Ireland: 'for he is just, and lov'd us well'.

It is apt that at the close of the scene the mutinous nobles catalogue his misdeeds, and Northumberland sees life peeping 'even through the hollow eyes of death': meaning that Bolingbroke is already on his way. Shakespeare does not mitigate the case against Richard's 'insolent misgovernment and youthful outrage', as Holinshed called it. To prefer flattery to sage advice, to be enthusiastic for sensuous verse and all the novelties of fashion, may simply be the natural weaknesses of youth. But Richard will never become any wiser. He will not outgrow the political obtuseness that commands a duel and then theatrically forbids it; makes an enemy of Bolingbroke but leaves him alive to nurse his resentment; goes off to Ireland[1] when by his own folly he has just provoked a crisis at home; and commandeers the Lancastrian estates so that every landowner in England is made apprehensive about his property. Next time we see him, he has come to meet 'the sick hour that his surfeit made'.

Shakespeare will presently use the little emblematic scene in the garden at Langley to remind us that Richard's duty was to govern and he had failed in it. The well-cared garden is a vision complementary to Gaunt's. But politics gradually become less important, giving way to the personal tragedy of Richard. Although his tragedy would be less dreadful if he were not a king, it is no longer all-important that he is a king. The issue is always greater than himself, for his fate is England's as well as his, but we forget this in the contemplation of an individual solitarily facing his destiny. From the moment of his appearance at Berkeley the end is clear.

That Richard should seem to be an accomplice in his own fall was congruous with the accepted tragic pattern, which required that sort of inevitability. Like James II, the historical Richard lost his throne because in the crisis he gave no lead to those who would have fought for him. Potentially he had a strong body of supporters, and with the least show of determination he could have confined Bolingbroke's ambitions to the recovery of his confiscated lands. His fleet was at Waterford, and Aumerle tried to persuade him to return to Ireland and gather an army. But he appeared to be incapable of action. He deserted his forces in Pembrokeshire and listlessly submitted to deposition and death. In the last months of his reign he was just a mumbling neurotic.

For a playwright these events were not in themselves dramatic, and Shakespeare has made his own reading of them. Richard's will is numbed, and he can only put his faith in his divine right and talk emptily about betrayal. He is indomitable when he thinks of what he ought to be, helpless when he realises what he has become. His strength is exhausted in recrimination and idle menace, and the very facility of his emotion robs him of the power of action. This, near enough, is the Richard of the sources, the man who destroyed himself by extremes of

[1] In historical fact his expedition to Ireland was made necessary by a dangerous revolutionary situation which he met with a policy of intelligent reconciliation. The seizure of Lancaster's estates may have been decided upon as a desperate means of paying for the expedition. Incidentally, Richard was shrewd enough to take with him as hostages the future Prince Hal, as well as the sons of other English noblemen.

apathy and passion. But 'sorrow's crown of sorrow is remembering happier things'. In the play he rises almost to tragic stature in the possession of his kingly memories. Although he is always self-regarding in his griefs, he has sufficient insight to realise what he has lost, and his suffering is transmuted into an outraged patriotism and an affront to the idea of royalty. Anointed and consecrate, he feels as no one else can the dreadfulness of what is being done to him, of what, in the final moment of his renunciation, he is doing to himself. His poetic imagination transforms his fall into a sacrificial rite.

In this way the idea of royalty is exalted to a peak where the unworthiness of a particular king cannot damage it.[1] The unkingliness revealed in the second half of the play is much more serious and fundamental than the frivolities and recklessness of Richard's prime. At the first touch of failure he capitulates utterly. As soon as misfortune releases his capacity for self-display, he is happy to wanton with his grief before his cause is really lost. 'O that I were as great as is my grief.' It is the image of sorrow rather than sorrow itself that takes hold of him, and he tortures his imagination to throw up language that shall be worthy of his sufferings. He rebukes Aumerle for turning him even for a moment from 'that sweet way I was in to despair'. He is the unloved stranger 'in this all-hating world', and defeat so sharpens his artistic susceptibilities that he loses himself in wondering contemplation of his ever-worsening predicament. Each new situation stimulates him to a richer poetic elaboration as his fertile fancy seizes on the possibilities inherent in the jostling conceptions of kingship and its ruin, trust and its betrayal, parting and the impregnable solitude of the man whose mind is its own kingdom. He has no thought for Green and Bushy in their ignominious death. Their fate, earned in his love and service, simply moves him to a marvellous descant upon the wretchedness of kings. The Queen's sorrow at their parting stirs him to compassion—for himself. When she tearfully reproaches his broken manhood, he can only bid her, 'tell thou the lamentable tale of *me*'.

Endlessly setting 'the word itself against the word', Richard sits like a gilded spider, spinning his variations on the theme of sorrow. He has Prince Arthur's trick of attributing feeling to inanimate objects, as though to ask all creation to shed tears for him. He would rather talk to things than to men. Men have been stonily unresponsive, but his

---

[1] Traversi suggests (*Shakespeare from 'Richard II' to 'Henry V'*, 20) that Shakespeare seeks to reconcile the apparently contradictory material of the play by exalting the royal office in such a way that the fall of a king revealed to be morally and politically worthless 'may leave the monarchic principle itself substantially untouched'.

fancy tells him that the earth has hearkened to his 'senseless con-
juration'. *Tongue*, as has often been noted, is one of the key words of
the play.[1] In crisis the Lancastrians are strangely silent. 'When words
are scarce, they are seldom spent in vain', Gaunt gnomically declares,
and at Coventry he asks his son, 'To what purpose dost thou hoard
thy words?' Henry replies:

> I have too few to take my leave of you,
> When the tongue's office should be prodigal
> To breathe the abundant dolour of the heart.
>
> I iii 255.

Richard's 'Mark, silent king', addressed to Bolingbroke in Westminster
Hall, acknowledges this difference between them. For it is in words that
Richard tries to immure himself against reality. His transforming
imagination cannot make any difference to his real predicament but he
does receive from it some personal consolation. In fact it gives him
the only sort of strength of which he is capable, since it is in defeat
that he at last becomes a king. His fancy has created for himself a
picture of a man who has once been royal. The face of the real man,
the sentimental weakling who fooled away a throne, is seen for the last
time in the mirror that shivers to pieces in Westminster Hall. In its
place stands the self-created portrait of one who can find even in his
own ruin a special significance that sets him apart from other men. The
artist has discovered how to heal his wounds.

It is in its way a beautiful performance, and we have to admire the
limpid, spineless verse that can turn any idea to melody; the grave,
reflective imagery, drawn not from any understanding of the human
heart but from folk-lore and fable, an idealised love of an England that
never was, and a mystical cult of kings. We must acknowledge, too,
the artistic tact which prevents this endless celebration of grief from
becoming too harrowing to our sensibilities.[2]

[1] Usually it speaks of sorrow and is burdened with a heavy tale. Banished
Mowbray's is engaoled in his silent mouth, Gaunt's is a stringless instrument,
Scroop's is care-tuned, the Gardener's harsh and rude. Only the loyal Groom
hints that actions speak louder than words: 'What my tongue dares not, that my
heart shall say.' Much of the imagery of the play acts as an undertone to the
King's sorrow, echoing the stricken outburst of Marlowe's Edward II:

> Whilst I am lodg'd within this cave of care,
> Where sorrow at my elbow still attends,
> To company my heart with sad laments,
> That bleeds within me for this strange exchange.
>
> V i 32.

[2] It is a gift that Constance lacked. But King Philip's chiding 'You are as fond
of grief as of your child' might, with *crown* substituted for *child*, be appropriate
to Richard's behaviour in the middle scenes of the play.

> Let him not come there,
> To seek out sorrow that dwells everywhere.
>   I ii 72.

But this is no way to keep a throne. The king who left for Ireland was at least erect and scornful in his follies, and he is barely recognisable, when next we see him, as the man who fondles the earth 'as a long-parted mother with her child'. It is in vain that Carlisle tells him that even God's deputies are beyond aid if they will not help themselves.[1] In his abasement, just as earlier in his pride, he is still impervious to counsel.

> Not all the water in the rough rude sea
> Can wash the balm from an anointed king;
> The breath of wordly men cannot depose
> The deputy elected by the Lord.
>   III ii 54.

The words are splendid but they bring short comfort to the speaker. As bad news comes fast, his irresolution, feeding gratefully on the luxuries of despair, prepares us for the capitulation in the following scene.

When this scene opens, the crown is still not irrevocably lost. Bolingbroke is still cautious. He will accept the arbitrament of heaven, and he tempers his bluster with references to his 'stooping duty' and his 'allegiance and true faith of heart'. If the event should run that way, he would still be the yielding water to Richard's fire. Fittingly, York is dazzled by Richard's show of majesty.

> Yet looks he like a king: behold, his eye,
> As bright as is the eagle's, lightens forth
> Controlling majesty.
>   III iii 68.

For a moment it seems as though Richard has seized his cue, for his long address to Northumberland (72–100) is the most controlled and effective of his utterances to his enemies. He rebukes Northumberland for failing in the duty of his knees; reminds him of the divine protection which guards anointed kings; and lays on the rebels responsibility for all the blood that will be shed if they persist in their treason. It is an argument to give pause to all waverers, and even Northumberland is sufficiently impressed by it to protest that, once granted his 'lineal royalties', Bolingbroke will ask nothing further than 'enfranchisement immediate on his knees'. These fair demands allowed, Bolingbroke

---

[1] III ii 27–32, 178–85.

would have had no moral right to continue his defiance; York would have seen the path of duty clear before him, which was all he ever wished to see; and the more prudent and honest of Bolingbroke's followers would have melted from his side.

Fatally, Richard chooses this moment to fall again to dramatising his position. Is it not humiliating, he asks, that a king should have to speak fairly to a rebel in arms? Aumerle tries to steady him:

> Let's fight with gentle words,
> Till time lend friends, and friends their helpful swords.
> III iii 131.

He is advising a show of compliance until an appeal to royalist sentiment shall enable Richard to restore his position. But he is too late. The doomed King has already yielded, captivated by the fancy of contrasting his present helplessness with the majesty that once sentenced Bolingbroke to banishment.

> O! that I were as great
> As is my grief, or lesser than my name,
> Or that I could forget what I have been,
> Or not remember what I must be now.
> III iii 136.

When Northumberland returns with a message from Bolingbroke, we are at one of the crises of the play. His estates restored, the message may promise submission and good behaviour. The odd thing is that we never know. Without ever stopping to enquire, Richard decides that it is a demand for his surrender, and he is heard resigning himself to the exchange of his crown for all manner of obscure destinies, vowing to flatten the corn and fret a grave in the dust with his wanton tears.

Gradually Richard sees his sacred authority broken by the pressure of events. In brave words he calls upon 'my master, God omnipotent' [1] to gather armies of pestilence against his enemies, but the bitter lesson he has to learn is that his assumption of irresistible power no longer squares with the facts. There are earthly forces which he 'must' obey. In these moments of insight he turns in self-disgust from the wordy conceits that would make 'this ill do well', sees himself as a mockery king of snow, acknowledges his need of bread and all material

---

[1] Again he recalls Edward II:

> Full often am I soaring up to Heaven,
> To plain me to the gods.
> V i 21.

sustenance. Then the agony of his present suffering is so intense that he cries out to be released from the prison of his memories and truly 'forget what I have been'. He begs his followers to throw away the 'respect, tradition, form, and ceremonious duty' that now mock him with their insincerity. But these moods do not last for long. It is not in his nature that they should. His faith in the divine sanctions of his office is strong enough to brace and exhilarate him even when he knows beyond doubt that God and the angels will not come to save him.[1]

But the nature of this faith undergoes a change which is the key to Richard's behaviour in the last two Acts of the play. When it was still possible to put up some resistance to Bolingbroke, his attitude merely revealed the futility of an exaggerated conception of Divine Right. Shakespeare is merciless to this conception. No good will come of empty invocations, for in a crisis men respect facts and only facts. The question then arises, has Divine Right any further validity when its fondest assumptions have plainly collapsed in the test of action? Bolingbroke answers that it has none. In the deposition scene he merely considers himself to be treating with a defeated enemy, and he stands by in silent contempt while Richard enacts his martyrdom. His own kingship will be founded on other sanctions. But Richard gives a different answer. With the insight granted to him as a man and as the anointed holder of a sacred office, he knows that his defeat has not altered anything. God still holds kingship in His special care and will demand atonement for the wrong done to His deputy elect. Richard is enabled to understand that his personal tragedy is simply his personal tragedy. The principle of royalty lives on.

His new faith, then, is no longer a sentimental hope of being somehow rescued from disaster. It is all the stronger because those facile expectations have been defeated and his own immediate and personal fate has almost become irrelevant. Deposition will be followed by death, and to all that he is now reconciled. But he is still assured of his inalienable kingliness and of the vengeance it will one day exact.

This assurance enables him to steal the scene in which he is brought before Bolingbroke to be formally deposed. Bolingbroke had planned this scene as a solemn ritual of confession and abdication, and in

[1] In his introduction to the Arden edition Peter Ure holds (lxii sq.) that Richard's tragedy is his failure to free himself from the burden of kingship even when its powers and responsibilities are lost. But surely it is this which saves Richard's sanity. The agony of his material loss becomes bearable when he discovers in his imagination, which is inviolable, that he is still royal, although fated to be deposed and die.

Northumberland he had a collaborator happy to execute the details with his own special brand of malice and efficiency. Even York had been persuaded that the act was necessary, and the intention was that Richard should make a public surrender, 'so we shall proceed without suspicion'. It was no part of the plan that he should succeed in making all the spectators accomplices in a crime.

Carlisle is the first to spoil the effect with his passionate protest against the condemnation of the figure of God's majesty by subject and inferior breath. When Richard is brought in

> To do that office of thine own good will
> Which tired majesty did make thee offer,
>   IV i 177.

he is by turns theatrical and pathetic. It is characteristic of his broken mind that he should not be absolutely certain of his touch, and the conceited expression of his grief is an indulgence that he cannot easily outgrow.[1] But it is no longer the mere image of sorrow that feeds his glowing fancy. Convinced now that no miraculous intervention will save him, he can stand and face his destiny. It is not true self-knowledge that he has attained, for that will always be beyond him, but it is some sort of reconciliation. He has accepted his fate. His concern now—the by-play with the mirror is a typically histrionic expression of it[2]—is to learn what sort of man he is who is both a king and not a king. It is a personal indulgence in a theme which he will find leisure to develop in the loneliness of prison. To his enemies he insists unwaveringly on his royalty. The volatile temperament that ought, once defeat was certain, to have collapsed into futile impotence has somehow achieved a mysterious virtue in the discovery that, in all the things that matter, he is still a king. Throughout the scene he clings passionately to that essence of his being. Northumberland tries in vain to make an end of these unrehearsed effects and confine Richard to the part allotted to him. Richard has no difficulty with Northumberland.[3] The 'haught

---

[1] A purely technical consideration is important here. The lament was the characteristic mediaeval form of tragic statement, and to the Shakespeare of 1595 it was not yet conceivable that Richard might be deposed without an appropriate demonstration of grief. In the corresponding scene in *Edward II* (V i) the King indulges in similar fancies, taking off the crown and putting it on again, alternately grieving at his harsh fate and calling on God to make him 'despise this transitory pomp'. Thus Richard's exaggerated language does not mean that his inner resignation has already deserted him. He does not expect to be saved; and he is reconciled.

[2] Ure points out that the long soliloquy in V v really begins at this point.

[3] Nor, of course, has Shakespeare. We shall meet again this unattractive symbol of the new political order, and for the moment Shakespeare is content to indicate his sullen ruthlessness in a few unmistakable touches. As in *Edward II*,

insulting man', mere ladder for Bolingbroke's ascent, is disposed of in language of new-found directness. Hesitation has vanished with the hope that God would send a thunderbolt from the skies. Richard is now so certain of his true nature that he can condemn his own participation in the crime that is being committed:

> For I have given here my soul's consent
> To undeck the pompous body of a king.
>
> IV i 249.

The 'sort of traitors' includes himself.

The irony that follows the breaking of the mirror is a new element in his character. He can even turn the incident against himself, so much superior to Bolingbroke has he now become. 'This sport' he teasingly calls his examination of the 'flattering glass'. He is not just playing with words when he cries that his real grief 'lies all within', for it is of a kind that his silent enemies cannot comprehend. The 'external manners of laments' is all that they can be expected to understand. Blandly—as though he were in need of instruction!—he thanks Bolingbroke

> For thy great bounty, that not only giv'st
> Me cause to wail, but teachest me the way
> How to lament the cause.
>
> IV i 300.

He penetrates the insincerity of Bolingbroke's 'fair cousin' with the wry conceit that, since a king now stoops to flatter him, he need not beg a request. The request, when it comes, is merely for 'leave to go': no matter where, so long as it is from their sights. With a final savage pun on *convey* he departs—to death—absolute master of the situation. Fifteen lines later the scene is over, but not before the audience have been admitted to an ecclesiastical conspiracy which shows that the true king's cause does not sleep.[1]

a distinction is made between the court, with its civilised standards and Italianate influences, and the world of 'accomplished barbarism' represented by Northumberland. It would not have impressed Northumberland that Richard was the man who introduced the handkerchief into England. Similarly, his dainty clothing was one of Mortimer's principal grievances against Gaveston.

In one respect, however, Northumberland comes off better than he might, for Shakespeare makes no use of the incident, fully described in Holinshed, of Northumberland's promise to Richard, then at Conway, of a safe-conduct to Bolingbroke for the purpose of negotiation. When Richard set out, Northumberland ambushed him and took him to Flint as a prisoner.

[1] In one of those telling anti-climaxes which Shakespeare manages so well but which scare producers into making ill-considered cuts. This tiny pendant is essential to the scene, to show that Richard's apprehension of his kingship is not mere vanity.

In the little episode with the Queen, Richard is still eloquent with self-pity, and the idea of parting furnishes new embroidery for his grief. But he still understands his real predicament.

> I am sworn brother, sweet,
> To grim Necessity, and he and I
> Will keep a league till death.
>
> V i 20.

He is no longer beating his beautiful, helpless wings in a cage. He knows what his fate is to be and has decided how he will meet it. But the Queen cannot realise what has happened to him. When he bids her regard his former state as 'a happy dream', she cries in amazement that Bolingbroke has deposed his heart and intellect. She reverts instinctively to Nature's primacies and reminds him that he is a lion, the king of beasts, and how

> The lion dying thrusteth forth his paw
> And wounds the earth, if nothing else, with rage
> To be o'erpower'd.
>
> V i 29.

He answers her reproaches in a single phrase, neatly turned:

> A king of beasts indeed; if aught but beasts,
> I had been still a happy king of men.
>
> V i 35.

'I had been still': he no longer has any illusions about the present and he is not now to be seduced by idle hopes. But—and it is one of the reasons why he does fall—he cannot avert his mind from the presence in his fate of an element of the casual and undeserved. It leads him to savour his fall as an epitome of human tragedy. Therein he is true to his conception of himself. If to ordinary people he seems to overstate the case, that is just the difference between himself and them. They are ordinary people, he is not.

From York's account, he behaves with the same detached submissiveness when he rides into the City at the tail of the triumphant Henry.

> But dust was thrown upon his sacred head,
> Which with such gentle sorrow he shook off,
> His face still combating with tears and smiles,
> The badges of his grief and patience. . . .
>
> V ii 30.

'The setting sun, and music at the close.' When we meet him for the last time, in the prison at Pontefract, Richard is reflecting on Edward's thought,

> But what are kings, when regiment is gone,
> But perfect shadows in a sunshine day?
> Marlowe, *Edward II* V i 26.

> Know that I am a king: O, at that name
> I feel a hell of grief! where is my crown?
> Gone, gone! and do I still remain alive?
> *ibid.* V v 91.

Richard's fancy is as fertile as ever, but the rhythms of his speech are more direct and colloquial, and—at least until he detects a resemblance between his tear-stained face and a clock—less burdened with lyrical conceits. Christian paradoxes are too subtle to give him comfort. 'Thoughts tending to ambition', which delude him with such 'unlikely wonders' as forcing his way out of prison, die in their own pride as they remind him of his impotence. He grasps finally at the consolation afforded to beggars in the stocks, that they are not the first of Fortune's slaves, others having endured the like. It is poor consolation for any-one with Richard's sense of dedicated separateness. Even without an audience his imagination has been creating roles for himself to play, and these succeeding fancies (the doubting Christian, the prison-breaker, the philosophic beggar) have been the thoughts with which he has idly peopled the world. With such brave fancies the human mind often seeks to relieve the instant pressure of pain and sorrow. But inevitably the hurt forces itself back into the consciousness, and in the end Richard sees himself playing the king again,

> and by and by
> Think that I am unking'd by Bolingbroke,
> And straight am nothing: but whate'er I be,
> Nor I nor any man that but man is
> With nothing shall be pleas'd, till he be eas'd
> With being nothing.
> V v 36.

'Nothing' to Richard is not being king, but it is also death. Only that 'nothing' can ease the nothingness that his life has become.[1]

---

[1] Cf. *Timon*:

> My long sickness
> Of health and living now begins to mend,
> And nothing brings me all things.
> *Tim.* V i 191.

Impregnable now in his self-possession, he can face the truth about himself when the world breaks in upon his musings.

> How sour sweet music is
> When time is broke and no proportion kept!
> So is it in the music of men's lives.
> And here have I the daintiness of ear
> To check time broke in a disorder'd string:
> But for the concord of my state and time
> Had not an ear to hear my true time broke.
>   V v 42.

Richard sees himself as the artist whose intuitions, rare and precious as they are, have not fitted him for the business of his life. 'I have wasted time, and now doth time waste me.' The harmony that is in himself has failed to achieve harmony in the state,[1] and so long as he is a creature of Time, his mind will know no peace. He welcomes death because it will release him from the time which he has broken.

But this perception has brought him only to the threshold of true self-knowledge. If we think of the insight granted to Lear and Timon, we shall realise how little Richard has really achieved. He has learned that the individual has somehow to accommodate himself with his own particular world, just as Lear and Timon learned that responsibility was not to be exchanged for sentimental indulgences. But with this partial knowledge he is satisfied to die. It has not given him the strength to rebuild his life. He could not, as Lear might have done, go back into the world and conquer it. Can we doubt that, given another chance, he would have failed again?

Henry VI, who also was a king, offers a fairer comparison than the heroes of tragedy. Hazlitt rightly says that the characters and situations of Richard and Henry were 'so nearly alike, that they would have been completely confounded by a commonplace poet'. Although Henry was too passive and acquiescent to be really tragic, his quiet courage moves a deeper pathos than Richard's more spectacular renunciations. Richard views his royal office primarily as the source of privilege and personal gratification, and he becomes peevish when the higher powers fail to protect his enjoyment of it. He never for a moment recognises that Divine Right imposes duties. But to Henry the office meant, first of all, responsibility. If he was called to any privilege, it was to the privilege of ruling with strength and justice. When men failed in their allegiance,

---

[1] The story of Henry V, the political success, complements that of Richard II, the political failure. Henry's personal harmony lay in a conception of honour which he was able to realise politically in a life of action.

their impiety saddened him but he did not regard it as a personal betrayal, for no man had so little vanity or so few illusions.[1] Knowing well the sort of man he was, he was ready to give up the crown whose rights and responsibilities he was incapable of exercising. We may feel that it was a spiritless performance, and Shakespeare does not hide the element of selfishness in Henry's readiness to abandon the duties of office in order that he may pass the time in what Hazlitt severely describes as 'monkish indolence and contemplation'. He was indifferent to its external pomps,

> a prince's delicates,
> His viands sparkling in a golden cup,
> His body couched in a curious bed,
>
> *3 Hen. VI* II v 51.

and his cry to be relieved from his anxieties comes from the heart. It is not so with Richard's extravagant resignation of

> my jewels for a set of beads;
> My gorgeous palace for a hermitage;
> My gay apparel for an alms-man's gown;
> My figur'd goblets for a dish of wood;
> My sceptre for a palmer's walking staff;
> My subjects for a pair of carved saints,
> And my large kingdom for a little grave.
>
> III iii 147.

This is perilously near fustian, and we must not be blind to the absurdity of the picture that Richard proposes: no man would have had less relish for the cloistered life. The distinction that Shakespeare makes between Richard and Henry is integral to his idea of kingship, and he lets us know that Richard was a man who never achieved complete self-understanding. Character and upbringing only fitted him to think of himself as a king. It was his great strength, and ultimately his means to some kind of victory over his enemies. Looking back at the past, he created an image of himself as more royal than he had ever been; exaggerating his gifts as an artist in the hope of gilding his failure as a king. He knew that he had failed, without ever understanding why. He never discovered that his office implied a duty.

And so the final Richard is not a fully regenerated figure. Some find consolation in his fighting end, but the last minutes of his life show some deterioration from his best manner. The recollection of his political failure drives him back to vain regrets. 'While I stand fooling

---

[1] See *3 Hen. VI* III i 76-101.

here', he says at the end of an elaborate conceit, but this is not a new-won gift for self-criticism. He has made this sort of remark before, and it has always seemed a mock-humble invitation to applaud the lyric flight still hovering on his lips. He does not really think that this kind of thing is 'fooling'. It has been the breath of life to him, and it has done more than anything else to cushion his fall. In renewed self-pity he calls the love that inspired the prison music 'a strange brooch in this all-hating world', and the entry of the Groom starts him again on the worst sort of railing, its conclusion being that the horse Barbary should be added to the growing list of Judases. He dies in violence, promising 'never-quenching fire' to his assassins. In the end he has been false to his vision of 'nothing', and his death is proud and ignorant and hopeless. On a like occasion Henry VI sought forgiveness for his sins and a pardon for his murderer.

In *Richard II* Shakespeare is not making a general condemnation of the artist as king. Given other qualities, the man of sensibility and imagination is likely

> had he been put on,
> To have prov'd most royally.
> *Ham.* V ii 411.

But Richard lacked stamina and a certain kind of discipline and dedication, and his imagination was incapable of directing itself outwards. The sophisticated aesthete may make a good enough king provided only that he does not try to substitute sensibility for action. Richard's fault was a self-engrossing imagination that peopled the world just as he wished to find it.[1] It did not direct itself upon things as they really are, and the creations of his fancy were always more real and vivid than the craggy truths of experience. It was the nature of his particular Calvary to have to learn, so far as he ever could, that the world had not conformed to his imaginings. But Shakespeare's way of telling the story leaves him with some sort of victory over his enemies, and he wins it through a final triumphant feat of the imagination that transforms experience into the betrayal of a Christ. It may be, too, that we are meant to understand that even an adolescent, egocentric imagination may sometimes be justified in its intuitions. Richard's facile conception of Divine Right is irritating and ineffective when he appeals to it to sanctify his whims and excuse himself from taking action. But disillusionment does not destroy his faith in his peculiar and ultimately invincible sacredness as the figure of God's majesty. To Bolingbroke's pragmatism he opposes this mysterious

---

[1] And even in prison he was still doing it.

sense of his own anointed separateness. The image that he creates of himself as a man essentially royal is fatuous if tested simply by his performance when the crown was his; but it proves itself to be finally valid both in the comfort it brings to Richard himself in his humiliation and in the strange uneasiness it causes to his enemies. Richard's political epitaph is the edged ambiguity contained in Exton's 'thy buried fear'.

Through the other main characters in the play Shakespeare revealed the intolerable dilemmas in which men may be put by the existence of a man like Richard. First there is York, a statesman of the old school, an essentially honest and middle-of-the-road sort of man whose defection to Bolingbroke may seem to approve the Lancastrian succession and so explain the play's contemporary reputation as a handbook for usurpers. Shakespeare certainly cast York for a special role of his own contriving, for he took liberties with the historical character.[1] Of all the seven sons of Edward III, Edmund of Langley was by nature and inclination the least fitted to bear responsibility at a critical time. 'A soft prince' is how Stow describes him. A Castilian bride was witness to some rather confused ambitions in Portugal in his younger days, but, as was only sensible in a prince with four elder brothers, he did not aspire to any great importance at home. As an enthusiastic huntsman he preferred sport to politics, and it was largely the accident of survival that led to his being appointed keeper of the kingdom when Richard left for Ireland. At the crisis he surrendered to the superior power of Bolingbroke as the quickest way of putting an end to an unhappy situation. So, up to a point, Shakespeare suggests, but for his own purposes he imagines York's extreme conscientiousness and the agony of his moral and political indecision.

York in the play shares Gaunt's uneasiness about Richard's dangerous irresponsibility, and the confiscation of the Lancastrian estates moves him to thoughts that he dare not entertain. But his criticism of Richard does not impugn his personal loyalty. It was his duty to give frank counsel, and Richard counted none the less on his love and allegiance in leaving him in charge of the kingdom. It was

---

[1] As he also did with Gaunt. The real Gaunt was not the time-honoured counsellor who in the play irks Richard with his 'intolerable consanguinity'. Holinshed writes of him as a 'turbulent and self-seeking baron', and he was almost as much a nuisance as his brother Gloucester. But Shakespeare needed a character who should be the traditional honest adviser, and he invested Gaunt with the homespun loyalty and candour which the author of *Woodstock* attributed, just as unhistorically, to Gloucester.

impossible, however, to rely on his capacity. He meets trouble with the fussy impotence of a Capulet trying to organise the household for a feast—in fact we can almost detect the worried accents of a Quince. His futility and indecision have made Bolingbroke's task half-accomplished even before Richard returns from Ireland. Disasters overwhelm him until he wishes he were dead, and his 'Go, fellow, get thee home; provide some carts' is a classic in the annals of military helplessness. Undoubtedly his conscience troubles him.

> If I know
> How or which way to order these affairs
> Thus thrust disorderly into my hands,
> Never believe me. Both are my kinsmen:
> The one is my sovereign, whom both my oath
> And duty bids defend; the other again
> Is my kinsman, whom the king hath wrong'd,
> Whom my conscience and my kindred bids to right.
>
> II ii 108.

He speaks in disjointed mutterings that are Shakespeare's clue to his predicament, and it is plain that his scruples have so far undermined a nature congenitally irresolute that he will be incapable of action.

> Well, somewhat we must do. Come, cousin,
> I'll dispose of you. Gentlemen, go muster up your men,
> And meet me presently at Berkeley Castle.
> I should to Plashy too:
> But time will not permit. All is uneven,
> And every thing is left at six and seven.
>
> II ii 116.

His encounter with Bolingbroke in arms momentarily revives his sense of outrage, and his language significantly gains in strength as he speaks of the deep sinfulness of rebellion. But the brave mood does not last. His resistance is already weakened by his feeling that Bolingbroke has a case, and he surrenders to something he now can do nothing about, the rebels' superior strength.

> Well, well, I see the issue of these arms:
> I cannot mend it, I must needs confess,
> Because my power is weak and all ill-left;
> But if I could, by him that gave me life,
> I would attack you all and make you stoop
> Unto the sovereign mercy of the king;
> But since I cannot, be it known to you
> I do remain as neuter.
>
> II iii 152.

Since he has been left to protect the country from the King's enemies, this is really no neutrality at all, and he then proceeds to involve himself further by offering a night's hospitality at his castle. When Bolingbroke announces that he intends next day to move against Bushy and Bagot at Bristol, York first says that he will go with him; but the next minute, because 'I am loath to break our country's laws', decides that he will not. He closes the scene with characteristic disingenuousness and resignation:

> Nor friends nor foes, to me welcome you are:
> Things past redress are now with me past care.
> II iii 170.

Before Flint Castle his spirits again revive and he seems to be hopeful that after all the true pieties will prevail. The very appearance of the King gives another fillip to his muddled optimism, and he persuades himself that the sight will dazzle men whose loyalties are less deeply rooted than his own.

> Yet looks he like a king: behold his eye
> As bright as is the eagle's, lightens forth
> Controlling majesty: alack, alack, for woe,
> That any harm should stain so fair a show!
> III iii 68.

But if in the past he has failed the King, now the King fails him. He can only stand in silence while Richard makes his wordy surrender, and thereafter his course is plain. He is no longer tortured by a divided allegiance. The habit of obedience is so strongly bred in him that his peace of mind is at once restored when there is only one man to claim it. A king there must be, and since it is not Richard it is Bolingbroke. Once this is settled by Richard's capitulation, York is as anxious as Bolingbroke himself to dispose of the necessary formalities. It is he who first proclaims the new king as 'Henry, of that name the fourth', and he who leads in Richard to seal the deed of abdication. He may not altogether like what has happened, but he belongs to that very large class of Englishmen whose perfectly sincere regard for principle will always at a crisis accommodate itself to facts.[1] If he has been weak, it is because the whole nation is already sick and because Shakespeare believes that even an honest man's will is paralysed by the least contact with rebellion.

[1] Can we doubt that Shakespeare himself belonged to it?

There are, too, certain excuses for his behaviour. Ties of kindred and an inborn respect for legitimacy bound him in loyalty to Richard, so long as Richard had the strength and virtue to command it. He would never have initiated rebellion on his own account. But as soon as Richard's misrule and disregard of counsel provoked a rebellion he could not suppress, York transferred his obedience to the man who was strong enough to take the crown without provoking a civil war. Not being a philosopher, York did not enquire into the causes of these events. He felt the pity of Richard's fall, but at the same time he thanked providence that a strong man was at hand to spare the country the miseries that must otherwise have followed. In this attitude was born the idea, naturally encouraged by Lancastrian apologists, that Henry was an instrument of providence; and York's moving account of Richard riding into London at the heels of his conqueror ends with the reflection that

> Heaven hath a hand in these events,
> To whose high will we bound our calm contents.
> To Bolingbroke are we sworn subjects now,
> Whose state and honour I for aye allow.
>
> V ii 37.

His *de facto* loyalty is at once put to a grievous test, and like his brother Gaunt, who had seen his son go into banishment in the name of peace, he too would sacrifice a son. Despite its comic bathos, the episode of Aumerle's conspiracy is a frightening revelation of the new order at work. With the scuttling of ancient loyalties, new and sinister motives are in control and there is a large element of panic in York's vehement insistence that Aumerle has earned a traitor's death. Throughout the play York is an important symbolic figure. He acts without courage or nobility, but his unhappy situation discloses the pitiless demands which the dogmas of the Tudor state could make upon personal honour and the claims of kindred.

Shakespeare's treatment of Bolingbroke is more equivocal. Standing always outside the bright light that falls on Richard, this man keeps his character and motives in shadow. That his usurpation was a crime Shakespeare never doubts, and Henry V, the mirror of England's greatness, would so regard it on the eve of Agincourt. But the play lends some substance to the traditional view that he did not seize the throne by deliberate calculation. This tradition was accepted by Daniel, who published the first four books of his *Civil Wars* early in 1595. They were registered during the previous autumn, and there can be little doubt that Shakespeare had read them. Daniel holds that, although the usurpation was wicked, providence was acting through Bolingbroke:

> Then, fortune, thou art guilty of his deed
> That didst set his state above his hopes erect,
> And thou must bear some blame for his great sin. . . .
>
> That he who had no thought so high to climb,
> (With favouring comfort so allur'd along)
> Was with occasion thrust into the crime,
> Seeing others' weakness and his part so strong.
>
> *Civil Wars* i 94–5.

This was Bolingbroke's own version of events, and Shakespeare at least allows it to be a possible interpretation.[1] We may, if we wish, think him innocent of far-reaching design. To some extent it was probably Shakespeare's intention that we should.

But that is not all. While he realised their immediate effectiveness in the theatre, the casual operations of Fortune never completely satisfied Shakespeare as a motive force of drama. Plot and character are indivisible. He searched the mind and heart of Richard to discover reasons for his fall, and in the same way, without drawing a fully-rounded character, he could not help sketching the outlines of the man whom Destiny summoned to be a king.

The picture already has the Machiavellian touches which Bolingbroke was to develop on the throne. Like Cromwell, he realised that he rises highest who knows not whither he is going. His actions have the flexibility permitted to men who do not have to declare their ultimate direction. It makes him dangerous from the first. Coleridge's keen ear detected the metrical deficiency in his opening line, and found it sinister:

> Many years of happy days befall
> My gracious sovereign.
>
> I i 20.

He remarked, too, the ironic courtesies that fall from Bolingbroke throughout this scene, and wondered by what right he should claim that Gloucester's blood cries 'to *me* for justice and rough chastisement'. The chosen of providence he may be, but he knows better than to leave everything to chance. Hazlitt found him a subtle opportunist, 'patient for occasion, and then steadily availing himself of it'; seeing advantage from far off but reaching for it only when he is sure that it has come within his grasp. We can see how tightly he reins his passions,

[1] See above, pp. 229–30.

how shrewdly his words and actions are subdued to the needs of the moment. If he is angry at his banishment, he does not publicly show it. He will not give his enemies that much satisfaction, and compared with Mowbray's unrestrained cry of grief, his response is controlled and deliberate. His two couplets,

> Your will be done: this must my comfort be,
> The sun that warms you here shall shine on me:
> And those his golden beams to you here lent
> Shall point on me and gild my banishment,
>
> I iii 144.

make an impersonal comment on the poetic falsity of the lines in which Richard has pronounced his sentence ('Till twice five summers have enrich'd our fields. . . .'). When at length he does give way to grief, there is only his father to witness it. On the other hand crocodile tears were readily available on demand. From Richard's wry description (I iv 24–36) we learn how skilfully, on his way to exile, he cultivated the arts of popularity, doffing his bonnet to every oyster-wench and 'wooing poor craftsmen with the craft of smiles'.

His promise that he returns as Lancaster, with no other object than to recover his lost estates, does not square with his high-handed treatment of Richard's creatures, 'the caterpillars of the commonwealth' whom he swears to 'weed and pluck away'. If Green and Bushy have indeed

> fed upon my signories,
> Dispark'd my parks, and felled my forest woods,
> From mine own windows torn my household coat,
>
> III i 22.

Bolingbroke, as party to the issue, should not be their judge. His sentence of death is, so far, an act of personal vengeance. But the rest of the speech, professedly delivered 'to wash your blood from off my hands',[1] goes farther than that. It is an assumption of sovereign power. His charges against his prisoners may be warranted, but it is not his place to sentence them; nor is their execution necessary to the recovery of his confiscated lands. This act of power, so personal and so deliberate, shows the true worth of the 'stooping duty' which, soon afterwards, he humbly lays at Richard's feet. In fact his usurpation has already begun.

---

[1] So that, he means, he cannot be accused of responsibility for their death. Cf. his insistence that Richard shall make a public abdication, 'so we shall proceed without suspicion'. He is clearly anxious to create the impression of a man who has always acted correctly. But for Hotspur's version of his behaviour at this time, see *1 Hen. IV* IV iii 54–105.

By all practical tests he justified himself, moving into unfamiliar positions with instinctive aptitude. Natural authority is evident in his handling of the quarrel in Westminster Hall,[1] astuteness in his attempt to stage-manage Richard's removal as a voluntary abdication. He is clever enough, too, to realise that, if the beneficiaries are shrewdly chosen, a reputation for mercy can be bought quite cheaply. He can afford to be lenient to Carlisle, who is honourable and essentially a man of peace; or to Aumerle, who is too unstable to be really dangerous and anyway has a zealous father to act as watchdog. On the other hand, he is ruthless to men he has cause to fear, and unlike Richard he does not threaten idly. 'Destruction straight shall dog them at the heels': and in the last scene his lieutenants report a succession of unmistakable victories. His evasiveness with Exton is a recognisable act of 'policy' in which everyone could see the resemblance to the story of the Queen and Secretary Davison. To lodge 'the guilt of conscience' in the bosom of a subordinate was to show a ready mastery of the arts of contemporary kingship.

Is then the deposition of Richard to be excused by the superior efficiency of the usurper? On the surface it seems that it may be, for evil counsellors have been removed, a capricious king has been succeeded by a man who has shown himself firm and temperate, and the change of government is acceptable to York, the honoured survivor of an older order, whom Bolingbroke himself greets, with uncharacteristic effusiveness, as 'thou sheer, immaculate, and silver fountain'. It would seem that England may expect fairer days. But Shakespeare forces us to enquire further into the true nature of Bolingbroke's success and Richard's failure. If Richard's futility in the everyday business of kingship could not in the end deprive him of his essential royalty, it may be that Bolingbroke's competence in these matters cannot suffice to make him truly a king. There is always something lacking in his address. Possibly it is because Richard's surrender brings him so easily to the throne, but he never meets the moral challenge to his position. He does not directly answer York on the issue of treason. Asked why he comes 'in gross rebellion . . . braving arms against thy sovereign', he offers the routine reply that he only wants his dukedom. York admits the justice of the cause but flatly tells him that this is not the honest way to win it:

> I have had feeling of my cousin's wrongs,
> And labour'd all I could to do him right;

---

[1] In contrast to Richard's ineffectiveness in I i.

But in this kind to come, in braving arms,
To be his own carver and cut out his way,
To find out right with wrong, it may not be;
And you that do abet him in this kind
Cherish rebellion and are rebels all.
                                                    II iii 141.

It is, of course, the crux, and Bolingbroke's actions stand irretrievably
condemned. But he is saved the necessity of reply by York's sudden
submission to the parade of arms he has just rebuked. 'I cannot mend
it.' For the moment the point goes by default, and in the practical
sense the issue is already over. But the moral question remains un-
answered, and we soon realise that Bolingbroke has no intention of
ever answering it. The only excuse he finds it necessary to offer for
his appearance in arms is, over and over again, that he wants his
hereditary rights. He still utters no further explanation when, with
these rights obtained, he is moving calmly towards a richer prize. It
can be interpreted as a conquest achieved by naked power and cunningly masked ambition, or as the march of necessity towards the throne
that Richard has abandoned. Whichever way it be, no usurpation has
ever been so matter-of-fact, so little attended by the justifications that
such occasions in decency demand. It is not only that Bolingbroke
lacks his father's traditional sense that it must be left to God to punish
a ruler's crimes. Except where it concerns his own deprivations (or
his affected interest in the fate of his uncle Gloucester), he is largely
indifferent to Richard's misrule. There is no scene in which he rallies
his followers by appealing to their sense of a common wrong; even
his patriotism, suitably uttered upon occasion, is conventional and
detached; and his denunciation of Green and Bushy is, on his own
admission, a bid to give a semblance of justice to an act of power. We
discover in the end that he has taken Richard's throne without ever
directly accusing him of anything.

Thus he is morally unequipped to meet Richard's final challenge in
Westminster Hall. His contribution to this scene is epitomised in the
brief observations which punctuate his silence. 'Are you contented to
resign the crown?'; or, 'Go, some of you convey him to the Tower.'
That is the extent of his interest in what he had designed to be a purely
formal ceremony. All the rest—Richard's reluctance at the last to
surrender his care-burdened crown, the agony of his self-betrayal, the
clinging to the potent shadow of his royalty—has apparently no
meaning for him. Gaunt would have understood; but the son, unconscious representative of a new order of things, does not. His

silence condemns him. If he does not understand what Richard is laying down, he cannot know what he himself is taking up.

By the end of the play Shakespeare has shown how insecure Henry's position really is, in spite of his practical efficiency. His 'unthrifty son' causes him anxiety by absenting himself from a victory celebration because 'he would unto the stews'. This may be only a private grief, but in his official self he cannot feel safe so long as Richard is alive. 'Have I no friend will rid me of this living fear?' Faithfully Exton executes his oblique commission and comes back with the body:

> Great king, within this coffin I present
> Thy buried fear.
> > V vi 30.

He means to assure Henry that the man he feared is now safely dead. To his limited perceptions that is the end of the matter. But the words contain another meaning, and for the first time in the play Henry's intuitions reach beyond the immediate event. It is borne upon him that there is more to kingship than simply stepping on to a convenient throne. He will never, so long as he lives, exorcise the secret fear of the man he has deposed and killed. Stone dead always has a fellow.

'To find out right with wrong, it may not be'. Here lies the rather pessimistic conclusion of the whole matter. The failure of the King implicates his people in a general suffering from which no act of state can rescue them. Even on the most favourable reading of Bolingbroke's motives or York's surrender to necessity, it is evident that none of the arguments available to them—pragmatism, expediency, innocent intentions, the misdeeds of Richard—is good enough. In their consequences their actions are indistinguishable from the open selfishness of Northumberland and his kind. Thus the symbolic little scene in the Duke of York's garden (III iv) is more than an indictment of improvident kingship. It specifically condemns all the participants in the drama: the King perhaps foremost, but the favourites too, who have devoured while seeming to support him, and 'the great and growing men' who might have lived to bear the fruits of duty. The theme of the tangled garden is here brought to a passionate climax as the two Gardeners discuss affairs of state. They have no reality as people, and nowhere else in his drama did Shakespeare pretend that countrymen speak as these two do. They are emblematic figures, spokesmen for the moment of their disordered and suffering country, like the son-slaying father and the parricide son who break into Henry's reveries at Towton. All that England has lately endured, by usurpation and misrule, treachery, irresponsibility and civil war, here fuses in Shakespeare's imagination into the image of the sea-walled garden where neglect has choked the flowers and herbs with noisome weeds. The Gardeners' talk holds no comfort for the future. Rue, sour herb of grace, is the only plant that will grow in the disordered garden.

In *Richard II* there are deeper implications than the simple issue between a good king and a bad king. In this unhappy conflict neither side is perfect, for both act selfishly and passionately; and government is clearly shown to be an act of participation in which ruler and ruled bear a proportionate responsibility. The tragedy of misgovernment is that it draws the whole people into the widening circle of its consequences; just as healthy plants are choked by weeds and ultimately share their corruption. Richard's guilt spreads like a blight through the fair garden, poisoning what had once been wholesome, until in the end all his subjects are touched by it. It contaminates the malcontents who raise their arms against him, and the flattering playboys who encouraged the follies it was their duty to correct. But better men are caught up in it too, like the warm-hearted impulsive Aumerle, reduced by these events to a typical 'mixed-up kid',[1] or the well-meaning York, who speaks the language of a traditional wisdom but fails wretchedly in the crisis. When death has removed Gaunt, the ideal of the good counsellor, his choric role passes to the Gardeners, whose dispassionate analysis spares neither the King's neglect nor the 'too fast growing sprays' and 'superfluous branches' which together have made the green garden an unprofitable wilderness.

Through the mirror of the ruined garden Shakespeare shows that the real victim of Richard's tragedy is England. When a king misgoverns, or is deposed, the country suffers. This conclusion is evident in the images of inheritance and generation that run through the play,[2] in Carlisle's dreadful prophecy, in Henry's apprehension of his 'buried fear'; and it would have been the stronger for the knowledge of every man in an Elizabethan audience that the predicted sorrows did in fact occur.

> I weep for joy
> To stand upon my kingdom once again.
> Dear earth, I do salute thee with my hand,
> Though rebels wound thee with their horses' hoofs.
>   III ii 4.

---

[1] The historical Aumerle was much less simple, and his treacheries were legion —he even betrayed Richard in 1399. The brave soldier at Agincourt hardly seems to be the same person.

[2] See C. F. E. Spurgeon, *Shakespeare's Imagery*, 238–41.

Throughout the play a wide range of speeches, imagery and associations is focused on this single passionate idea of England and the
suffering she brings to herself through dissension and civil war. 'This
earth shall have a feeling,' Richard says, and as the beautiful English
landscape lies before us—its 'high wild hills and rough uneven ways',
the castle fringed by 'yon tuft of trees', the pale-faced villages, the
parks and forest woods, the proud-topped eastern pines, the un-
seasonable stormy day 'which makes the silver rivers drown their
shores', old folks by the fireside in tedious winter nights, the summer's
dust, and bay trees withered in the heat—'the fresh green lap of fair
King Richard's land' becomes a sentient being, to bleed at the touch
of marching feet and recoil from the 'boist'rous untun'd drums . . . and
grating shock of wrathful iron arms'. These pictures of the fair countryside, threatened with a tempest of blood, give the play, despite the
gravity of the political argument, its essentially lyrical atmosphere. If
Richard is the most poetic of Shakespeare's kings, it is because his
theme is England.[1] The *Sonnet* mood permeates the play, with its
dedication to the idea of Beauty, its intense love of the world, and its
sorrow that all things lovely must sometime die.

> The setting sun, and music at the close,
> As the last taste of sweets, is sweetest last,
> Writ in remembrance more than things long past.
>   II i 12.

But in the play the enemy is not Time, it is man himself.

Postscript

The changing fashions in the interpretation and popularity of
Richard II make an interesting footnote to the play. In Shakespeare's
own time, as we know, it was thought to offer dangerous inducements
to sedition: an impression that may rather have been due to the nature
of the historical facts than to Shakespeare's personal handling of them.
Anyhow it was a subject more wisely avoided, and it was still powerfully mistrusted when Tate made his unfortunate venture at the time
of Oates and 'exclusion'. Once it had outgrown this unwelcome
topicality, the play had to endure a long period of contempt and dis-
interest. The eighteenth century was bored by it. Johnson's well-
known comment, that *Richard II* cannot be said 'much to affect the

---

[1] Although his grief is self-centred, he consistently identifies his own suffering
with England's, and he more than once points out that, when his own personal
tragedy is over, the country's suffering must continue.

passions, or enlarge the understanding', was echoed in the same generation by George Steevens, who observed that, although critics might admire it, 'the successive audiences of more than a century have respectively slumbered over it, as often as it has appeared on the stage'.

Even more singular, by contrast with the play's reputation today, is the opinion of a critic writing early in the present century: 'As a stage drama it has never appealed to the ordinary theatre-goer owing to the nature of its interest being too subjective, too much concerned with subtle passions and affections, and too little with those grand elemental emotions which constitute the *milieu* in which nine-tenths of humanity live, move, and have their being.' [1] This remark at any rate explains why *Richard II* did not particularly appeal to the more heroic days in which the writer lived, and it shows by implication why it has become popular in our own. The eighteenth century's neglect of the play persisted into the Victorian age. The great actor-managers either ignored it or misunderstood it. At Sadler's Wells in the middle of the century Samuel Phelps went through most of the canon (incidentally keeping close to Shakespeare's text and making this unusual experiment pay), and this was one of the six plays he did not attempt. The other five were the three parts of *Henry VI*, *Troilus and Cressida*[2] and *Titus Andronicus*: astonishing company in which to find Richard. Irving, who made a problem play of *The Merchant of Venice* and usually was very sensitive to complexities of character, apparently failed to realise the opportunity that Richard would have given him. Charles Kean and Beerbohm Tree both mangled the text to make room for needless pageantry, and earlier Hazlitt had objected to Edmund Kean's interpretation, presented in a corrupted version in the year of Waterloo, because the actor made Richard 'a character of *passion*, that is, of feeling combined with energy; whereas it is a character of *pathos*, that is to say, of feeling combined with weakness'. Kean was wrong to make his gestures 'fierce and heroic, instead of being sad, thoughtful, and melancholy'. Hazlitt knew how Richard should be played if he was to be played at all. For some two hundred years, it seems, Shakespeare's dramatic interpreters failed to realise the poet in Richard, the bright but inward-looking imagination, the streak of perverseness and femininity. They thought of him as a choleric tyrant who could not make good his lofty pretensions, and being out of patience with that sort of thing, they made nothing of the character.

---

[1] Oliphant Smeaton, *Shakespeare: his Life and Work* (Everyman), 137.
[2] *Troilus and Cressida*, which was even more neglected than *Richard II*, has also found an audience in recent times.

It was left to the athletic Benson to discover Richard's rare and subtle sensibility, his infatuation with each succeeding idea of kingship, ruin, sorrow and betrayal. Our own age, mentally less robust than many that have preceded it, knows more about its Richards and is better able to sympathise with them. Psychological drama has made us familiar with those 'subtle passions and affections' which a more confident generation rejected as unworthy of its attention. After two world wars, and the collapse of numerous assumptions which for our grandparents bore the reassuring stamp of eternity, we are possibly more interested in failures than successes. In this climate a man like Richard can flourish. We are likelier to appreciate the engrossed subjectivity of his vision, and there is no fear now that he will appear before us as something too heroic. The danger is rather that the moody but gifted dreamer, absorbed in his thick-coming fancies, may lean too heavily on our sympathy and upset the balance of the play.

We must not allow Richard to bewitch us. The play is roughly contemporary with *Romeo and Juliet* and *A Midsummer Night's Dream*, when Shakespeare was in a mood to mistrust excess. He was unsure of the realms to which even his own imagination might beckon him, and in his drama at this time he shows us men betrayed by strained emotion and excess of fancy. Quick bright things find their way to destruction. The likeness between Richard and Romeo is much more than verbal, for there is some defect in each which prevents his story from being genuinely tragic. *Romeo and Juliet* is in the main a comedy of bungled social relationships, of a needless family quarrel, and a boy and a girl who demand more of the world than their particular world can at the moment give them. At the climax Romeo's arraignment of the everlasting stars is as brash and inappropriate as Richard's assumption of a personal Calvary. *Richard II* is more complex and much harder to assess, chiefly because it is impossible for us to feel about him as the Elizabethans did. His failure affected them as it can never affect us, and the true nature of his fault, as of the pathos he inspired, is not easily grasped by generations for whom government has lost its mystery and resistance may sometimes be a solemn duty. Intolerable as a king, Richard can yet charm us as a person, for we are better able than the Elizabethans to separate the man from the office. When political failures can be removed from power without injury to the structure of government, it is possible to retain some sympathy for them personally and look forward with considerable interest to reading their biographies.

So we shall never quite be able to see Richard through his creator's eyes. In our time men of his sort are very common indeed, and perhaps they get a more respectful hearing than they deserve. Shakespeare would warn us that this is dangerous. While the play draw its strength from the pathos of Richard's fall and the lovely, lingering echoes of his plaintive verse, it fails to reach the heights because the heights were always out of Richard's reach. Great art, it was said long ago, needs a great soul to nourish it. Men like Richard win the tribute of an idle tear, may rise, at their finest, to a certain pallid splendour, but they do not breed great tragedy, nor even stirring history. Richard was not merely an amateur of politics, he was also—as Shakespeare revealed him—an amateur of life.

V. 'KING JOHN'

Except that Mr. John Masefield has found it a 'truly noble play', and Dr. Johnson applauded its 'very pleasing interchange of characters and incidents', *King John* has received little favour from critics and has only occasionally appealed to audiences in the theatre. That there is no record of Elizabethan or Jacobean performance need not mean very much, as these records are scanty and haphazard, and the two re-issues of the quarto of the source-play, *The Troublesome Reign of King John*, argue a certain amount of public interest in the theme. It is not a play that it would have been prudent to offer at the court of Charles I's Catholic queen; nor, it seems, did anyone venture to revive it during the crisis of the Popish Plot. In fact there is no record of a performance until 1737; and a few years later, in 1745, with a Stuart rebellion brewing in Scotland, Colley Cibber produced a tendentious adaptation which he called *Papal Tyranny in the Reign of King John*. Unlike many of the botched versions of Shakespeare's work, this did not hold the stage for long, and subsequent productions in the eighteenth century, by Garrick, Thomas Sheridan, John Philip Kemble and others, were tolerably respectful towards the folio text. It was a favourite piece in Kemble's repertoire, and Constance provided Mrs. Siddons with one of her most dramatic parts.

In the following century the play was chiefly valued for the opportunities it gave for spectacle and a pedantic antiquarianism. In 1823 Charles Kemble, with J. R. Planché as his designer, presented it 'in the precise Habit of the Period, the whole of the Dresses and Decorations being executed from indisputable Authorities, such as Monumental Effigies, Seals, Illumined MSS, &c.' Macready, who acted the play more than once during the crisis of Catholic Emancipation, was almost equally intent upon pageantry and historical accuracy, and in 1852 Charles Kean, with Planché again the designer, aimed at 'a total puri- fication of Shakespeare, with every accompaniment that refined know- ledge, diligent research and chronological accuracy could supply'. Irving ignored the play, but in 1899 Beerbohm Tree put on a charac- teristically sumptuous production that included a lavish dumb-show of 'The Granting of Magna Carta'.

In the present century *King John* has never been very popular. It is not a satisfactory play, since it lacks a focal point. Shakespeare's cus- tomary insistence on the themes of patriotism, obedience and unity is here entangled in his stern exploration of Commodity. Faulconbridge, by far the most attractive and memorable of the characters, has a curiously equivocal function. Although closely drawn into the action, especially in the closing scenes, he is always in a sense standing apart, as commentator and symbol. Dramatically the central figure is, or should be, the King himself, and this is where the play's artistic weakness lies. For John is not an integrated character. At times he is a fumbling, un- certain, self-reproachful villain, a sort of meaner Macbeth; at times— because he is king—the great ocean towards whom all English loyalties should flow in tributary obedience; but never a man whose personal and political dilemmas insist upon being understood.

Unable to find in the play any central animating idea, Chambers dis- missed it as 'a bit of hack work,' [1] and possibly that is what it was. It may be that Shakespeare was bored: not, certainly, with the play's underlying issues, which still had enormous contemporary importance, but with the stale setting in which he was now obliged to examine them. Conceivably *King John* was a theatre chore demanded of him by his fellows because a rival company had had a success with a similar theme. This sort of thing was apt to happen in the Elizabethan theatre. The immense popularity of *Henry IV* prompted the Admiral's Men to their heavily-carpentered *Sir John Oldcastle*, and a few years later Shakespeare was himself called upon to write a romance with a wood- land setting to match the success of the rivals' *Robin Hood*. He re- sponded on that occasion with *As You Like it*, but the outcome might not always be so felicitous. If, then, it was the persuasions of his com- pany that turned him to the story of King John, and they considerately put into his hands a copy of *The Troublesome Reign* (1591) to save him the labour of research and start his imagination working, he would at once have found that he had handled most of this stuff before. The virulent anti-Popery was new, but he found that uncongenial. All the

[1] *Shakespeare: a Survey*, 100.

rest—the pasteboard characterisation, the fighting in France, the treachery and vituperation, the meaningless iteration of defiance and lament—was wearisomely unsubtle and familiar: so familiar that he could not rouse himself to avoid the chronicle method to which *The Troublesome Reign* monotonously adhered. Certainly that is how it appears, and the unusual abundance of personifications and images of bodily action seems to betray a sense of conscious strain, as though Shakespeare realised his shortcomings and tried to flog the verse into an artificial energy.[1]

King John was probably written in 1596, after *Richard II*. Naturally this date is not favoured by critics who like to think that the sequence from *Richard II* to *Henry V* was composed as a deliberate tetralogy, a sort of dramatic epic, but the four plays of a tetralogy (if there was one) do not have to be written immediately one after the other, and Shakespeare's choice of theme was often dictated by the requirements of his company. *Much Ado About Nothing* certainly interrupted the Lancastrian sequence, which may explain its rather scornful title. The autumn of 1596 has been suggested as a date for *King John* on the ground that in Constance's grief over Arthur, Shakespeare was mourning the death of his own son Hamnet, who was buried at Stratford in August of that year. 'For grief is proud and makes his owner stoop.' Of course it could be so (and has anyone thought of dating *Hamlet* by the death of Shakespeare's father?), but this is not the way that artists usually work. Shakespeare was quite able to live a mother's sorrow without the sting of personal bereavement, and if he uttered his own feelings at all, it is likelier to have been through those characters who blamed Constance for lamenting overmuch. 'Lady, you utter madness, and not sorrow.'

Stylistically *Richard II* and *King John* are linked in several ways, notably in the marked absence of prose, but also there are striking differences. While nearly a fifth of *Richard II* is in rhyme, a natural characteristic of Shakespeare's sonneteering period, *King John* has very little rhyme outside the couplets that bring each scene to a conventional close, and the proportion of blank verse—2438 lines out of 2570—is the highest in the canon. It is in many respects a transitional play. Shakespeare is discarding the self-consciously lyrical drama of Romeo and Richard for a more realistic treatment of history and comedy. *King John* is lyrical only in the outbursts of grief and in those passages where Shakespeare's imagination is stirred again to contemplate the horrors of invasion and civil war.[2] In other passages the play

---

[1] See C. F. E. Spurgeon, *Shakespeare's Imagery*, 245–52.
[2] As at II i 23–30, 66–75, V vii 112–18.

seems to have brought him to the threshold of the period in which prose would be his happiest medium, and this is especially evident when Faulconbridge is on the stage. Although there is not a single line of prose in the whole play, this is the medium that Faulconbridge instinctively needs for the expression of his quizzical, earthy personality. A play or two later he would have found it.

While the conceits of Constance have a clear affinity with the language of Romeo, Richard II and the *Sonnets*, her way of speaking is not allowed to dominate the play. Arthur, too, has his pretty pathos, and moves it in other poeple, but Faulconbridge is always a counterbalancing presence, infecting even courtly persons with his own laconic colloquialism, so that they come to mistrust the 'wasteful and ridiculous excess' that likes

> To gild refined gold, to paint the lily,
> To throw a perfume on the violet,
> To smooth the ice, or add another hue
> Unto the rainbow, or with taper-light
> To seek the beauteous eye of heav'n to garnish.
>
> IV ii 11.

Of this excess the play itself is by no means innocent, but excess is at war with a more compressed and less declamatory way of saying things. As a whole the play is stylistically self-conscious and experimental. Shakespeare is less often disposed to linger upon a conceit and watch it grow, which had been the characteristic language of Richard II. Instead he often lets the imagery race ahead before an idea has been fully worked out, as in Salisbury's comment on John's second and unnecessary coronation:

> In this the antique and well-noted face
> Of plain old form is much disfigured;
> And, like a shifted wind unto a sail,
> It makes the course of thoughts to fetch about,
> Startles and frights consideration,
> Makes sound opinion sick and truth suspected,
> For putting on so new a fashion'd robe.
>
> IV ii 21.

King John also marks a transition in Shakespeare's political ideas. It is a bridge between his earlier histories and the maturer thought of the Lancastrian plays, and it announces his discovery of the true nature of political man.

Basically the play uses the same situation as *Richard II*, and not merely reaches the same conclusions but states them more emphatically. Richard was a bad king, but John is worse. Shakespeare declares him to be a usurper—which was doubtful—and gives him a greater responsibility for Arthur's death than his sources warranted; at the same time taking a few years off Arthur's age in order to underline the horror of the deed. John's flawed title, followed by his palpable wickedness, brings into question a subject's relationship with a man so evidently bad; and the answer, given in Faulconbridge's carefully weighed allegiance, says again that rebellion is the worst of evils. When he addresses Pandulph or the French, John is still, for all his faults, the voice of England, and this is the royalty that Faulconbridge momentarily inherits. The duty of obedience to a *de facto* king, however bad, could not be more explicitly stated; and because under the right leadership the English nobles return to that duty, the country is once again united. Faulconbridge makes the right decision, and he is the reason that majesty does not cease.

So far Shakespeare has only repeated himself. The new discovery that he makes in *King John* is that public and private morality do not always march together. England's saviour in the play is not a saint, nor even a particularly good man; but he is a man able to adapt himself to what his experience has shown him to be the necessities of political life.

A proper understanding of John himself was made impossible by his peculiar place in Elizabethan historiography. In the Middle Ages history was written by the clergy, whose enemies always came in for their unmitigated censure. John's bad reputation thus began early, long before constitutional historians discovered the importance of Magna Carta. He was branded as predatory and irreverent, scornful of the Church's teachings and covetous of its earthly treasures. As Holinshed put it, he was 'little beholden to the writers of that time in which he lived', and for some generations he was regarded as one of the least satisfactory of kings. We saw in an earlier chapter how he was suddenly transformed in Bale's propagandist play into the brave and godly king who first threw down the gauntlet to Rome.[1]

So John, in whom the Victorians were to discover a resourceful opponent of English liberties, was reconstructed in Bale's reading of events as the earliest champion of our independence, frustrated in his high intent because his enemy was ubiquitous, implacable and strong and his own subjects unfortunately something less than heroic. Foxe the martyrologist also saw him as the baffled forerunner of mighty happenings, and Holinshed, who was usually content to accept what-

---

[1] See above, pp. 69–70.

ever he read in the mediaeval chronicles, rejected their version of a king who, in his view, 'had a princely heart in him and wanted but faithful subjects to have wroken himself of such wrongs as were done and offered to him'. In official circles the beatification of John proceeded no farther than the express condemnation in the Homilies of the subjects who had revolted from him, but Shakespeare grew up in a generation that had come to think of him at least as the king who made the first brave stand against Roman tyranny. He was Moses to Henry VIII, the saviour to come.

This was the John of *The Troublesome Reign*, which apart from Holinshed was probably the only source that Shakespeare used.[1] In the Induction to the printed text audiences who have taken pleasure in the triumphs of the Scythian Tamburlaine are now invited to do appropriate homage to a native champion of equal lustre.

> For Christ's true faith endur'd he many a storm,
> And set himself against the Man of Rome,
> Until base treason (by a damned wight)
> Did all his former triumphs put to flight.
>
> Ind. 6.

John is made to promise all that Henry VIII was later to accomplish. As a true servant of God he is 'in arms against the Romish pride', and he swears to seize 'the lazy abbey-lubbers' lands' and outlaw 'the trental obsequies, mass, and month's-mind' that are the scenic apparatus of the Papal yoke. Clerical luxury and idleness are conventionally satirised, and 'the Pope and his shavelings' come off ill in coarsely humorous episodes of 'sport among the smooth-skin nuns' and 'revel with the fausen friars'.

[1] This has lately been questioned, notably by E. A. J. Honigmann in the Arden edition of *King John*. Honigmann believes that *The Troublesome Reign* is a corrupted version of Shakespeare's play, which must therefore have been written some little time before 1591, probably under the impact of Mary's execution and the Armada. This is not the place for a detailed discussion of this thesis, but it does not convince. Honigmann's theory that *King John* was earlier than *The Troublesome Reign* was considered and demolished in anticipation by J. Dover Wilson in his Cambridge edition (1936), and there have been more recent refutations by F. P. Wilson (*Marlowe and the Early Shakespeare*, 114–19) and J. Isaacs (*Shakespeare's Earliest Years in the Theatre*, the British Academy Shakespeare Lecture, 1953). Whatever debasement took place between *King John* and *The Troublesome Reign*—and it is suggested that there may have been an intervening play—it is surely surprising that the copy used only one line of the supposed original, the commonplace 'For that my grandsire was an Englishman' (*KJ* V iv 42). Nor was it the usual practice of actors who plundered someone else's play for their own use, usually in the provinces, to lengthen the text and enlarge the cast. Yet *The Troublesome Reign* is 300 lines longer than *King John* and has 40 speaking parts compared with 23.

But John is not able to achieve all that he has promised. The un-known author cannot wholly escape the historical facts, and by the end of the play John is lamenting that

> I am not he shall build the Lord a house,
> Or root these locusts from the face of earth.
>   Pt II sc viii 106.

In this disappointment he finds consolation in his vision of the future:

> But if my dying heart deceive me not,
> From out these loins shall spring a kingly branch,
> Whose arms shall reach unto the gates of Rome,
> And with his feet tread down the strumpet's pride
> That sits upon the chair of Babylon.
>   108.

Up to a point his failure is easily explained. All, as Faulconbridge observes, 'is the fruit of Popery'. John's troubles began when, deserted by his nobles, he submitted to Pandulph to get help against the French.

> Since John did yield unto the Priest of Rome,
> Nor he nor his have prosp'rd on the earth:
> Curst are his blessings; and his curse is bliss.
>   100.

No doubt: but why was John deserted by his nobles? Even this can be blamed in part on clerical influence, for the machinations of the Pope are everywhere; but it is here that the author of *The Troublesome Reign* gets into difficulties and his picture of John as the warlike Christian hero begins to fall apart. Not so disingenuous as Bale, who conveniently overlooked the whole episode, he has complicated his theme by introducing the story of Arthur, which occupies the central portion of the play. John struggles against the need to order Arthur's death, and in so far as the play concerns the personal tragedy of John, this is the crucial dilemma. Either way, alive or dead, Arthur was a danger to his crown: as Mary to Elizabeth's.

> For on his life doth hang thy sovereign's crown;
> But in his death consists thy sovereign's bliss.
>   Pt I sc ix 32.

But his death does not bring the hoped-for security:

> Arthur is dead; ay, there the corsie grows:
> But while he liv'd, the danger was the more;
> His death hath freed me from a thousand fears,
> But it hath purchast me ten times ten thousand foes. . . .

> His life, a foe that levell'd at my crown;
> His death, a frame to pull my building down.
> My thoughts harpt still on quiet by his end,
> Who, living, aimed shrewdly at my room.
> Pt I sc xiii 234.

As John discusses it here, the problem is more political than moral, but later he accepts the moral responsibilities of his crime and recognises that it has rendered him unfit to lead his people into freedom.

> Thy sins are far too great to be the man
> T'abolish Pope and popery from thy realm:
> But in thy seat, if I may guess at all,
> A king shall reign that shall suppress them all.
> Pt II sc ii 169.

Through mere opportunism he submits to Pandulph in order to save his throne. The deterioration in his character is not concealed, and he ends the play devoid of virtue, a remorseful, self-confessing sinner, grasping only at the hope that where he has failed, a greater than he will succeed.

> Methinks I see a catalogue of sin
> Wrote by a fiend in marble characters,
> The least enough to lose my part in heaven.
> Methinks the devil whispers in mine ears,
> And tells me, 'tis in vain to hope for grace:
> I must be damn'd for Arthur's sudden death. . . .
> How, what, when, and where, have I bestow'd a day
> That tended not to some notorious ill?
> My life, replete with rage and tyranny,
> Craves little pity.
> Pt II sc viii 71.

His hero having failed him—for this abject John is not really tragic even by the undemanding convention of 'the fall of princes'—the author patches up the remainder of his play with a number of patriotic affirmations.[1] In date of composition *The Troublesome Reign* belonged to the anxious years of Mary's execution and the Spanish invasion. It was much safer to plead for national unity than to probe too closely into a sovereign's relationship with an inconvenient kinsman. So it was for Shakespeare too, even if he was writing seven or eight years later, and *King John* suffers from the same ambiguity in the treatment of the central character.

Read side by side, the two plays bring us very close to Shakespeare

[1] See above, pp. 82-4.

as he worked.[1] The language of *The Troublesome Reign* was not for him,[2] and it is fascinating to watch him give vigour and individuality to the speech of the Bastard, re-state the Papal claims for Pandulph, or lay a gloss of 'wit' on the protracted grief of Constance. But he was broadly content to follow the general design of his original, preserving its chronological sequence and merely omitting, compressing or expanding to suit his own version of the story.[3]

A short comparison of the opening scenes will sufficiently illustrate his method. Both enact the episode in which Faulconbridge discovers his royal but sinister parentage. Shakespeare takes 276 lines over it, against *The Troublesome Reign's* 431, and it is noticeable at once how he gets straight down to business, dispensing with the lifeless preliminaries of his source and opening dramatically with John's challenge to the ambassador of France, 'Now, say, Chatillon, what would France with us?' In the fourth line Chatillon refers to John's 'borrowed majesty' and already the play is in motion, with the audience early made aware that the King's title is in question. Where *The Troublesome Reign* takes 66 lines to get Chatillon off the stage, Shakespeare accomplishes this in 30 and then inserts a 14-line colloquy between John and his mother to develop the theme of usurpation and plant it firmly in the spectator's mind. This theme is something that Shakespeare has himself introduced into the plot. In *The Troublesome Reign* the opening speeches imply that John inherits in natural succession from his brother.

John's brief 'Our abbeys and our priories shall pay This expedition's charge' (48–9) is shortened and transferred from lines 316–21 of the source, and the Faulconbridge family then appear, to be greeted in *The Troublesome Reign* with the fussy, ineffectual 'Say, Shrieve, what

---

[1] In this particular instance. His treatment of his sources varied from play to play, and the comparison with *The Troublesome Reign* illuminates his methods in one case only, and one in which he may not have been very much interested. Usually he borrows much more freely from the actual language of his source.

[2] He reduces the classicism and Latinity in which the source abounded, e.g. at Pt I sc i 250–2, 348–9; sc ii 8–9; sc iii 3–5.

[3] He retained also many of the glosses and inaccuracies of the source, his method, as in all the histories, being to reduce the facts to a pattern that served his dramatic purpose. Thus he gathers all John's difficulties—with Arthur, with the barons, with France and with Rome—into a single theme, although John did not in fact have to face them all simultaneously; he makes Arthur a child, in place of Holinshed's young knight; because she would be more pathetic as a widow, he conveniently forgets that Constance's third husband, Guy of Tours, was still alive, and fails to note that she died before Arthur; and he brings into a single scene the death of Constance (1201), the death of Elinor (1204), John's second crowning (1202) and the French invasion (1216).

are these men? What have they done? Or whereto tends the course of
this appeal?'; and by Shakespeare with the crisp 'What men are you?'
The earlier play indelicately makes Lady Faulconbridge be witness to
her humiliation, whereas Shakespeare does not bring her on until the
claim is decided and the Bastard Philip has already been knighted as
Plantagenet; and although in both plays she eventually admits her
lapse from virtue, Shakespeare allows her only 57 lines, compared with
108, for the purpose. In *The Troublesome Reign* Philip roughly forces
the confession from his mother, hammering away at her until she
breaks down into involved and tedious utterance (400–21). Shakespeare resolves this into a brief, spontaneous admission:

> King Richard Cordelion was thy father.
> By long and vehement suit I was seduc'd
> To make room for him in my husband's bed:
> Heaven lay not my transgression to my charge!
> Thou art the issue of my dear offence,
> Which was so strongly urg'd past my defence.
> *KJ* I i 253.

Again, in the source Philip receives the confession without a thought
for his mother's feelings, but Shakespeare closes the episode by finding
him lines that will heal her wounds:

> Some sins do bear their privilege on earth,
> And so doth yours; your fault was not your folly. . . .
> With all my heart I thank thee for my father!
> Who lives and dares but say thou didst not well
> When I was got, I'll send his soul to hell.
> *KJ* I i 261.

To reduce the length of the scene Shakespeare cuts the altercation
between the two brothers, his lines 134–62 compressing more than a
hundred lines of the source, and he adopts a much more convincing
means of resolving the question of Philip's parentage. *The Troublesome
Reign* sends Philip into a trance (250–77) wherein, speaking in 'a
frantic madding vein' and vomiting gobbets of Latin, he senses 'fumes
of majesty' and discovers that he was royally fathered. Shakespeare
does not care for these lunary intimations, and in his version the truth
is learned when Queen Elinor reads 'some tokens of my son in the
large composition of this man'. John and his mother have made up
their minds before the wretched Robert has begun to argue. Philip
himself comes to a similar conclusion when it occurs to him to wonder
why he should be so unlike his brother; and it is revealing to see how

Shakespeare develops and compresses an idea given by his source. This is *The Troublesome Reign*:

> Can Nature so dissemble in her frame,
> To make the one so like as like may be,
> And in the other, print no character
> To challenge any mark of true descent?
> My brother's mind is base, and too too dull
> To mount where Philip lodgeth his affects;
> And to his external graces that you view,
> Though I report it, counterpoise not mine:
> His constitution, plain debility,
> Requires the chair, and mine the seat of steel;
> Nay, what is he, or what am I to him,
> When anyone that knoweth how to carp,
> Will scarcely judge us one-country-born?
>
> Pt I sc i 365.

This is Shakespeare:

> Madam, an if my brother had my shape,
> And I had his, Sir Robert his, like him,
> And if my legs were two such riding-rods,
> My arms such eel-skins stuffed, my face so thin
> That in mine ear I durst not stick a rose
> Lest men should say 'Look, where three-farthings goes!'
> And, to his shape, were heir to all this land,
> Would I might never stir from off this place,
> I'd give it, every foot, to have this face.
>
> I i 138.

Here is the characteristic Shakespearean concreteness; and here, as they do not in the generalised picture given in *The Troublesome Reign*, the unheroic lineaments of Sir Robert rise lifelike from the printed page.[1] In Shakespeare's text the laconic, bantering tones of the Bastard invigorate the whole scene, which in the source-play is insipid and protracted. His speech on 'worshipful society', in which he delightedly contemplates the pitfalls and opportunities of his new-won state, is entirely Shakespeare's invention.

It is illuminating to pursue these comparisons throughout the play, but we must turn now to Shakespeare's handling of the religious and political ideas he discovered in the source. Except in a few short and inoffensive passages, he eliminates the crude anti-Catholic bias, and he

---

[1] Shakespeare here owed something to the actor who almost certainly played the part, the grotesquely thin John Sincklo, the 'mere anatomy' and 'father of maypoles', see *SWW*, 257.

deliberately refrains from presenting John as the Moses of the Reformation. He ignores the whitewashing process introduced by contemporary Protestant zeal. At the same time, when he does come to deal with the Papal pretensions, his analysis is more lethal than anything the earlier author was capable of. He knew exactly where Pandulph's arguments would lead, and he felt too deeply about them to be able to make his answer in a spirit of cheap comedy and vulgar abuse. His way is to allow Pandulph to speak his own implicit condemnation, in the scene where he orders France to dissolve the recent compact with England. This episode is enlarged by Shakespeare (*KJ* III i 135–347) from a much shorter scene in *The Troublesome Reign* (Pt I sc v 65–153). In the source, to establish a contrast with John's insolent defiance, the French King yields without protest to Pandulph's demands and rebukes John for his impiety. But Shakespeare gives him a long speech in which he accuses Pandulph of dissolving sacred vows and causing France and England to

> Unswear faith sworn, and on the marriage-bed
> Of smiling peace to march a bloody host,
> And make a riot of the gentle brow
> Of true sincerity.
>
> *KJ* III i 245.

The Cardinal's reply is a grave statement of the prime allegiance owed by princes to the Church.

> O, let thy vow,
> First made to heaven, first be to heaven performed,
> That is, to be the champion of our church.
>
> III i 265.

But he then goes on to enmesh France in casuistries:

> The better act of purposes mistook
> Is to mistake again; though indirect,
> Yet indirection thereby grows direct,
> And falsehood falsehood cures, as fire cools fire
> Within the scorched veins of one new-burn'd:
> It is religion that doth make vows kept,
> But thou hast sworn against religion,
> By what thou swear'st against the thing thou swear'st,
> And mak'st an oath the surety for thy truth
> Against an oath: the truth thou art unsure
> To swear, swears only not to be forsworn:
> Else what a mockery it should be to swear.

Pandulph is allowed a full and dignified presentation of his case,[1] and damns himself with his own falsity. Shakespeare's method is far removed from the naïve crudities of *The Troublesome Reign*. Here, in all its specious subtlety, men could recognise the Jesuit 'double talk' that played 'fast and loose with faith' and brought confusion to their daily pieties. To rally the people against the Catholic threat *The Troublesome Reign* could do no better than stir up the memory of vanished abuses. Shakespeare sees the present danger. France's surrender to Pandulph,[2] the more significant for his earlier defiance, warns Elizabethans of the subtler enemy now in their midst.

But the exposure of Roman sophistries—except that he was concerned with any threat to national unity—was not the purpose of Shakespeare's play. In *King John* he gives fresh emphasis to the problems he has lately examined in *Richard II*. Richard was an insufficient ruler but he was none the less the legitimate, anointed king. The issue was whether he should be deposed by a usurper who might govern better, and the play seemed to conclude that legitimacy was inviolate and indefeasible. In *King John* the ethics of rebellion are re-examined in circumstances much more favourable to the rebels. Richard was the legitimate king, and although he ruled badly, he was not a criminal; John was a usurper, and in plotting the death of Arthur he was guilty of a dreadful crime. Yet the fundamental questions remain. Is rebellion justified? Who is really responsible for the country's dissensions: the usurping King, or the subjects who falter in their obedience?

Shakespeare begins the play by insisting on John's unlawful title. Chatillon's 'borrowed majesty', for which there is no authority in Holinshed or *The Troublesome Reign*, is followed by Elinor's sharp reply when her son boasts that 'our strong possession and our right' will dispose of the French challenge:

> Your strong possession much more than your right,
> Or else it must go wrong with you and me.
>
> I i 40.

John is king *de facto*, and possession is his only 'right'. But this must suffice even when his actions put a heavier strain on his subjects'

---

[1] Of this case Johnson justly remarks, 'The propositions, that the *voice of the church is the voice of heaven*, and that *the Pope utters the voice of the church*, neither of which Pandulph's auditors would deny, being once granted, the argument here used is irresistible; nor is it easy, notwithstanding the jingle, to enforce it with greater brevity or propriety.'

[2] The original audience would have seen in this surrender a reference to Henry IV's conclusion that 'Paris is well worth a Mass'.

loyalty. In the opening scene he is shrewd and energetic, defying Chatillon with the spirit expected of an English king and meeting the Faulconbridge deputation with a generous readiness to acknowledge princely qualities in a subject. But thereafter, both as a king and as a man, he deteriorates: partly through defects in himself that swiftly become apparent, and partly through the working of the Shakespearean mystique that decreed that usurpers would not prosper:

> A sceptre snatch'd with an unruly hand
> Must be as boisterously maintained as gain'd.[1]
>   III iv 135.

The scene outside Angiers reveals his shifty opportunism, the conviction that every man has his price, the innate dissimulation imperfectly masked by declarations of patriotism and principle. The capture of Arthur then exposes him to grimmer temptations, and he proceeds with little hesitation to the crime which will make his people ready to 'kiss the lips of unacquainted change'. In his instructions to Hubert (III iii), although he pretends, Macbeth-like, to wish for darkness in which to unfold his purposes, he is not stayed by the moral caution or expedient doubts which made the John of *The Troublesome Reign* speak in riddles. His orders are unambiguous: Arthur is to die.

In thinking, later, to see the King's colour come and go 'between his purpose and his conscience', Salisbury is probably misreading the signs, for it is not until the nobles have left the stage in rebellious fury that John expresses any sort of penitence, and then it is apparently something of a surprise for him to discover that

> There is no sure foundation set on blood,
> No certain life achiev'd by others' death.
>   IV ii 104.

With the resilience of the naturally amoral he has soon recovered and is telling Faulconbridge that he has 'a way to win their loves again'. His satisfaction at being able to lay the blame on Hubert finally restores his courage and assurance, and in words that recall Bolingbroke's repudiation of Exton he declares that

[1] John's usurpation is emphasised in several references throughout the play, e.g. by Philip of France at II i 95; by John himself when he says before Angiers, 'Doth not the crown of England prove the king?' (II i 273); by Elinor at II i 471, 'thy now unsured assurance to the crown'; by John's own insistence on a second coronation, and Salisbury's misgivings about the wisdom of this, IV ii 21–7; and by Faulconbridge in IV iii, where he speaks of Arthur as 'the life, the right and truth of all this realm' and foresees in the expected reprisals against John 'the decay of wrested pomp'.

It is the curse of kings to be attended
By slaves that take their humours for a warrant
To break within the bloody house of life,
And on the winking of authority
To understand a law, to know the meaning
Of dangerous majesty, when, perchance, it frowns
More upon humour than advis'd respect. . . .
How oft the sight of means to do ill deeds
Makes ill deeds done!

IV ii 208.

It was Hubert's villainous aspect, he says, that turned his thoughts to murder, and he denies that he expressly commanded Arthur's death.

In one respect this is the critical episode of the play, since it decides John's stature. He lacks the insight of Macbeth, who cursed the juggling fiends but always knew in his heart that they did but direct him the way that he was going. Macbeth accepted moral responsibility, and John does not. John, concerned only with the political consequences of his crime, can still his self-questionings by verbal paltering. Up to this point *King John* could have developed into the personal tragedy of a monarch tempted to take the evil way; the play, in fact, that the author of *The Troublesome Reign* might have written if he had been capable of it. But this was not the play that Shakespeare chose to write. He was not yet ready to bare a murderer's soul, and in keeping the play firmly on the level of politics he deprived John of grandeur.

After this decisive scene with Hubert, John has little further part in the story. Faced with rebellion at home and an invasion by the French, he craftily divides his enemies by submitting to the Pope. Shakespeare recognises no patriotic martyrdom in this. He is careful to insist that surrender was not forced on John by desperate necessity, as it is in *The Troublesome Reign*. It is a deliberate act of expediency; and the crown is scarcely back upon his head before he is urging Pandulph to keep Rome's side of the bargain:

Now keep your holy word: go meet the French,
To stop their marches 'fore we are inflamed;

V i 5.

and, left alone, he congratulates himself that his submission has not been made 'on constraint'. 'Heav'n be thanked, it is but voluntary.' As such, it is more shameful in English eyes, and it is John's abdication as a king. His royal function passes to Faulconbridge, who makes a last vain attempt to rouse him to his duty:

Be great in act, as you have been in thought;
Let not the world see fear and sad distrust

> Govern the motion of a kingly eye:
> Be stirring as the time; be fire with fire;
> Threaten the threatener, and outface the brow
> Of bragging horror: so shall inferior eyes,
> That borrow their behaviours from the great,
> Grow great by your example and put on
> The dauntless spirit of resolution.
>
> V i 45.

All that John can answer is, 'Have thou the ordering of this present time.'

Melun's reference to 'the old, feeble, and day-wearied sun' describes the King as the 'black, contagious breath' of night envelops him. In a fever John is carried to Swinstead Abbey, where we are suddenly and surprisingly told that he has been poisoned by a monk: surprisingly because Shakespeare has scarcely mentioned the actions that might have exposed him to monkish vengeance.[1] Brought out to die, he multiplies the images that tell of death's swift encroachment, comparing himself in a last fine flash of language with a body cramped for space, a parchment shrunken by the fire, a vessel torn by storms. But his thought, as always, is only for himself. He dies, 'a clod and module of confounded royalty', impenitent because bereft of understanding.[2]

Shakespeare has pared away all that was heroic in the John bequeathed to him by *The Troublesome Reign* and sixteenth-century tradition. Significantly, the play contains less cosmic lore than any other of the histories, for it does not suit Shakespeare's purpose to remind us that John may be the eagle or the sun.[3] When Faulconbridge bids him play the lion, he responds with a smug reference to his treacherous league with Pandulph and simply gives up his functions. The only greatness allowed him is an occasional choric greatness, when he becomes a symbol to embrace recovered loyalties or to defy Chatillon and the Pope. Shakespeare's purpose is to present an extreme example of a situation in which, if ever, rebellion might be justified. Salisbury's argument that 'The king hath dispossessed himself of us' is much more than specious: Salisbury is no Northumberland. This is the cue for

---

[1] The omission is due to Shakespeare's casual use of *The Troublesome Reign*. In removing the anti-Catholic buffooneries of the source, he forgot that he had failed to provide a motive for the priests' hostility to John.

[2] Miss Caroline Spurgeon noted (*Shakespeare's Imagery*, 248–50) how Shakespeare has reduced John's stature by frequently picturing him as only a portion of a body. This symbolism 'in a play crowded with pictures of dancing, wrestling, whirling human figures, lets us see the king as a portion of a body only, and that portion steeped at times in human blood'.

[3] He bears these qualities only when Faulconbridge is speaking in his name, as at V ii 149.

Faulconbridge, who heals the country's wounds by pointing the way
to a higher duty.

> Now hear our English king;
> For thus his royalty doth speak in me.
> V ii 128.

His moment comes when Arthur's mutilated body is found at the
foot of the castle walls. The 'distemper'd lords' immediately conclude
that this is Hubert's work, done on the orders of the King, and they
abandon themselves to a quite excessive display of horror. 'This is the
very top.' It is indeed. Salisbury forbids his soul obedience to the
King who has decreed this murder, and Pembroke and Bigot are similarly unrestrained. Their protestations are plainly influenced by aristocratic dislike of the low-born Hubert—'Out, dunghill!' Bigot shouts
at him: 'Dar'st thou brave a nobleman?'—but the scene loses its effect
if we do not believe that their horror is genuine.[1] Faulconbridge is no
less appalled than they:

> It is a damned and a bloody work;
> The graceless action of a heavy hand.
> IV iii 57.

But he is less hasty to decide the guilt, and he swiftly lowers the emotional temperature by a characteristic order to Salisbury to put up his
sword,[2]

> Or I'll so maul you and your toasting-iron,
> That you shall think the devil is come from hell.
> IV iii 99.

The nobles angrily depart, to join the French invaders, and it is the
Bastard's decision now that will decide England's fate.

The deed is 'graceless' and will put its perpetrator 'beyond the infinite and boundless reach of mercy'. The world is an even wickeder
place than Commodity's anatomist had thought it. But his mood is
that judgment shall be hereafter. If Hubert is guilty, a thread from a
spider's web shall be strong enough to hang him on; meantime the
pressing need is England's, where a vast confusion waits and a thou-

---

[1] E. M. W. Tillyard (*Shakespeare's History Plays*, 223–4) speaks of the ill-
considered 'levity' of their actions, apparently because they explode in anger
against the King without first checking their facts, but this hardly seems to be
the appropriate word. If the lords have been actuated only by 'levity', the very
different behaviour of Faulconbridge loses much of its gravity and significance.
Shakespeare takes great pains to show that the rebels have a very serious case.

[2] His 'Your sword is bright, sir; put it up again' anticipates a famous line from
Othello.

sand businesses are brief in hand. He hurries to the King and takes his master's regality upon himself. Given the dreadful choice between rebellion and the service of a ruler whom he suspects to be indirectly responsible for this crime, he decides against sedition. By giving further offence to God, rebellion would only add one sin to another and make the punishment more terrible.

By the time the disaffected lords have joined the French, the single-mindedness of their late resolves has somewhat evaporated. It is a means of conveying, in terms of drama, that the Bastard's leadership has already begun to turn the tide, and it prepares us for their subsequent repentance. Salisbury is already deploring that 'the infection of the time' has made an earthquake of nobility.

> I am not glad that such a sore of time
> Should seek a plaster by contemn'd revolt,
> And heal the inveterate canker of one wound
> By making many.
>
> V ii 12.

Sedition is no longer the clear and unmixed duty that passion had so recently declared it, and in the presence of the French he grieves

> That, for the health and physic of our right,
> We cannot deal but with the very hand
> Of stern injustice and confused wrong.
> And is't not pity, O my grieved friends!
> That we, the sons and children of this isle,
> Were born to see so sad an hour as this?
>
> V ii 21.

Faulconbridge then enters to add definition to these uncertainties. The monarch is in arms, 'like an eagle o'er his aery towers',

> And you degenerate, you ingrate revolts,
> You bloody Neroes, ripping up the womb
> Of your dear mother England, blush for shame:
> For your own ladies and poor-visaged maids
> Like Amazons come tripping after drums,
> Their thimbles into armed gauntlets change,
> Their neelds to lances, and their gentle hearts
> To fierce and bloody inclination.
>
> V ii 151.

He defies France and defies Pandulph, excusing John's late compact with the Pope as executed 'rather for sport than need', and speaking in the name of England he promises the destruction of all her enemies.

It is simple, stirring stuff that reduces all the complex issues of the reign to the single one of patriotic duty. In the heat of the ensuing battle Salisbury breaks off to confess, 'I did not think the king so stored with friends.' This unexpected resistance puts them in a mood in which they are already half-prepared for Melun's revelation of France's intended treachery, and it is a relief to them to see the path of duty clear again.

> I do love the favour and the form
> Of this most fair occasion, by the which
> We will untread the steps of damned flight,
> And like a bated and retired flood,
> Leaving our rankness and irregular course,
> Stoop lowly within those bounds we have o'erlook'd,
> And calmly run on in obedience,
> Even to our ocean, to our great King John.
>   V iv 50.

The final promise of unification under the young Prince Henry marks God's forgiveness of the former acts of revolt; a forgiveness made possible only by Faulconbridge's decision not to be a rebel too. Henry is 'the cygnet to this pale faint swan', born

> To set a form upon that indigest
> Which he hath left so shapeless and so rude.
>   V vii 26.

In this closing scene, with its sober patriotism and grave, incantatory rhythms, John is become an alien figure, an unwished reminder of a sickness that is passing. He dies recounting the agonies that torment his 'unreprievable contemned blood', and with his death, the burden of his evil is lifted almost palpably from the scene while the Bastard talks of sweet, healthy things, of 'the lineal state and glory of the land', of *submission*, *faithful services* and *true subjection*, and ends the play with his final invocation of an England impregnable in unity.

This unity has been his achievement, and his character, although dramatically it is often anomalous, adds a new dimension to a play in which Shakespeare otherwise says little that he has not said before. Faulconbridge owes his success to the inspired authority and purpose lent him as the vessel of royalty. Like Gaunt, he comes to speak for England, and there is a vast difference between his earlier self and the symbolic figure whose importance consists in what he stands for. We shall be mainly interested in the lessons he learns in the course of his transformation.

Shakespeare developed the character from the brash and noisy boaster he found in *The Troublesome Reign*, and used him in the first half of the play as the bystander whose function was to comment upon the action. The morality writers often employed this choric figure, and his role covered the whole range between credulity and cynicism, between naïve acceptance and a sort of railing complicity. At this second extreme stood Thersites, and let us admit that there is more than a touch of Thersites in the early Faulconbridge. He may not have the acrid tongue or scabrous mind, but between him at Angiers and Thersites at Troy the difference is only one of degree.[1] A schoolboy relish for personal abuse and the *tu quoque* is coupled with an unerring eye for the moral and tactical weakness in everyone else's position. A soiled mind affects to wonder at the evil in the world but is all the time adding to it. Like Thersites, too, he is frequently rebuffed and snubbed by the other characters. His scheme for the reduction of Angiers—much the grubbiest proposal put forward in a scene remarkable for its unblushing *realpolitik*—is not in the end accepted; and after Angiers he is off the stage for a long time, except for a short moment when he has just slain Austria as an act of personal vengeance for his father. When he does reappear, we find that the King has not been employing him on any great business. He has merely 'sped among the clergymen' to collect their enforced contributions to the war.

'I am I, howe'er I was begot.' This glorying in his lack of kinship puts him in the company of the other stateless men, like Iago, Parolles, Falstaff, Richard III or Coriolanus. It may account for the uneasiness that seems to affect all the characters in *King John* when they are in his presence; and on the personal level he continues to be strangely unsuccessful. Even when John has virtually abdicated and he has become the embodiment of England, it seems that, strictly as a military leader, he has achieved remarkably little (V i 30, V vi 39, V vii 58–64).

In his morality role of Simplicity he is just a blunderer, and he succeeds only when he is identified with *Respublica*. Shakespeare has his own way of preparing the audience to accept this new identification. As a Plantagenet and the son of Lion-heart, a high destiny may be indicated for Faulconbridge in the opening scene, but we are not sure of it until the tang of his speech shows it unmistakably. He speaks of England before fate calls him to speak for England. His sturdy shoulders bear all that the play contains of comedy and pictures of Elizabethan life, and with an energy that overruns the plot and the solemn

---

[1] His liking for coarse insult is made evident in the source, e.g. Pt I sc ii 145–9, where he calls Limoges 'loathsome dunghill swad' *et al.*

political theme, his inexhaustible eloquence packs the stage with eel-skins, toothpicks in the mess, the absey-book, Good Friday fast, young maids of thirteen with their puppy-dogs or old men at their bowls, 'Old Time the clock-setter, that bald sexton Time', citizens crowding the streets to hear the prophet's harsh-sounding rhymes, toasting-irons, dogs that tug and scamble for a bone, spiders, beardless boys and cockered silken wantons, buckets dipped in wells, men crouching in stables and lying hugged with swine, thimbles, needles, maidens tripping to battle behind the town-crier's drum, or the unhaired sauciness of boyish troops. His 'mere Englishness' breathes in every syllable of his racy, trenchant speech, ultimately resolving the ambiguities of his character and marking him as the man who will rouse the sleeping majesty of England.

Thus Faulconbridge redeems and crowns the play, since the action is seldom as interesting or important as his independent vision of it. Shakespeare has sometimes used this sort of character before (Berowne and Mercutio are examples), but it is new to the histories. Although implicated in the action, Faulconbridge stands outside it and surveys it, not consistently but at least with enough detachment to be able to deepen its significance by his commentary. He condemns rebellion, but that is only one of the things he says about it. He also offers a self-sufficient explanation of the mainspring of political behaviour.

King John is the most cynical and disillusioned of the histories. By comparison *Richard III* is just a cautionary tale about a wicked magician, and in the political jungle of *King John* Richard himself would early lose his way in its thorns and dangers. Among its characters we may make an exception of Constance, whose mother-love, although she carries it to excess, is a decent human instinct, and she revolts from the treacheries and impersonal opportunism of the politicians. We may also except Arthur, with the reservation that Shakespeare's boys are seldom among his more endearing creations; and Blanch is just an innocent pawn in the game of power politics. But no one else in the play is a person of integrity, not even Faulconbridge, who cheerfully admits that he is tarred with the same brush as the people he condemns. Of the lesser characters, Robert Faulconbridge is ready to defame his mother and brother for a parcel of land; his mother has betrayed her husband; Lymoges is a bloody-minded blusterer, Melun betrays his master's secrets, Philip of France veers with every wind, Queen Elinor contrives for her son without honour or scruple; the men of Angiers propose a cynically treacherous compact for the saving of their city; Salisbury and his fellows find that sedition is a losing game before they decide to abandon it. Those who play a larger part bear a larger guilt. John, already a usurper, is also a killer; Pandulph deploys moral forces in pursuit of worldly ends; the Dauphin, once teased for being so green and fresh in this old world, learns his lesson well enough to be ready to betray his allies when he has used them; and even Hubert, on the whole a sympathetic character, accepts a wicked mission and decides to 'fill these dogged spies with false reports' when he has been talked out of executing it.[1]

It is a dark picture. Issues of right and wrong are debated freely, and every time the wrong prevails. Force and expediency appear in all the distorting colours of conscience, honour, patriotism, domestic piety and religious duty. Never before has Shakespeare's world been so ubiquitously and subtly evil. The dark, gesticulating figures of the Roses plays are wicked in a way that is easily understood. Noisy, passionate, violent, treacherous, ambitious, they never pretend to be other than they are; and their vices are offset by the decent ordinariness of the men and women whom they entangle in their schemes. Even Richard of Gloucester, who callously exploits all kindly emotions for his own purposes, disarms rebuke by his relish of his own virtuosity. Can so exquisite an artist be wholly bad? In *Richard II*, a play maturer and more thoughtful than any of these, we begin to be conscious of an evil of a different sort, that hides itself as virtue and knows how to temporise. When ambition has learned to play a waiting game and

---

[1] Hubert is strangely unsatisfactory. The King orders him to put Arthur to death, although by the time he appears in the prison the commission has apparently been changed to blinding. The stage is thus set for a classic discussion of the conflict between duty and conscience. The issue was at least as old as Antigone, and it was generally agreed in the sixteenth century that for a Christian the duty of obedience to the king stopped short of the commission of a crime. The Executioner puts the point when he says, 'I hope your warrant will bear out the deed', but Hubert surprisingly disposes of the objection as 'uncleanly scruples'. In the end Hubert neither kills nor blinds, but conscience is not his reason. Shakespeare chooses instead to have him overwhelmed by a rhetorical set-piece, and Arthur saves himself from the hot irons simply by piling up verbal points against an opponent who begins by wiping away remorse ('foolish rheum' and 'tender womanish tears') but ends, in his own quibbles about heating the iron and reviving it with his breath, by falling into the same rhetorical tricks. When he finally admits defeat, he has not yielded to pity or any other emotion; he has been confounded by Arthur's superior dexterity (*KJ* IV i).

To achieve this result Shakespeare departed from his source. In the corresponding scene (*TRKJ* Pt I sc xii) Hubert acknowledges the traditional dilemma. The deed is bad, but 'a king commands, whose precepts neglected or omitted, threateneth for the default'. Once again Arthur prevails, but he does it here by reminding Hubert that he is imperilling his immortal soul (xii. 65–80); and Hubert finally desists because the 'great Commander counterchecks my charge'. Shakespeare deliberately refused this issue, and it is hard to see why.

ruthlessness is masked as patriotism, the world becomes a more complicated and dangerous place. Bolingbroke's fair words and cool assessment of the odds show a sophistication that makes intriguers like Buckingham and Warwick seem innocent. But *Richard II* stops far short of being an unpleasant play. Its lyricism keeps it sweet, Gaunt's patriotism is idealised and clean, and York may hope for the best because he honestly believes in it. The atmosphere of *King John* is very different, for the whole currency of emotion has been debased. Evil no longer speaks as itself, it speaks as wisdom, justice, honour and religion. Commodity is the only wear.

Faulconbridge is the character through whom Shakespeare mirrors this sense of the baseness of political life. The difference between him and York, who also has a choric function, explains the different atmosphere of the two plays. York is a representative of the nobler and more optimistic tradition in which he was nurtured, but Faulconbridge has no roots—his illegitimacy is symbolic. As a creature of his time, he is naturally adept at delivering sweet poison for the age's tooth, and his strength is his power of rapid assimilation. His earlier simplicity is swiftly accommodated to the ways of the strange new world in which he finds himself. Armoured in his self-possession, an immense and irresistible adequacy, he learns by practice and example. Before he is thus acclimatised, the regular runners in the rat race find him boorish and naïve, and more than once he falters, momentarily astonished at their enormity, before he proves himself as apt as they. His resilience and intuitive adaptability will always restore his personal mastery of the situation.

At first he thinks it is all going to be great fun, and the exuberant boyishness of his first soliloquy (I i 182–219) shows how much the world has yet to teach him. Knighthood promises all sorts of harmless amusements, like pretending in a superior way to forget people's names, or pulling the legs of travel snobs, or practising the polite shams of social intercourse. These he supposes to be the delights of the 'worshipful society' to which he now belongs. But once he has seen high politics in action, he never speaks in this mood again. Coming with the King and his forces to the conference before Angiers, he listens in silence to the angry parley: a silence that lasts for fifty lines before the insolence of Austria excites him to speech, youthful and intemperate speech that only sidetracks the discussions. A cracker, Austria calls him, uttering superflous breath; and France contemptuously bids the 'women and fools' to leave off their wrangling. Except for another short skirmish with Austria, Faulconbridge is then silent for a further two hundred lines, and when he does speak again he has learned the first rule of diplomatic conferences, which is that they have no rules. It is absurd, he says, for the people of Angiers to quibble about surrendering their wretched little city to its lawful master. They have no power of arms, and so the obvious solution is for France and England to combine against the 'peevish town' and resume their differences when it has been levelled with the ground.

The citizens trump this audacious trick by proposing 'fair-faced league', namely the marriage of Blanch, niece of England, to the Dauphin. To this alliance they will open their gates forthwith. When this plan is accepted, Faulconbridge has at last taken the full measure of his opponents, and the famous 'Commodity' speech expresses his new-won knowledge. Never again will he be 'bethumped with words' that dress policy in the language of virtue. He has seen his master John surrender part of his inheritance in order that Arthur shall not have the whole of it; and France, 'God's own soldier' whose armour conscience buckled on, deflected from an honourable purpose to 'a most base and vile-concluded peace'. The agent is Commodity, 'purpose-changer' and 'daily break-vow', ceaseless foe of impartiality and straightforward action. Why, he finally asks himself, does he complain of this 'bias of the world'? Only because he has not learned the trick of it; and when he has,

> My virtue then shall be
> To say there is no vice but beggary:
> Since Kings break faith upon Commodity,
> Gain be my lord, for I will worship thee.
> II i 595.

In the following scene he will be pupil to a consummate exhibition by Pandulph that will establish the accuracy of his conclusions. But first we are shown a very different reaction to the marriage compact. Faulconbridge has called this a 'mad composition', since he has always wanted to fight Angiers, but he has learned to admire the technique. Constance, Arthur's widowed mother, is more directly involved, and she reacts in the traditional way—in the way of one who still expects to find honour in public life—to the slippery evasiveness of her friends. She is the last, and significantly the last, of the long and vociferous sequence of women who in the earlier histories have been the mouth-piece of conscience. In them, all the countless victims have found a voice, for they have always spoken for more than their personal suffering. Their own part in the action has seldom been guiltless, but when, bereft of husbands and sons, they cry out against the unnatural violence and treachery of war, they protest for all humanity. Shakespeare has preserved a moral balance by allowing them to testify to the common pieties which the politicians blasphemously ignore.

Constance, then, is apt to her cue. Her personal outrage at Arthur's disinheritance assumes a larger and nobler indignation as she contemplates the wickedness that daily masquerades as statesmanship. In this finer mood she will instruct her sorrows to be proud, for it is not only of her own grief that she speaks. On the stage Constance is hard to endure; and even to read, despite the rich imagination which finds in each succeeding metaphor the stepping-stone to yet another, her utterances 'only serve to shew', as Johnson sourly remarked, 'how difficult it is to maintain the pathetic long'. But the substance of her grief preserves a magnificent consistency. She acknowledges Commodity but will not come to terms with it, and her superb invective flays all its adherents impartially.

That is the difference between herself and Faulconbridge, and the gradual change, which this play unmistakably reveals, in Shakespeare's developing outlook on the political scene. Faulconbridge is the first character to embody without compromise the exclusively political morality in which all the remaining histories are conceived.

Eventually he brings the play to an orthodox and familiar conclusion. Contemporaries had to be reminded of the need for unity, and so it is as the saviour of society that he is finally presented to us. It would be foolish to pretend that this is not his main function. But this is also the man who came to accept the Angiers pact, the Dauphin's treachery and Pandulph's smooth equivocations as the norm of political action. He espoused Commodity as a man might woo a courtesan who had yet to cross his path: if others enjoyed her favours, why should not he? In its venial forms Commodity is just the barrow-boy's goddess or the instinct to scramble aboard the band wagon; but it can also, as Faulconbridge discovered, mean betrayal, deceit and murder. Once he has accepted this, there can be no reconciliation between himself and Constance. In her simpler morality, wrong is wrong and no political needs or calculations can make it right. In the later histories there is no Constance. She disappears as finally as the sort of language she and her kind have spoken, and there is an obvious relation between the two.

But this does not mean that Constance is wholly right and Faulconbridge wholly wrong. Right and wrong, in this context, are question-begging words, and the emphasis of *King John* is on the idea that virtue may have more than one aspect. Whatever Faulconbridge may say in praise of Commodity, his actions show him to be far removed from the out-and-out Machiavellianism of Commodity's other disciples. To him it means something more than self-interest and expediency. It is a means to effective action, the code of behaviour that a wise man will use if in public life he wants to get results. In politics it is often necessary to fight evil with evil. This is a doctrine which in the moral sphere can only end disastrously, as Hamlet found, but the political world has its own principles and usages, frequently at variance with the ethics of ordinary life; and the ultimate paradox of this discovery is that political morality, which from the traditional Christian standpoint is often no morality at all, may be a means to the highest good, the safety, strength and unity of society.

Because he realises this, Faulconbridge, who is in many ways a bumptious bounder and seems to make a hash of his personal undertakings, is the right man to crown the play as defender of the established order. That order has survived because he has set the country's safety before the punishment of a 'graceless' act for which only God can exact the fitting penalty. Thus the 'surety of the world' is the mended faiths of the lords who have been momentarily blind to the fundamental issues. He greets them as stars now moving again in their proper spheres, asserting his morality against theirs and showing them that *right*, even if a little tainted by Commodity, means only one thing when the country's safety is at stake.

Faulconbridge is a link with the Prince Hal of the plays to come. Hal is a slightly different and a better man, or it would not have been necessary for these plays to be written. But the appearance here of this concept of the political man, suggested only vaguely, if at all, in the earlier histories, means that *King John* is not a play to be ignored. Indeed the subsequent histories, although they are much better plays, develop and explore this idea without making any discovery of comparable importance. In Faulconbridge, the political man is humanised by his robust wit and intense patriotism; and while the wit is not indispensable (as Henry V will demonstrate), the patriotism undoubtedly is. As well as dedication, a certain disinterestedness of aim was necessary to give this figure validity in its own limited sphere. Shakespeare's feeling is that the political man is not a wholly amoral conception, since his cynicism and ruthlessness acquire some sort of sanction when they are devoted to the country's interest. Without patriotism the character is nothing.

In *Henry V* the political man is idealised and, within his limitations, entirely successful; and thereafter Shakespeare is no longer interested in this kind of success.

VI. 'HENRY IV'

1. Time's Subjects

So shaken as we are, so wan with care,
Find we a time for frighted peace to pant,
And breathe short-winded accents of new broils
To be commenc'd in stronds afar remote. . . .
1 Hen. IV I i 1.

The limp, exhausted rhythms of the opening speech announce the nature of Bolingbroke's England. Without any direct allusion Shakespeare looks swiftly back to the events of *Richard II* and sums up their meaning as he shows us this tired and impotent king whom we last met in the confident beginnings of his reign. This is the man who took a crown because he would wear it better than the king he had deposed; and the quality of his act is to be judged by his decline from efficiency and decisiveness to the haggard uncertainty in which we find him now.

Henry is prematurely old,[1] and he knows, none better, the reason why. His 'holy purpose to Jerusalem' acknowledges a weight of sin which this hallowed expedition possibly may lift. The aspiration was not hypocritical and not absurd. In mediaeval England, to dedicate oneself to the crusading ideal was believed to expiate all other crimes (even, so the chroniclers thought, the abnormal lusts of Richard I), and Henry hoped that at 'the sepulchre of Christ' he would find forgiveness for the sin of usurpation which had brought to nothing all his good intentions. In fact he was destined never to leave these shores; and his eventual death in the palace chamber called Jerusalem sharpens the irony and hopelessness of his predicament. Immediately, in the very first scene, his expectation of peace is dashed by the 'post from Wales loaden with heavy news' that Mortimer has fallen to Glendower; and his satisfaction in the victory over the Scots at Holmedon is turned to anger at the report of Hotspur's dangerous insolence in refusing to surrender his prisoners. Then private grief intrudes upon his official anxieties when he wishes for a son who would be 'the theme of honour's tongue' and not a tavern-hunting wastrel. The next scene reveals the Prince's low companions as themselves a symptom of the land's

---

[1] The play opens in 1402. Henry IV, like Richard II, was born in 1367, and they were both of them three years younger than Hotspur. But for the sake of dramatic contrast Shakespeare turns Henry into an old and ailing man, and makes Hotspur about the same age as Prince Hal, who was born in 1387.

disorder—the image of the sun is asked to promise that, when he is king, the law shall wink at those who conduct their business by the light of the moon (I ii 26–33). It suggests, too, that Hal likes to associate with these dissolute men because there is something in the atmosphere of the court, with its thin-blooded care for the official proprieties, that stifles humanity. All the responsibility for the country's sickness fastens itself on Henry, who is trapped in the prison of his own misdeeds.[1]

The third scene shows that he does not occupy it alone. Here he is in angry conflict with the Percies, his allies in the events that brought him to the throne. As Richard predicted,[2] their common complicity in these events has now locked them in a struggle that will be fatal to the country and fatal to themselves. The Percies cannot forgive Henry for taking the richest prize: if he were to give them half the kingdom, Richard had said, they would think it too little, having helped him to win it all. The present relationship between them is therefore grounded in mutal fear: the Percies' fear that Henry, knowing them for what they are, will not rest until he has robbed them of their power to strike in the same way again; and Henry's corresponding fear that men who have been rebels once are likely to be rebels for evermore. It is a contest in which there can be no winners. Both sides are the helpless victims of their own past.

This sense of being borne along by necessity deepens as the play develops. In his first interview with his erring son (Part One III ii) Henry tries to rouse him to his princely responsibilities, but the sum of his advice is merely to show how irrevocably the dangerous present is linked with what has happened in the past. Henry is sincerely anxious to see the country ruled in justice, peace and order,[3] but the inescapable past always rises to prevent it. It is thrown in his teeth again when his offer of an amnesty is refused before the battle at Shrewsbury. Worcester and Hotspur both recite their version of the events of 1399, and Worcester finally refuses to take Henry's offer to the rebel camp. He simply does not believe that the King would be able to fulfil its conditions:

> It is not possible, it cannot be,
> The king should keep his word in loving us;

---

[1] See his admission in Part Two IV v 182–97, where he says that his whole reign has been a scene acting the argument of the retribution that his usurpation had brought about.   [2] *Richard II* V i 55–68.

[3] Shakespeare's sense of the mystical power of kingship is so strong that he feels that Henry has been ennobled by his office. Although much less competent than Bolingbroke, he is more sympathetic as a man.

> He will suspect us still, and find a time
> To punish this offence in other faults:
> Suspicion all our lives shall be stuck full of eyes;
> For treason is but trusted like the fox. . . .
> Look how we can, or sad or merrily,
> Interpretation will misquote our looks.
>
> Pt I V ii 4.

In Part Two Henry seems to lose all ambition to control events. Yielding to the pervasive decay and infirmity of the times, he sinks into a fatalism in which he wonders how things could have been persuaded to happen differently. In a scene which parallels Richard's spiritless collapse when both Carlisle and Aumerle tried to stir him to his duty (*Rich. II* III ii), Henry rejects Warwick's optimistic counsel that the 'rank diseases' of the kingdom may still be healed by determined physic. If we could read the book of fate, we should only learn that human effort is inevitably condemned to fail, and he will not be persuaded by Warwick's argument that the past does not irrevocably engage the future. Wisely read, Warwick says, it may be a guide to decisive action:

> There is a history in all men's lives,
> Figuring the nature of the times deceas'd;
> The which observ'd, a man may prophesy,
> With a near aim, of the main chance of things
> As yet not come to life.
>
> III i 80.

But Henry only answers him with apathetic resignation ('Are these things then necessities? Then let us meet them like necessities.') and a further reference to his crusade, the illusory ideal in which he tries to find some emotional compensation for his failure. The open misconduct of the heir is additional punishment for his fault, and he expects nothing but ruin for the country when he is dead.

> The blood weeps from my heart when I do shape
> In forms imaginary the unguided days
> And rotten times that you shall look upon
> When I am sleeping with my ancestors.
> For when his headstrong riot hath no curb,
> When rage and hot blood are his counsellors. . . .
>
> IV iv 58.

The words are a conscious echo of the death-bed prophecies of his own father, ironic in their similarities but tragic in the huge gulf that divides them. Henry's 'other Eden' is a world where all the pretences are down, where even the petty evasions and compromises that hedge our daily life are observed no longer. 'If the young dace be a bait for the old pike, I see no reason in the law of nature but I may snap at him.'

The rebels are in even worse case than the King, being subject to the blindness and paralysis of will that inevitably accompanied rebellious acts.[1] They too carry the crushing burden of past wrongdoing, and throughout the two parts of the play they drift helplessly towards a defeat which they have expected for so long that it no longer has any meaning for them. In I iii the Percies have their own family disagreements, and the traitors' divisions widen in the petty disputes at Bangor. The play is constructed to show a correspondence between the growing weakness and disunity of the rebels and, on the other hand, the steady growth of the King's power as Prince Hal becomes more royal. In the preliminaries at Shrewsbury, Vernon's description of the Prince and his knights

> All plum'd like estridges that wing the wind,
> Baited like eagles having lately bath'd,
> Glittering in golden coats, like images,
> As full of spirits as the month of May,
>   IV i 98.

bursts upon the rebels while they are still reeling from the shock of Northumberland's absence. Hotspur and Douglas, the warriors, discount the military consequences, but Worcester, with his clearer insight—on the rebel side he is the counterpart of the King—perceives that this defection of one of their leaders will have repercussions that they cannot at present estimate. This is not, he says, a matter for precise calculations. When rebellion is afoot, the imponderables are always against it; and the reaction to Northumberland's absence will prove one of these. Men will wonder why he is not there,

> And think how such an apprehension
> May turn the tide of fearful faction
> And breed a kind of question in our cause;
> For well you know we of the offering side
> Must keep aloof from strict arbitrement,
> And stop all sight-holes, every loop from whence
> The eye of reason may pry in upon us:
> This absence of your father's draws a curtain,
> That shows the ignorant a kind of fear
> Before not dreamt of.
>   IV i 66.

Worcester admits, in fact, that rebellion is conceived in passion and

[1] See above, pp. 116–8, where reference is made to the predicament of these particular rebels.

cannot stand up to rational examination: its adherents, inevitably, are
deluded men. Of this point he is soon to give a personal demonstration,
for it is he who suppresses Henry's offer of peace, thinking in his passionate blindness that it cannot be sincere. His words show too how
rebellion is vulnerable to the sort of rumour, or false report, that is
described in the Induction to Part Two.[1] Sedition breeds 'surmises,
jealousies, conjectures', and is itself destroyed by its own offspring.
The action then begins with a post-mortem on the defeat of Shrewsbury. Morton describes the paralysis that came upon Hotspur's men,
and Lord Bardolph later blames Hotspur for peopling his army with
recruits who had no existence outside his imagination. The rebels greet
the Archbishop of York as a powerful convert to their cause, assuring
each other that his presence will overcome all religious objections to
the enterprise, but they soon discover that they have only recruited
another fatalist. Although engaged to 'consecrate commotion's bitter
edge', he speaks of the rising in tones of extreme distaste and disillusion. He regards the whole thing as the manifestation of a diseased
surfeiting—the people who were once tired of Richard are tired now of
Bolingbroke.

> The commonwealth is sick of their own choice;
> Their over-greedy love hath surfeited.
> A habitation giddy and unsure
> Hath he that buildeth on the vulgar heart. . . .
> > What trust is in these times?
> > > I iii 87.

Later in the play, when Westmoreland has denounced rebellion and
asked how a respected prelate, 'whose beard the silver hand of peace
hath touch'd', comes to be mixed up in it, the Archbishop once again
speaks of it as a universal disease.

> We are all diseas'd;
> And, with our surfeiting and wanton hours
> Have brought ourselves into a burning fever,
> And we must bleed for it.
> > IV i 54.

In these circumstances he suggests that the rebels should be thought of
as physicians who have come

> To diet rank minds sick of happiness
> And purge the obstructions which begin to stop
> Our very veins of life.

---

[1] Some critics have thought that Rumour's rather clumsy speech means that
Shakespeare was groping for a way to get his sequel started, but Worcester
has clearly anticipated it.

The Archbishop argues that they should not be charged with personal responsibility for their actions, as they are merely victims of their generation:

> We see which way the stream of time doth run
> And are enforc'd from our most quiet sphere
> By the rough torrent of occasion.

The point is taken up by Mowbray, son of the Norfolk, whom Richard banished. He urges that forgiveness and understanding are due to all

> That feel the bruises of the days before,
> And suffer the condition of the times.
>   IV i 100.

This even gains a partial admission from Westmoreland, who allows that if one should 'construe the times to their necessities' (suppose that events are determined by some inescapable compulsion), then indeed it would be true that

> It is the time,
> And not the king, that doth you injuries.

When Prince John appears, the Archbishop insists again that

> The time misorder'd doth, in common sense,
> Crowd us and crush us to this monstrous form,
> To hold our safety up.
>   IV ii 33.

It is as much an accusation as a defence. The Archbishop regards the King and his party, equally with the rebels, as the powerless victims of circumstance. The men who are now posing as the defenders of society were rebels once themselves, and their present show of righteousness cannot protect them from their past.

It is in this picture of impotent confusion that Shakespeare finally presents the nemesis of rebellion. Both sides, the adherents of the established order as well as its enemies, feel themselves to be the dumb actors of roles that necessity has prescribed. They are victims of a general malady; or, as they more often think of it, they are the sport of Time. Especially in Part Two, Time is the dominant symbol of the play, and all the characters confess their helplessness as Time's subjects. Life itself is just Time's fool, and Hotspur will accept death as release from its tyranny. In this common subjection to Mutability, rebels and royalists seem to lose all separate identity and become, as Mr. D. A. Traversi has said, 'complementary aspects of a dramatic unity conceived by the poet in terms of the rooted infirmity which threatens society with dissolution'.[1] The final sickness of rebellion is a universal impotence in which it no longer matters who is a foe and who a friend.

2. *Falstaff*

This total loss of majesty is redeemed by the lonely figure of Prince Hal. Although as deeply implicated as anyone in the ubiquitous and oppressive decay of his father's kingdom, he alone is not Time's subject, and against this background of approaching dissolution the play follows his solitary struggle, often against the pull of his immediate inclination, to rise to his princely duty. The Archbishop's bid to present his own party as physicians come to apply a purge to the country's sickness is the sort of delusion to which self-blinded rebels are often liable. The true physician could only be a man who, whatever the outward appearance of things, had never really been sick.

In the official Tudor reading of history the glorious reign of Henry V was a brief interlude in which God was moved to suspend the punishment incurred by the deposition of Richard II; being persuaded thereto by the extreme virtue of Henry, which was complemented in the historical pattern by the unnatural wickedness of Richard of Gloucester. The two parts of *Henry IV* therefore treat of the education of a prince, and Shakespeare considers in political and personal terms the sacrifices and disciplines he will be compelled to accept. In its design the play is constructed to present in alternating scenes the opposed courses of honour and dishonour, and Falstaff, the gross emblem of sloth and sensuality, is not the only corrupted agent to try to tarnish Hal's majesty. *Henry IV* is the story of three tempters. Falstaff is one; the others are Hotspur and the King.

The legend of Hal's sudden change from wildness to an acceptance of his royal burdens was firmly established in popular tradition. It had small historical foundation, but the allegory of the prodigal son is one of which every generation has need, and it appealed to the dramatic sense of the chroniclers to be able to describe the conversion of an irresponsible youth into one of the noblest of English kings. Thus Fabyan's *Chronicle* (1516) tells how he formerly 'applied him unto all vice and insolency, and drew into him all riotous and wild disposed persons; but after he was admitted unto the rule of the land, and anon and suddenly he became a new man, and turned all that rage into soberness and wise sadness, and the vice into constant virtue'. Hall commended

[1] *Shakespeare from 'Richard II' to 'Henry V'*, 134.

him for profiting from the examples of Edward II and Richard II in deciding to put away 'his old playfellows, his privy sycophants and ungracious guard as authors of all mischiefs and riot', appointing in their places 'men of gravity, persons of activity, and counsellors of great wit and policy'. The story of his being committed to prison by the Lord Chief Justice was told by Sir Thomas Elyot in *The Governor* (1531) and repeated in Shakespeare's time by Stow, and the whole dissolute saga of Hal's adventurous youth was uncritically accepted in the compilations of Holinshed.

From the chroniclers it had found its way on to the stage in Tarleton's *Famous Victories of Henry V*. This immensely popular play paid no heed to fact or motive or historical progression. It simply offered the groundlings in the public theatre all that was likely to interest them in Hal's career, which meant the early riots and the later glories; and it covered in an episodic way the incidents to which Shakespeare was to devote a trilogy. In this play Hal appears as a noisy prodigal who boasts that his coming reign will be a pageant of misrule. 'If the old king, my father, were dead, we would all be kings.' Oldcastle is the knightly companion of his riots, and to another of his cronies, called Ned, he promises the office of his enemy the Lord Chief Justice. A carrier is robbed on Gadshill, Hal is arraigned before the mayor and sheriff, and the story is told of his boxing the Lord Chief Justice on the ear. Eventually he takes a dagger to kill his sleeping father, but when he tries on the crown he is suddenly and sensationally converted. The author has given no previous hint that this will happen, and there has been nothing in the character to make it probable. Hal is then reconciled with the representatives of order and he coldly tells his old companions that his affections have changed.

Shakespeare made use of most of these incidents,[1] and broadly he accepted the popular estimation of his hero. He would enlarge it with new and profounder implications, but it gave him a satisfactory starting-point for the last and most exhaustive of his studies of political power.

Falstaff, who was originally called Oldcastle,[2] is the misleader of

[1] *The Famous Victories* only survives an incomplete version, but Shakespeare must have known the original.

[2] The real Sir John Oldcastle was an earnest Lollard who was acquainted with the young Prince and is said to have tried to convert him, but he was never a boon companion or the tutor of his youthful riot. Eventually he tried to raise a rebellion in the west, for which he was 'hung and burnt hanging', a most un-Falstaffian fate, and whatever the faults of this wayward, determined man, they had little in common with those which Tarleton and Shakespeare fathered on their dramatic characters. Oldcastle's second wife was heiress to the barony of

Hal's youth, and everything that we need to know about their relationship, including the certainty of the ultimate rejection, is contained in the first scene in which they appear (I ii.) Falstaff launches his attack with shattering audacity. His opening remark—'Now, Hal, what time of day is it, lad?'—is likely to have left an Elizabethan audience staring open-mouthed at the familiarity of this address to the heir-apparent. He follows it with an impudent plea on behalf of 'the squires of the night's body',[1] a staggering reversal of established degrees, and then he goes on to elaborate his expectations of a better world 'when'—three times he uses these words—'thou art king'. With the gallows rotting at the wayside, no longer will lads of mettle be curbed by 'old father Antic the law', and the pickings of office shall be shared according to each true man's sense of his deservings.

This Falstaff is many persons. He is our Saturday selves; or the sort of man we should most of us like permission to be for at any rate one week in the year. Strictly he is not the Vice, since *Henry IV* is not really a morality: the hero's mind and spirit are never debauched and the outcome is not for one moment in the balance. But he has many of the Vice's incidental qualities and persuasions, and as the embodiment of Riot and Misrule he is the official companion of the hero's unbuttoned hours. A touch of the *miles gloriosus* comes from another of the familiar strains of popular comedy; and in yet another triumphant impersonation he derives from his original identification with Oldcastle a streak of Puritanism which he is always turning to our delight.[2] Poins's 'Monsieur Remorse' alludes to this favourite affectation of melancholy and repentance. He will be troubled no more with vain things. 'I would to God thou and I knew where a commodity of good names were to be bought,' he informs the Prince. Evil associations have corrupted his innocence. 'Before I knew thee, Hal, I knew nothing, and now am I, if a man should speak truly, little better than one of the wicked.' The assumption of piety is as outrageous as the assumption of courage, and in these he is giving his imagination the

---

Cobham, and when the family complained of the slanderous treatment of their ancestor, Shakespeare and his company changed the name to Falstaff. At the same time Russell and Harvey, companions of Oldcastle but also familiar names at Elizabeth's court, were re-named Peto and Bardolph. See *1 Hen. IV* I ii 47 and the Epilogue to Part Two; and cf. the Prologue to the significantly-titled *True and Honourable History of the Life of Sir John Oldcastle, the good Lord Cobham*, which the Admiral's Men, the rival company, acted in 1600: 'It is no pamper'd glutton we present. . . .'

[1] See p. 154-5.

[2] D. A. Traversi (*Shakespeare from 'Richard II' to 'Henry V'*, 57-8) observes that this Puritanism complements the deliberate self-discipline of the Prince.

free and irresponsible play allowed to the Lords of Misrule. Even so, there is a world of difference between these knowing pretences and the frail, pathetic deceits of Shallow. 'Ha! cousin Silence, that thou hadst seen that that this knight and I have seen.' He has seen nothing, as Falstaff immediately tells us. Shallow lives among illusions and the treacherous magnifications of memory, and all that he is falteringly trying to say is summed up in Falstaff's single magnificent and evocative phrase, 'We have heard the chimes at midnight, Master Shallow.' Falstaff's lying is always a spontaneous overflow of the imagination, an absurd and endearing richness of character in one who is instinctively absolute for life.

In almost any dramatist but Shakespeare the character would be mere 'comic relief', a vulgar, boisterous alternation with the heavy scenes of state, like Hodge in *The Life and Death of the Lord Cromwell* or Nobs in *Jack Straw*. But to suppose that when we meet Falstaff we are just going below stairs for a laugh and a smoke is to misunderstand the fullest implications of Shakespeare's idea of majesty. Falstaff is as much a victim of the action as the author of it. In a healthy society he could not exist, and his presence, and still more the apparent reach of his influence, are a symptom of the decay and corruption of the age. Bred of corruption, he is a parasite that prevents the body's recovery of its health. Yet in the unparalleled variousness of his dramatic function he is also a critic, and to a large extent a valid critic, of the values by which he is very properly condemned. It is a paradox that possibly reflects Shakespeare's growing uneasiness with the values of a purely political world.[1] Confessedly Falstaff is Time's subject. 'Do not bid me remember mine end': death is the enemy against whom not even this invincible master of circumstance will be able to improvise a victory. But at the same time he has an imaginative freedom that constantly denies the body's limitations. His mental energy and resilience are a repudiation of the decay of which he is a symbol. Although his final rejection is certain and asks to be approved, his irresponsibility contains a considered criticism of the imperfect values of public life. True majesty must be sweetened by humanity.

In their first encounter Falstaff emerges as an indolent petty crook who supposes that his usefulness in filling a prince's idle hours will procure his everlasting happiness when the prince succeeds to the throne. But it is easy to see why Hal enjoys his company. His quickness of mind stimulates even a prince whose own inherent wit and legerity of spirit have been sharpened by courtly training. In the cut-and-thrust

[1] See Chapter VI.

of their verbal exchanges, in range of imagery and telling instances, in immediate apprehension of changes of mood and purpose, the two are finely matched: a point that needs to be remembered, since Hal's brains and quality are often denigrated. But that is where their association stops. Hal remains, cool, detached and uncommitted, speaking mostly in reserved and wary tones that contrast with Falstaff's exuberant spontaneity. He refuses to catch at the bait of 'when thou art king'. There *shall* be gallows, he says, and says it twice when Falstaff refuses to believe him. He never hides his contempt for Falstaff's way of life. All the serious questions, the probing about gallows and the justice due to thieves, are lightly turned aside, and always the conversation is brought back to evil living and the need for amendment. The most that he allows to Falstaff is an affectionate tolerance, and Dr. Tillyard has pointed out that in his very first speech he brands his companion as the symbol of misrule.[1] 'What a devil hast thou to do with the time of the day?' Time being the symbol of a regular, ordered life,[2] Falstaff is 'superfluous', or inappropriate, when he enquires about it.

This significant rebuke indicates Falstaff's formal role in the play. The gap between Hal and himself is of a kind that will never be bridged, and in the end there will be no betrayal. Falstaff is treated as he should always have known that he would be treated. But to leave no doubt of his intentions Shakespeare closes the scene with Hal's assurance that the sun has not left its orbit.[3] This speech also explains why Hal does not leave his old companions at once. There is something defective in his expression of his thoughts. Hal is here very much his father's son, speaking the language of 'policy' in terms that Henry would have much approved, and this display of cold-blooded calculation shows how much—despite the impeccable propriety of his resolves—he has yet to learn. He will need to see more of Falstaff before his apprenticeship is complete; for his Eastcheap escapades are at the same time a trial of his self-discipline and dedication and a means to the self-knowledge and human understanding demanded of a prince. That the tempter is also a teacher is an unvarying psychological truth. Warwick, at least, knows what Hal is about:

> The prince but studies his companions
> Like a strange tongue, wherein, to gain the language,
> 'Tis needful that the most immodest word
> Be look'd upon, and learn'd; which once attain'd,
> Your highness knows, comes to no further use

---

[1] *Shakespeare's History Plays*, 278. [2] Cf. *Rich. II* V v 49–60.
[3] See above, pp. 154–5.

> But to be known and hated. So, like gross terms,
> The prince will in the perfectness of time
> Cast off his followers; and their memory
> Shall as a pattern or a measure live,
> By which his Grace must mete the lives of others,
> Turning past evils to advantages.
>   *2 Hen. IV* IV iv 68.

Shakespeare has toned down the riotous exploits described in *The Famous Victories* and has entirely rejected the sudden conversion. There is no conversion, since Hal's dedication to his duty is made plain from the first. Warwick points out that he has put on a kind of moral disguise, in order to know his people better and one day rule them better. In practice he does not abuse his easy familiarity with the London underworld—the crimes he commits are trivial, if they are crimes at all. 'In everything the purpose must weigh with the folly.' Through Poins's fairway mind he discovers by his low-life contacts in what estimation he is really held; and we must not be blind to the connection between the clumsy, rather brutal fooling with Francis the Drawer and that 'little touch of Harry in the night' that brings new hope and courage to a dejected army.

Having once made clear the true relationship between Falstaff and the Prince, Shakespeare can afford to move leisurely towards his climax, plotting the way with controlled, instinctive mastery. The gap between them steadily widens as the one moves towards care and responsibility and the other surrenders to the illusion of pampered ease. After the buffoonery at Gadshill we see, in the most richly comic scene Shakespeare ever wrote, the splendid high-noon of their relationship. This is the scene (II iv) of the men in buckram, or in Kendal green, and the final, exultant, unanswerable 'By the Lord, I knew ye as well as he that made ye . . . the lion will not touch the true prince. Instinct is now a great matter—I was now a coward on instinct.' There follows the 'excellent sport' of Falstaff standing for the King and examining the wayward heir upon the particulars of his life; and when the Sheriff and the Watch come to find the men who have robbed the travellers, Hal repays the entertainment by using his authority to call off the search. Falstaff meanwhile is innocently snoring behind the arras, in his pocket the reckoning, certainly unpaid, for a monstrously liquid meal.

Even in this scene the future casts its shadows. Besotted with his vision of golden days 'when thou art king', Falstaff starts the perilous game of allowing the Prince for the first time to act his father's role; and underlying the humours that so convulsed Mistress Quickly were stern, uncompromising words that he would have done well to heed. Reverend vice, grey iniquity, father ruffian, vanity in years, abominable misleader of youth: Falstaff tries to laugh them off, but at his plea that he of all the world should not be banished from his Harry's company, the Prince ends the play-acting with a brief and ominous 'I do, I will'. But effective criticism is not all on one side. Falstaff too finds the mark with some telling strokes at the expense of the cold official world to which Hal belongs. He has a disconcerting way of puncturing the virtues for which he has no inclination, and his riotous burlesque of Henry's public manner touches shrewdly on the shams and insincerities of palace life. Under the comic exaggeration he is making a serious plea for the human spirit before it is extinguished by the chilly exigencies of 'policy', and later events will show that Hal has taken his point. The vital difference between the two men during the play-acting episode is that Hal learns something while Falstaff does not. If Falstaff even hears what is said to him, he does not heed it; whereas Hal is beginning to realise that even though there may be no place for the fat rogue himself in the company of a king, a king cannot be indifferent to the things he stands for. Leaving for the court at the news of war, Hal promises him a charge of foot: not perhaps a very wise or responsible appointment in a military sense, but Falstaff will have illuminating things to say when rebels are in the field, since they 'offend none but the virtuous'.

Before they meet again, Hal receives from his father just the sort of treatment that Falstaff had indicated. He confesses the vanities 'wherein my youth hath faulty wand'red and irregular', but his promise that he will hereafter 'be more myself' does not stem the flow of paternal admonition and at length he swears again:

> I will redeem all this on Percy's head,
> And in the closing of some glorious day
> Be bold to tell you that I am your son. . . .
> This, in the name of God, I promise here:
> The which if He be pleas'd I shall perform,
> I do beseech your majesty may salve
> The long-grown wounds of my intemperature.
>   Pt I III ii 132.

It is a solemn and unmistakable vow, but by bringing him again into Falstaff's company in the following scene Shakespeare reminds us how much of his inclination is still with the carefree life of the streets and taverns. A stage-direction brings on 'the Prince and Poins marching. Falstaff meets them, playing on his truncheon like a fife'. It is the spirit in which countless young Englishmen have gone to war, jesting because their own courage embarrasses them, and it is very much in character that Hal should stay for a while to fool with Falstaff before dropping significantly into verse—in this play the language of high occasion—to issue crisp instructions for the campaign and speak with a gravity he has never shown before in Falstaff's presence:

> The land is burning; Percy stands on high;
> And either we or they must lower lie.
> > Pt I III iii 225.

Falstaff stays behind to order his breakfast and wish that the tavern were his drum. Despite his magnificent improvisations on the theme of Bardolph's nose, the scene has done him little credit and we have the first hint that in his off-moments, when he lacks Hal's company to fire his wit, he is given to the shabbier vices, to petty degradations of the code of thieves. Not only does he swindle the Hostess by borrowing money from her and refusing to pay her bills; he now accuses the poor woman of having his pocket picked while he slept. These revelations are made about him while Hal is answering the call of duty.

They meet again on the eve of battle, after Falstaff has exposed the ways of the Elizabethan press-gang, and the Prince has no time for his distracting chatter. 'Say thy prayers, and farewell . . . thou owest God a death.' Hal, who for so long has 'a truant been to chivalry', has realised at Shrewsbury a conception of honour that is neither Falstaff's nor Hotspur's, and when he turns from his noble epitaph on the fallen Percy to find his old friend lying on the ground in apparent death, there is no hypocrisy or falsity of sentiment in the grave, affectionate words he speaks in repudiation of his former life:

> What! old acquaintance! could not all this flesh
> Keep in a little life? Poor Jack, farewell!
> I could have better spared a better man.
> O! I should have a heavy miss of thee
> If I were much in love with vanity.
> > Pt I V iv 102.

Falstaff is not dead, and Hal carelessly lets him have the credit for the killing of Hotspur. But where he would once have stayed to rally Falstaff upon the outrageous audacity of his lie, he now accepts it with contemptuous indifference. 'This is the strangest fellow' is his only comment; and

> For my part, if a lie will do thee grace,
> I'll gild it with the happiest terms I have.
> > Pt I V iv 161.

The glories and material rewards of victory may go to them who want it, and in the same mood he releases Douglas 'ransomless and free'. The important victory is that which he has won over himself. At the closing of a glorious day he has put away vanity and shown himself a true prince of chivalry. Now he may leave it to his brothers to put down the rebels still in the field, for the final stage in the apprenticeship of a prince is to work out his atonement with the principles of law and justice. That is the theme of the second half of the play.

In Part Two Hal and Falstaff pursue increasingly divergent paths until at the end there is no ground of contact between them. Falstaff has lost much of his old calibre. Like the politicians, he is infected with the moral and physical dissolution of the times, and his criticisms of the established order now lack point and vigour. The inverted order that he represents has sunk into decay, and he no longer has the vitality either to tempt Hal from the way of duty or to instruct him in the human needs of kingship. In this play Hal's battles are fought in other fields, and they meet only once, in II iv, before Falstaff leaves London to seek the easier conquests appropriate to his diminished powers.

Shakespeare reveals the change in him by instantly confronting him with the Lord Chief Justice, symbol of the harmonious order that Hal must bring himself to accept. Falstaff is as impudently witty as ever— wittier, perhaps, since it is his only means of concealing the gap between what he would be and what he is—and he taunts the Lord Chief Justice with his years ('some smack of age in you, some relish of the saltness of time'), laments the decay of virtue, and lays claim to a voice turned hoarse by hallooing and singing of anthems. He even tries to touch his opponent for a thousand pounds, and in a culminating impertinence tells him that the distracted Quickly 'says up and down the town that her eldest son is like you'. But his shafts no longer penetrate. We want him to win, of course, and we could listen to him for ever. The stilted figure of the Lord Chief Justice is not of a kind to inspire affection nor, except in what he represents, any particular respect. But once we stand outside the immediate action, we know that Falstaff has to lose, for he is pitting himself against the embodiment of the rule of law. He has to hear some hard things. 'You have misled the youthful prince'; 'you follow the young prince up and down, like his ill angel'; 'God sent the prince a better companion': the charge of corruption is reiterated and made absolutely explicit, and then, when Falstaff starts fantasticating about his supposedly youthful energies, he is cut short by devastating reminders that he is 'as a candle, the better part burnt out', a man 'blasted with antiquity'. He is touched with the same senility as the court he so much hates, and as he has said himself, his powers have begun to bate and dwindle. The Lord Chief Justice brushes aside all his equivocations and evasions ('I am well acquainted with your manner of wrenching the true cause the false way'), and the final, crushing 'Thou art a great fool' is the judgment of a man who is neither impressed nor amused. Falstaff has been tilting at an impregnable righteousness beyond the reach of his moral understanding, and his defeat by it is inevitable.

Hal meanwhile is restless and uneasy, and he forces Poins to play the uncomprehending Horatio while he takes serious stock of his position. 'Doth it not show vilely in me to desire small beer?' He is on the rebound from Shrewsbury and the release provided by physical action, and although his ultimate choice has been made, he is not finding it so easy to escape his light-hearted past. He has entered imaginatively into an understanding of what it will mean to be king, and he is honest enough to know that in some ways his 'appetite was not princely got'. 'These humble considerations make me out of love with my greatness', for greatness is infinitely demanding and oppressive, and calls a spirited young man who loves gay company to a solitude where he will seldom be able to open his heart. Resentment of this burden of impersonality boils up when he turns on the unoffending Poins with a curse that he should know anything of the sordid life of such companion, or even bring to mind his face and name.

> What a disgrace is it to me to remember thy name, or to know thy face to-morrow! or to take note how many pair of silk stockings thou hast; viz, these, and those that were thy peach-coloured ones! or to bear the inventory of thy shirts. . . . Pt II II ii 15.

He would not, we might think, be so oppressed in spirit if Falstaff were there to share a game of wit, but we soon learn what else is troubling him. His father is ill, but he fears that if he were to weep, no one would believe that his grief was sincere. In popular estimation he is still the rapscallion only waiting for the King to die to start an orgy of misrule. Poins tells him that he has not misjudged. The world believes him 'as far in the devil's book as thou and Falstaff for obduracy and persistency'. But 'let the end try the man'. The world will be astonished yet.

At that moment Bardolph enters with a saucy letter from Falstaff, and when he learns that the old boar is feeding in the old frank, accompanied by a lady 'as common as the way between Saint Alban's and London', Hal cannot resist a final visit to the *Boar's Head*: 'from a god to a bull! a heavy descension! it was Jove's case'. Disguised as drawers, he and Poins steal briefly into the scene before duty summons them away. Hal is on the stage for only 150 lines, and for 50 of them he is unobserved by the company. His stilted, sententious verse as he departs half-regrets the indulgence he has allowed himself.

> By heaven, Poins, I feel me much to blame,
> So idly to profane the precious time,
> When tempest of commotion, like the south,
> Borne with black vapour, doth begin to melt
> And drop upon our bare unarmed heads.
> Give me my sword and cloak.
>
> Pt II II iv 395.

At the door he turns and takes his leave: 'Falstaff, good night.' When next they meet, it will be at Westminster and Hal will be king.

By then, too, Falstaff will have fallen very low. Part Two finds him the dupe of the glory won at Shrewsbury. Although achieved by a trick and by consent of Hal's good nature, his reputation for military skill and courage had made its mark. It was enough to make Sir John Colevile (himself also a fugitive from the main battle) surrender without a blow; Prince John coldly acknowledged it, it had penetrated into Gloucestershire, and even the Lord Chief Justice allowed that the service done at Shrewsbury gilded over the exploit at Gadshill. Falstaff himself is intoxicated by his fame.

> If your father will do me any honour, so; if not, let him kill the next Percy himself. I look to be either earl or duke, I assure you.
>
> Pt I V iv 144.

He is made a knight, and at once assumes the airs he thinks appropriate to his new dignity. He acquires a page and garbs him fantastically; gets fashionable diseases, sending his water for medical analysis; fusses about his appearance, ordering satin for his short cloak and slops; and proposes to adorn his status by obtaining a horse. He is 'Sir John with all Europe'. In these posturings there is a large element of self-deception. The Falstaff of Part One was always the first to see the joke against himself, but now, when he takes himself seriously as a man of parts and the terror of the enemy, he has become the prisoner of his own comic fancies, already showing some likeness to the blundering dupe of *The Merry Wives of Windsor*. Almost like Malvolio, he is the victim of his own lack of awareness.

Presumption and complacency have always been the targets of comedy, and the close of *Henry IV* follows a conventional pattern. In Gloucestershire, where Silence and Shallow 'sit affectionately over the year's dilapidation', Falstaff rises to the fullness of deluded pride that goes before the final reckoning. Here, in the quiet fields of the coloured counties, there is leisurely talk of apples and bullocks and the land that is to be sown with red wheat. In the fair promise of fertility we seem to have been miraculously transported from the intrigues of court and camp, but the contamination has spread even into the countryside. These two Cotswold scenes offer a remarkable illustration of Shakespeare's fecundity in finding fresh symbols for a theme that he has presented variously enough already. The two old men are locked in the past, although, unlike Henry and the rebels, they find it sweet. Time has buried them already, and they are just faded emblems of age and impotence. The various responses of Bardolph's phantom army recall attitudes that we have met on the political level elsewhere in the play—the resignation of Feeble's 'a man can die but once; we owe God a death' echoes the King's defeatism as well as the familiar philosophy of the battle scenes. Necessity seems to have laid its hand even on this rural backwater, and corruption is present too, in Davy's request to his master to let justice sleep when William Visor of Wincot makes his appearance at petty sessions.

Into this equivocal world there now comes Falstaff, the famous warrior condescending to his country cousins, the sophisticated rogue who—after he has monstrously abused the Queen's press—is quick to sense the atmosphere of his new surroundings.

> I do see the bottom of Justice Shallow. Lord! Lord! how subject we old men are to this vice of lying. . . . If the young dace be a bait for the old pike, I see no reason in the law of nature but I may snap at him. Let time shape, and there an end. Pt II III ii 326.

When he returns to Gloucestershire, crowned with the dubious laurels of Gaultree, the audience have just seen Hal dedicate himself to his new responsibilities at the bedside of the dying King. So it is a little pathetic, as well as ironical, when Falstaff promises himself that his tales of these country simpletons will 'keep Prince Harry in continual laughter the wearing out of six fashions . . . O! you shall see him laugh till his face be like a wet cloak ill laid up.' The irony deepens when Falstaff, of all people, remarks upon the importance of keeping good company. He has noticed that by constant acquaintance Shallow and his servingmen have become more like one another, and he concludes that 'either wise bearing or ignorant carriage is caught, as men take diseases, one of another: therefore let men take heed of their company'. It is an unconscious recognition of the loss of degree and the contagiousness of corruption.

When Pistol arrives with the news that Hal is king, Falstaff soars to his consummating insolence.

> Master Robert Shallow, choose what office thou wilt in the land, 'tis thine. Pistol, I will double-charge thee with dignities. . . . Master Shallow, my Lord Shallow, be what thou wilt, I am Fortune's steward. . . . I know the young king is sick for me. Let us take any man's horses; the laws of England are at my commandment.   Pt II V iii 126.

This wanton defiance of the rule of law, an arrogant assumption of complete irresponsibility, is his final outrage. Not the tavern only but the whole kingdom is to be his drum. Chaos has here made his master-piece, and the time has come for the act of atonement that shall restore the sovereignty of justice and order.

The coronation opens with the arrest of Doll, carrying a child or pretending she does, and Quickly, 'for the man is dead that you and Pistol beat among you'. Here is the truth about the associates of the man who now jostles his way to the front of the expectant crowd, sure that he is to be loaded with honours and favour. 'I know thee not, old man.' If the words of rejection are harsh, it is because they are true. But we cannot perceive the distance that has opened between Hal and his old companion without feeling that something has been lost to them both. Hal feels it too, for even on this most solemn occasion, the first public act of his reign, he cannot resist a final jest about Falstaff's size, so often the subject of his playful fancy in idler days. It is a momen-tary revelation of human weakness, very moving in a scene commonly regarded as remorseless and cold-blooded. 'Know the grave doth gape for thee thrice wider than for other men.'

But he instantly recovers himself and wipes from Falstaff's lips the saucy answer that is already half-uttered;

> Reply not to me with a fool-born jest:
> Presume not that I am the thing I was;
> For God doth know, so shall the world perceive,
> That I have turn'd away my former self;
> So will I those that kept me company.
>   Pt II V v 60.

Hal has made his submission to the embodiment of justice, and the old relationship is cancelled absolutely. But in this moment of affectionate banter he involuntarily acknowledges all that the relationship has meant to him. The rejection of Falstaff has been foredoomed and merited, and there can be no place for him in the life that his old friend has re-solved to make for himself. The end has proved the man. But Hal would know that the men who fought at Agincourt were men who liked small beer; and this sort of understanding, essential to his kingship, has come to him through his wanderings in the streets. He has confessed it to Poins, to whom he always speaks simply and frankly. 'I am sworn brother to a leash of drawers and can call them all by their christian names. . . . I am so good a proficient in one quarter of an hour, that I can drink with any tinker in his own language during my life': and all this with such instinctive poise and dignity that to Francis he is 'the king of courtesy'. Thanks to his wide experience of the men he will one day govern, he is 'now of all humours', and there is no one he cannot understand. In the stews he has 'sounded the very base string of humility'. He can sink no lower. But a prince's art was like a composition in music—the phrase has two meanings—and no instrument must be too humble for him to play.[1]

3. Hotspur

For a prince of chivalry, as Hal was determined to be, Hotspur offered a different kind of seduction. This was the man whom the King wanted his own son to resemble, calling him the theme of honour's tongue, in a grove the very straightest plant, Mars in swathling clothes, and much else in eulogistic vein. He even wished it could be proved that 'some night-tripping fairy' had exchanged the infants in their cradles: which only shows how little he understood either Hotspur or his son.

Hotspur is a conspicuous example of the non-political man; and although there may always be some disposition to sneer at politicians and the necessary disciplines of political life, this means that he is a rather inadequate person altogether. His attractive qualities are all visible on the surface, and apart from physical courage they are not of a kind to enthuse over, even in an individual. Shakespeare has favoured him with a richly idiosyncratic way of speaking that perfectly matches his restless, passionate nature, and this is apt to misdirect one's judgment of him. It is difficult to resist such a fascinating talker, and he has usually received the indulgence allowed to those who refuse to grow up. Hotspur is 'humorous' in the Elizabethan sense—warm-hearted,

---

[1] An intimate knowledge of all levels of society was one of the qualities the Renaissance expected of its princes, see Tillyard, *Shakespeare's History Plays*, 272–9. Cf. *Henry V* I ii 266–8, when the Dauphin scornfully sends Hal some tennis-balls:

> We understand him well,
> How he comes o'er us with our wilder days
> Not measuring what use we made of them.

choleric, unpredictable, vigorous in the expression of likes and dislikes that usually depend upon a passing whim. He is generous, because congenitally improvident; he detests 'policy' or calculation in others, because he is himself totally lacking in judgment or persistence; and having a contempt for ideas, he is quick to denounce what he suspects to be boasting or insincerity. These qualities have a good side, for Hotspur has sufficient charm and eloquence to make their opposites seem very unattractive. But he has all the crudity and innocence of the early Faulconbridge,[1] and unlike Faulconbridge he does not outgrow them. It is characteristic of him that although he pounces quickly enough upon Glendower's mystical fantasies or the trickeries of the King, he never realises how he is being deceived and betrayed by his own father.

As so often, Shakespeare fully reveals the character on his first appearance. Hotspur's account of the popinjay courtier who came to him at Holmedon (I iii 29–69) is splendidly embellished. It is hot with resentment of pansies and civilians, and below the rhetorical surface Shakespeare has discovered the attitudes of the born fighter. But the speech is meaningless beyond its revelation of the speaker. It does not explain why Hotspur has still held on to his prisoners after the battle, and that, as Blunt points out, is the crucial question. Hotspur then reacts with passionate loyalty in defence of his kinsman Mortimer, and in this outburst he shows the impulsive generosity and quick-growing anger that his father and uncle are shrewd to exploit for their own purposes.

> To your quick-conceiving discontents
> I'll read you matter deep and dangerous,
> As full of peril and adventurous spirit
> As to o'erwalk a current roaring loud,
> On the unsteadfast footing of a spear.
>   I iii 189.

In the last three lines Worcester is craftily appealing to Hotspur's love of excitement, and the absurdly exaggerated response is automatic:

> Send danger from the east unto the west,
> So honour cross it from the north to south,
> And let them grapple: O! the blood more stirs
> To rouse a lion than to start a hare. . . .
> By heaven methinks it were an easy leap
> To pluck bright honour from the pale-fac'd moon,

---

[1] He resembles Faulconbridge also in his preference for a homely imagery which broadens the picture of England. See III i especially.

> Or dive into the bottom of the deep,
> Where fathom-line could never touch the ground,
> And pluck up drowned honour by the locks;
> So he that doth redeem her thence might wear
> Without corrival all her dignities.
>
> I iii 195.

This is famous but it is fustian. It is quoted (inaccurately) by Ralph in the Induction to *The Knight of the Burning Pestle* when he is asked to 'show the gentlemen what thou canst do; speak a huffing part'. To huff was to bluster or swell with pride and arrogance, and Ralph, who 'will fetch you up a couraging part so in the garret, that we are all as feared, I warrant you, that we quake again', was in love with swaggering roles, having played Jeronimo and Mucedorus. This is how Hotspur was taken at the time, and doubtless how Shakespeare meant him to be taken. At best he is invoking virtues that have been less dangerously mediated through the institution of compulsory games. 'He apprehends a world of figures' is Worcester's comment, and for the rest of the scene he and Northumberland try to restrain Hotspur's reckless passion. They tell him that he is drunk with choler, a wasp-stung and impatient fool plunged into a 'woman's mood' where he will listen to no voice but his own. But action will now be the only salve for his resentment, and Worcester has to rebuke the over-eager haste that would release the dogs before the game has been flushed. It is all quite useless, and Hotspur goes off begging that

> The hours be short,
> Till fields and blows and groans applaud our sport.
>
> I iii 302.

Hal and Hotspur do not touch each other closely. It is conceivable that if Hal really had been dissolute and had then undergone the conversion described in *The Famous Victories*, Hotspur is the sort of man he might have become in his reformed state. But in Shakespeare's play the two young men express fundamentally different values, and it is only the King, always blind to anything but the superficialities of character, who supposes that they could be judged by the same standards. Hal thinks of 'this northern youth' as a crude provincial who is the victim of an obsession.[1] In a stupid altercation with his wife Hotspur has again shown his inadequacy for any kind of personal

---

[1] Hotspur's incompleteness is evident again in III i, where he picks a quarrel over trifles and boasts of a whole crop of prejudices, including music, poetry, bourgeois self-control and the Welsh language.

relationship, estranging her as he boastfully puts a further gloss upon his idea of honour. When she begs his love, he answers

> This is no world
> To play with mammets and to tilt with lips:
> We must have bloody noses and crack'd crowns.
> II iii 96.

In the following scene Hal makes a comment on this limited outlook:

> I am not yet of Percy's mind, the Hotspur of the North; he that kills me some six or seven dozen of Scots at a breakfast, washes his hands, and says to his wife, 'Fie upon this quiet life! I want work!' 'O my sweet Harry,' says she, 'how many hast thou killed to-day?' 'Give my roan horse a drench,' says he, and answers, 'Some fourteen,' an hour after, 'a trifle, a trifle.'   II iv 116.

Even in conversation with his father he shows some reservations, admitting Hotspur's valour (Holmedon was not an achievement that could be brushed aside) but responding to Henry's exorbitant praises with a cold and slighting reference to him as 'but my factor . . . to engross up glorious deeds on my behalf'.

It is evident that Hal will find his own way to an idea of honour that is very different from Hotspur's. Whereas Hotspur's chivalry is a complex of attitudes personal to himself, Hal evolves a truer conception in response to society's needs, and the battle at Shrewsbury lights up this contrast. There it is left to Falstaff to pass final judgment on Hotspur's creed of 'bloody noses'. 'What is honour? a word. What is that word, honour? Air.' It has no skill in surgery, cannot set a leg, is blown away by envy. Here is the true complement to Hotspur's adolescent heroics, which are seen to be futile and dangerous when tested by events. Echoed by Douglas, whose wit is in his forearms, he hails Northumberland's desertion as something to lend

> A lustre and more great opinion,
> A larger dare to our great enterprise.
> IV i 77.

This gallant futility, refusing 'strict arbitrement' to the rebels' cause, is followed at once by Vernon's spontaneous tribute to Hal as he

> Vaulted with such ease unto his seat,
> As if an angel dropp'd down from the clouds,
> To turn and wind a fiery Pegasus
> And witch the world with noble horsemanship.
> IV i 107.

Lacking generosity to his enemies, Hotspur finds this praise worse than the sun in March, which nourishes agues. Reckless defiance is the only answer he knows how to make.

> Let them come;
> They come like sacrifices in their trim,
> And to the fire-ey'd maid of smoky war
> All hot and bleeding will we offer them:
> The mailed Mars shall on his altar sit
> Up to the ears in blood. I am on fire
> To hear this rich reprisal is so nigh
> And yet not ours.
> IV i 112.

When Vernon again stresses the Prince's modesty and discipline, Hotspur's angry, ill-considered answer shows how far he is from possessing these qualities himself; and how far he is, too, from even valuing them. All human qualities seem to him inadequate before the immense authority of Time.

> O gentlemen! the time of life is short;
> To spend that shortness basely were too long,
> If life did ride upon a dial's point,
> Still ending at the arrival of an hour.
> V ii 81.

With life's deeper values thus casually disposed of, he rides off to battle uttering incantations to the idea of glory in which he monotonously seeks compensation for his emotional immaturity.

It only remains to gather the various epitaphs spoken upon him. There is Morton's uncomplicated praise of the man 'whose spirit lent a fire even to the dullest peasant in his camp': a merited acknowledgment of the brave and generous leadership whose loss

> Took fire and heat away
> From the best-temper'd courage in his troops;
> For from his metal was his party steel'd.
> Pt II I i 114.

Lady Percy's wifely commendation speaks for all who found in him the 'expectancy and rose of the fair state', and her scorn for the ignoble evasions of the other conspirators lends her passion:

> By his light
> Did all the chivalry of England move
> To do brave acts: he was indeed the glass
> Wherein the noble youth did dress themselves. . . .
> He was the mark and glass, copy and book,
> That fashion'd others. And him, O wondrous him!

> O miracle of men! him did you leave,—
> Second to none, unseconded by you,—
> To look upon the hideous god of war
> In disadvantage; to abide a field
> Where nothing but the sound of Hotspur's name
> Did seem defensible.
>
>   Pt II II iii 19.

But there are other views. Lord Bardolph and the Archbishop both criticised the feckless generalship which rushed into battle with only the feeble sinews of 'conjecture, expectation, and surmise of aids incertain'. Hotspur

> Lin'd himself with hope,
> Eating the air on promise of supply,
> Flattering himself with project of a power
> Much smaller than the smallest of his thoughts;
> And so, with great imagination
> Proper to madmen, led his powers to death,
> And winking leap'd into destruction.
>
>   Pt II I iii 27.

This is, of course, a personal as well as a military criticism, reflecting upon the spiritual emptiness which Hotspur himself admitted in his own last words. He could more easily bear the loss of life than 'those proud titles thou hast won of me'. The glory that had been his adoration had failed him at the last, and there was nothing left.

> But thought's the slave of life, and life time's fool;
> And time, that takes survey of all the world,
> Must have a stop.
>
>   Pt I V iv 81.

That is all. It is the miserable end of a life that dies in futility because it has learned nothing that might brave Time's scythe. Hal's own tribute is full of curious reservations. He will pay the respect that courtesy demands, but his understanding of Hotspur's true nature forbids him to be more than conventionally generous. His words simply echo Hotspur's own sense of futility:

> Ill-weav'd ambition, how much art thou shrunk!
> When that this body did contain a spirit,
> A kingdom for it was too small a bound;
> But now, two paces of the vilest earth
> Is room enough. . . .
> Adieu, and take thy praise with thee to heaven!
> Thy ignomy sleep with thee in the grave,
> But not remember'd in thy epitaph!
>
>   Pt I V iv 88.

He speaks in quite a different spirit when he turns to what he believes to be the body of Falstaff.

The Prince's distant epitaph on his enemy utters the full man's contempt for the adolescent. The master of all the humours has long ago realised the inadequacy of the brave, inflated creature whose moral unawareness has made him a danger to society, and it is one of the ironies of the play that Hal's association with Falstaff[1] saves him from ever being anything like Hotspur. The dense obliquity of Falstaff's life at any rate protects his friends from the more destructive forms of innocence. At bottom Hotspur's gallant glorification of honour is as deeply flawed and selfish as Falstaff's professional disillusionment, and it is important to understand that these two complement one another, leaving the Prince to learn a little from each but to be infected by neither.

Hotspur is admirable in his courage and his freedom from the meaner forms of calculation, and to this extent, like Falstaff, he helps to soften in Hal the wooed austerities of political man. The self-denial becomes less painful for each recognition of acts that come from flesh or heart. But Hal rises in this first half of the play to an ideal of honour that has nothing to do with rewards and titles or with Hotspur's technicolour heroism. It is an ideal of service, requiring of him only the sober performance of his duty. Looking ahead to the subtle dissections of honour in *Troilus and Cressida*, he derives it from his own sense of a lofty purpose, and not from the opinions that men may chance to have of him. Thus he can endure his father's rebukes and the country's scorn because he knows that there will come some glorious day when he will be 'more myself'. On this day 'this same child of honour and renown, this gallant Hotspur' will surrender his ephemeral glories, and Hal himself, indifferent to the outward prizes, will carelessly lay his plume and sword on Hotspur's body and leave to Falstaff and Prince John the credit for the day's achievement. His own consciousness of having done his duty is the only reward he needs.[2]

---

[1] About which Hotspur is heavily contemptuous, e.g. I iii 230-3, IV i 94-7. But whereas Hal never lets Falstaff lead him into baseness, Hotspur's idea of honour makes him the noble but disastrous tool of men who do not know what the word means.

[2] Superficially there is a considerable resemblance between Hotspur's thoughts on honour (lack of numbers brings 'a larger dare' to our enterprise, and so forth) and Henry V's famous speech before Agincourt, in which he admits that he cherishes honour above everything else and says, just like Hotspur, 'the fewer men, the greater share of honour'. But Henry is then looking for words to inspire his troops in face of daunting odds, and with his instinct for the common touch he discovers exactly the right address. He says nothing that diminishes his own

4. Father and Son

Of Hal's three tempters, Henry IV perhaps comes nearest to success. Despite the family reconciliation at the end of the play, Henry equally with Falstaff and Hotspur offers an idea of political behaviour that is at odds with Shakespeare's conception of majesty. We already know something of his hopeless situation. As the author of a violent past, he was condemned to be the victim of a violent present, bound with the rebels in an endless chain of circumstance. He could not rule as the strong, pacific king that he had hoped to be, and his plan for a crusade, through which he might expiate his sin, would never be more than an ironically distant mirage. His daily problem was simply to find a means of keeping by force what force had won him.

Long before the end the proud and confident Bolingbroke has shrunk into a sleepless neurotic helplessly revolving the theme of 'if only we had known'. But this was a weakness that he revealed only to his family and the few counsellors he could trust. The public Henry is never unimpressive, and Shakespeare lets us feel that here is a shrewd, courageous man doing his best in conditions in which, through his own original fault, success was impossible. Unlike King John, he does not require the presence of foreigners to rouse him to kingly gestures. In business he is swift and efficient, and he addresses all rebels in terms that would be impeccable if only he and they could forget that he was once a rebel himself. But they never could forget, and in consequence Henry never possesses the authority for the proper exercise of royal power. He is reduced to shifts. His is a threadbare, makeshift majesty, and his idea of statesmanship aims no higher than the devious manipulation of opposing forces. He is a sort of poor man's Machiavelli, using the gifts and dedicated purpose of political man simply to keep himself in power.

Nothing is more typical of his limited understanding than his failure to perceive his son's true nature. He does not understand Falstaff or Hotspur either, for he is a man who judges by appearances. This, as he now realises, had been his mistake before he took the throne, when he misjudged the Percies and perhaps misjudged Richard too. But he has not learned wisdom from his failure, and at their first meeting in the play he treats Hal to an extended lecture on the importance of wearing the right sort of public face.

personal sense of honour, which he has lately re-defined in his conversation with Bates and Williams. 'Methinks I could not die any where so contented as in the king's company, his cause being just and his quarrel honourable.'

Had I so lavish of my presence been,
So common-hackney'd in the eyes of men,
So stale and cheap to vulgar company,
Opinion, that did help me to the crown,
Had still kept loyal to possession
And left me in reputeless banishment,
A fellow of no mark nor likelihood.

Pt I III ii 39.

This is from the man who sufficiently understood the vulgar arts to
woo poor craftsmen with the craft of smiles,[1] but his point is clear. The
statesman's public behaviour should always be suited to the occasion
and should avoid familiarity unless the circumstances particularly
require it. He goes on to tell the Prince how he won the throne, by an
affectation of courtesy and humility that kept his person ever 'fresh
and new'. This he contrasts with the alleged behaviour of Richard,
who

Mingled his royalty with capering fools . . .
Grew a companion to the common streets,
Enfeoff'd himself to popularity. . . .
So, when he had occasion to be seen,
He was but as the cuckoo is in June,
Heard, not regarded; seen, but with such eyes
As, sick and blunted with community,
Afford no extraordinary gaze
Such as is bent on sun-like majesty
When it shines seldom in admiring eyes.

III ii 63.

This, it will be noticed, is purely technical advice, without roots in
character or feeling. Henry is admitting his son into the tricky secret
of how he formerly drew attention to himself by a policy of deliberate
effacement. It has nothing to do with royalty as Hal is coming to
understand it, and he makes no comment whatever upon these seamy
disclosures. In fact his reply is a definite rebuke:

I shall hereafter, my thrice gracious lord,
Be more myself.

III ii 92.

Shortly before he dies Henry begs Clarence to use his personal influence with Hal and to encourage those good qualities in him that
may restrain his passions. But Henry is by this time too defenceless
and disillusioned to have any sanguine hopes about the future, and he
continues to torment himself by imagining 'the unguided days and

[1] *Rich. II* I iv 24-36.

rotten times' that will come after him. These anxieties seem to be confirmed when he finds the Prince prematurely wearing the crown, and
he falls again into the prolonged and nagging self-pity that would
have justified any of his sons in keeping out of his way.

> Pluck down my officers, break my decrees;
> For now a time is come to mock at form.
> Harry the Fifth is crown'd! Up, vanity!
> Down, royal state! all you sage counsellors, hence!
> And to the English court assemble now,
> From every region, apes of idleness!
>
> Pt II IV v 116.

He forgets, apparently, the continuous disorder that his own reign has
been, and on and on he goes, declaring that Harry will pluck from
curb'd licence the muzzle of restraint until, with appetite roaming
unrebuked, the country will again be peopled by its old inhabitants,
the wolves.

This is Henry in his accustomed vein, and the significant passage in
the scene occurs when he has swiftly and without question accepted
the Prince's explanation of his putting on the crown. Persuaded at last
that Hal does not intend to waste the crown in dissipation, he gathers
his strength to utter 'the very latest counsel that ever I shall breathe':
the final witness of a king. It turns out to be typical Lancastrian stuff,
confounding statesmanship with trickery and proposing to the heir
the trumpery devices of a street-corner Machiavelli.

> God knows, my son,
> By what by-paths and indirect crook'd ways
> I met this crown.
>
> IV v 182.

This is oddly at variance with what Henry has only just been saying
to Warwick, to the effect that necessity so bowed the state that he and
greatness were compelled to kiss (III i 73–4), and there is no reason
why he should have lied to Warwick, who was the most loyal of his
servants. It could be that in the final grip of sickness he had come to
accept the least creditable interpretation of his own actions; a diseased
mind does make that sort of submission. On the other hand, this is just
the kind of inconsistency that Shakespeare often commits for the sake
of the immediate effect. He is concerned at the moment with Henry
the Machiavellian, who goes on to tell his son by what ambiguous ways
he sought to keep the crown thus indirectly got. Hal's throne will be a
little more secure, since he comes in the line of inheritance, but recent
memories are still fresh and he will not be able to count on anyone.

Henry explains how he had tried to divert the enmity of the intriguers who helped him to the throne.

> All my friends, which thou must make thy friends,
> Have but their stings and teeth newly ta'en out;
> By whose fell working I was first advanc'd,
> And by whose power I might well lodge a fear
> To be again displac'd: which to avoid,
> I cut them off; and had a purpose now
> To lead out many to the Holy Land,
> Lest rest and lying still might make them look
> Too near unto my state.
>
> IV v 203.

So much for the pretended crusade: it was just a trick to turn the more dangerous of his former friends from enquiring too closely into his own title. Since these men are only tamed and not subdued, he recommends the same technique to Hal:

> Therefore, my Harry,
> Be it thy course to busy giddy minds
> With foreign quarrels; that action, hence borne out,
> May waste the memory of the former days.

The Prince is thus advised to seek an excuse for campaigns overseas, as a means of preventing civil war at home, but once again he avoids direct comment on these proposals. To Henry's final prayer that he may be permitted to keep this dubious crown in peace, he simply answers,

> My gracious liege,
> You won it, wore it, kept it, gave it me;
> Then plain and right must my possession be:
> Which I with more than with a common pain
> 'Gainst all the world will rightfully maintain.
>
> IV v 219.

These pantomime couplets announce the indefeasible rights of possession, a commonplace upon which even King John was able to insist. It is in the circumstances the only conceivable answer, a public and formal acceptance of responsibility. What is significant is that Hal refuses complicity in his father's idea of statecraft.

Hal is moving in the youthful gravity with which he lays the heavy burden on his head (IV v 20–46); and even if his previous uncertain relationship with his father makes him protest too much when he explains his action (141–75), he leaves no doubt of the spirit of dedication in which he admits the due of 'tears and heavy sorrows of the blood'. Joy and vainglorious pride are altogether absent as he receives the crown as an enemy whose cares have killed his father. He takes it as a trust too sacred to be soiled by the politic advice to which he has just been compelled to listen, and his submission to the Lord Chief Justice, in which he formally recants the wildness of his youth, has deeper significance as a repudiation of his father's devious ways:[1]

> There is my hand:
> You shall be as a father to my youth;
> My voice shall sound as you do prompt mine ear,
> And I will stoop and humble mine intents
> To your well-practis'd wise directions.
> And, princes all, believe me, I beseech you;
> My father is gone wild into his grave,
> For in his tomb lie my affections;
> And with his spirit sadly I survive,
> To mock the expectation of the world,
> To frustrate prophecies, and to raze out
> Rotten opinion, who hath writ me down
> After my seeming. The tide of blood in me
> Hath proudly flow'd in vanity till now:
> Now doth it turn and ebb back to the sea,
> Where it shall mingle with the state of floods
> And flow henceforth in formal majesty.
> V ii 117.

Hal has accepted the principles of justice and the rule of law, and as the bearer of a title in which there was no personal dishonour he would be able to rise above the shifts of 'policy'. It is his final test and his greatest victory. Neither Falstaff's fleshly seductions nor Hotspur's envious emulation have attached him in quite the same way as the claims of kinship and office exerted by his father, and it would have been easy for an inexperienced youth to confuse craftiness with statesmanship and accept Henry's separation between the private and public faces of a ruler. Hal recognises this attitude to be false, but without absolutely denying Commodity's place in the conduct of society: there are times when the most honest of rulers has to dissemble and times when he must be more ruthless than a private citizen need ever be.

Hal will be a good king because events have schooled him in knowledge and responsibility. He realises what the 'polish'd perturbation, golden care' will mean in the denial of human instinct and the acceptance of loneliness and impersonality. Youth's warm impulses must be

---

[1] It is significant that Hal is not implicated in the treachery committed in Gaultree Forest (IV ii.) It is evidently Prince John who inherits the parental notions of statecraft.

steeled into disciplined courage and dedicated to honourable ends. He will have to judge all causes with a 'bold, just, and impartial spirit' that despises the short-cuts which authority always knows how to find. It is required of him also that he shall know his people in all their strength and weakness, so that he and they may live together in the harmonious relationship that is the supreme condition of majesty. Hal understands all this; and with understanding he has the drive to success —there is no harm in calling it ambition—without which all these other qualities are only ornaments.

VII. 'HENRY V'

After the sustained conflicts of the two preceding plays, *Henry V* is in the main a demonstration. The hero is no longer in the toils. The end has proved the man, and his victory over himself has been much more than a personal victory. Riot and dishonour have been put to flight, reason is passion's master, and England has at last a king who can physic all her ills. Because he has proved himself a valiant and chivalrous prince, and one who acknowledges the sovereignty of law and justice, the crown comes to him 'with better quiet, better opinion, better confirmation', and all the soil of the Lancastrian achievement has gone with his father to the grave. In *Henry V* Shakespeare celebrates England's recovered majesty through the deeds of 'the mirror of all Christian kings'.

A formidable body of critical opinion is hostile to this view. In general it is held that, if this really was what Shakespeare was trying to do, he failed to bring it off; his natural scepticism could not help revealing the essential hollowness of this idealised and unlikely figure. Obviously there is something in this. Shakespeare was much too conscious of the human pressures that weigh on a public man to believe that a whole reign—even a short one that enjoyed God's special care—could be conducted on this rarefied level, and he has allowed the human material to be transformed by the universalising tendencies of epic. But the hostile critics have various kinds of objection to the play. They are united only in their dislike of Henry, and they find different ways of rationalising their prejudice. Purely subjective notions paralyse their judgment, and they write as pacifists, republicans, anti-clericals, little Englanders, moralists, even as arbiters of etiquette, until one is astounded at the prejudice Henry has managed to arouse. In all the canon only Isabella, in *Measure for Measure*, has stirred so much personal distaste. In the meantime all contact is lost with Shakespeare's purpose and achievement. Dr. Johnson wrote of the play without much enthusiasm, but at least he noted (with reference to Shakespeare's endless enjoyment of the joke about the warming properties of Bardolph's nose) that 'this poet is always more careful about the present than the future, about his audience than his readers'. The immediate effect in the theatre was what concerned him most.

Hazlitt went full-tilt at the play, branding Agincourt as a royal Gadshill and describing the Archbishop of Canterbury as a pander to riot beside whom Falstaff was only 'a puny prompter'. Henry made war on his neighbours because his own crown was doubtful and he did not know how to govern the country anyway. Hazlitt concedes that 'we like him in the play. There he is a very amiable monster, a very splendid pageant', to be admired rather as one gazes at a caged panther in the zoo. But objective criticism of the play was made impossible by the writer's Francophil republicanism. He admired Napoleon but not 'this star of England'. A hundred years later Mr. John Masefield, in not dissimilar terms, found in Henry 'the knack of life that fits human beings for whatever is animal is human affairs': a back-handed compliment at the best, but almost the only one he is willing to pay to a man whom he reckoned to be 'commonplace'. Bradley, who could not stomach the rejection of Falstaff, allowed Henry a certain coarse efficiency but thought him to be inescapably his father's son, 'the son of the man whom Hotspur called "a vile politician".' The key to the reign is therefore to be found at *2 Henry IV* IV v 176–218; and presumably there is not much point in reading *Henry V* at all. Granville-Barker found the play to be lacking in any 'spiritually significant idea': which is patently absurd, since in Shakespeare's time the wise government of states was one of the highest destinies to which God might call a man. But Chambers says much the same thing: 'Here you have a Shakespeare playing on the surface of life, much occupied with externalities and the idols of the forum. And with the exception of a few unconsidered words that fall from the mouth of a woman of no reputation, there is nothing that is intimate, nothing that touches the depths.'

More recently, and more soberly, Dr. Tillyard has given Shakespeare credit for good intentions but concludes that he set himself an impossible task. Shakespeare's Hal, so warm and human, was irreconcilable with the copy-book hero of popular tradition; and Tillyard blames the sources for the fact that the king is a lesser person than the chivalrous prince who won Vernon's heart (*1 Henry IV* IV i 97–110.) Mr. Traversi finds human flaws in Henry's total self-dedication to the business of being a king, and, like Bradley, he feels the father's influence to be still pervasive. The coldly official manner masks a personal inadequacy of which Shakespeare was evidently aware.[1]

There is no means of persuading people to like Henry if they lack the inclination, but at least we should recognise what Shakespeare was trying to do and how he set about it. Popular legend gave him a paragon, as Tillyard says. It was sufficiently potent to cause Polydore Vergil to break off his mainly critical narrative and insert a most uncharacteristic eulogy. Hall, Daniel, Drayton and Raleigh all came under Henry's spell, Hall in particular finding him the cradle of all the royal virtues: 'a king whose life was immaculate and his living without spot . . . a shepherd whom his flock loved and lovingly obeyed . . . he was merciful to offenders, charitable to the needy, indifferent to all men, faithful to his friends, and fierce to his enemies, toward God most devout, toward the world moderate, and to his realm a very father'. This was Shakespeare's feeling about him too; and it is important to remember that he did not accept the legend without examining it. In two plays devoted to the education of a prince he built up Henry's character so that men could believe in it, showing the human weaknesses as well as the dedication and conveying the magnitude of the responsibility by hinting at the personal sacrifices which it demanded. He does not allow us to think of Henry as an angel temporarily borrowed from above. The character gains its strength and conviction from all that has gone before, not from *Henry IV* only but from all the poet's earlier studies of kingship and society. In these studies he has shown us not only the sort of man the ideal king will be but also the roots from which he must grow; good government results from a complex of social and moral relationships, and *Henry V* is a play about England as well as about a single heroic man.

Is it a successful play? The proof is in the theatre; and critics who dislike the play may fairly be asked to give an honest answer to the question of what their response has been when—if they ever have—they have seen it acted on the stage. No play of Shakespeare's has such a simple, unvarying effect. It is absolutely proof against the perversity of directors. It is quite impossible to do anything 'clever' with it, and the only way of producing it is the way the author indicated long ago. Nor does it fail in its impact. In times of war and national danger men

---

[1] W. Hazlitt, *Characters of Shakespeare's Plays*; J. Masefield, *Shakespeare*; A. Bradley, *Oxford Lectures on Poetry*; H. Granville-Barker, *From 'Henry V' to 'Hamlet'*; E. K. Chambers, *Shakespeare: a Survey*; E. M. W. Tillyard, *Shakespeare's History Plays*; D. A. Traversi, *Shakespeare from 'Richard II' to 'Henry V'*.

have been inspired by it; but even at ordinary times, when one per-haps goes to the theatre in no mood to be stirred by elementary heroics, the play's energy and its uncomplicated sentiment unite the audience in common surrender. In the theatre it is no longer possible to have any doubts about Henry himself. If Shakespeare had any secret reservations about the character, they are not apparent on the stage, where Henry is virtuous, strong and gay, a born leader of men. It is quite evident that Shakespeare approves of him; just as, in his own dramatic terms, he approves of Isabella and does not approve of Shylock.

Of course the play's appeal and interest are limited, and this very limitation makes its unfailing success in the theatre the more remark-able. Technically it is a considerable achievement, since Shakespeare was writing in a mode that he recognised (and he admits it often enough) to be extremely difficult.[1] 'O for a Muse of fire.' He decided that the noble deeds of Henry V, which were of a kind to inspire won-der and imitation, could not be fittingly celebrated except through the medium of epic; and epic and drama are not naturally congenial to one another. The well-known admissions in the Prologue are not just an apology for the theatre's failure to accommodate marching armies: Shakespeare was quite ready to stage a battle when it suited him, and with no apology for the small numbers engaged in it. The Chorus was a device that he seldom used, and never so extensively as in *Henry V*. Its function here is to apologise for the unsuitability of any stage for the breadth and sweep of epic; but at the same time Shakespeare uses it with great boldness and ingenuity to make good some of the deficiencies he so modestly admits. He tells the story of the reign in a sequence of episodes, linking them by speeches in which the Chorus supplies gaps in the narrative and generally sets the mood for the fol-lowing scene. This is a practical function of some value, as we can discover from those episodic chronicle-plays where no such assistance is supplied. But the verse of the choruses, corresponding to the pas-sages of heightened description which a narrative poet habitually employs, has the further function of establishing the epic stature of the hero.

Properly the hero's qualities should be established through the dramatic action, and the prominence of the Chorus, like the element of rhetorical strain often detectable in the verse, is a weakness that neces-

[1] Cf. the judgment of J. H. Walter in the introduction to the new Arden edition, p. xvi: '*Henry V* is daringly novel, nothing quite like it had been seen on the stage before.'

sarily results from the use of the epic mode: Shakespeare was trying to do something that did not wholly belong to drama. His method was to illuminate his hero in a succession of facets. Dover Wilson calls them tableaux,[1] and they may be compared with magnificent stained-glass windows whose panels unfold a story. But tableaux and stained-glass windows do not move. Their nature is to crystallise an emotion, and it is a just criticism, so far as it goes, that the ritualistic style of the play confines the hero to certain rigid, one-dimensional attitudes. Henry's character is immediately established in the opening conversation between the two ecclesiastics, and it does not develop thereafter. Nor, despite the immense surface energy which keeps the play moving in the theatre,[2] is there any real conflict. Henry has risen above temptation, and there is nothing to excite us in his calm pursuit of an assured destiny. Doubts assail him only twice, when his bedfellow betrays him and when ordinary soldiers question the justice of his war. But even then—so it is said—the official manner does not relax. He always seems to be speaking 'for the record', and even in soliloquy he addresses himself as though he were a public meeting.

The familiar criticisms start from here. Henry is smug and hypocritical; or he exists only on the surface and is simply too good to be true. Then it is only a short step to more serious accusations, and Henry's behaviour is condemned by standards not in the least applicable to his time and state. It is easy to see how this has happened. Epic praises heroes and denounces villainy. It does not deal in light and shade, and its blacks and whites have a definition too simple for the give-and-take of ordinary life. Aeneas is always *pius*, Odysseus always πολύμητις, because the poet does not mean to complicate the fundamental issues. So with Henry: if in the play his virtues seem to be superhuman, this does not invalidate the seriousness of Shakespeare's purpose nor, within the restrictions imposed by his medium, the success of his execution. Henry is an appointed symbol of majesty, and the action of the play is directed with the most elaborate care to show him doing everything that the age expected of the perfect king.[3] If real life is not quite

[1] In the introduction to his Cambridge edition, xii.

[2] On the lower levels, obviously, the play was composed with great technical assurance. There is conflict of a kind in the clashes between the English and the French both at court and on the battlefield; the two camps are excellently contrasted, and Shakespeare has found room for a rich variety of character and incident, all of it related to the central theme.

[3] See J. H. Walter, Arden edition, xvii–xviii. Thus Henry is the intimate of scholars and divines and seeks the advice of wise counsellors; he banishes idlers, parasites and flatterers, although he can unbend in the company of ordinary men; he is master of his passions and does not give way to lust or anger; he accepts

as simple as that, no matter. Human virtue is always muddied, or it would not be human; epic is the art that on special occasions transforms it into the ideal.

Shakespeare opens the play with two churchmen marvelling at Henry's recent conversion. 'His addiction was to courses vain; his companies unletter'd, rude, and shallow,' and so on; but

> The breath no sooner left his father's body
> But that his wildness, mortified in him,
> Seem'd to die too; yea, at that very moment,
> Consideration like an angel came,
> And whipp'd the offending Adam out of him.
>   I i 25.

This does not mean that Shakespeare has turned his back on *Henry IV*. Spectators familiar with these two plays would understand the true character of the Prince and would know that there had been no unpremeditated change in him. But there is no reason why the two bishops should have known it too, and their assumption of a heaven-sent conversion is an effective and economical way of emphasising the reputation that Henry now enjoys. It is the reputation that matters, not the manner of it; and it would be odd if the Church did not find in it the occasion for a certain amount of professional congratulation. In any case Ely does also allude to the explanation of Henry's behaviour that had earlier been given by Warwick:

> The strawberry grows underneath the nettle,
> And wholesome berries thrive and ripen best
> Neighbour'd by fruit of baser quality:
> And so the prince obscur'd his contemplation
> Under the veil of wildness; which, no doubt,
> Grew like the summer grass, fastest by night,
> Unseen, yet crescive in his faculty.
>   I i 60.

They enter the King's presence and at once he raises the question of his claim to France. This is the crux of the play. Henry's detractors say that he had not forgotten his father's advice to busy giddy minds with foreign quarrels, and that he was base enough to seek the clergy's

all the cares of state, burdensome as they are, and recognises titles and ceremony at their true rate; he has the sinews to protect his kingdom, and, if necessary, to conduct a righteous war, but at the same time he knows that war has many evils and he acknowledges his duty to see that it is not waged without real cause; personally brave, he raises the spirits of his men; he rules mercifully but justly, being ready to sacrifice his friends if they threaten the public safety; he maintains order and the country is united under him.

blessing for a war for which he had no better excuse than this need for diversionary activity, coupled later with his personal anger at the insulting message sent by the Dauphin. The clergy, for their part, sanctioned the campaign, and even made a handsome donation towards expenses, because there was a bill before parliament to confiscate their temporalities.[1] If this is a just interpretation, Henry is beyond our pardon. The idea of the godly ruler fails at once, and all the later heroism and fair words and gallant comradeship in battle cannot gild the fault. Henry's reformation would be mere expediency, and Shakespeare's picture of him as the mirror of all Christian kings would be a shocking irony.

It is improbable that Shakespeare would have deliberately wrecked his play in the first ten minutes: not even in his so-called 'bitter' period was he as outrageously as cynical as that. In fact we have only to read these two scenes carefully to realise that he did nothing of the kind, and two recent editors of the play[2] have convincingly argued that, however it may appear to us to-day, the French war was a righteous war which a virtuous king was bound in honour to undertake. Shakespeare deliberately departs from the sources in order to make this plain. Hall's untempered Protestantism, echoed in spirit by Holinshed, seized on the opportunity to accuse the clergy of seeking to divert the attack on their property by urging the King to conduct the anticlerical laity upon a campaign in which, if God were just, many of them would be killed. Shakespeare will have none of this. In I i Canterbury says that he has offered money to the King. It may indeed be a bribe to ward off sequestration, but that is not how Henry receives it. He gives Canterbury the most solemn warning not to twist the facts when he pronounces on the English claim to France. To consult his spiritual advisers on a matter of this gravity was the correct thing for a king to do, and it is ironical that Henry's critics should have regarded it as a brazen invitation to the clergy to consecrate commotion's bitter edge. But Henry warns Canterbury of the dreadful responsibility that rests on him:

> For God doth know how many now in health
> Shall drop their blood in approbation
> Of what your reverence shall incite us to.
> I ii 18.

---

[1] See I i 7–19. A fairly comprehensive bill for the appropriation of ecclesiastical property had been brought before Parliament in 1410. It did not pass into law, other distractions coming to the clergy's rescue, but it was reintroduced at the Leicester Parliament of 1414.

[2] J. H. Walter (Arden), xxiii–vi; J. Dover Wilson (Cambridge), xix–xxiv.

Canterbury follows with his exposition of the English claim, more than 60 lines of it. It would be a remarkable audience that did not fidget, but we must remember that the English pretensions to the crown of France, for us long buried in a distant past, were by no means a dead issue when Shakespeare was writing. The loss of Calais was still in living memory, and Elizabeth had not in theory surrendered either this or any other French possession that was lineally hers. Dover Wilson believes[1] that Shakespeare's audience would have thrilled at this reminder that their claims on France had not been abandoned but only slept; and might indeed, if the hour produced the man, one day be revived. Henry V was such a man, and Canterbury assures him that his cause is just: a point on which Shakespeare has to satisfy us if we are to believe in his conception of the King. Historically Canterbury was quite right. The Salic Law had been in the particular instance a dishonest contrivance by French jurists to deny the claims of Edward III; and in addition to these claims Henry had also inherited the rights of his own Angevin ancestors. The present century has made us suspicious of the excuses invented to countenance aggression, but in feudal law Henry's war was justified.

Even so, he will not leave until he is satisfied that the kingdom is safe from the Scots. It is Henry himself who raises this point, showing himself to be aware of his duty to protect his people from attack; and he is rewarded by Exeter's assurance of the unity of the realm.

> For government, though high and low and lower,
> Put into parts, doth keep in one consent,
> Congreeing in a full and natural close,
> Like music.
>
> I ii 180.

It is a wonderful evocation, especially significant in this context, of the harmonious relationship between Henry and his people, and it is followed by Canterbury's elaborate comparison between society and the hive:

> Therefore doth heaven divide
> The state of man in divers functions,
> Setting endeavour in one continual motion;
> To which is fixed, as an aim or butt,
> Obedience: for so work the honey-bees. . . .
>
> I ii 183.

Its biological accuracy has been challenged but it is a classic statement of the Tudor theory of status. At its close Henry announces his deci-

---

[1] Cambridge edition, xxiv.

sion to enforce his claims, and the French envoys are summoned to be made acquainted with it. They produce the Dauphin's gift of tennis-balls, a painful reminder of carefree days in the company of Falstaff. It is absurd to pretend that the French war was a personal vendetta to avenge this trivial insult. That decision had already been made, and in his reply Henry leaves the French in no doubt of the real issues.

> This all lies within the will of God,
> To whom I do appeal; and in whose name
> Tell you the Dauphin I am coming on,
> To venge me as I may and to put forth
> My rightful hand in a well-hallow'd cause.
>
> I ii 289.

Actors of Henry tend to go through a certain amount of foot-stamping during this speech, but the text does not seem to warrant it. Henry is sarcastic, masterful and icily determined; there is no evidence of lost control, and the chief impression given by the speech is that it is the Dauphin who is the irresponsible playboy now.

The next scene introduces us to the reprobates, but not to Falstaff. His presence was promised in the Epilogue to *2 Henry IV*, 'if you be not too much cloyed with fat meat'. It seems, too, that the author went sufficiently far towards keeping the promise by including him in the original draft of the play, where it was he, and not Pistol, who ate Fluellen's leek;[1] and where he may have had a meeting with the King in the night before Agincourt that we should dearly like to have over-heard.

It has been suggested that the Cobhams, not content with getting his name altered from Oldcastle, now managed to get him off the stage altogether; and so it needed nothing less than a royal command to get him back again in *The Merry Wives of Windsor*. But the influence of the Cobhams in these matters tends to be overrated, and they were seemingly powerless to prevent the use of their family name of Brooke as a *nom de guerre* for the jealous Ford. Falstaff's disappearance is also attributed to the departure of the comedian Will Kempe, who left the company at about this time. But it is by no means certain that Kempe ever played Falstaff: the part may have been created by Thomas Pope. Moreover, Kempe was still in the company when the Globe was built during 1599, being one of the small group of actors who shared the

---

[1] See J. Dover Wilson, Cambridge edition, 113–16; J. H. Walter, Arden edition, xliii–iv. The triumph over the spineless Le Fer (IV iv) is such a characteristically Falstaffian exploit that it would be difficult to believe that the scene was not originally written for him.

financial risk;[1] so it seems likely that he was available to play Falstaff if it had been required of him.

What then did happen to Falstaff? It has escaped notice that his omission may have been Shakespeare's deliberate artistic choice. The Epilogue to *2 Henry IV* is suspect anyway. It contains two further paragraphs after the prayer for the Queen which should have closed the entertainment, and it is evident that there is more matter in the printed text than was ever spoken at a single performance. The promise that Falstaff should reappear seems to have been added at some time after the original performance: possibly for an appearance at court, in regard for the Queen's known affection for the character, or possibly to appease the public outcry at his most unpopular rejection. It may well be that, at the request of the company and to please the audience, Shakespeare genuinely tried to introduce Falstaff into *Henry V* but later abandoned him as alien to the spirit of the play.

If he had appeared in person, it would have been necessary to degrade him out of recognition—or else to diminish the conception of Henry that Shakespeare was trying to create. Shakespeare's eventual compromise is brilliant. Falstaff is present only to die one of the most moving deaths in all our literature. It is not just anyone who dies, and the emotion that this scene creates is born of our happier memories of him in his prime. It is hard to believe—and Shakespeare could not make it harder, either for himself or for us—that it is a better world in which this man has no place. The Arden editor writes that 'the "finer end" that Falstaff made changes the tone of the play, it deepens the emotion. . . . The play gains in epic strength and dignity from Falstaff's death, even as the *Aeneid* gains from Dido's death, not only because both accounts are written from the heart with a beauty and power that have moved men's hearts in after time, but because Dido and Falstaff are sacrifices to a larger morality they both ignore.' [2] In the England of Henry IV, Falstaff was a symbol and source of the corruption that he was confident would still prevail in the following reign, but Shakespeare allows us to forget the dishonour that now dies with him. 'Dost thou think, because thou art virtuous, there shall be no more cakes and ale?' There is a heavy loss in the death of so large a morsel of our common nature, and Shakespeare gives us leave to think, if we are so inclined, that there is something frigid and unnatural in the

[1] See *SWW*, 212–13, 263–6. The original performance of *Henry V* may be dated with some certainty between March and September, 1599, this being the time that Essex was in Ireland (V Chorus 29–32).
[2] J. H. Walter, xxvi.

perfectly disciplined soul. He even has the audacity to allow his hero to be cursed for ingratitude, by the honest Gower as well as by the disreputable Nym. But the point is this: the better we can be induced to think of Falstaff, and the more we regret his absence, the higher is the tribute which, consciously or not, we are paying to Henry and the larger virtue that he represents.

The country's unity demands a further sacrifice before Henry sets out for France. The unmasking of the conspirators is not a comfortable episode, but that kind of thing never is. It can never be pleasant to see men bared to the soul. But the scene further illustrates Henry's kingly qualities, in his willingness to pardon the drunkard whose railing was offensive to his person but did not harm his royal office; and then in his severity to the close friend who had plotted to destroy him.

> Touching our person seek we no revenge;
> But we our kingdom's safety must so tender,
> Whose ruin you have sought, that to her laws
> We do deliver you.
>
> II ii 174.

For the country's good he rises above personal affection and suppresses any impulse he may have to show mercy to men he had loved and honoured. Their fate shall be according to the course of law.

But this is one of the few occasions in the play when we are admitted to Henry's inner thoughts.

> O! how hast thou with jealousy infected
> The sweetness of affiance.
>
> II ii 126.

This is at the heart of his grief and disappointment. Breach of trust weakens the defences of society, and even while he is publicly denouncing the traitors he is on the rack of bitter self-questioning. He is moved to dwell upon the harsh realities that may lie beneath the 'glistering semblances of piety'. The fair face of unity may conceal a thousand other treacheries in men who seem to be dutiful, free from gross passion and constant in spirit. Scroop's fault strikes him as another fall of man, because of its implicit threat to loose all the hideous forces of appetite and anarchy. The speech, which many critics regard as an insufferable piece of sanctimonious ranting, exposes the tensions in which a king must live. The revelation of this treachery has opened up for Henry the gulf that separates his own conception of honour from the passions of the men he has to rule.

He derives genuine consolation from the thought that God has revealed the plot before it could do any actual harm, and this strengthens his faith in his mission as he leaves for France. Many things in his conduct of the war have been disliked because they have not been understood. He is a man well versed in 'the disciplines of the wars', and Fluellen's praise of him is not to be taken lightly. Where he seems to modern ideas to have been quite astonishingly insensitive, he was in fact directing the campaign according to the recognised principles of his age. Thus he begins by sending Exeter to give the French a further opportunity to avoid the whole bloody business. The justice of his cause, 'no sinister nor no awkward claim', is reasserted and France is warned to surrender

> The borrow'd glories that by gift of heaven,
> By law of nature and of nations 'long
> To him and to his heirs.
>
> II iv 79.

If the warning is not heeded, the King's reply will be 'bloody constraint', and the French will be responsible for all the innocent blood that will be shed. Before Harfleur Henry in person threatens terrible destruction if the town will not surrender. It sounds the utmost in hypocrisy to call the citizens 'guilty in defence' if they try to save their town from a foreign invader, but if in justice Harfleur was his by rightful inheritance, then they would indeed be guilty of impious defiance in attempting to withhold it from him. That is what the rules of war prescribed, and the effectiveness of Henry's highly-coloured threats does succeed in preventing bloodshed, so that in the end he is able to tell Exeter to 'use mercy to them all'. At Agincourt his order to the soldiers to kill their prisoners has again been misunderstood, and Dover Wilson's analysis of the situation—which was historical—deserves to be carefully studied.[1] Henry's action has the immediate endorsement of Gower, who was a professional. 'The king most worthily hath caused every soldier to cut his prisoner's throat. O! 'tis a gallant king.' This is followed, again significantly, by Fluellen's enchanting comparison of Henry of Monmouth and Alexander of Macedon, and of the fish that swim in the rivers at both these towns. Then Montjoy appears to bring the French surrender to the leader whose determination and tactical insight have averted an ugly situation.

It may well be that no amount of explanation will make these incidents acceptable to modern taste. There are many matters on which Shakespeare's thinking is so utterly different from ours that reconciliation is impossible. It never seems to have occurred to him, for instance,

---

[1] Cambridge edition, xxxiii–viii.

to question the morality or wisdom of capital punishment as a social expedient: he lived in a world where this drastic medicine was probably necessary. Warfare similarly had a code of behaviour that was found to be satisfactory for the short-season campaigning of feudal armies, and the civil war of the seventeenth century was fought broadly by the same conventions as Shakespeare accepted for Henry V.

In any case these blemishes, if they are blemishes at all, do not spoil Shakespeare's wonderful picture of the King as he leads his tiny force to victory. This is no lay figure just striking the right attitudes. The battle scenes glow with the warmth and inspiration of a man leading his people in fulfilment of a sacred trust bequeathed to him by his ancestors. Already his personality has healed the bitter wounds of civil war, and from 'that nook-shotten isle of Albion' his armies come 'as fierce as waters to the sucking of a gulf', the youth of England all on fire with his spirit. The French King fears his dreadful prowess, 'the native mightiness and fate of him' (II iv 48–64), and the scenes in the enemy camp, with their boastfulness and bickering and essential triviality, show by contrast the doom of a nation that has lost its soul. Weakened by disease and their losses before Harfleur, the English army limp through France with colours dimmed by 'rainy marching in the painful field', and here Shakespeare bids us remember the band of scarecrows that Falstaff led across the midland plain to Shrewsbury. But in the face of overwhelmning numbers[1] the English are united by the King in that sort of fatalistic courage of which great deeds are born. In Henry's speech on the eve of battle Shakespeare rises unmistakably to the height of his epic theme.

> And Crispin Crispian shall ne'er go by,
> From this day to the ending of the world,
> But we in it shall be remembered.
> IV iii 57.

The literal-minded hasten to point out that this prophecy has been disappointed: we no more remember Agincourt than we remember who Crispin was. But they are wrong. The English race have remembered Agincourt whenever the odds were long and the future dark and doubtful, and Henry superbly touches the strings that move men to be greater than themselves. 'How thou pleasest, God, dispose the day.' Almost, in such a mood, it does not matter. This is the triumphant cry of one who has done all within the reach of man.

[1] One against ten, Drayton says (*Ballad of Agincourt*, iv 3), but he was claiming a poet's licence. The English had just over 6000, the French about five times that number.

Henry's 'band of brothers' is composed of men who are free. They are human enough to 'have no great cause to desire the approach of day', and Falstaff's Boy is not the only one who would give all his hope of fame for a pot of ale and safety. But they would not be there unless they chose to be. Henry wants no lagging spirits, and if any have no stomach for the fight, he will find their passages home to the safety of their English beds. In a heroic hour there is no place for Bardolph, whose fire is out. In the whole army only Pistol asks for greater indulgence than perhaps we ought to give him, and Shakespeare has many ways of showing the single-mindedness and quiet comradeship of the men whom Henry leads. Fluellen, an indomitable cocksparrow, is given latitude to develop a richly idiosyncratic character within the framework of the honesty and loyalty that are his most significant virtues. The interlude that he plays with Gower, Jamy and MacMorris offers, as Johnson very rightly said, only 'poor merriment', but these four men of different races are a further symbol of the unity and spirit that Henry has inspired. 'By the mess, ere theise eyes of mine take themselves to slumber, aile do gud service, or aile lig i' the grund for it.' Finally, in a lull in the action before the stirring movement of the battle, three ordinary soldiers show the true nature of their loyalty in the very act of asking themselves why they give it.

This is an important episode in several ways. It demonstrates, 'as may unworthiness define', the royal leadership promised in the fourth chorus, and we see Henry comforting his troops, 'even as men wracked upon a sand, that look to be washed off the next tide'. It is not done in a few empty phrases drawn from the cheap currency of military exhortation. Henry reasons quietly with his men, soberly admitting the dangers and conceding their right to hold the doubts and reservations they have expressed. It was a king's duty to feel his responsibility for the men he was leading into battle, and his claim on their obedience is complemented by his obligation to satisfy them that the cause is just and 'his quarrel honourable'. The relationship between king and subjects in this scene crystallises Shakespeare's idea of majesty. All know their duty. The subjects owe obedience, for 'to disobey were against all proportion of subjection'; but 'if the cause be not good, the king himself hath a heavy reckoning to make'. The soldiers' blunt questioning moves Henry to a further examination of his conscience, and when he is alone he contemplates the terrible responsibilities of his office. 'Every subject's soul is his own': wherein he is luckier than the King, whose public conscience faces problems beyond the understanding of ordinary man. In Henry's speech on ceremony (IV i 250-304)

Shakespeare relaxes the epic mood to sum up his earlier reflections on power and the nature of kingship. We are back in the taverns[1] as Henry longs for the 'infinite's heart's ease' that his subjects are free to enjoy, and human feeling makes a momentary challenge to the austere disciplines of royalty. His recent conversation with the soldiers has reminded him again of the isolation which he has forgotten in the free-and-easy comradeship of the camp. But the moment of weakness passes, and Henry's acceptance of his burden is the more impressive for his admission of a personal sacrifice. His speech acknowledges the sleepless hours of care and service, and dismisses the pomps of office as the baits in which flatterers offer their deceiving poison. The scene closes with Henry committing his cause to God and praying that his father's usurpation shall not decide the issue of the coming day. In the course of some 320 lines he has shown almost every quality that Shakespeare thought to be fitting for a king.

Johnson believed that Shakespeare found himself short of material for the final Act, but Henry's wooing, so often criticised as heavy-handed and hypocritical, was in the accepted manner of the light-hearted gallant.[2] It is important to Shakespeare's purpose to have the righteous war crowned by a peace that unites the two countries, and of this new and wider unity Henry's marriage is the fitting symbol. Burgundy's lengthy declamation (V ii 23–67) urges the need for harmony, for war is not man's right condition. This play, which shows like no other the particular virtues that war can breed, also examines its horrors with penetrating disillusion. It has been hailed both as a glorification of war and as an exposure of its corruption and brutality. Both views are correct. Suffering, bloodshed and cruelty are always implicit in the action; the foibles of the professional soldier are mocked, although not unkindly, in the blinkered pedantry of Fluellen; war's heroics are debunked in the response made by Pistol and his crew to Henry's speech before Harfleur; and Pistol stands also for the type of man to whom war brings the opportunity to line his pocket and acquire at the same time a bogus reputation as a hero (II iii 58–9, V i 90–4). The desolation pictured by Burgundy is a final condemnation

---

[1] The play's frequent references to Falstaff, like the reiteration of the joke about Bardolph's nose, may indicate, as Johnson suggested, that Shakespeare was reluctant to part with him 'and has continued his memory as long as he could'. But they have a more important purpose in constantly reminding us what Henry has given up.

[2] Dover Wilson points out (Cambridge edition, xliii) that this is how most of Shakespeare's bachelors have gone about the business of getting married. Except that he would have been much wittier, it might be Benedick talking.

of war as destructive and unnatural, and the signing of an honourable peace is therefore to be regarded as Henry's concluding achievement.

But only through war could Shakespeare fully express the sort of man that he wanted Henry to be. As well as frailty and weakness, war develops special qualities. Possibly they are the highest virtues, possibly not; but at any rate they are particular virtues and they are valuable. Shakespeare insists on this in *Henry V*. In the ordinary way we come to know many things about Henry—that he is self-controlled and dedicated, superior to flattery, pious and God-fearing, and so forth. But war is the ultimate test of a country's unity and spirit, and the ultimate challenge to the men who rule it. This was the challenge that Shakespeare needed if he was to draw Henry in the fullness of his majesty.

It may not be a wholly convincing portrait: in the bold, bright colours of epic it is not always easy to recognise a human being. It is natural, too, to react against a surfeit of perfection, and without going to the extreme position of Henry's more implacable critics, many readers of the play have found him too coldly official for their taste. But Shakespeare's ideal king is a composite figure, and in Henry VI he found qualities of humanity and compassion that the stylised epic mode prevented him from revealing in the son. It is perhaps easier to admire Henry V than to like him. But an Elizabethan audience may not have had this difficulty, and it does not seriously weaken the effectiveness of the play that Shakespeare was intending to write. He brought his historical sequence to an end with a heartening picture of a society cured of its sickness and united under a prince whose own redemptive experience corresponded with that of his people. To an England living under the shadow of the Queen's approaching death, with all that this might mean, he offered this final assurance that under strong and disciplined leadership men had nothing to fear.

CHAPTER SIX

Beyond Politics

Banish plump Jack, and banish all the world.
1 Hen. IV II iv 534.
Would I were with him, wheresome'er he is, either in heaven or in hell.
Hen. V II iii 7.

ALTHOUGH *Henry V* was written only about halfway through Shakespeare's professional career, it was to be the last of his histories.[1] There was a wealth of political observation still to come, and very few characters in his remaining plays would manage to avoid being judged by standards that were in some degree social. But after *Henry V* he wrote no further play in which political virtue was the dominant idea. His characters find 'a world elsewhere', and to some of them it is permitted to make the assertion that the claims of public life have no right to extinguish personal freedom.

There is no need to ask why Shakespeare moved beyond politics. No doubt there were certain practical reasons for it, as in Shakespeare's career there usually are. Soon after *Henry V* Essex returned from Ireland in disgrace, and his fatal rebellion in 1601 made it additionally dangerous for any writer or dramatist to treat of public affairs. It was not that there was nothing to be said, but it would not have been safe to say it. Then the Queen died, and the long-awaited crisis came and went without even rippling the surface of public life. With James and his family secure on the throne, the need no longer existed for the sort of homiletic drama that Shakespeare had been writing intermittently for the past ten years. The lesson, maybe, had been learnt, and historical didacticism had once again justified itself. But the main reasons for the re-direction of Shakespeare's interests were personal and artistic. In writing a sequence of plays in which political values excluded all others and the conception of order controlled characterisation as well

---

[1] Except, of course, *Henry VIII*, written in 1613. In the main this is conceived in the spirit of the later romances, with a good deal of pageantry and spectacle, and it is characteristic of Shakespeare's closing phase that the infant Elizabeth should give promise of regeneration. Shakespeare does not trouble to revive the political themes that he has stated in earlier plays, but at least he says nothing to contradict them; and his insistence upon the heavy cares of statesmanship is a clear echo from the past.

as plot, he had accepted restraints that seriously constricted his freedom. Where the only test is political, a political failure is just that and no more; the dramatist has no freedom to consider its personal implications, and throughout the histories Shakespeare had been prevented by his artistic discipline from developing the tragic potentiality of his characters. But in comedy and tragi-comedy he had been examining other aspects of human experience, and in history itself the relation of the ruler to his office had suggested other ways in which the problems of responsibility might be considered. He had said what he needed to say about man's duty to the state. In his future plays he demanded wider terms of reference.

But he never retracts the conclusions he has reached about the specialty of rule. It is sometimes argued that in the tragedies and bitter comedies, and even in the romances with which he ended his life in the theatre, he became so sceptical about the human condition that he questioned whether any man could be virtuous enough to be trusted with power. So perhaps he did. One after another, men in possession of place and authority are revealed in various states of sin and weakness that make them quite unfit to rule, and their personal tragedy invariably implicates the society to which they belong. But the existence of evil does not exclude the possibility of good. In the histories Shakespeare has said what majesty is and stated the conditions of a healthy society. These conditions are still valid, and it is impossible to find any passage in his plays where Shakespeare says that they are not. The great political virtues of obedience, love and disciplined dedication have a strength and permanence that carry them triumphantly through the disordered world of Shakespearean tragedy. Their emphatic restatement by Malcolm and Macduff (*Macbeth* IV iii) shows them to be still the foundation for the eventual restoration of society, and in almost every play (*Troilus and Cressida* seems to be the only exception) there are characters uncontaminated by the prevailing evil who are an assurance that the ordered life of the state will be certainly resumed. Shakespeare never wavers in his conviction of the qualities needed for the proper government of man.

It is perhaps unavoidable that a book about Shakespeare's histories should create an impression that politics dominated all his thinking. In these histories, it must be said again and for the last time, political values were paramount and the only valid test of any character was his social fitness. Society could not be effectively analysed on any other terms. But no one knew better than Shakespeare the huge loss in human potentiality that these austere standards entailed. Man may be, as Aristotle notoriously said, a political animal, but he is something more besides.

There must always be a dualism, and often a serious conflict, between the claims of the social order and the natural self-realisation of the individual. Not every man will find his highest fulfilment within the group, and for some the group's demands may be so exacting as to amount to a frustration of personal development. The natural conformists, men who by and large acknowledge their obligations to society and are willing to accept them, probably form the majority of mankind, but even they will try to preserve some part of their lives from its intrusions. It is a very limited world in which the political good is an exclusive standard of reference; and this political good is in any case a delicate balance of moral and ethical qualities, each of which has its own particular, occasionally divergent values. Although the state is a moral idea, it cannot lay claim to the whole moral energy of man, and even in the severely political climate of the histories Shakespeare is constantly responding to a wide range of action and feeling that lies outside the immediate requirements of his story. May not mercy, which is 'an attribute to God himself', be above the 'sceptred sway' of kings? There is a hint here of the divine potentiality in man to which even majesty itself should bow the knee. Hotspur's brave, intensely personal cussedness is virtue of a kind. Banished Falstaff pleads for all of us who have heard the chimes at midnight. On the humblest level, Parolles' 'Simply the thing I am shall make me live' echoes too insistently to be ignored.

Most to be pitied as occasional victims of the social order are the rulers themselves.

> Power hath great scope; she walks not in the ways
> Of private truth.
> > Greville, *Mustapha* I ii 5.

Henry V is admirable, but something inevitably withers when duty demands so much of a man.

> And almost thence my nature is subdu'd
> To what it works in, like the dyer's hand:
> Pity me, then, and wish I were renew'd.
> > *Sonn.* CXI 6.

His meditation on a ruler's cares is urgent with his desire for a renewal of the humanity that he has been obliged to subdue,[1] and Shakespeare is

---

[1] Cf. his earlier denunciation of the crown as a life-stealing enemy, *2 Hen. IV* IV v 20–39, 156–63.

always aware that office may be an impediment to the realisation of something precious in its own right. Brutus recognises this when he fears Caesar's elevation to power, and his own personal tragedy arises from his exploitation by men better versed in the ways of Commodity. Cassius believes that

> Thy honourable metal may be wrought
> From that it is dispos'd,
>
> *JC* I ii 314.

but this turns out to be a faulty analysis. Brutus brings into public life conceptions of truth and honour that destroy both society and himself. It is not in him to make the accommodations of which a coarser but more flexible mind would have been quite easily capable,[1] and the play illustrates the remorseless truth that there are situations in which even the most estimable virtues may be disastrous. The political ineptitude of Coriolanus is finally redeemed by an inner victory that is entirely personal; Antony and Cleopatra choose a destiny liberated from the pressure of the world. Order may be the enemy of individual greatness, and even in Shakespeare's English histories it would be wrong to regard political failure as absolute. Men may fail in the immediate context of their times because of qualities that in other circumstances would be useful to society as well as to mankind. There is an independent value in the piety of Henry VI or Humphrey of Gloucester, in Richard II's sense of '*qualis artifex pereo*', in the wonderful energy and concentration displayed by Richard III. In the histories the moral nature of man is observed in its social manifestations, but obviously there are other ways in which it might be examined, and as in his tragedies Shakespeare always leaves us free to think that the failures may be men who have refused to make compromises unworthy of their higher natures. Man was not born merely to 'hold the world but as the world'. Even rebellion may be the misdirection of qualities that in another generation might have been brought to the service of society; so that it is a needlessly restricted vision that sees 'proneness to rebellion simply as the headsman sees it'.[2]

However much, therefore, the characterisation and values of the histories may be determined by political orthodoxy, the universalising pattern is always large enough to contain individual variations. They express themselves chiefly through the richness and subtlety of Shakespeare's language. Men like Richard II or Cade or Hotspur would not

---

[1] See U. M. Ellis-Fermor, *The Frontiers of Drama*, 48–9.
[2] Arthur Sewell, *Character and Society in Shakespeare*, 47.

speak as they do if what they say were not important. By sheer style they demand to be heard for what they are, and for the moment they are able to subdue the choric voices endlessly chanting in the background. Sir William Lucy is not allowed to stand unchallenged as the final arbiter of virtue, because in fact the deceptively simple structure of the histories conceals a complex of personal values in which such things as love and honour and religious piety may eventually have to be sacrificed to the virtues that Lucy stands for. Often the triumphs of the social order throw off ironic echoes, often there are awkward, question-raising correspondences and juxtapositions. It might be thought that the epic spirit in which Shakespeare conceived *Henry V* was a device to hold at a safe distance the doubts that keep on arising in plays where the language is more personal.

The challenge to orthodoxy is of course epitomised in Falstaff, the foremost of the 'irregulars' who throughout Shakespeare's drama are permitted to question the assumptions of the Establishment. Although he is eager enough to take privileges and titles if they come his way, Falstaff is the spokesman of the huge army of the unprivileged and the undeserving. His rejection is certain, but in the meantime he offers an important corrective to the official view of society by speaking for all those who, having no share in government and its perquisites, doubt its integrity and mistrust its pronouncements. Its calls to duty are dismissed as mere propaganda, and from what Falstaff says about honour it is evident that to him it was just an Establishment word.

This is the creed of 'Number One'. It denies any sort of obligation, and to the kindly virtues that are the real bond of society it simply opposes a steady devotion to chicanery, self-seeking and unearned bonuses. Yet 'if sack and sugar be a fault, God help the wicked'. Falstaff is not to be confined in any single attitude. His very shamelessness seems to contain an imaginative energy that takes the glow of health from the virtues by which he would be condemned.[1] Sack and sugar may indeed be a fault, in a certain view of society; but not everywhere and always. Falstaff's assertions are seldom invalid within their own equivocal limits, and Shakespeare in fact allows him to be a very considerable critic of the world in which he finds himself. Faulconbridge could both deplore Commodity and decide to make use of it. Falstaff, similarly, claims attention for a comic vision which, although partial and inadequate in itself, is unfriendly to the accredited virtues of public life. Honourable merit seems to have lost much of its savour by the time he has done with talking about it. Suddenly it ceases to be a

---

[1] See D. A. Traversi, *Shakespeare from 'Richard II' to 'Henry V'*, 74–7.

virtue to refrain from strong drink; and a few moments later an adher-
ent of 'thin potations' has perpetrated a frightful treachery. This is a
direct hit, but it need not have been; Falstaff can also wound obliquely,
and eventually we realise that he is not in the play just to embody the
direct opposite of virtue, for life is not quite as simple as that. He presents a complementary vision that cannot be omitted from Shakespeare's reading of public life. We are in a strange world of ambiguities
and hidden meanings, and it is through Falstaff's inexhaustible burlesque that Shakespeare adjusts the official, policy-conditioned explanation of events. Historical comedy is the dramatist's way of indicating
the human contradictions present in the idea of successful political
action. It should be possible to win the battle of Agincourt without
recourse to the press-gang. Henry V embodies the chivalry that would
win it thus or not win it at all. Falstaff represents the unbiddable world
of fact where if it were not for his methods of recruitment, there would
be no army for the hero to lead; and he knows that the hero knows it.

It may seem that a few pages have demolished all that has gone
before, and, if Shakespeare were a tractarian, that probably would be
so. But a poet may do what a tractarian cannot. Shakespeare's view of
society, which embraces Falstaff, has a consistency that belongs to art
and not to logic. It probably happens that whenever an artist attaches
himself to a particular moral scheme, his work spontaneously reveals
all the flaws in the scheme and becomes in some sort a criticism of it.
Shakespeare worked with a double vision which simultaneously saw
two conflicting and apparently irreconcilable truths, each of them valid.
(It accounts for his compulsion to express himself through words like
boil, which is an imposthume, or gathering of evil humours, and also
an action that purifies.) Politically this two-eyed vision is illustrated
by the plight of Enobarbus, an honourable man whose sorely divided
loyalties reflect the dilemma of the master he loves. Affection turns him
one way, duty another; and because of this conflict, neither course is in
the way of honour. So he dies in a welter of paradoxes, with heart
bruised by the flint and hardness of the fault to which that same heart
has willed him. The master who is 'nobler than my revolt is infamous'
is yet the cause of his revolt, and his only answer, hopeless but at the
same time triumphant, is to take the life that has become 'a very rebel
to my will'.

In Enobarbus the opposites are only reconciled in death, but the
lesson of Shakespeare's more optimistic studies of society is that
reconciliation is possible in terms of fruitful and continuing life. His
idea of majesty is not indifferent to other conceptions of virtue, in

which, for instance, Prince John's treachery is a sin, however useful his action may be to the state; or the rejection of Falstaff, politically right, bears the mark of ingratitude, and ingratitude is not a virtue. Various moral pressures are always rubbing the shine off the image of political perfection, and Shakespeare's questioning probes much too deep for comfort. Logically, no doubt, his perception of majesty should be demolished by this awareness of alternative and often divergent values. But because he speaks with an artist's authority, it is somehow strengthened. We know the worst; but the nature of political duty does not change.

Index